HOW **SOCIETIES** WORK

HOW **SOCIETIES** WORK
CLASS, POWER, AND CHANGE
5TH EDITION

JOANNE NAIMAN

Professor Emerita, Ryerson University, Toronto

Fernwood Publishing • Halifax & Winnipeg

Editing and text design: Brenda Conroy
Cover design: John van der Woude
Printed and bound in Canada by Hignell Book Printing

Published in Canada by Fernwood Publishing
32 Oceanvista Lane, Black Point, Nova Scotia, B0J 1B0
and 748 Broadway Avenue, Winnipeg, Manitoba, R3G 0X3
www.fernwoodpublishing.ca

Fernwood Publishing Company Limited gratefully acknowledges the financial support of the
Government of Canada through the Canada Book Fund and the Canada Council for the Arts,
the Nova Scotia Department of Communities, Culture and Heritage, the Manitoba Department
of Culture, Heritage and Tourism under the Manitoba Publishers Marketing Assistance
Program and the Province of Manitoba, through the Book Publishing Tax Credit, for our
publishing program.

Library and Archives Canada Cataloguing in Publication

Naiman, Joanne, 1946-
How societies work: class, power, and change / Joanne Naiman.
-- 5th ed.

Includes bibliographical references and index.
ISBN 978-1-55266-481-0 (bound).--ISBN 978-1-55266-465-0 (pbk.)

1. Sociology--Textbooks. 2. Canada--Social conditions--1991- --Textbooks. I. Title.

HN103.5.N35 2012   301   C2011-908391-4

Contents

most of us take it for granted. But in sixteenth-century Europe, a religious world-view rather than a scientific one was dominant. At that time, the Catholic Church was a very powerful institution that promoted belief in a world ordered and understood only by God. Most people at that time were illiterate and made sense of what they saw around them either through religious precepts or common-sense folk wisdom.

In sixteenth- and seventeenth-century Europe and England, philosophers began to develop a new way of understanding the world. This scientific world-view recreated the systematic thought about the universe that had been lost since the time of the ancient Greeks and Romans. Science is rooted in two key elements: first, knowledge must be based on empirical observation, that is, on data that can be observed through the senses; second, information must be analyzed through logic and rational thought. But science was much more than simply a method. It was also a totally new way of seeing the world, based on the belief that both the physical and social environment could be altered by humans through the thoughtful application of reason.

This was the world in which the field of sociology began, predominantly in England, France, and Germany, where industry was developing rapidly, cities were expanding, and the new scientific world-view had firmly taken hold. The methods of science were not only employed in the world of industry and commerce but also came to be used in the study of human beings. Attempts to utilize science in the study of the human body, mind, and social behaviour all advanced during this period.

However, none of these developments took place in a neutral context. The period we now refer to as the Industrial Revolution brought with it great social dislocation, increasing disparities between rich and poor, and growing oppression of peoples around the world. For those who were benefiting from the new economic order, the new social sciences became a means of justifying the current social arrangements. For the disadvantaged, the new tool of social science was seen as a way to change the world. Thus, from the very outset, there was a tension in sociology about the ultimate use of social analysis.

One of the earliest social theorists to try to apply scientific principles to social analysis was Frenchman Auguste Comte (1798–1857). He is remembered today primarily because he coined the term "sociology" (after he discovered that the term "social physics," his first choice for the new science, had already been used). Comte was among the first intellectuals since the time of ancient Greece to emphasize the importance of empirical observation of the external material world in the study of social phenomena. Today most social theorists would consider Comte's attempts to apply the methods of the physical sciences to the social world too mechanical and simplistic. Nonetheless, he laid out many of the basic tenets for social science that remain valid to the present day.

Sociology as a field has changed a great deal since Comte's time, and the meaning of what constitutes a "science of society" continues to be debated. North American sociology of the twentieth century became much more focused on quantitative analysis and proximal social relations while European sociology remained closer to philosophy, focusing on broader social questions. From the 1950s onward, a distinctively Canadian sociology began to flourish, and sociology departments expanded across the country. The 1970s saw the growth of both feminist and anti-racist orientations, which examined and critiqued the systematic domination of males and Whites in both society and the field of sociology itself. Postmodernism as a theoretical approach to the arts, philosophy, and social sciences developed in this period as well. Put simply, it placed increasing emphasis on individual subjective experiences, and moved away from the broader, more comprehensive theories of earlier sociologists.

Think About It
As late as the 1970s, almost all sociology textbooks used in Canadian colleges and universities were from the United States and were written by White males. Do you think it matters who writes a textbook?

The Inevitability of Bias in Science
It is generally assumed that the value of science lies primarily in its objectivity; that is, we believe that science is free from bias. In one respect this is true—legitimate science must base its conclusions on observable information that can be evaluated by others. For example, to link cigarette smoking to lung cancer, one cannot simply assert, "I'm sure there's a connection." Data must be provided and other competent scientists must assess the methodology and the conclusions. Early sociologists such as Durkheim and Max Weber (1864–1920), trying to build a legitimate science of society, thought that the social world had to be studied in a neutral or non-biased way. However, no knowledge—not even scientific knowledge—can be totally unbiased, since it is always collected by humans with already-formed opinions, who decide what to study, how to study it, and so on.

After reading a few chapters of this book, you may feel that it is biased. Of course it is, as is every course you will ever take, any book you will ever read, and any newscast you will ever watch. In order to teach a course, a professor has to decide what material to include and what to leave out, which books or articles to assign, what order to present the material in, and so on. The reason we seldom notice these biases is either because they are in fields we know nothing about or because the biases match our own. We most commonly notice bias only when it conflicts with our own views.

Does this mean that we can know nothing for certain because everyone has a personal opinion and therefore objective reality does not exist outside of our own individual perceptions of it? Most scientists reject this view. The role of science is to validate or invalidate individual observations of the world. A piece of information can be true or false regardless of the bias of the observer. Put differently, information can be biased and true or biased and false. While sociology cannot, therefore, be value free, it must none-theless satisfy the rigours of scientific investigation. Moreover, whether it is academic writing or material from the mass media, all information should be examined with a critical eye. This is particularly true now that anyone can post material on the Internet. It is always wise to consider where the information came from, what methods were used, how the research was funded, how the information is being presented, and so on.

Think About It

In 2006, some ten thousand scientists in the United States signed a statement protesting political interference in the scientific process. The American Union of Concerned Scientists claimed that scientists working in U.S. government agencies were being asked to change data to fit policy initiatives in areas such as global climate change, international peace and security, and water resources. Similar trends are now being seen in Canada. Why might governments pressure scientists this way?

Examine the four principles of dialectics in Box 1.3. These are very useful tools for helping us make sense of our complex social world. The last principle is probably the most important, yet also the most difficult to understand due to its abstract nature. This is because we are taught to think in a linear, rather than dialectical, fashion. In reality, humans—in seeking what they need or want—often end up with the very opposite of what they seek. For example, most students today go to college or university because they want the credentials in order to find employment. But as more students follow this path, too many students graduate with degrees and diplomas for the number of jobs available, and many graduates fail to find appropriate employment. Thus, an individual choice results in a collective outcome that is the opposite of what was intended. Such contradictory tendencies are not uncommon in society; thinking dialectically helps us look for such complexities.

Think About It

Can you think of any examples where an individual or group of individuals, in seeking what they need, may actually achieve the very opposite of what was intended?

If you find the concept of dialectics difficult to grasp, don't despair—this philosophical term is, indeed, hard to understand except as it is applied to real situations. This term re-appears in later chapters of the book, so when you see it used again, a quick re-reading of this section may help make this abstract concept easier to comprehend.

Box 1.3 Science and Dialectics

The concept of dialectics, that change is a result of internal stresses, is an old one, going back as far as Greek philosopher Heraclitus, approximately 2500 years ago. The ideas of Heraclitus did not reappear until the modern era. Karl Marx (1818–83) and Friedrich Engels (1820–95), drawing on the work of German philosopher Georg Wilhelm Friedrich Hegel (1770–1831) as well as new advances in the physical sciences, developed the modern concept of dialectics. The principles of dialectics are similar to many non-European world-views that have also existed for thousands of years. They may be briefly listed as follows:

- *Everything is related.* Nothing in the universe is isolated, but, rather, all things are dependent on everything else. The particular nature of the relationship may be direct and significant or relatively indirect and less significant, but it is always there. It follows, therefore, that nothing can be understood in isolation.
- *Change is constant.* Nothing in the universe is final, absolute, eternal, perfect, and immutable. Everything is in the continual process of becoming and passing away. But the replacement of old forms by new ones always preserves the viable elements of the earlier form in the later one.

- *Change proceeds from the quantitative to the qualitative.* Generally, the way things change is gradual, with the relatively slow accumulation of modifications through time. At a certain point, these cumulative or quantitative changes achieve a radically different nature resulting in a distinctly new quality. An easy example is the bringing of water to the boil. If we start to heat water at 20 degrees Celsius at sea level, it will get hotter and hotter through a gradual process (quantitative change). However, at 100 degrees, the water no longer simply gets hotter, it actually begins to convert to a different form of matter, a gas (qualitative change). This example also helps us understand that both types of change are necessary, but that one is the ultimate outcome of the other.
- *Change is the result of the unity and struggle of opposites.* Most of us are taught that things are either one thing or another: they are alive or dead, true or false, in motion or at rest, good or evil, and so on. Dialectics, on the other hand, emphasizes the unity of opposites—that is, things can embody within them two opposing tendencies at the same time. Thus there are opposing tendencies within societies, and it is the tensions, or irresolvable contradictions, that can often become the basis for social change.

Theories: Why Is There More Than One Explanation of Human Behaviour?

Most of us believe that the world is made up of "facts" that, like apples on a tree, are just waiting to be picked. Once we have a basketful of facts, we can put them all together into a coherent bundle known as "the truth." Since most of us accept such notions, it can be confusing to discover that there is more than one explanation, or theory, for the same set of phenomena. Put differently, there are a number of competing broad theoretical frameworks (sometimes called *paradigms*) that explain the same facts in different ways. Indeed, the theory used may even affect which facts get picked.

The term *theory* can be a confusing one, because in everyday language we often think of it as meaning "something that has not yet been proven." For example, if someone offers us a solution to a problem and we are not sure the proposal will work, we may say, "Well, that's a good idea, in theory." In the world of science, a theory starts out as a framework for analysis, a proposal to explain something observed in the world. But most often in science, a good theory already has sufficient supportive evidence (the "data") that we can consider it to have been proven. For example, although we still speak of Einstein's theory of relativity or Darwin's theory of evolution, the supportive evidence for these theories is so extensive that they may therefore be designated as true or factual at this point in time. Of course, unlike religion, science never considers truth to be eternal or absolute; all notions of reality can be modified as new facts are discovered.

A simple analogy can help make sense of how science works. All of us have seen movies or television shows that have as the central plot a mystery or crime that needs to be solved. Let's imagine that a theft has occurred, and the police have to find the robber. First, they have to find some clues. Once they have the data (in this case, the clues), they can hypothesize about who did it and build a theory to explain how the crime occurred. If the clues are good and they build their theory well, they are more likely to find the perpetrator. This is exactly what science does—it constructs a hypothesis, gathers data to confirm or deny the hypothesis, and builds a theory to explain the data.

In the physical sciences, it is common for a single theory or explanatory framework to dominate until a better explanatory framework comes along. For example, it was long believed in medicine that stomach ulcers were primarily the result of stress. It wasn't until 1982 that an independent-thinking Australian physician offered a new explanation after he found a previously undetected bacterium, *H. pylori*, in tissue biopsies taken from people with ulcers. In this way, a new theory—drawing on new data—replaced a long-accepted one.

However, in the social sciences there are normally a number of theories competing with each other at the same time. This occurs for a number of

Figure 1.1. Contradictory Elements in Society

Stability — Change
Individual — Social Group
Social Structure — Human Agency
Sameness — Difference
Genetic Traits — Social Learning
Personal Relationships — Broader Social Institutions
Perceptions — Behaviour

reasons. First, societies are complex entities that are full of contradictory elements (see Figure 1.1). As a result, not everyone approaches society in the same way. Some sociologists try to focus on broad social or cultural phenomena, while others focus on personal social relationships. Some focus on the structures themselves, while others focus on human perceptions of the structures. Some focus on the elements that draw humans together, while others focus on the stresses that push them apart. Some focus on how society imposes on the individual, while others focus on how the individual imposes on society.

Second, as already noted, most of us already have strong feelings and opinions about the social world in a way that few of us have about, say, ulcers. As a result, we do not come to the study of the social world from a neutral place. From the outset, we all bring with us our past history and memberships in various social groups, such as our religion, gender, nationality, social class, and so on.

It should not be surprising, therefore, that there are many differing—and often competing—theoretical frameworks in sociology. But rather than simply trying to explain a single social phenomenon, most social theorists—like the philosophers in centuries past— also attempt to answer some of the "big" questions: Is this a just world? How did things get to be this way? Can the world be changed? What can we expect in the future? (Sears 2005, 30). At this point in the book, it is not necessary to describe the many theories in detail; for now, a general introduction will suffice. One of the themes stressed throughout this book is that ideas both arise out of the social world and have consequences for it. So it is with the various sociological frameworks. Robert Mankoff's fish cartoon can help us begin to make sense of this difficult proposition.

The cartoonist has taken an "iconic" image—that is, one commonly used to visually express an abstract concept, which in this case is social

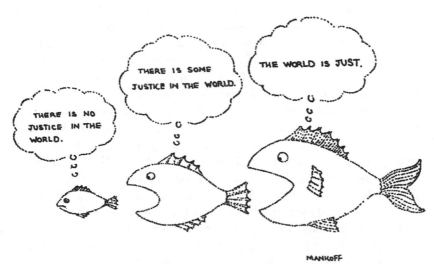

inequality—and made it humorous by giving the fish "human-like" moral thoughts about the justice of such inequality. Despite being lighthearted, the cartoon also has a key sociological idea embedded in it: how we see things is largely determined by our place in the world. Here, structured inequality—a topic central to the field of sociology—is viewed differently depending on whether one is an eater or an eatee (the one in the middle, who is both, is, logically, ambivalent on the question).

In the human fishpond there are also different-sized "fish"; in other words, there are people who are situated in different places within the social structure or who identify with those situated in a place other than their own. Because all of us, including social scientists, are situated somewhere in the social structure, there can be no such thing as neutrality or unbiased social thought. (One of the fascinating questions that is addressed later in this book is why so many human "little fish" hold the view that "the world is just.") To repeat a point made earlier, theories in sociology—as in all the sciences—have a bias, or a point of view. One of the key distinctions between schools of social thought is whether they see current social arrangements as just or unjust. We could say, then, that there are "big fish" theories, "middle-fish" theories, and "small-fish" theories. In the human fishpond, size matters.

Think About It
Which size "fish" do you think you are? Why?

The Major Sociological Frameworks

As already noted, the world of social theory can be overwhelming to the first-level student. To help us get our bearings, let us once again use the cartoon. In this hypothetical fishpond, it is easy to see that the big fish have a better situation than the small ones; as a result, they are more likely to be happy with the present scheme of things. In contrast, the small fish are more likely to be dissatisfied with the current situation and desirous of changing it (so as not to get eaten). As for the middle fish, it is likely that their commitment to the current arrangements would depend on whether, at any given moment, they are about to devour a little fish or are about to get eaten.

If these cartoon fish were actually able to study and analyze their fishy world, it would make sense that the big fish would be interested primarily in explanations that helped maintain the arrangement in the fishpond. We might refer to these as **order theories**, since they would focus on and support the current order of things. In contrast, the theories of the little fish would be more likely to highlight the lack of justice in the current arrangements and the ways the little fish lose out in the present situation. These theories would focus on how things have changed in the past and ways they might change in the future. Because the little fish would benefit from an alteration of the status quo, we might refer to such explanations as **change theories**. This term is not the one generally used in sociology.

Rather, such theories are usually referred to as either *conflict theories* or *critical theories*. However, the problem with these traditional terms is that both the words "conflict" and "critical" have quite negative connotations, particularly when compared to the word "order." To avoid this potential problem, the term "change theories" is being used so that students are not tempted to prejudge either approach simply on the basis of its name.

Whether acknowledged or not, all social theories either support the present social arrangements or advocate changing them. This doesn't mean that only "big fish" in human society (exactly who they are is explained in a later chapter) actually think up the order theories themselves, and only "small fish" think up change theories. In other words, we need not be concerned with the social position of the individuals who actually develop or promote a particular analysis (we seldom know this in any case); instead, we need to assess whether a particular theory ultimately supports the present social arrangements or advocates changing them.

It is much easier for students to identify change theories than order theories. This is mainly because we tend to notice those views that differ from our own, and change theories are not well known outside of academia in North America. All change theories are, in one way or another, informed by the ideas of Karl Marx. Marx's analysis should not be viewed as his alone. Although the name Marx and the term Marxism are often thought to reflect a single individual's ideas, they should more correctly be thought of as representing a school of thought that first developed in the mid-nineteenth century. In particular, Friedrich Engels should always be remembered when we discuss the ideas of Marx. Indeed, many of the writings often considered as the core Marxist texts were actually written by both Marx and Engels.

Although it is sometimes thought that the downfall of most twentieth-century communist governments meant the end of Marxist thought, the ideas of Marx and Engels continue to permeate much social analysis, even among those who dispute their arguments. In fact, it has been said that most social thought of the twentieth century was little more than a debate with the ghost of Marx. Marx was not a sociologist in the official sense of the term. Indeed, since the sociology of Marx's time was fairly conservative, he would have strongly objected to this categorization. In reality, Marx was at once a historian, philosopher, social agitator, political economist, and sociologist. One writer (Collins 1994, 56) feels that it was Engels who was the more sociological writer of the two and who, in many ways, made the more lasting and solid contributions to social analysis.

Like other thinkers in late nineteenth-century Europe, Marx was surrounded by a world in rapid and tumultuous social, political, and economic change. But while most of the thinkers of that period were, like the big fish, trying either to justify and maintain the social

> Very few thinkers have changed the course of history as decisively as Marx.
> —Terry Eagleton, Why Marx Was Right

> Today Marx is, once again, very much a thinker for the twenty-first century.
> —British historian Eric Hobsbawm

world of that period or to alter it in minor ways, Marx identified his interests with the "little fish." Thus, he tried to demonstrate how the entire social system would eventually be transformed. Moreover, while most social theory of the time placed emphasis on the world of ideas, thoughts, and feelings, Marx gave prominence to the material basis for human behaviour, primarily the economic conditions of people's lives. The general framework that draws on Marxist notions is often referred to as the *political economy* approach to sociology. In recent years, others, including some feminist and anti-racist theorists, have expanded on nineteenth-century Marxist notions, making the analysis more relevant to today's world.

Order theories are harder for students to identify, not only because they seem more neutral or familiar, but also because there are so many different approaches. All such theories, however, help maintain the present social arrangements. One of the most clear-cut is that of **biological determinism**, which is examined more closely in Chapter 2. Biological determinist theories locate the key to explaining human behaviour in some aspect of human physiology, such as anatomy, hormones, or genes. If a human behaviour is biologically based, it cannot easily be changed. It should be noted that biological determinist theories are not strictly sociological theories (they are most commonly developed by psychologists), but they find their way into all the social sciences and into the popular press as well.

Probably the best known of the order theories within the sociological tradition is that known as **functionalism**, or **structural functionalism**. This school of thought had its roots in the early sociology of Auguste Comte, Herbert Spencer, and Émile Durkheim, and became widely accepted in North American sociology following World War II and right up until the 1970s. Talcott Parsons (1902–79), an American, was probably the best-known structural functionalist of that period. Functionalist theories, to simplify somewhat, analyze the function of various elements that exist within a society. For example, it could be argued that war is functional to a society because it fuels the economy, provides employment to many young people, and unites the population against a common enemy. While such an analysis can be useful, it can also lead to the unfortunate conclusion that anything that serves a social function—as in the case of war—must be an inevitable part of that society.

There are numerous other order theories, but for the purposes of this general introduction it is not necessary to detail them at this point. The hardest of the order theories to understand are those that promote *some* changes to our social world, but seek only readjustments within the same basic structural arrangements. These are essentially "middle fish" theories, which argue that "there is some justice in the world." These and other theoretical approaches are introduced and expanded upon in later chapters.

Up to this point, only theories that are generally included under the term **macrosociology** have been addressed. These theories focus on the ways individual human behaviour is influenced by the broader society; that is, they concentrate on analyzing social structures. In contrast to this approach is **microsociology**, which focuses primarily on the way individual behaviour and perceptions influence society. For those sociologists who utilize this approach, human agency is primary.

Macro- and microsociology are not necessarily in opposition to each other but, rather, are two different ways of looking at social phenomena. For example, suppose we want to examine social inequality in Canadian society. Both macro- and microsociologists might be interested in this issue. Microsociologists would be interested in the "person to person" ways that inequality is maintained—for example, how forms of communication are used to signify inequalities. They would be interested in power relations primarily at the proximal level. Macrosociologists, in contrast, are more interested in the "big picture": what are the origins of inequality, and how is it maintained or eroded over time? These theorists are generally more interested in examining broad questions of distal power and control within societies as a whole. As a result, change theorists are more often connected with the macrosociological approach.

It should not be surprising that different theoretical frameworks view power in different ways. If we think of that fishpond again, it makes sense that the last thing the big fish want the other fish to know is how big they are and how much power they have. Hence, the order theories do not generally focus on the nature of power in societies or how it is unequally distributed. In contrast, change theories place more emphasis on the allocation of power in society. This is because little fish can only benefit from making other little fish aware of how little power they have relative to the big fish in the fishpond. It might be said that one of the greatest legacies of Marx is the attention he draws to the issue of distal power within societies—who has it, how they get and maintain it, who lacks it, and how those who lack it ultimately struggle to change the distal relationships of power.

However, as with our earlier discussion of society, we must be careful not to oversimplify. In the real world of theory building, things are often not clear-cut. While the various change theories address the issue of power, there are disagreements about the basis of power inequalities and the direction for change. Moreover, while all change theories may draw on Marxist theory, there can be strong disagreements among them. On the other hand, some order theories do address the issue of power and change, although they may not construct as overarching a framework as Marx's.

The Boundaries of Sociology

To this point we have been discussing sociology as if it were a well-defined discipline that can be distinguished from other disciplines. To some extent this is true: sociology has its own distinctive history, founders, theoreticians, and body of knowledge. Yet the boundaries between the various areas within the humanities and social sciences are not as clear-cut as they may at first appear. This is as it should be, because, of course, the real world is not one

9. All knowledge has a bias embedded in it, and human understanding is affected by where we sit in the social universe. Nonetheless, sociology must satisfy the rigours of scientific investigation by providing concrete evidence to support or refute theoretical constructs.

10. Dialectics can help us make sense of our social world by offering a basic set of tools we can use in social analysis.

11. The two major approaches in the social sciences are the order theories and the change theories. The former tend to support the status quo, while the latter try to alter it.

12. Although sociology is a distinct discipline, the boundaries between the various areas within the humanities and social sciences are not clear-cut.

FURTHER READING

Beamish, Rob. 2010. *The Promise of Sociology: The Classical Tradition and Contemporary Sociological Thinking.* Toronto: University of Toronto Press.
A good overview of some key classic thinkers in sociology.

Charon, Joel M. 2010. *Ten Questions: A Sociological Perspective.* 7th ed. Belmont, CA: Wadsworth.
An easy-to-read introduction to basic questions in sociology by an American sociologist.

Collins, Randall, and Michael Makowsky. 2009. *The Discovery of Society. 8th ed.* Boston: McGraw-Hill.
A useful exploration of the main ideas and analysts who have shaped modern sociology, from the perspective of two U.S. sociologists.

Eagleton, Terry. 2011. *Why Marx Was Right.* New Haven & London: Yale University Press.
A short work in which a prominent British philosopher responds, in non-academic language, to ten common objections to Marxism.

Hobsbawm, Eric. 2011. *How to Change the World: Reflections on Marx and Marxism.* Yale University Press.
A renowned British historian offers thoughts on Marx's role in history and Marx's place in today's world.

Mills, C. Wright. 1967. *The Sociological Imagination.* New York: Oxford University Press.
A classic work by an American sociologist.

Morrison, Ken. 2006. *Marx, Durkheim, Weber: Formations of Modern Social Thought.* Revised edition. Thousand Oaks, CA: Sage.
An in-depth look at the key ideas of three authors whose works form the basis of the classical tradition in sociological theory.

Sears, Alan, and James Cairns. 2010. *A Good Book, In Theory: Making Sense Through Inquiry.* Toronto: University of Toronto Press.
Students often have a hard time grasping the concept of what constitutes a theory. This book offers a very accessible introduction to thinking theoretically.

2 Is Human Behaviour the Result of Our Biology?

In This Chapter

- Is there such a thing as "human nature"?
- Why are theories that see human behaviour as determined mainly by our genes so popular?
- What is the process of evolution and where do humans fit in?
- What makes us unique in the animal world?

When I introduce this chapter to students in a classroom setting, I always start with a fable. In this made-up story, I ask them to imagine two unrelated infant children—a baby boy and a baby girl—being washed up on a deserted island after a cruise ship sinks. Through an amazing set of circumstances they survive and grow. I then ask my students the following question: When they reach puberty, will these two young people mate? I have asked this question over many years. Without fail, I can be certain that the majority in every class will answer that, yes, absolutely, they will mate. When explaining why, the answer they give is always the same. They will mate, according to most students, because to do so is "instinctive," "just natural," or "human nature."

My students are not unique in responding this way. Humans have always speculated about why we do what we do, and my students' approach is one of the most common ways of explaining a human behaviour. Today the mass media frequently reinforce our belief in inborn patterns by telling us that such diverse human characteristics as sexual preference, intelligence, emotions, and behaviours such as aggression, male dominance, criminality, alcoholism, or even celebrity worship may all be genetically determined. These sorts of explanations are collectively referred to by social scientists as *biological determinism*.

Before we can proceed with an analysis of our social world, it is essential to examine whether such explanations are valid. If we accept that certain behaviours are determined by our biology, then we must accept that we cannot change them. Thus, if we argue that many of the social problems facing us today—such as war, social inequality, and criminality—are rooted in a biologically based human nature, then our ability to eliminate them is out of the question. On the other hand, if we conclude that the social world is created by humans living together, then the possibility of altering our world becomes a possibility.

Almost all social scientists agree that humans are not born as "blank slates" capable of any behaviour under the right conditions. We, like all animal species, *are* biological entities, and our behaviour must therefore be, to some extent, limited by both our genetic matter and physical capabilities. No matter how hard we try, for example, humans cannot become airborne without the aid of technological devices, nor can we stay underwater for extended periods of time. We are not constructed to run like a gazelle or swing from trees like a gibbon. But are we "hard-wired" to act human? Can scientists identify specific behaviours that are, as most biological determinists argue, solely or predominantly the result of our genetic make-up? Is there such a thing as a human nature?

One important clue that biological determinist explanations of human behaviour have their limitations is the diversity of human social organization and behaviours. Anthropologists have undertaken field studies of many societies, and their summaries, referred to as *ethnographies*, have described many forms of human social organization and culture. Of course, in the major cities of Canada, where there are people who have arrived from every part of the globe, most of us can observe this diversity on a daily basis. Such variations in human societies—over time and across cultures—call into question the argument that our behaviour can be explained as simply the result of biology. On the other hand, as noted in Chapter 1, there are certain similarities among all cultures. Therefore, before we can reject biological determinist arguments, we need to examine them in more detail.

Do Humans Have Instincts?

Let's begin with the argument made by my students that the fictional young boy and girl on the island would naturally have sex because it is instinctive for them to do so. An **instinct** is an inborn complex pattern of behaviour that must normally exist in every member of the species and, because it is embedded in the genetic code, cannot be overcome by force of will. It should be distinguished from a *reflex*, which is a simple response of an organism to a specific stimulus, such as the contraction of the pupil in response to bright light or the spasmodic movement of the lower leg when the knee is tapped. Instincts, in contrast, are complex sequential stimulus-response patterns; such behaviours can be easily identified in non-human animals and have been extensively studied by zoologists and biologists.

Could it be possible that at least some basic elements of human behaviour are universal and therefore must be instinctive or natural? Is there a "sex instinct"? What about the "survival instinct" or "maternal instinct" that are so often spoken of in everyday conversations? We may all eat different foods, but we do all eat, so isn't eating instinctive? It is certainly true that, as living things, humans have a number of basic requirements: in order for our species to physically survive, we must ingest food and water and excrete wastes, we must spend some time at rest, and at least some of our species must reproduce.

But while these are general tendencies in all living things, it would be overly simplistic to speak of these as natural or instinctive. A moment's thought reveals many examples of behaviours that contradict these supposedly universal tendencies. If survival is a human instinct, how do we explain suicide? Likewise, how can we make sense of those who go on hunger strikes for a cause and refuse to eat? And if women have a maternal instinct, how is it possible that many women today consciously choose not to have children, or that some women give up their children for adoption?

Let us return to the fable about the two infants that began this chapter. Would the two infants in fact mate? When I use this story with students, I tell it two more times, but with slight variations. The second fable is of two babies washed up on a deserted island, but this time they are brother and sister. The students become more hesitant about the sexual activity of these two. The third time, the story has both children being males. Now there is a really serious debate in the class about what will happen. What at first seemed "just natural" is, in fact, not at all easy to determine.

If we look at sexuality in our species, we find an enormous range of possibilities. Some of us prefer a member of our own sex, some a member of the opposite sex, some self-stimulation, while others are only satisfied with a threesome. Some people have sex as frequently as possible, while others are interested in having sex only occasionally. Some of our species engage in sexual acts only after they have been legally or religiously sanctioned through marriage, while others have sex only outside of marriage. Some people, for religious, political, or personal reasons, decide not to have an active sex life at all.

In addition, a moment's thought tells us that we don't actually have sex every time we feel the biological urge. Thus, while it can be assumed that everyone (or almost everyone) at your college or university has sexual feelings—and many may be thinking sexual thoughts all day long—there aren't masses of students and faculty having sex all over the campus. In order to live together, humans had to bring such "natural" urges under social control.

The notion of a natural sex drive or a sex instinct that mechanically leads to a behavioural outcome does not adequately explain sexual behaviour in our species. The same can be said of other behaviours commonly deemed to be "just natural." The key question, then, is not whether we have universal, inborn tendencies; rather, it is how members of a species, all bringing with them the same basic genetic matter, end up displaying a variety of behavioural outcomes. No other species displays this kind of diversity.

Humans are *of* the animal world, but unique within it. Only humans have the ability to alter nature in complex ways and to transmit, through language, new ideas and accumulated knowledge through generations. This makes us the most flexible and adaptable of all species. We are the only species capable of conscious thought and abstract reasoning, able to look back on the past and plan for the future. Whatever genetic push exists in our species toward certain types of behaviour is highly generalized. In other words, while all members of our species may carry genes with a tendency to push behaviour in certain directions, there nonetheless remains a range of possible behavioural outcomes.

Because it is so much a part of our common-sense understanding of human behaviour, many of us have a problem giving up the notion of human instincts. Sometimes it is argued that, while we all have certain instincts, we are able, under particular conditions, to reject or repress them. Thus, in this line of reasoning, students don't have sex every time they feel the urge because they have learned to repress their feelings; it would be socially embarrassing if they didn't. Similarly, some might argue that a man who takes his own life has successfully repressed his survival instinct, or a woman who gives up a child for adoption has repressed her maternal instinct.

The problem with such arguments is that they simultaneously explain everything and nothing. If we can overcome our nature or instincts by force of will, how do we know which behaviours are the instincts and which the rejection of the instincts? How do we know we don't have a jumping-up-and-down-stark-naked-and-shrieking instinct that we have all repressed because it is so embarrassing? Or perhaps we all have a nose-picking instinct, which most of us repress because it is so disgusting. But late at night, while we're alone studying and there's no one around, out pops the instinct!

Arguments that focus on the centrality of human instincts are an example of biological determinist explanations of human behaviour. In the end, focusing on the biological *alone* is neither useful nor adequate in explaining human behaviour. That is not to say that there is no biological or genetic component to human behaviour; this is as false and simplistic as the opposite argument. As previously noted, humans *are* biological beings and do bring with them at birth a range of potentials, both at the level of our species and as individuals. Unfortunately, only some of us have the capacity to become a talented pianist, a brilliant scientist, or a professional hockey player. Human behaviours are thus the result of a complex interplay of biological elements and social learning, with each feeding back on and altering the other in a never-ending process.

Think About It
Can you think of human behaviours not mentioned here that are frequently said to be "just natural"? Why do you think this is such a common explanation?

The Popularity of Biological Determinist Arguments
Sociologists study not only human behaviour, but human ideas as well. One fascinating question is why ideas retain their popularity even when proof of their legitimacy is weak or absent entirely. For example, it is interesting to ask why so many people read their horoscopes when there is

no substantive evidence to support the validity of astrological predictions. Likewise, the question arises as to why biological determinist theories keep reappearing—not only in the popular press, but also within social science itself—even though such approaches have long been discredited. Again and again these theories have been critiqued for their shoddy science. These theories remain popular not because of their academic credibility, but rather because they help maintain the belief that our current social arrangements are unchangeable.

A recurring theme of biological determinist arguments is that social inequality is based on underlying biological differences. According to these arguments, since social inequalities are the result of individual differences that are innate, then clearly little can be done to eliminate the inequalities.

As we will see in the next chapter, structured social inequality developed

---

Box 2.1 Can We Identify Criminals by Their Appearance?

Among the earliest theorists to formulate a biological explanation of human behaviour was Cesare Lombroso, an Italian physician who, in the late nineteenth century, argued that criminals could be identified by certain physiological characteristics. According to Lombroso, certain body markers demonstrated that "born criminals" were evolutionary throwbacks to our apelike past. As a result, Lombroso felt criminals would display this apishness not only in their behaviour but also in their appearance. Among the characteristics Lombroso thought were identifying characteristics of a criminal were a large jaw, relatively long arms, large ears, absence of baldness, darker skin, and the inability to blush. He even argued that one could identify prostitutes by their feet, which he thought were similar to apes, with the big toe widely separated from the others. Lombroso also saw some social traits as markers for criminality. It is rather humorous to note—given today's fashion—that Lombroso identified tattoos as one such marker (Gould 1981, 125–32).

Lombroso's theory was taken quite seriously in its day, and Lombroso was often called in as an expert at criminal trials. Many individuals were convicted of crimes solely on the basis of Lombroso's testimony that they must be guilty since they *looked* like a criminal.

We like to think that things have changed a great deal since then, but have they? Some years ago, a friend, who is a university graduate and government employee, told me of an incident that happened to him in Toronto. He was riding home one evening on his bicycle, when he was stopped by the police, thrown against the police car, and had his hands twisted behind his back. After extensive questioning, he was let go. The next day he called his local police station to complain and insisted he be told why he was apprehended. He was furious. The police officer eventually explained that there had been a theft of some musical equipment in the neighbourhood, and he fit the description of the thief. He was a Black male.

Although almost all policing agencies deny that there is such a thing as racial profiling, most people of colour have experienced it. Racial profiling means that people get targeted on the basis of perceived membership in a group associated with particular stereotypes rather than anything they have done (Sears 2005, 79). Since 9/11, this tendency has increased. People who fit some vague description of a "terrorist" may find themselves stopped for questioning by security officials, unable to fly on an airplane, refused entry into a country, or even arrested.

around seven to ten thousand years ago, and we can assume that there have been explanations for this inequality as long as it has existed. Prior to the modern industrial age, however, there was little expectation that there should be, or could be, equality for all. Certainly, disadvantaged groups opposed—often violently—their conditions of life. What they were generally demanding, though, were material improvements to those conditions (Lewontin 2001, 199). In contrast, the industrial era, as we will see in the next few chapters, offered its citizenry the possibility of social equality. The great rallying cry of the French Revolution was "Liberty, Equality, Fraternity." The founding constitution of the United States stated that "all men are created equal." Of course, the slogans seldom fit with reality. While some people did improve their lot, most social inequality continued as before, often—as in the case of slavery—with horrific consequences.

Think About It

Biological determinist arguments began to expand at the end of the nineteenth century, primarily in the United States and Great Britain. This was shortly after slavery was abolished in both countries. What might be the link between these two developments?

By the second half of the nineteenth century, theorists began to use the developing tools of science to "prove" that structured inequalities were the result of natural biological differences between populations. Darwin's *Origin of Species*, published in 1859, provided a key analytical framework. The core of Darwin's argument revolved around the competition for survival that existed in nature. Although this work did not actually deal with our species, others concluded that, since we are part of the natural world, the competition between individuals and groups in human society must also be a biological given. Thus, some theorists explained social inequalities by arguing that the richest and most powerful in any society were meant to succeed because they were most "fit"; social inequality was simply the working out of the laws of nature. Such arguments came to be known collectively as **social Darwinism**. It is worth noting that the phrase "survival of the fittest" was not in fact coined by Darwin, as is usually assumed, but rather by Herbert Spencer, a British sociologist considered to be one of the "founding fathers" of the discipline and an early social Darwinist.

In addition to a focus on social inequality, a second underlying theme of biological determinism has been that human aggression, competition, and territoriality have a biological basis. These arguments were particularly popular in the immediate post–World War II period and were promoted by writers such as Konrad Lorenz, Robert Ardrey, Desmond Morris, and Raymond Dart. This theme can also be seen in William Golding's still-popular novel *Lord of the Flies*, about a group of British schoolboys marooned on a deserted island. Removed from the social constraints of "civilization," their "true" bestial and predatory natures, previously held in check, come out into the open.

Both the notion that inequality is the result of individual characteristics and the belief that aggression and territoriality are innate help to justify the world as it is currently structured. As all of us know, we live in a world of war, extreme social inequalities, and widespread poverty. Biological determinist arguments are "big fish" theories that argue "the world is just" by drawing our attention away from the social origins of human behaviour.

From Theory to Practice: The Eugenics Movement

Biological determinist arguments are not simply incorrect; they are dangerous, for they have actually been put into practice in the form of **eugenics** (from the Greek word meaning "well-born"). An examination of eugenics helps us see that social theories are not just abstract thoughts developed by professors in ivory towers; rather, theories are often used by social groups to further their aims. Eugenics started as a theory, shifted to a social movement, and later became government policy in many countries, including Canada and the United States. The argument went this way: If certain human behavioural traits are inherited, and if some of these traits are deemed by a society as negative, then it is a simple enough task to "improve" the species. For eugenicists, if adults display characteristics thought to be hereditary handicaps, such individuals should simply be sterilized. This argument was first developed in the late nineteenth century by Francis Galton, Charles Darwin's cousin.

It is not hard to see that this is a slippery slope with no end: characteristics are simply assumed to be genetically based, and the number of characteristics deemed to be inferior continually expands. For example, the Model Eugenical Sterilization Law, drawn up in the United States in 1922, advocated the compulsory sterilization of all people judged to be members of the "socially inadequate classes"; these included all those with physical or mental disabilities (including epilepsy, blindness, and deafness), alcoholics, the "criminalistic," and the "dependent (including orphans, ne'er-do-wells, the homeless, tramps and paupers)" (quoted in Chase 1977, 134). While few governments actually went as far as sterilizing all these people, sterilization on the basis of criminality, epilepsy, and what was then termed "feeblemindedness" was fairly common.

In Canada, both British Columbia and Alberta passed legislation allowing for the sterilization of the "feebleminded" and the setting up of eugenics boards. Most of the victims were foster children or had been raised in institutions. Elsewhere in Canada, eugenical arguments became quite popular. For example, in 1935,

> The growth of a large business is merely a survival of the fittest.... The American Beauty rose can be produced only by sacrificing the early buds which grow up around it. This is not an evil tendency in business. It is merely the working out of a law of nature and a law of God.
> —American financier John D. Rockefeller, 1902

> Natural Selection, otherwise known as the Rotman [School of Business] Admission Process: Species in the wild constantly find themselves in a struggle for survival. And candidates eager to join the Rotman School are no different. The competition promises to be fiercer than ever.
> —advertisement for the Rotman School of Business, University of Toronto, 2002

Box 2.2 Eugenics in Alberta

Leilani Muir spent most of her childhood living in foster homes. In 1955, when she was ten, she entered Alberta's Provincial Training School for Mental Defectives. The following year, based on the results of an IQ test and a short interview, the Alberta Eugenics Board labelled her a "moron" and approved her for sterilization. When she was fourteen she was told that her appendix was to be removed. During the operation, the surgeons—without informing her—also cut her fallopian tubes, preventing her from ever having children. She married at twenty-five and tried to start a family. Only later did she discover why she was unable to become pregnant. She and her husband were later divorced.

More than 2800 people in Alberta were sterilized between 1928 and 1972 before the Sexual Sterilization Act was finally repealed. In 1996, Muir and her lawyers brought her case before the Alberta Provincial Court. She was awarded $740,000 for wrongful sterilization and wrongful confinement. Over 1200 of the victims eventually brought similar suits against the Alberta government.

Agnes Macphail, Canada's first woman member of Parliament, argued at a meeting of United Farm Women that it was immoral to allow "defectives" to breed (McLaren 1990, 121). After a royal commission in Ontario in 1930 recommended sterilization legislation, the province's lieutenant-governor warned of the "alarming consequences if idiots are permitted to procreate their kind" (quoted in Henton 1996).

Once one has accepted such arguments, it becomes possible to move to the next step. If characteristics are both inferior and genetically based, sterilization may not be adequate. Some individuals may escape the process and continue to "contaminate" the population. To prevent this from happening, some eugenicists argued that such inferior types should be eliminated, for their own good and the good of society. In 1933, the German government instituted a law similar to that in the United States, which called for the sterilization of all persons suffering from diseases considered hereditary, including mental illness, learning disabilities, physical deformity, epilepsy, blindness, deafness, and severe alcoholism. However, in 1939 Hitler proceeded to the next step by personally initiating a decree that gave physicians the power to grant a "mercy death" to "patients considered incurable according to the best available human judgment of their state of health." Those with physical and mental disabilities were the first to be sent to the Nazi death camps, and approximately 275,000 disabled people were killed.

The evidence detailing the horrific outcome of such theories largely discredited the eugenics movement for a long time after World War II. However, eugenical arguments tend to reappear from time to time. For example, in the November 1994 newsletter for Mensa, an organization for people with high IQ test scores, one author suggested that "society must face the concept that we kill off the old, weak, the stupid and the inefficient," while another proposed that most of the homeless "should be done away with, like abandoned kittens" (*Toronto Star*, January 11, 1995).

Genetics and "Inherited Tendencies"

The early biological determinist arguments have now been replaced by arguments focusing on genetics, with its underlying assumptions that a large proportion of human anatomy, physiology, and behaviour is "controlled" or "determined" by our genes (Lewontin 2001, 205). Thus, or so it is commonly believed, the Human Genome Project, a major project by geneticists that mapped the sequencing of DNA in the human organism, will allow scientists—with the aid of the multi-billion dollar private biotechnology sector—to "improve" individuals and societies in a way that the eugenicists never imagined.

However, even though a characteristic may be *heritable*—that is, passed on through the genes—it is still possible that the physical or social environment can have an effect on it. For example, although both body shape and height are highly heritable traits, they can nonetheless be affected by diet, general health, lifestyle habits, and so on. Obesity is a growing phenomenon around the world even though our genetic make-up has remained essentially the same. Likewise, a person may inherit a genetic predisposition toward cancer, but whether a person actually develops the disease will depend on many other factors, including some that have nothing to do with genetics, such as stress, diet, socioeconomic status, and contact with carcinogens. What is even more fascinating, evidence indicates that one's health may be related to broader social variables that are not "inside" the individual at all. For example, extensive research has shown that people living in more equal societies—regardless of their personal income—are healthier overall than those living in unequal societies (Wilkinson and Pickett 2010, 84).

The issues become even more complicated when we analyze behaviour rather than physiology. What does it mean to define someone as "mentally defective," "criminalistic," or "alcoholic"? Such categories are not scientifically precise; they are socially created and subjectively determined. In addition, it is simply impossible to separate out the genetic component of a particular behaviour, since the genes themselves are in constant interaction with their environment. There are simply so many possible environmental influences and such a complex interplay between environmental and inherited factors that a simplistic "cause" of the condition is impossible to detect (Hubbard and Wald 1993, 103).

Those who are identical twins, or those who know them, will agree that genetically matched individuals do not grow up to become identical people. While the number of shared traits of such individuals is greater than that of non-related individuals or even non-identical twins, identical twins are by no means a mirror image of each other, even with regard to illnesses known to be genetically transmitted. Clearly, genetics alone does not mechanically determine human characteristics. Put somewhat differently, both "nature" (our biological potential) and "nurture" (what we learn) make us who we are.

Recent revelations from the Human Genome Project and the decades of research that preceded it have helped us understand that human behaviour is more complicated than the biological determinists would have us believe. The latest genetic research seems to show that our genes are not fixed and unchangeable, but rather are themselves affected by their environments, beginning in the womb. Thus, modern genetics is demonstrating what most sociologists have long argued: human behaviour is the result of a complex interaction between inherited predispositions and the social world.

Despite growing questions about biological determinist explanations of human behaviour, such theories remain very popular. This is partially explained by the fact that such arguments are both simple and, on the surface, appear to be self-evident. For example, some might argue that although governments have spent millions of dollars trying to help the worst off in our society as well as trying to eliminate crime and gross social inequalities, crime and social inequality continue to exist. The conclusion might therefore be that the causes of crime and poverty must lie within the individual. Such arguments allow us to acknowledge social problems without having to consider the possibility of any type of social transformation. If poverty is the result of low intelligence, or criminality of a genetic predisposition, then there is no more need to waste money on social reforms.

In contrast, most sociologists agree that understanding what it means to be human requires a more complex analysis of our species, as well as some examination of how our behaviour came to be less rigidly tied to its biological roots. This necessitates a brief look at the place of humans in evolution.

The Process of Evolution

While the concept of evolution will forever be connected to Charles Darwin (1809–82), many prior to Darwin—indeed, as far back as the ancient Greeks—had formulated similar notions. Darwin's contribution was that he was the first to provide a comprehensive and well-documented explanation, which he termed *natural selection*, for the way evolution occurred. The experimental work of Gregor Mendel (1822–84) on heredity some years later confirmed the process and added to our scientific understanding of how species survive and change.

Both Darwin and Mendel discovered that what appear on the surface as opposites—*similarity* (of members of a species when compared to another species) and *variation* (of individual members within a species)—were actually two interconnected aspects of the same reality (Lewontin 2001, 68).

Think About It

Imagine a world in which everyone was the same as you. Could our species survive if we were all the same?

It is interesting to note that Darwin never actually used the term *evolution*. Prior to Darwin, evolution was thought of as a process of advancement, of movement from lower to higher, from worse to better (Gould 1977, 36). Within this framework, humans were seen as the highest form of development in a hierarchy from simpler to more complex organisms. In contrast, Darwin saw a species as well developed if it survives in its natural habitat and produces viable genetic offspring, whatever its place in the natural world. A central principle of natural selection is that the process is both random (that is, it occurs without a specific pattern) and unplanned.

It is often falsely assumed that species evolve in some kind of planned way. For example, a young children's book on dinosaurs (Watson 1980) notes that, in order to protect themselves from the bloodthirsty *Tyrannosaurus rex*, some creatures grew long legs, some learned to fly, and others took to the sea and swam. This perspective is also seen in academic literature: an introductory sociology text explains that "the savanna-dwelling apes evolved into our ancestors because the environment of the savanna forced them to develop a new set of characteristics" (Thio 1994, 41). While it might not have been the intention of the authors, such arguments leave the reader with the impression that evolution moves in specific directions as a conscious response to changing conditions.

In reality, organisms cannot plot their genetic futures. Rather, there are a number of unplanned processes that cause species to change. Because there are variations in the basic genetic matter of humans, certain minor alterations might suddenly confer a benefit to the organism that contains it. This variation would then likely be passed on to offspring and might eventually spread throughout a population. This is most likely to occur where environments are changing. If certain genetic variations or new characteristics accumulate within a population to the point where the organisms contain substantially different genetic matter from the original parent generation, a new species has come into existence.

It is most easy to observe this process with regard to changes *within* species. Houseflies, for example, have developed a resistance to DDT, a pesticide originally used to eliminate insects. However, because of variation within the genes that affect the sensitivity of flies to DDT, some flies were more resistant and some less. With the widespread application of DDT, the flies sensitive to this pesticide were killed—and their genes lost—while those resistant to the pesticide survived and reproduced, passing their genes on to future generations. Eventually the entire species became resistant to DDT (Lewontin 2001, 55). In the same fashion, as a result of excessive use of antibiotics, many bacterial infections in humans that were once easily eliminated with these medicines are now resistant to them.

In order to comprehend the full process of evolution, we must understand the vast period of time in which it normally takes place. (The above examples are interesting to us because we can observe the evolutionary process within a short period of time; however, these entail only small alterations within species.) It is also crucial to understand that the entire process of evolution is not linear; we do not begin with a single-celled organism and move neatly to multicellular organisms, up through, say, fish to reptiles to mammals to humans. Rather, we must picture evolution as a winnowing-out process, in which a vast array of varying life forms did not survive because of failure to adapt to changing environments or as a result of recurring mass extinctions. Surviving species, while genetically similar, branched and evolved in fairly distinctive ways.

In the context of evolution, behaviours that are a result of instincts or inborn patterns are neither better nor worse than those acquired through learning. Each works well under certain conditions. In unchanging environments, inborn patterns confer a certain advantage—each member of the species will automatically acquire certain mechanisms required for survival. Learning, however, can be useful in changing environments.

Humans and Evolution

Humans are mammals that are members of the order Primata, the primates. This order also includes various families of monkeys, as well as the great apes—chimpanzees, bonobos, gorillas, and orangutans—to whom humans are most closely related. Our species, *Homo sapiens*, belongs to the family Hominidae, the hominids, and is the only remaining member of this category. Humans share certain characteristics and genetic coding with other primates. However, despite this connection, we are here today as a species because we became distinct from chimps and apes. This distinction makes us unique among living things.

As mentioned earlier, humans are the most flexible and adaptable of all species. This means that humans are not particularly well adapted for a specific environment as are most other animals. For example, think of the polar bear, with its thick non-pigmented fur and other physiological traits that allow it to survive in the extreme cold of the far north. Unfortunately, as a result of global warming, the species is now under threat because it is physiologically not well suited to the changing environment.

Humans, in contrast, have been able to find ways of surviving in almost every environment, from the Arctic Circle to the equator, from the ocean floor to outer space. This is so because hominids, in the process of evolution, gradually acquired a package of characteristics that has allowed survival under near-impossible odds. We may be quite genetically similar to chimpanzees and bonobos, but just a small difference means a huge distinction in our species. What eventually became the "human package" includes **bipedalism** (standing upright on two feet), which freed the hands for the production and use of tools; an increase in the size and capacity of the brain; complex communication through language; and the control of sexuality. But these changes would have mattered little—indeed, they likely would have never occurred—if humans were not able to live together in social groups. Our evolutionary ancestors certainly show the beginnings of both empathy and sociability, but it becomes most developed in our species, with its capacity to share. Indeed, it is the characteristic of sharing, of both food and knowledge, which sets us apart from other species. A number of inter-related developments help explain the basis for human existence. While they are being separated out here for theoretical analysis, in reality each developed as a part of a complex package, with every element feeding back on, and reinforced by, the others.

Bipedalism and Toolmaking

It has long been theorized that bipedalism evolved in our hominid ancestors after the changing ecology in Africa pushed them from a tree-dwelling existence onto open grassy plains; in this environment it was thought that bipedalism would have provided a number of survival advantages, including the ability to see predators above the tall grasses. However, debates are still occurring about the actual process and the time when bipedalism first appeared.

Whatever the actual process, it is clear that bipedalism was an advantage for survival once our ancestors lived on open plains, called savannas, where one could be easily spotted by predators. Bipedalism, even if only temporarily, made an animal look bigger to other animals and allowed it to brandish sticks or hurl objects at its enemies. Standing upright also allowed for a wider view of the surroundings. Most importantly, bipedalism freed our hands for making and using tools. The earliest tools were probably sticks, used for digging at roots or for threatening other animals. In addition to bipedalism, other characteristics—superior eyesight with stereoscopic vision, an opposable thumb, and precision grip—made possible the full use of the forelimbs for manipulating the environment. Toolmaking eventually led to the development of hunting as an activity. It would also have encouraged communication between members, as well as some forethought and planning. All of these elements, in turn, helped develop brain function.

Meat Eating

It is also likely that we are here today as a species because our ancestors began to have meat as a more regular part of their diets. Although some apes and chimps occasionally feast on an animal, vegetarianism is the norm. Hominids, on the other hand, are omnivores; that is, they eat both meat and vegetable matter as a normal part of their diet. It is believed that for our hominid ancestors in Africa, meat may have constituted as much as 30 percent of the diet (Leakey and Lewin 1977, 159).

Hunting and meat eating did not turn our ancestors into aggressive, bloodthirsty killers. Quite the opposite—meat eating is important to our species' existence because it propelled us toward cooperation and sharing. Herbivores (non-meat eaters) can survive as individuals, tearing off leaves and berries; in contrast, hunting, especially the large-game hunting undertaken by the hominid line, requires collective planning and action. It also encourages the collective consumption of the spoils.

We now understand that meat constitutes a readily absorbed complete protein, and those of our prehuman ancestors who began to consume it would likely have had a physical advantage for survival. But far more important are the consequences of hunting with regard to social development.

Leakey and Lewin argue: "The key to the transformation of a social ape-like creature into a cultural animal living in a highly structured and organized society is sharing: the sharing of jobs and the sharing of food. Meat eating was important in propelling our ancestors along the road to humanity, but only as a package of socially-oriented changes involving the gathering of plant foods and sharing the spoils" (149).

Hunting and gathering, or foraging, societies are examined in more detail in Chapter 3. However, it is worth noting at this point that hunting required a dividing up of jobs (referred to as a **division of labour**), with some members hunting and others gathering the roots, nuts, and berries that constituted the major part of the diet. This, in turn, required forms of cooperation, sharing, restraint of individual impulses, and a dependence on others that is not seen in any other species. Once this tendency to share food began, it went far beyond the mere requirements of nutrition or basic survival. In all human societies, sharing seems to be the glue that binds individuals together—it becomes a social ritual that promotes social solidarity (White 1965, 79). And it is this social solidarity that, in turn, maximizes the chances of individual survival in a very precarious world.

Think About It

What traditions exist in your ethnic or religious community that involve the sharing of food? How many holidays have the sharing of food as a central activity, even if—in theory—they are religious events? Why might so many cultures have a period of fasting as part of their traditions?

Language and Symbols

Of course, the ability to hunt and live together in communities would have been severely limited if our prehuman ancestors had been unable to communicate with each other. Other animals communicate—even insects and birds can communicate such things as readiness to mate or imminent danger. But only humans can communicate using elaborate systems of symbolization. Humans communicate primarily through the use of **symbols**, which are physical, vocal, or gestural signs that have arbitrary, socially learned meanings attached to them. Some sociologists argue that our ability to create symbols, along with our social essence, is the core of what makes us human.

Words are a good example of symbols. Suppose we want to communicate to another person the notion of a small furry animal that many of us have as pets. If we speak English, we could say *cat*. But that sound is arbitrary, in the sense that there is no automatic attachment between the word and its meaning. We could just as easily say *gato*, *pusa*, or *kedi*. Whatever the word, however, it has meaning only if the receiver has been taught beforehand to comprehend the meaning of the sound being made.

Objects can also be symbols. Think, for example, of the following diverse objects: a swastika; a gold ring worn on the third finger of the left hand; a white cloth with a stylized red leaf in the middle and two red bars on either side; the letter M in the shape of two large arches. Each of these objects has a symbolic meaning to those who have been taught to understand it. We learn the meaning of such symbols through our various social institutions, such as the family or schools. The advertising industry spends billions of dollars creating symbols to sell products. For example, the De Beers Corporation created one of the most successful advertising campaigns in modern history by turning the diamond engagement ring into a symbol of love.

Verbal symbols ultimately become codified into spoken and written language systems. These highly elaborate systems consist of more than strings of words; they also have a shared set of rules and structures. These systems allow humans to communicate extremely complex thoughts and to go beyond the concrete here and now. We can assess the past or ponder the future. We can deal with reality, or we can consider the mystical. We can discuss feelings, theories, or aesthetics. And we can pass on all our ideas and knowledge to the next generation. All this is possible not simply because of our language systems, but also because of the capacities of the human brain.

A number of authors have recently argued that hominids made music before they made language, and, in fact, music may be the key to understanding how we developed language. One author (Mithen 2006) believes that before our ancestors had language, it was music that advanced their sociability. Music helped them calm a child, find a mate, and work collectively; it helped bind people together. Even today, music—especially singing together with others—is a universal component of all cultures.

Think About It
Do you like listening to music, singing, or playing an instrument? Can you explain why? What does it feel like when you sing or play in a group? Is there music that can make you cry?

Large and Complex Brain
The brain of *Homo sapiens* is unique in the animal world. It is not simply the size of the organ that makes it special—although the primate brain is distinctively large relative to body size—but rather it is its complexity that makes it unique. Within the primate line, a gradual increase in the size of the brain can be seen along an evolutionary time frame, with the brain of *Homo sapiens* the largest. In evolutionary terms, those who could come up with the best ideas for survival—and who could pass them on to offspring who could then build new ideas upon them—had the best chance of survival.

This large and complex brain allows us to communicate through language and other symbols; it also allows us to live in social groups where complex understandings of social interaction are required. Humans seem unique in having what psychologists refer to as a "theory of mind," the ability to understand what others of their species are feeling or thinking. In everyday terms, we usually refer to this ability as *empathy*. In order to inter-

> J.K. Rowling created narrative magic with the character of Harry Potter. Her books about the boy wizard... re-established the importance of one sadly outdated commodity: human empathy.... Harry Potter stands on a foundation that plays to the very noblest of human abilities: our capacity to love each other, forgive each other, and work together to overcome divisive and selfish forces of evil.
>
> —film reviewer Katherine Monk

> Next to death, solitary confinement is our most extreme form of punishment. Our bodies and minds are not designed for lonely lives. We become hopelessly depressed in the absence of human company, and our health deteriorates.
>
> —primatologist Frans de Waal

act with others and live in social groups, we need to have the ability to both understand and predict what others are thinking. One author (Baron-Cohen, 2011) argues that empathy in fact has two aspects. The first is our attempt to identify another person's thoughts and feelings, and the second is our attempt to respond appropriately to those thoughts and feelings. It is an extension of the human capacity to share, in this case, to share our emotions. Put differently, it involves our ability to "put ourselves in someone else's shoes."

For most of human history, as we will see in Chapter 3, humans lived in relatively small, highly homogeneous groups. For these hunting and gathering people, their ability to "read" what another person was thinking and feeling was made easier by the fact that they came into regular face-to-face contact with others in their social group, and those others were relatively similar to themselves.

Today, most of us live in large anonymous cities where we may not even know the people who live in the same building as us. We go to schools where we often have little connection to the people in our classes. We get into private automobiles to get from one place to another, or we sit on public transit and avoid making eye contact. We are instructed as children "not to talk to strangers," and even as adults we feel uncomfortable when total strangers start talking to us in public places. Nonetheless, our ability to be empathetic remains a core element of what it means to be human.

Think About It

In the twenty-first century we spend increasing amounts of time interacting with others electronically via phones or the Internet, rather than face-to-face. Do you think this affects our ability to be empathetic?

Control of Sexuality

Humans have a different pattern of sexual activity than any other mammal species. Most mammals are generally sexually inactive, copulating only when females are ovulating and capable of being fertilized. Moreover, female mammals will solicit copulation specifically when they are ovulating; in contrast, human females can never be absolutely certain that they are ovulating. Since sexual intercourse for humans occurs at any stage of the reproductive cycle, and even during pregnancy or after menopause, much of it can have nothing to do with reproduction. This is another reflection of our liberation from the purely biological. For humans, sex takes on additional social, psychological, and recreational functions that have nothing to do with conception.

Our need to form social groups, to share and cooperate, required some kind of restraint of individual behaviours, and this must have included the realm of the sexual. All societies that have been studied by social scientists seem to have rules putting some limits on sexual behaviours. Although *specific* behaviours can vary from society to society, all societies seem to tolerate or encourage some kinds of sexual behaviours while discouraging or prohibiting others. There are, however, two universal social customs relating to sexuality that are of interest to social scientists. First, humans generally have sex in private, while all other group-living animals copulate in public. The other pattern is the **incest taboo**, which forbids sexual relations between those defined as kin, or family. No one knows for certain why these two behaviours are practised in our species, and many theories to explain them have been formulated.

What is known is that extended kinship networks were essential to early human societies through their provision of mutual aid. Keeping sex private and adhering to the incest taboo clearly must have helped families remain stable, thus giving them a better chance of survival. In this way, human biology was brought under social control. Of course, despite its prohibition incest continues to occur in most societies, including our own, as does adultery. Humans don't need to create rules preventing behaviours that we have no capacity to do; the human fear and detestation of incest, as Freud noted, is proof that we have a biological capacity to engage in it.

Think About It

Try to imagine a society where everybody could have sex with anyone they felt attracted to at any time. What problems might this create for the social group?

Humans as Social Animals

Humans are, above all, a sociable species. Living together allows for the sharing of knowledge, as well as for increased protection against predators. If, as hypothesized, a climatic change in Africa led to the decline in forested areas, species that were pushed into the open grasslands would have been in competition for food with species better adapted to that environment. It is a reasonable hypothesis that the basic sociability of our prehuman ancestors is the likely reason for their survival under virtually impossible odds. This sociability was subsequently selected for over time (the most sociable individuals tended to survive and mate), pushing our prehuman ancestors even further in this direction.

Other animal species—including bees, ants, and many of the primates—live in social groups. Orangutans and chimpanzees even show some ability to transmit knowledge and skills from one generation to another, thus creating elements of culture once thought to be the exclusive domain of humans. The appearance and development of what is now termed social intelligence allowed hominids to live together. It likely also became part of a feedback loop that allowed our prehuman ancestors to engage in more collective activities such as hunting, to converse more, and to develop their social networks and social skills. This, in turn, likely helped hominid brains develop and encouraged more sociability.

The origins of our increasing sociability are unknown, but bipedalism may have played an important role. Unlike virtually all mammals, human females do not deliver their offspring alone; rather, they get help from other women, which probably saves the life of both mother and child. One reason that humans need help from others is because the baby emerges from the womb in a manner that makes it very hard for a woman to deliver her child alone, as she needs help making sure it is free from the umbilical cord and mucus. In addition, the length of time that infants need to be cared for and fed is much greater than for other species. This longer period of dependency probably led to an increase in the need for food sharing and long-term male-female bonding. Strong bonding would also have developed between offspring and their mothers, as well as bonding between siblings (Ehrenberg 2001).

Conclusion

This chapter has shown that, although humans are part of the animal world, we are unique within it. Humans are born in a pronounced state of physical immaturity, and we have an extremely long dependence period relative to our lifespan. Thus we can survive only by becoming part of a social group for an extended period of time. Given this reality, it is absurd to envisage society as something that constrains us, or as something that controls our true selves. There is no "self" that can exist outside the social world of which it is a part. It is also senseless to imagine a "biological" human outside of a social context. From the moment of birth, our physiological selves are in constant interaction with our social world, with each acting on and affecting the other. The biological determinist assertion—that behaviours as complex as aggression, addiction, or homosexuality can be the result of a single gene or genes—is far too simplistic.

It is important, therefore, to repeat that there is no substantive proof to support such arguments. The information currently available to us from fields as diverse as anatomy, genetics, zoology, anthropology, and palaeontology negates the commonly held view that human behaviour is simply a natural expression of our biology. Rather, the overwhelming body of evidence indicates that human behaviour is the result of a complex interaction between our biological inheritance and the social world in which we live.

KEY POINTS

1. There is little evidence that human behaviour is the result of instincts.

2. Humans are of the animal world but unique within it. Humans are the most flexible and adaptable of all species.

3. Biological determinist arguments, which see certain aspects of human behaviour as being primarily the result of inborn characteristics, remain very popular. A substantial body of scientific research has repeatedly discredited such arguments, which help to justify and maintain social inequalities.

4. The eugenics movement turned biological determinist arguments into social policy, with horrifying outcomes for many individuals. Eugenics is not only morally bankrupt but also scientifically flawed.

5. Traits may be heritable, but the environment can still have an effect. Recent studies indicate that even genes themselves may be affected by their environment.

6. In the process of evolution, our prehuman ancestors acquired a package of traits that allowed them to survive under near-impossible odds. This package includes bipedalism and toolmaking, meat eating, increase in the size and capacity of the brain, complex communication through language, and the control of sexuality.

7. Above all, humans are social animals. Being human means being social.

8. Human behaviour is the result of a complex interplay between the biological and the social.

FURTHER READING

Gould, Stephen Jay. 1989. *Wonderful Life: The Burgess Shale and the Nature of History*. New York: W.W. Norton.
This work presents some key issues related to evolutionary processes, told as a detective story. Gould, who died in 2002, wrote a monthly column for *Natural History* for many years; many of these columns were gathered into collections and published as books. All of them are highly readable and are an excellent introduction to issues of natural history and evolution.

——. 1996. *The Mismeasure of Man*. New York: W.W. Norton.
This is a revised and expanded version of the original 1981 book, which provided a detailed historical overview of biological determinist theories. Of particular interest is Gould's critique of the methods and forms of statistical analysis used by many social scientists.

Johnson, Olive Skene. 2007. *The Sexual Spectrum: Why We're All Different*. Vancouver, B.C.: Raincoast Books.
Skene—a neuropsychologist and mother of two gay sons—examines from both a professional and personal viewpoint the many elements that influence gender behaviour and sexuality.

Laland, Kevin N., and Gillian R. Brown. 2011. *Sense and Nonsense: Evolutionary Perspectives on Human Behaviour.* 2nd ed. New York: Oxford University Press.

In the 1970s and 1980s, a debate raged between academics who saw human behaviour as primarily rooted in our genes and others who felt culture was the key variable. This book attempts to draw out the best from both arguments.

Mithen, Stephen. 2007. *The Singing Neanderthals: The Origins of Music, Language, Mind, and Body.* Boston: Harvard University Press.

The author—drawing on many academic fields—tries to explain why humans seem so compelled to both make and hear music.

Quammen, David (ed). 2011. *Charles Darwin On the Origin of Species: The Illustrated Edition.* New York: Sterling Signature Publishing.

Darwin's classic is re-issued here with a new introduction that makes it accessible to beginners.

Ryan, Christopher and Cacilda Jethá. 2011. *Sex at Dawn: The Prehistoric Origins of Modern Sexuality.* New York: Harper Collins.

A well-researched and fascinating look at human sexuality through the ages, as well as an examination of how our taken-for-granted assumptions about it may be incorrect.

de Waal, Frans. 2009. *Empathy: Nature's Lesson for a Kinder Society.* New York: Three Rivers Press.

Responding to sociobiology, this primatologist argues that empathy is rooted in our paleontological past.

Wilson, David Sloan. 2007. *Evolution for Everyone: How Darwin's Theory Can Change the Way We Think About Our Lives.* New York: Delacourt.

As the title notes, this is a beginners' introduction to Darwinian theory, written for a general audience by a professor of evolutionary biology.

3 Culture, Society, and History

In This Chapter

- What is culture, and how do we study it?
- Is there such a thing as Canadian culture?
- What did early societies look like, and what is the point of looking at societies that preceded ours?
- How did social inequality arise?

Why is it common today to see flowers left by total strangers at a spot where someone has recently died a violent death? Why do Canadian business people shake hands when meeting, while the Japanese bow? Why do Sikh men wear turbans? Why do we say "thank you" when someone has done us a favour? Why do Canadians eat with forks and knives, while other nationalities eat with chopsticks? The answer to all these questions, in a word, is culture. Culture is essentially the complete way of life shared by a people, including both the material and non-material elements. The non-material elements of culture include the *cognitive*, that is, the knowledge and beliefs of a people; the *symbolic*, which include verbal and non-verbal forms of communication; and the *normative*, or values, beliefs, and behavioural expectations of a people. The material elements of a culture include all of a group's material artefacts and products created by its members. The two elements are, of course, inter-related. For example, the existence of a mosque (material culture) is linked both to an Islamic belief system and a set of practices (non-material culture). Socialization is the ongoing process by which we learn the various cultural components and behavioural expectations of our social world.

There are four primary characteristics of culture (Sanderson 1999, 32). First, culture is learned, rather than being simply the result of some biological inevitability. Second, culture is rooted in symbols—physical, vocal, or gestural signs that have arbitrary, socially learned meanings to them. It is symbols that are the building blocks of all cultures. Third, culture is a system shared by all members of a society. It is the embodiment of a collective of individuals, past and present, rather than simply the behaviour of any one of them. Lastly, the elements of culture are generally integrated, in that the various components fit into a coherent whole, even though there may be contradictory or conflicting elements within the whole.

Box 3.1 Cultural Universals

We learned in the previous chapter that humans are social animals. We have always lived in groups, working out collective strategies for physical survival of ourselves and especially our offspring.

Despite the cultural diversity we see all around us, it must be remembered that we are all one species with the same basic biology and the same basic needs, such as physical survival, reproduction, sexual gratification, care of the young, keeping the group together, and so on. And because our species has the ability to think abstract thoughts and ponder the past and future, all cultures address what might be termed the "existential" questions of human life, such as these: Why are we here? Why is there so much suffering in the world? Where do we go after we die? Thus, while each culture is unique, they all share certain common elements, or *cultural universals*. In other words, all cultures are patterned in more or less similar ways.

There are many elements that are common to all societies, including the following:
- personal names
- family or household, i.e., kin groups
- rules delineating rights and obligations of group members
- rules defining right and wrong, good and bad
- inequalities of prestige
- statuses and roles, minimally by gender and age
- cooperative labour
- collective decision-making
- use of shame to limit unacceptable behaviours
- sports
- beliefs about death
- beliefs about disease
- beliefs about fortune and misfortune
- dream interpretation
- story-telling
- proverbs, sayings
- childbirth customs
- rites of passage (from one stage of life to another)
- music, rhythm, and dance
- death rituals, mourning
- food rules
- feasting
- creation stories

In the previous chapter it was argued that humans have few, if any, inborn patterns, or instincts. In other words, we are not preprogrammed for survival. Rather, in the process of living together, we work out appropriate patterns for survival under certain conditions. We develop technologies, expand our means of communicating with each other, construct social institutions, develop rules of social behaviour, and create values and belief systems that allow us to live together in groups. Collectively, this socially created package is referred to as a society's culture. Once developed, these cultural elements are passed on from one generation to the next, with each subsequent generation adding to, or modifying, them.

Humans must be taught the means of survival through the process of socialization, a process in which the members of each generation learn the cultural beliefs and patterns of those who preceded them. Luckily for us, as noted in the previous chapter, we have a long period of physical dependency after birth that allows us to learn culture from the adults around us. We have no choice in the matter; without learning language and societal norms, beliefs, and values, we would not be able to survive. The culture we learn throughout childhood and adolescence is a key part of who we become. In this sense, culture is "in us" as much as it is "out there." Not surprisingly, then, most of us are deeply attached to our language and culture; for many of us, the fear of being separated from our culture is equal to losing part of ourself. This helps us understand why recent immigrants to Canada so often seek out others who share their language, cultural traditions, or religious practices. Even Canadians who have simply changed locales may try to connect with others from "back home."

Think About It

Ask your parents or other relatives why they have (or have not) retained their connection to their ethnic, linguistic, or regional communities. Have you?

Box 3.1 gives us some indication of how similar all humans and their social groups are. However, these cultural universals must be understood as universal only in their most general aspects. We all have to eat to survive, but what, when, and how we eat are culturally determined. As we will see later in this chapter, a delicacy for one group of people may be inedible for another. We all have to deal with death and dying, but how we do so varies from culture to culture, and what is practised in one group may be offensive to another. Once these cultural practices—as well as the beliefs and values that are connected to these practices—come into being, they take on a life of their own and are handed down from generation to generation, whether or not they any longer have direct relevance to the survival of a people. Indeed, the fact that some customs continue even when there is no longer any particular reason tells us that we also seem to have a strong need for cultural traditions.

Embedded in all cultures is the assumption that the ways we do things—the food we eat, the beliefs we have, the way we organize ourselves, and so on—are normal and superior, while the ways of other people are strange or possibly even immoral. This tendency to see the world in terms of our own culture is referred to as **ethnocentrism**, and it exists in all societies. This universality makes sense, since no society could survive for long if most of its members continually questioned the validity of their cultural practices and beliefs (see Box 3.2).

Is There a Canadian Culture?

It is impossible to do an analysis of culture without taking a short side trip to assess whether there is such a thing as "Canadian culture." If one travels to France, Great Britain, China, or Iran, the people there will happily dis-

> As we interact and become part of a society or group, we generally come to feel something good about belonging to that group.... Becoming part of a group encourages a sense of loyalty, and that loyalty encourages ethnocentrism. Loyalty means a commitment to something we regard as important and right. It brings a feeling of obligation to serve and defend. Criticism and threats to the group are defended against.
> —*sociologist Joel Charon*

> If someone were to put a proposition before humans bidding them choose, after examination, the best customs in the world, each nation would certainly select its own.
> — *Herodotus, ancient Greek historian*

Box 3.2 "Us" versus "Them"

While each of us exists as an individual, we are simultaneously members of social groups. Whether it is going to a family reunion, wearing our favourite hockey team's colours, defending our country's military by literally wrapping ourselves in its flag, financially contributing to our religious community's building fund, or participating in a gay pride parade, it is clear that we generally feel good about being a part of a group. And in today's complex world, most of us belong to many groups. But being a member of a group can mean that others are excluded. The joy we feel at being part of "us" can easily escalate into a dislike or even intense hatred for "them," that is, those not part of our group. This can range from mild hostility to genocide and massacres of innocent people. The creation of an "us" versus "them" mentality has regularly been used by the powerful to promote their own political and economic interests. Moreover, many groups cling to disputes long past, with some ethnic and religious groups still seeking revenge for events that happened hundreds of years ago. Sadly, under certain political conditions the human propensity to be empathetic becomes highly selective. Modern history has repeatedly shown that we can have good friends from a different tribe, religion, or culture who live next door to us, and suddenly—urged on by others—our positive feelings can quickly be transformed into a hate so extreme that we can slit their throats, shoot them, or send them off to die in prison camps without any hesitation.

The good news is that the tension between "us" and "them" is not embedded in our genes. Rather, it is socially created and often passed down from one generation to the next. Certain groups that today may seem to be inevitably locked in a history of hatred had actually lived cooperatively for long periods of time, such as Jews and Moslems in Spain and in many parts of the Middle East. And some groups with recent histories of violence toward each other—such as the Catholics and Protestants of Northern Ireland—are slowly learning to live together in peace. Thus it seems possible for humans to move past the horrible consequences of a world divided into "us" and "them."

cuss their cultural traditions and what makes them distinctive. Canadians (with the exception of francophones in Quebec) are far less certain about who they are and whether there actually is such a thing as a distinctively Canadian culture. This is largely because Canada is such a young country in relative terms.

Think About It

What is there that could be defined as distinctively Canadian? Remember, culture consists of both material and non-material elements. What does being Canadian mean to you? Are there any foods you would consider distinctly Canadian? Do you think the region where you live has a distinct culture?

Our country began with the varying cultural traditions of numerous Indigenous peoples, plus two "charter" groups that originally came from Britain and France. The twentieth century saw the arrival of immigrants from every part of the globe; each group brought with it new cultural elements. But there was no real "melting pot" in Canada as there was in the United States, and these varied traditions did not quickly join together into a single culture. Because of Canada's size and relatively small population, it remained highly regionalized. In some ways, it is still easier to identify a distinct Newfoundland culture or an Acadian culture than a Canadian one. To make things even more complex, the cultures of the world are merging as a result of new technologies and globalization, with American culture dominant in this process. The United States has had a particularly strong influence on our culture, given its proximity and our shared English language.

> Canada is a large, diverse, and divided country. It covers almost ten million square kilometres spanning six time zones.... The population is widely dispersed; there are fewer than four persons per square kilometre. Almost 90 percent of Canadians live in a long east-west ribbon within 150 kilometres of the American border.... Canada is not an easy country to define, to govern, or to imagine.
> —Mary Vipond, Professor Emerita, Concordia University

Although there are common practices, norms, beliefs, and values that most Canadians share, these elements are by no means universal. Sometimes the differences break out into open hostilities, such as in debates about abortion, euthanasia, gay marriage, marihuana legalization, or gun control. In addition, French-speaking Canadians and the Indigenous peoples of Canada have felt that their cultural traditions and languages are being eroded through the dominance of English-Canadian social institutions and an English-speaking North American culture.

Canadian culture, like all cultures, must be viewed as fluid and malleable. Not only is culture created by humans, it is also perpetually being *re-created* by them. We are not automatons who mechanically accept and repeat what we learn from our parents and teachers. This does not mean that there are not elements of a culture that remain constant over time: indeed, some of our beliefs and patterns of behaviour are thousands of years old. Such an analysis simply implies that culture must not be studied as a closed, unchangeable system.

For example, let us examine the notion that the roles of men and women in Canadian society are largely determined by our cultural expectations regarding gender. To some extent, this is true. Certainly the many agents of socialization—such as family, schools, religious institutions, and mass media—reinforce traditional expectations regarding gender roles. At the same time, however, these very expectations are changing. For example, some women continue to be taught that certain jobs are inappropriate for their gender. Nonetheless, in spite of learning such notions, many women enter these occupations. They in turn become role models for the next generation of women, who further alter cultural expectations—and so on, in a never-ending process.

What we refer to as "Canadian culture" is an entity constantly being changed by Canadians themselves. For example, think of our flag, something most of us would consider an essential component of our culture. Yet this flag is relatively new, having been introduced—amid much controversy—in 1965. Similarly, although "O Canada" was written over a century ago, the English words were altered in 1968, and it officially became our national

Box 3.3 Changing Views About What It Means to Be Canadian

Story-telling is a core part of being human, and every cultural group has stories defining who they are and what they value. In nations of the modern age, government officials or their agents often create stories to advance their political agendas. In late 2009, a sixty-two-page citizens' guide, *Discover Canada: The Rights and Responsibilities of Citizenship*, was released by the Conservative government. The *Calgary Herald* lauded the new document, claiming that it "teaches Canada's key values and history that are a crucial part of Canada's identity as a nation."

The *Globe and Mail* compiled the most frequently used words in the new guide. Leading the list are obvious words like Canada (385 uses), Canadian (208), citizenship (83), government (71), and Quebec (66). However, there was no tabulation of words that were missing from the document or used infrequently, words one might expect to see in a discussion of Canadian society. For example, the word "unions" doesn't appear in the guide despite the fact that 4.2 million Canadians—or nearly 30 percent of working people—are union members. The word "feminist" is absent from the guide and "activist" appears only twice.

Nor does the guide mention prisons, poverty, medicare, landlords, tenants, or wealthy Canadians. The word "unemployment" is used four times, but for historical purposes only, the most recent being the introduction of unemployment insurance in 1940. The term "environment" is used nine times, but never in relation to environmental issues, and there are no concerns expressed about climate change. In contrast, the term "Dominion" is used sixteen times and the word "war" fifty-five times.

This guide fits with the shift to a much more militarized image of Canada. Whereas a decade or so ago Canada's armed forces were almost invisible, today they are very much a central part of our culture. They are highly visible in the media, celebrated at sporting events, and mythologized as the core of what it means to be Canadian. Images of the military as heroes are everywhere, and several major highways where fallen soldiers are transported have been renamed as a "highway of heroes." In 2011, the Winnipeg Jets hockey team unveiled their new jerseys (with a logo depicting a military jet placed over a maple leaf) by having players come out of the back hatch of a Canadian Forces Hercules jet fighter at the local Canadian air force base; in 2012 the Toronto Raptors basketball team unveiled their new camouflage–style jersey at the annual Canadian Forces night.

Sources: Gutstein 2010; Volpy 2009.

anthem only in 1980. Thus, newer elements are constantly becoming incorporated into the older culture, and the controversies that may have surrounded their introduction are normally forgotten. Likewise, certain cultural patterns become outmoded and disappear.

Think About It

Language is an important component of culture and is always being changed by those who use it. For example, we no longer speak the English of Shakespeare's day, although we can still understand it. Listen to the way your friends and classmates speak. In what ways do you talk differently from your parents' generation? Do you find yourself laughing at their quaint expressions? Do they ever ask you to explain what you're saying?

Toward a Dialectic of Culture

We can see that humans create culture because they live together in social groups to survive. But how do these cultures arise, why are there differences between groups, and why do cultural practices and forms of social organization change? How do we identify common patterns while acknowledging distinctive elements? Put plainly, how do we make sense of a sociocultural system? Can we ever really understand how societies work? Clearly, from the title of this book you can guess that the answer is yes. But where do we begin? For many centuries, philosophers have debated the relationship between the material world and the abstract world of human thoughts, feelings, and perceptions. Do humans create culture because of what is inside their heads or in response to what is in their environment? Obviously, if we think dialectically, it is a bit of both. However, many social scientists argue that the starting point is a society's material infrastructure, that is, how people within a society get their basic needs met. Box 3.4 provides an example of how food preferences can be explained from a materialist perspective.

In a similar fashion we can see that many aspects of Canadian life, including the "ideal" personality type and the dominant value system are linked to the material realities of our lives. Given the emphasis on the marketplace, on profit, and on perpetual economic growth in societies such as ours, it is not surprising that competition, hard work, individual enterprise, and personal accumulation of wealth are highly valued in our culture. While these values may seem natural and eternal to the reader, we will soon see that such ideals are not universally admired.

Karl Marx tried to explain how societies and cultures worked by focusing on what he called their **mode of production**. This term draws attention to the fact that the way humans get the things they need for survival—their food, clothing, and shelter—must be central to how they organize their societies and construct their cultures. Marx emphasized a society's *economy*, which is the organized production, distribution, and exchange of goods and services. In turn, a society's economy must be linked to three other interconnected factors (Sanderson 1999, 43): in the process of acquiring and distributing their means of existence, humans must work with what nature provides (*ecology*) and the characteristics of their own population (*demography*) to develop their tools and methods of survival (*technology*). And since humans are social animals, they must pursue their survival by entering into certain social relations with each other. A society with a specific mode of production can more precisely be referred to as a **socioeconomic formation**.

There are certainly other ways of looking at culture and society. However, the emphasis on a society's material infrastructure, that is, its mode of production, reminds us that the basis of all social life is physical survival. Humans must obtain the basics of life—food, clothing, and shelter—before they can do anything else, and they must do so by working together in social groups. If used in a dialectical rather than mechanical fashion, the concepts of mode of production and socioeconomic formation can help us understand

Box 3.4 Why Do Some Groups Shun Pork or Beef While Others Love It?

If you ask an observant Jew or Muslim why they don't eat pork, they will tell you that, according to their religious precepts, pigs are unclean animals. Similarly, observant Hindus, who don't eat beef, will tell you that the cow is considered holy. Anthropologist Marvin Harris (1989) was fascinated by religiously based food prohibitions. All religious groups believe that their food taboos are dictated by their god or gods. However, as a social scientist, Harris was interested in linking the origins of these religious practices, not primarily to beliefs, but rather to issues of environment and survival.

In the case of the Hindus in India, the cow was more useful if uneaten: it was an essential traction animal, and its dung could be used for fuel, building materials, and fertilizer. Those who ate their beasts during a famine would not survive for long. The question of the Jewish and Muslim prohibition of pork was particularly fascinating to Harris because peoples in New Guinea and the South Pacific Melanesian Islands not only ate the meat but also valued it so highly that they treated their pigs as family members. Harris linked the prohibition of pork to the particular ecology of the Middle East. Pig farming was poorly suited to the hot, dry climate of the region, making pigs costly to raise and in direct competition for resources required by humans. Since they were a tempting source of protein and fat, the best guarantee for limiting pig farming was to forbid the consumption of pig flesh.

According to Harris, the construction of certain food taboos can help increase the likelihood of survival. For the Hindus of India, where the cow performed essential functions, it could not be eaten. It therefore came to be revered. Among ancient Jews and other peoples of the Middle East, for whom the pig served no useful function but instead constituted a threat, pork came to be defined as unclean and an abomination.

This is not to say that those who practise such food prohibitions *see* their behaviour from this viewpoint; in fact, they rarely do. However, social scientists look for the underpinnings of human behaviour in the material conditions of our lives. It should also be noted that shared eating patterns are both a way to bind people together and to distinguish them from others. The fact that modern Jews, Muslims, and Hindus in completely different geographic and cultural environments continue to adhere to food taboos is an indication that economic factors alone do not explain them. Nonetheless, it is valuable to understand how many of our cultural practices are rooted in economic and material conditions.

the common underpinnings of societies at their most general level, without denying the uniqueness of each society's history and culture.

Foraging Societies: The First Socioeconomic Formation

Every culture seems to have some way of acknowledging the importance of ancestors, for example, via traditions such as worshipping their spirits or giving a newborn the name of a relative. Clearly, humans understand that, in some way, we are all linked to our past. Likewise, a full understanding of today's social world requires that we examine its social and cultural roots. We discussed earlier how science seeks patterns; that is, it seeks to draw out the general from the specific. Sociologists must therefore become historians, not to study the specific details of our past, but to look for the broad patterns of change that have brought us to our current social arrangements.

This brief overview focuses on the major modes of production and how they have changed over time. It illustrates how each transformation from one socioeconomic formation to another led to widespread social change.

Until around 10,000 years ago, every human who had ever lived obtained their food by foraging, that is, by hunting and gathering. What did these foraging societies look like? In fact, we can't know for certain. While our preliterate ancestors left remains of their skeletons and their material culture, they didn't leave behind any written record of their social lives.

Fortunately, foraging as a dominant mode of production continued in some societies right into the twentieth century, and some of you reading this book may be the modern descendants of these people, as they include most of the First Nations in Canada. The records of early traders and explorers as well as the more recent (and more precise) studies of anthropologists have helped describe a general pattern of life for foraging people. Since foraging societies, despite their many differences, seem to share certain common elements, it can be assumed that the earlier foraging societies were in general fairly similar.

Because foraging peoples produced no food of their own, they were totally dependent on what nature provided. All that was obtained from gathering and hunting was immediately consumed; in other words, no surplus was produced. Nomadic bands moved from place to place, drawing on the resources of one locale until they were depleted and then moving on to the next. A band might eventually return to its original point of settlement after the resources had replenished themselves and then start a new round of movement. For those foragers who lived off non-depleting abundant resources (such as fish), settled villages and some economic surplus became possible.

Most foraging people survived primarily by gathering fruits, nuts, berries, and roots. One anthropologist (Lee 1978) has estimated that modern foraging societies obtain about 65 percent of their diet from gathering. (Obviously, in certain environmental conditions there is less gathering; for example, the Inuit of the Arctic traditionally relied much more on hunting.) However, in spite of the fact that gathering was the more regular source of caloric intake, hunting was the more valued activity in foraging societies. This is likely connected to the fact that meat is both a more readily absorbed source of protein and a means of increasing the sociability of the population. It was also likely to be more valued because it was scarce.

Let us construct a composite picture of the typical hunting and gathering society of the past. Foraging people lived together in small groups of approximately fifty to eighty people. Each band existed as a fairly self-sufficient unit, although bands were commonly connected through ties of marriage to a broader network of bands. This wider network shared the same general cultural patterns and was part of a common language group, although there may have been local variations. It was not uncommon for people to move from one band to another, often on a day-to-day basis.

Kinship was the central organizing feature of foraging people. When it came time to marry, most groups practised **exogamy**; this meant that marriage partners had to be sought outside the local band. Aside from the important consequence of keeping the gene pool open, the practice of exogamy served the vital social purpose of maintaining kin links with neighbouring bands. This helped minimize tensions between bands in possible competition for resources, allowed for movement of individuals between bands, and increased the likelihood of sharing and cooperation.

Foraging peoples relied on simple but effective technology to obtain food, build their dwellings, and so on. Because all possessions had to be carried to the next site, hunters and gatherers had little in the way of personal possessions. The main productive forces, the land and natural resources, were not privately owned.

The division of labour—that is, how various tasks in a society are divided up—was a simple one, with the only division being that of sex and age. Everyone contributed to the essentials of survival except the very young and the very old. The **gender division of labour**—that is, assigning different tasks to men and women—varied from society to society, although big-game hunting was almost always a male activity, and women were more often food collectors. However, most animals that were regularly caught were relatively small, and women did, at times, participate in hunting them.

The differing tasks assigned to men and women were not primarily linked to differences in strength (for example, food gathering is often a strenuous task, especially when combined with the carrying of young children and necessities such as water or firewood). Rather, the fact that women gestate, bear, and suckle their young would likely have constituted a central organizing feature of foraging societies. It makes sense that there would have been a survival advantage for women (at least of childbearing age) to perform tasks that were less risky and more compatible with pregnancy and lactation. Whatever its functions, the gender division of labour did *not* seem to automatically lead to male dominance. Women's role in foraging societies—as the main economic providers, as the likely inventors of the earliest tools and other technological innovations, and as the bearers of children—meant that status inequalities between men and women were not dramatic. In other words, men and women were essentially equal in early foraging societies.

In this context, most anthropologists feel that the incidence of warfare among early hunters and gatherers was relatively low. Even those anthropologists who believe that warfare did occur fairly frequently among foraging peoples acknowledge that various social constraints made it less frequent and less deadly than what appears after the development of agriculture. It is not that foragers were naturally peaceable people, but rather that, under conditions of economic scarcity, fighting battles would have been highly risky for group survival. In a world where every adult member had to participate in getting food or in other essential activities, the loss of even a few band

Box 3.5 The Human Relationship to Nature

[Today] we spend 90 percent of our time indoors and five percent in our cars. Yet human beings evolved in nature, and for that simple reason nature is important to us. And there are a lot of ways in which being in nature and viewing nature can be beneficial. From the global to the domestic, nature is fundamental to our health…. Without it, how do we know our place in the universe? (Trevor Hancock, University of Victoria School of Public Health and Social Policy)

For most of our species' history, we lived at one with nature—we were surrounded by it, we depended on it, we were part of it. Not surprisingly, then, our ancestors saw the natural world as something holy. Many researchers now feel that nature provided far more than simply our food and material objects. Rather, it was being a part of nature that made us feel fully human. Today, with most of us living in large urban environments, we may be losing far more than we know.

Richard Louv recently coined the term "nature deficit disorder" to describe the physical, mental, and spiritual loss people (particularly children) experience when they are disconnected from nature. It is not a medical diagnosis, but rather a term used to draw attention to what we are losing in today's world. More and more of us spend almost all our time indoors or in cars. Parents' fear of the dangers to be found out-of-doors—traffic, child molesters, germs, and so on—has prompted most parents to keep children indoors or in structured play areas.

What children are losing may be profound. Nature has been shown to be calming, therapeutic, and restorative. It connects us to something far broader and more eternal than ourselves. Studies show that being in nature is associated with a positive mood, reduced mental fatigue and exhaustion, boosted immunity, and enhanced productivity. It is good for both the body and the soul.

Source: Johnson 2011; Louv 2005.

members could have tipped the balance of survival. Those individuals who could live together in relative harmony had a better chance of surviving and passing on their genes and cultural patterns.

Within bands, relations were maintained largely through a generalized set of social obligations binding band members to each other. No major inequalities existed in these societies; the few differences that existed were of prestige due to a special skill or talent rather than heredity, and brought no special privileges or power. Even in bands that had a "headman," he could attempt to influence others but could not compel them to do his bidding. Decisions were commonly arrived at by consensus.

Anthropologists have noted that modesty and humility are essential behaviour expectations in foraging societies. For example, Richard Lee extensively studied the !Kung of southern Africa (the exclamation mark stands for a clicking sound in their language). He found that the most serious charges one could level against another were those of stinginess or arrogance. To be stingy meant not sharing one's goods with others. Arrogance was considered an even worse offence. To limit such behaviour, writes Lee (1978, 888), "levelling devices are in constant daily use, minimizing the size of others' kills, downplaying the value of others' gifts, and treating one's own efforts in a self-deprecating way. 'Please' and 'thank you' are hardly ever used in their vocabulary."

Of course, disputes between individuals did occur on occasion. Hunters and gatherers were human after all, and conflicts could arise, even in societies that emphasized cooperation and sharing. However, in foraging societies it was important to minimize tensions that could threaten group solidarity. If disputes could not be settled informally, elders might be called upon to help negotiate a resolution; when disagreements could not be resolved, one of the parties involved simply moved to another band.

Think About It
Read Box 3.5. Do you make a point of spending some time in a natural environment every day? What does it make you feel like when you do? Do you agree that young people today are suffering from a "nature deficit disorder"?

What Foraging Societies Tell Us

For about 99 percent of our species' life we hunted and gathered; all of us have foragers for ancestors if we trace our lineage back far enough. If anything is "natural" to humans, we should see it in this socioeconomic formation. However, unlike the image presented by most biological determinists, humans living in these kinds of societies have not displayed the behaviours of competition, dominance, or aggression. Nor do we see warfare or structured inequality as a major social pattern. On the contrary, we see women and men working together in small cooperative units to obtain the things they need to survive.

The examination of foraging societies allows us to understand the way in which the economic arrangements of a society provide the base for the other components of a sociocultural system. Knowing that these societies were at subsistence level—that people hunted, gathered, or fished with basic tools, and that there were cooperative relations of production in which no one privately owned the means of production—helps us make sense of the total life pattern, or culture, of foraging people. That is not to say that every foraging culture throughout history has been identical, but rather that there is a similarity in all of them. In a world centred on cooperation and sharing, where productive property is not privately owned and there are no major social cleavages due to unequal access to resources, certain values and behaviours are likely to dominate. Such societies tend to emphasize the notion of *reciprocity* as well as the notion of *redistribution* (Polanyi 1957, 68). Reciprocity means that each member of a society has duties and obligations to all others. The notion of redistribution means that the community transfers wealth to those who have less.

The study of foraging societies also helps us understand that extreme inequalities of wealth and power have *not* been a part of most societies down through the ages. In fact, for most of human history people seem to have lived in relatively cooperative, egalitarian societies. Two questions now need answering. First, given that this socioeconomic formation seemed to work for humans for such a long period, why did we cease being hunters and gatherers? Second, since it is obvious that most people today live in societies structured quite differently from the foraging societies, how did we get from there to here?

The Decline of Foraging and the Development of Farming

Some foraging societies were so well adapted to their environment that they continued to exist right into the twentieth century, and, were it not for their contact with more developed socioeconomic formations, they might have continued ad infinitum. But hunting and gathering societies that survived until recent times were geographically isolated. The majority of such societies had transformed themselves much earlier. The shift to domesticated plants and animals as the major food source, sometimes referred to as the **Neolithic Revolution**, began at varying times around the globe. Few events in the history of our species can match this development in its importance. Over time, humans gained an increasing measure of control over the natural environment and were no longer simply dependent on the ups and downs of nature. It is impossible to overstate the changes in human social organization that came about as a result of the shift to farming and herding.

Although we cannot know for certain, the sea change that affected human patterns of life forever was probably the result of a number of factors. These included population pressures, the decline in availability of wild foods, and the cumulative development of new technologies. Climate change led to the increasing availability of wild plants that could be domesticated. Once food producers began to increase in numbers, it is also likely that they either displaced or killed hunter-gatherer populations (Diamond 1999, 109–113).

Three of the most important changes that resulted from the cultivation of plants and the herding of animals were the further growth of human populations, the greater permanence of settlements, and the possibility of a stable economic surplus, that is, of acquiring more than was immediately consumed. Settling in one place and producing regular surpluses in turn allowed for increased specialization of tasks as more and more people no longer had to be food producers. Increased specialization led to new technological innovations, greater surplus, greater specialization, and so on, in a never-ending process.

Calling this long process the "Neolithic Revolution" gives the false impression that it was a one-time event. The widespread adoption of agriculture probably occurred first in the area that is now Iraq around eight to ten thousand years ago, about a thousand years later in the New World, and about three thousand years after that in China and Southeast Asia. It may have begun as late as the year 500 in parts of the eastern United States and in southern Africa.

While it may appear to us that farming was just a logical development on the road to greater prosperity, hunters and gatherers likely took to it gradually and hesitantly. It may seem obvious to us today that farming means increased control over one's environment, the possibility for producing surplus, and greater productivity of labour output, but the reality for early garden farmers was a life with more work and restrictions on their freedoms. Plant cultivation, certainly at the beginning, usually meant hard work for small (and eventually diminishing) returns, in addition to the necessity of being tied both to the physical place and to cultivation cycles. That the domestication of plants and animals does eventually come to replace foraging worldwide must reflect its necessity for survival.

Farming is usually divided into two forms: *horticulture*, or garden farming, which is labour intensive, utilizing only basic technology such as the digging stick or hoe; and the more advanced form of *agriculture* (also referred to as agrarianism), in which the new technology of the plough is utilized. Societies that survive through the herding of animals and do little or no farming are known as *pastoral societies*. Pastoralism developed around 3000 to 3500 years ago in areas where farming was either difficult or impossible.

The Beginning of Structured Social Inequality

The key to understanding the rise of structured inequality lies in the gradual development of private property. But what exactly is private property? Some people would argue that all those things owned by individuals—whether it is their house or a factory—are forms of private property. However, forms of property vary. A house is actually part of one's *personal possessions*, while a factory is *productive property*, part of the means of production. The **means of production** includes all the things that humans use to produce what we need, including tools, natural resources, the land on which production occurs, and the buildings where production takes place.

Why should we bother to distinguish between the two forms of property? The answer to this question lies in the fact that only productive property gives one power. If you own a factory, you gain control over others—you can hire or fire them and gain control over the productive process. You can expand the factory or shut it down and move it to another city or country. Personal possessions do not give that kind of power; at best, if one is rich and can acquire valuable possessions, one can gain status. The question of property is often confusing because people who own productive property usually have enough wealth to have valuable personal possessions as well.

Today we live in a world where private ownership of productive units seems natural, as does the notion that people in any society will compete with each other to attain the power and wealth that come with such ownership. It is therefore surprising to learn that for most of human history our species did not have a developed concept of private ownership of the means of production. However, as this chapter demonstrates, once a surplus comes to be produced, advances in technology and the expansion of the division of labour enlarge inequalities between individuals. Eventually private property—mainly land—comes to be in the hands of some whose ownership or control allows them to be completely removed from production. It also enables them to accumulate great wealth. Others not so fortunate are forced, in one way or another, to be the producers. Once forms of structured social inequality come into existence, they become, to a fair degree, self-perpetuating. This is mainly due to the fact that advantaged individuals are highly motivated to maintain, and even enhance, their position.

On the surface, it appears as if property relations are between humans and things—you own or you don't own something. In reality, property relations are between people. The only reason individuals need to identify an object as belonging to them is so that others will know it is not theirs. Someone shipwrecked on a deserted island does not need to assert ownership of the land. A property relationship, therefore, is between an owner and a non-owner.

As private property expands, some people are able to take things that have been produced by others and keep them for themselves. This process takes on different forms through history, but its essence remains the same: workers produce a surplus beyond their own requirements, and a large part of that surplus is privately appropriated by non-producers as a result of their ownership or control of some form of property. In classical Marxist analysis, each of these groups, which has a distinct relation to the means of production, is referred to as a **social class**.

The issues of structured inequality and social class are among the most controversial in sociology. In later chapters the ongoing debate about the meaning of social class is discussed; for the present, however, the above definition will prove sufficient and useful. In societies where private appropriation of surplus occurs, there are always *at least* two major classes: a relatively large subordinate class that produces the surplus and a relatively small appropriating class that, through ownership or control of the means of production, gets to keep all or part of that surplus. There are usually minor classes within a society as well. The reason that the owning class is always much smaller than the productive class is quite simple—until recently, at least, limited technologies meant that there had to be a large number of workers to produce what was required for everyone's survival.

Think About It

Why would the majority of people have let a few others have a position of dominance over them, a position that allowed such individuals to take much of what they produced away from them?

To understand how social inequality arose, we need to briefly examine the gradual transition of societies from egalitarian foraging societies to class-based agrarian forms. This development occurred over thousands of years and at different speeds in different parts of the world. In this chapter we examine how inequalities began, and in the next chapter we conclude our historical overview by looking at how we changed from agrarian societies to ones dominated by technology and the marketplace.

Horticultural Societies

Horticultural societies can be divided into two types: simple and advanced (or intensive). Advanced horticultural societies experience greater productivity as a result of the use of a hoe and the practice of certain techniques, including basic irrigation, fertilization, and metallurgy. As technologies advance, productivity increases. This, in turn, leads to increased population size, greater surpluses, and increased societal divisions, both in occupational specialization and unequal allocation of power, privilege, and prestige.

While foraging societies are usually egalitarian and have no formally structured leadership, simple horticultural societies more often show evidence of formalized political leadership. Inequalities become even more pronounced in advanced horticultural societies, and we sometimes see the appearance of monarchs. Social inequalities are thus beginning to appear.

The question, of course, arises as to why humans allowed social inequality to develop. Why couldn't our species farm and have increased surpluses and more complex forms of social organization while retaining egalitarian relations of production? The most likely answer is that societies that developed greater inequalities at that stage of production seemed to have had an improved chance of survival. Early horticulturists didn't hold meetings to decide whether they should retain cooperative forms of production or move in a different direction; social inequality appeared on the scene because, at that time, it worked. The development of a political structure with one or more people in control seems to have improved labour productivity and helped increase chances of survival. However, it also led to the gross inequalities of wealth and poverty that are visible to this day.

Societies often have more than one form of property relation within them and therefore have different methods of extracting surplus. However, one form usually dominates at a particular point in time. The private appropriation of surplus, regardless of its form, always requires at least some degree of coercion, or force. Otherwise, to put it simply, why would those who produce or create surpluses for others keep on doing this? Sometimes this force is violent and obvious; at other times in history it becomes less visible and more subtle.

[The rise of structured inequality created a world] in which every step forward is also relatively a step backward, in which prosperity and development for some is won through the misery and frustration of others.
—*Friedrich Engels*, The Origin of the Family, Private Property and the State, *1884*

In foraging societies everyone contributed their labour except the very young and the very old. In agrarian societies, some people came to be excused from work. Most likely, the first people to be freed from productive activity were those who had some connection with the supernatural or who had special knowledge and skills related to production or warfare. Such individuals became leaders in their society and were able to obtain surplus through forms of tribute and, later, via taxation. The majority probably accepted this regular payment as an early form of insurance policy. For example, a family might be prepared to give a weekly tribute to their temple priest if they felt the priest had the ear of the gods, which would guarantee a good harvest the following season. Once structured inequality came into being, it did, to some extent, take on a life of its own. For those who had more than others, there was an increasingly vested interest in maintaining, or even expanding, the inequality. The more institutionalized the inequality became, the more difficult it was to imagine any alternative.

Warfare also becomes increasingly common once a regular surplus is produced, and it is often connected to giveaway feasts. With a surplus, warfare becomes more feasible and more profitable. Defeating the enemy can mean acquisition of both material goods and land. Warfare also serves

---

Box 3.6 What Is Potlatch?

The *potlatch* is a gathering held regularly—usually in winter—by a wide number of Indigenous peoples in the Pacific northwest of Canada and the United States. When Europeans first colonized the area, they thought it a strange and "useless" custom, and in Canada it was actually banned from 1884 until 1951.

At these gatherings—for example, to celebrate births, rites of passage, weddings, namings, and honouring the deceased—a family or hereditary leader hosts a feast for the guests. A variety of events take place, including singing, dancing, theatrical performances, and at times spiritual ceremonies. In this sense, these gatherings sound little different from the cultural practices of most Canadians today who celebrate their major life markers with similar parties.

What distinguishes the potlatch—and what made it seem so foreign to the European colonizers—was that a key purpose was the redistribution of wealth. In these ceremonies, held every few years, chiefs attempt to validate and protect their position by giving away as much food and other goods as possible to neighbouring bands. The guest leaders and their followers, after being laden down with an embarrassment of riches, vow to hold even bigger feasts and give away even more to show their superiority. For those coming from a developing industrial economy where the hoarding of personal wealth in the form of money was highly valued, it seemed strange and even dangerous to see people giving away their possessions. However, from a sociological perspective, the practice of potlatch makes a great deal of sense.

Simple horticulturists—as well as some foragers—can produce a surplus, but the surplus is unpredictable and likely to decline over time, since improved economic conditions raise population size. For such societies, the occurrence of giveaway feasts serves a number of important functions that enhance survival. They mainly act as a means of redistributing surpluses among neighbouring groups, thus maximizing each group's chances of making it through lean times that result from regional and seasonal variations in resources. Giveaway feasts also push individuals to be more productive, hence providing a margin of safety in crises such as war or crop failures (Harris 1989, 118).

This does not mean that those who held potlatch ceremonies fully understood the advantages of their activities. Rather, in a manner similar to the food taboos mentioned earlier in the chapter, these cultural practices were tied to deeply felt spiritual beliefs. Social scientists, on the other hand, are interested in understanding why certain behavioural patterns seem to appear in certain times and places but not in others. By linking these ceremonies to the survival needs of those who practised them, we can more clearly understand this particular social custom.

as a means of controlling excessive population growth in circumstances where population grows faster than the capacity to feed everyone. In this context, good warriors come to be highly valued, and leadership is often connected to the bravest and most successful in battle. Since women, due to their reproductive capacity, are almost universally prohibited from battle, it is likely that the expansion of warfare lowered women's status and increasingly excluded them from circles of power.

All these tendencies become even more evident in advanced horticultural societies, where hoe technology and other developments allow even greater surpluses to be accumulated either through production or seizure. The unequal distribution of resources—material, political, and symbolic—continues to grow, although the redistributive ethic is retained. This limits the degree to which chiefs can use surplus for their own ends. Greater inequalities between groups either by gender, geographical origin, or occupational specialization are in evidence.

As farming advances, certain kinship groups acquire a great deal of land, which also gives them power; with this land comes a need to have some organized way to defend and protect it. As a result, more complex military and administrative structures develop over time. But how are they financed? Usually some of the surplus is taken from subordinate groups, commonly via taxation. The institution that carries out such activities in a society is known as the *state*, and advanced horticultural societies show the beginnings of state structures. *For the first time in human history, there comes to be a rigid separation between those who are producers and those who produce nothing. Those who produce nothing survive by keeping for themselves what is produced by others.*

Once surpluses are regularly produced, societies begin to change from cooperative egalitarian forms of social organization to social forms with private appropriation of wealth, formalized leadership, and structured inequalities. These changes, in turn, lead to changing values, beliefs, and behavioural patterns. In other words, changing the economic arrangements of a society changes its cultural components as well. These cultural components then further alter economic elements within a society.

Agrarian Societies

Over time, a series of inventions and discoveries—including the plough, the harnessing of animal energy, irrigation systems, crop rotation, the smelting of metals, the wheel, and the sail—all bring about major transformations in production, transportation, and communication. As a result, the amount of surplus produced increases substantially. These developments lead to even greater population size, increased social densities, growing need for large-scale projects such as irrigation, and more internal and external conflicts. Such conditions require increasing the degree of organization, leadership, and social control. The need for increased coordination and increased productivity leads to the centralization of power in the hands of a few.

The growth in size and complexity of societies, the growing centralization of power, and the gradual erosion in importance of kin networks eventually lead to the disappearance of the redistributive ethic common to horticultural societies. This paves the way for the emergence of major social inequalities. Power that has previously been invested in leaders as a result of personal qualities is gradually replaced by dominance based either on inheritance or the seizure of power. It can be said that at this point a new form of society appears on the scene. This major transformation is not the result of some clever design or of a collective decision on the part of the participants; rather it arises out of the cumulative changes within the societies themselves.

Agrarian systems represent a *qualitative* change from what preceded them. Kinship now takes an increasingly secondary role to other social alliances and networks that often span whole societies or even empires. Divisions within agrarian societies increase, not only on ethnic, gender, and geographical lines, but in occupational differences as well. Most importantly, with the disappearance of the redistributive ethic, the separation between those who own or control productive property and those who don't becomes sharper and more extreme.

Slavery in Agrarian Societies

Slavery is the most direct way to appropriate the surplus produced by someone else; workers are themselves considered a form of property, owned by the master, and all the surplus they produce, save the barest minimum necessary to keep them alive, is taken from them. Slaves in antiquity were almost always obtained by conquest, which made it easier to see a slave as "the other," a thing less than human. Because they were property owned by their master, slaves had almost no control over any aspect of their lives. Some slavery began to appear in early horticultural societies, but it is in the agrarian empires of ancient Athens and Rome that we see a fully institutionalized system for the large-scale employment of slave labour. Although there were various ways to appropriate the surplus, slavery was the defining form, broadly integrated into the political and ideological spheres of society.

While slavery is the most direct way of appropriating surpluses from workers, it is always a highly unstable form of surplus extraction. This is largely because it is so oppressive, and because there is no incentive—except punishment—for the slave to work harder. While various forms of slavery have continued until the present day in many parts of the world—with many millions of individuals still living in various states of enslavement—there are relatively few moments in history where slavery has been the *dominant* form of surplus extraction. The more common form of surplus appropriation in agrarian systems, discussed at greater length in the next chapter, involves a class of landlords who force another class of dependent economic producers to transfer the surplus to them via some combination of taxation, forced labour services, or rent (paid in goods or money).

The development of social classes inevitably leads to what is referred to as **class conflict** or class struggle. This struggle occurs because the interests of the owning and producing classes are in direct opposition to each other, since the greater the amount of surplus that goes to one class, the less the amount that goes to the other. It is important to note that this struggle is of a *structural*, not personal, nature. It has nothing whatever to do with whether people like or don't like each other. In many cases, members of structurally opposed classes can actually be very close, as was sometimes the case between domestic slaves and their masters.

Such personal relations do not minimize the fact that their class interests are directly opposed. The tensions between opposing classes can often be held in check for long periods of time, but the underlying structural conflict remains just below the surface, always ready to emerge under certain conditions. We can see this struggle reflected in such things as peasant and slave revolts or labour strikes in industrial societies.

Power and Structured Inequality

Structured social inequality means not only the unequal distribution of resources, but also the consequent unequal distribution of power. The increased complexity of the division of labour and the growth of the state leads to increased hierarchies of power and status. One clear example, discussed in more detail in Chapter 12, is the erosion of women's position inside and outside the family, which gives men increased power over them. But the greatest power in any society is held by those who own or control the means of production and, as a result, are able to extract surpluses from large numbers of people who must do their bidding in order to survive. Later in the book we will see how this economic power is also linked to political power and the power over ideas.

It is for this reason that any understanding of the cultural patterns within a society must begin with an investigation of its economic arrangements, in order to determine which individual or group of individuals dominates within that society. Once we have discovered who controls the major means of production in any society, we will have a key tool for making sense of the other elements within that society. That is not to say that the economic arrangements mechanically determine a society's culture. However, the historical analysis provided in this chapter makes clear that the economic relationships in a society are primary in affecting who has power. In turn, the individuals who hold power are most able to shape a society's norms, beliefs, values, and social institutions.

Such analysis also helps us understand the underlying tensions between those who have power and those who lack it, and it is these tensions that ultimately pave the way for social change. Our culture determines not simply what we do but also who we are. If we want to fully understand our own society—indeed, if we want to understand ourselves—we must determine which people hold power, how they came to get it, and how that power is maintained.

KEY POINTS

1. Humans are cultural animals. In order to survive together under particular conditions, we develop technologies, social institutions, means of communication, rules of social behaviour, values, and belief systems.

2. Socialization is the process of learning our society's cultural components.

3. All cultures believe that the way they do things is normal and superior, while the ways of others are strange or even immoral. This tendency is referred to as ethnocentrism.

4. Components of culture remain relatively stable over time, even as they are simultaneously being altered and reworked by humans. New cultural elements are always appearing, while some traditional elements may disappear. In complex societies such as ours, there is no single culture to which all Canadians adhere.

5. The central organizing element of all cultures is their economic arrangements, that is, the way people get the basic necessities of life.

6. A society's economic underpinning is referred to as its mode of production. A society with a specific mode of production is referred to as a socio-economic formation.

7. Foraging societies constituted the first socioeconomic formation. Such societies, with subsistence-level economies, were small, kin-based, and nomadic. The division of labour was simple and there was no private ownership of the means of production. There was no structured inequality, and warfare was rare.

8. With the eventual production of surpluses, cleavages within societies began to appear. In early surplus-producing societies, the surplus was redistributed in occasional lavish feasts. With the production of regular surpluses, warfare became more common.

9. As private property developed, one group of people was able to permanently take and keep what another group produced. In classical Marxist analysis, these groups, each of which has a distinct relation to the means of production, are referred to as social classes.

10. In societies where private appropriation of surplus occurs, there are always at least two major classes: a superordinate class, which through ownership or control of the means of production appropriates the surplus, and a subordinate class, which produces the surplus.

11. The first and most direct form of surplus appropriation was that of slavery.

12. Structured social inequality means both unequal allocation of resources and unequal distribution of power.

Cherot, Daniel, and Clark McCauley. 2006. *Why Not Kill Them All? The Logic and Prevention of Mass Political Murder*. Princeton, New Jersey: Princeton University Press.
  Despite some limitations, this book is a challenging examination of mass murders, past and present. The authors show how an "us" versus "them" world—whether past or present—can lead to horrible outcomes.

Berreby, David. 2005. *Us and Them: Understanding Your Tribal Mind*. New York: Little Brown.
  While not an academic, Berreby undertakes a serious yet highly readable analysis of why humans have a need to identify with groups and the implications of this for both individuals and societies.

Harris, Marvin. 1989. *Cows, Pigs, Wars and Witches: The Riddles of Culture*. New York: Vintage Books.
  Although he can be overly deterministic at times, this American anthropologist offers fascinating explanations on the "riddles of culture."

Sanderson, Stephen K. 2001. *The Evolution of Human Sociality: A Darwinian Conflict Perspective*. Lanham, MD: Rowman & Littlefield.
  An attempt to integrate sociology, anthropology, and evolutionary biology.

Sasson, Jack M., ed. 1994. *Civilizations of the Ancient Near East*. New York: Charles Scribner's Sons.
  An extensive examination of the development of some of the world's earliest civilizations, with contributions by many authors.

4 The Basis of Modern Societies

In This Chapter

- What kind of society preceded ours?
- How did capitalism develop?
- What exactly is capitalism?
- How has capitalism changed over time?

In the previous chapter we discussed foraging, horticultural, and agrarian societies. Obviously, such terms do not describe Canada today. Some social scientists might refer to Canada as an industrial society, focusing on the way we produce the goods we require. Others might refer to it as an urban society, in contrast to the rural-based societies of the past. Yet others, focusing on how our political system differs from earlier forms, might refer to Canada as a democratic society. All these descriptions would be valid. However, in the last chapter we addressed the centrality of a society's mode of production, which includes both the technology and the relations between people in the process of production. Using this approach, Canada can be described as a capitalist form of society. In order to better understand what this means, we need to first understand the historical roots of capitalist socioeconomic formations.

Studying our past is an essential part of the sociological imagination. Just as we can learn a great deal about individuals by examining their past experiences, we can really only understand societies through an examination of their roots. This is particularly important since capitalism gives the appearance of being both eternal and unchangeable. This chapter demonstrates that capitalism is not a natural and inevitable outcome of human existence; rather it should be seen as the result of certain events that occurred in the past few centuries in one small part of the globe.

The Roots of Capitalism: Feudalism

Most of us are familiar with images of the Middle Ages from childhood fairy tales—a time of queens, kings, castles, and knights in armour. Much of Western literature, art, architecture, beliefs, and religious practices have their origins in that period. And yet, aside from these mythical childhood images, few of us know anything about what life was really like at that time.

> The past hundred years, the century or so which has seen the world-wide expansion of industrial capitalism, have...brought about social changes more shattering in their consequences than any other period in the whole previous history of humankind.
> —sociologist Anthony Giddens

The Middle Ages of Western Europe are commonly dated from around the fifth century until the sixteenth century. The dominant socioeconomic formation that developed during this period is usually referred to as *feudalism*.

Feudalism was an agricultural system that grew out of the ruins of the old slave societies, especially in what are now France, Germany, Italy, and Great Britain.* The classical age of feudalism occurred between the tenth and thirteenth centuries. Feudalism was a complex system—social, economic, and political—of duties and obligations between individuals. Since this was a system of private ownership of the productive units, there was an appropriating class of owners, the *nobility*, and a producing class of *serfs*, or peasants. There were also minor classes such as artisans, soldiers, and clergy, and there was a hierarchy of wealth and power *within* the two major classes.

In feudal societies, the land was divided into manors or estates that were held by royalty and then parcelled out to lords or knights. Almost all social relationships were tied to these estates, which could not be bought or sold in the way we know it; other than through inheritance, land could be acquired only through seizure, through bestowal, or through marriage. Virtually all that was produced was consumed locally.

In the early form of feudalism, the feudal lord acquired the surplus primarily from forced agricultural service. Serfs worked most of the week on the lord's land, with all production taken by their lord. For a small part of the week they worked to produce their own food either on their own allotment of land or the commons, which was land held for public use. Why did the peasant agree to this state of affairs? It was mainly because of various *non-economic forms of coercion*—in other words, via the use of political, legal, or military force. Bad things would happen to you if you didn't fulfill your obligations to the lord of the manor.

Think About It
Many people today work at jobs they hate. They don't appear to be coerced. Why then do they continue to do it?

The *rent system* gradually replaced the system of forced agricultural service. Now the peasants worked their own parcel of land and were required to give the lord a portion of what they produced. By the end of the fifteenth century, money payment largely replaced both agricultural service and rent in the form of goods. Over time, both lord and peasant were increasingly drawn into markets and a money economy. The growth of a new type of

---

* European feudalism is discussed here because central Europe and England are where capitalism developed. However, feudal forms have existed in most other parts of the world, and remnants can still be observed in the less-developed countries.

market—a capitalist market—is key to an understanding of how feudal relations of production declined over time.

Commodity Production and the Growth of Markets

Humans have probably always engaged in some form of trade with each other. At first, trade must have been sporadic and achieved through some kind of barter system. However, the barter system is impractical as markets develop, because it requires that the seller and buyer need each other's goods. A **market** exists when people offer goods and services for sale to others in a more or less systematic and organized way. The concept of the market embodies not simply a physical place but rather a set of social relationships organized around the buying and selling of objects. An object that is produced specifically for exchange is referred to as a **commodity**.

If most of us were asked how feudal societies became capitalist ones, we would probably guess that it was simply a case of markets growing bigger and bigger, until feudal markets became capitalist ones. However, markets alone cannot explain the rise of capitalism and the decline of feudalism. Many parts of the world—including various parts of Europe—had large urban areas and extensive trade but retained feudal class relations. Capitalism was an outgrowth of feudalism but distinct from it. The growth of capitalism—a socioeconomic formation that had at its core the need to intensify labour and improve productivity to increase profitability—seems to have been most clearly rooted in England (Wood 1999).

The Decline of Feudalism

Let us suppose you could enter a time capsule and be transported back to fourteenth-century England. After a pleasant lunch with the Baron of Byng, you inform him that the system in which he lives, from which he so grandly benefits, is on its way out and will shortly be replaced by a totally new form of social organization. You also inform him that he, in part, is contributing to this process. Needless to say, he doesn't believe a word you're saying.

Of course, it is far easier to analyze the past than predict the future. In this case we know what the baron could not, that capitalist societies arose out of—and eventually replaced—the feudal forms of central Europe and England. For approximately 400 years, starting in about the fourteenth century, feudalism decayed from within, until its last remnants finally disappeared and were replaced by a capitalist mode of production.

> Human beings have existed on this planet for approximately 200,000 years. They had an economy all of this time…. Capitalism, in contrast, has existed for fewer than 300 years. If the entire history of *Homo sapiens* was a 24-hour day, then capitalism has existed for 2 minutes.
> —*Jim Stanford*, Economics for Everyone

> It was [in Europe at the beginning of the sixteenth century] that capitalism introduced the idea of using scarcity as a deliberate tool of economic organization. By intentionally creating scarcity (for the many), capitalism used scarcity to generate wealth (mostly for the few).
> —*Linda McQuaig*, All You Can Eat

The question of what led to the decline of feudalism has been hotly debated in the social sciences, and there is not full agreement regarding the exact processes of change. If we think dialectically, we will recall that change is the result of a complex interplay of connected elements, each feeding back on and reinforcing the other. As a result, the process of social transformation is neither linear nor uniform in all places. Thus, while it is impossible to give a simple explanation of what led to the development of capitalism, it is possible to examine some of the key changes—most reaching their full development after 1500—that eventually altered feudalism forever.

New Class Relations: The Rise of Agrarian Capitalism and Growth of Capitalist Markets

For thousands of years prior to capitalism, classes existed. The dominant class was able to take the surplus from the producing class through force. Slavery was the most extreme form in which extra-economic coercion was used; feudal forms were somewhat more moderate. In both slave and feudal formations, the producing classes gave up most of what they produced because the alternative was some form of severe punishment. In these societies there was generally no incentive for either the slave or the peasant to increase labour productivity, because no matter how hard they worked, their lives remained more or less the same.

The first major change to feudal class relations occurred in England, where a variable rent system began to replace a system of fixed rents; in other words—as in today's world—a landlord could independently set the amount that the peasant had to pay in rent to work the land. If one peasant family was less productive than another, nobody would beat them or put them in jail. However, they might not be able to pay the going rent when someone else could; consequently, they might lose their livelihood. *Thus, for the first time, economic coercion—in contrast to the earlier non-economic forms of coercion—began to play a role in the production of surplus.* As a result of the shift to a variable rent system, both feudal landlord and tenant farmer became interested in "improvement," or increasing productivity for profit (Wood 1999, 80). In other words, an idea we take for granted today—working harder and harder to create more and more in competition with others—is a relatively recent development.

Urban centres, meanwhile, saw an expansion in the number of merchants and craftspeople. In the pre-capitalist marketplace, merchants were nothing more than traders who made profits through the difference in the buying and selling price of the product. But gradually some merchants, rather than simply buying and selling goods, realized that they could improve profits via greater control over the productive process. Thus, they began to provide the raw materials and, later, the tools to those who made products for them. In this way they were becoming a class of owners, which Marx referred to as the **bourgeoisie**. Nowhere did this group develop more clearly than in England.

The driving force for the growing bourgeoisie, or capitalist class, was the need for ever-expanding profits. Each capitalist enterprise is in competition with others, and if capitalists hope to maintain a place in the market their enterprises must continue to expand. From the outset, the overarching theme of capitalist economic activity has been that "you grow or you die." Because of this reality, it is not simply profits that the capitalist seeks, but rather the *maximization* of profits.

Think About It

Suppose I am a caring factory owner. I don't want to make a lot of money, just enough to live modestly. I pay my workers higher than average wages, give them better benefits and longer holidays, and make lower profit than others in my industry. Why might I have trouble keeping my business going?

The capitalist owning class, of course, could not survive without a class of workers. Marx referred to these new wage workers as the **proletariat**. This class of workers was made up of the displaced peasants, artisans, and craftspeople who now could survive only by selling their labour power in exchange for a wage.

Accumulation of Capital

What did the feudal nobility do with their wealth? Most of us probably assume that they invested it. That is because in our world it seems an obvious thing for rich people to do with their money. But what exactly is meant by "investing" money? Put simply, it is a way of using money with the specific goal of obtaining more money. Money used this way is referred to as **capital**. Investing money is pre-eminently a capitalist notion and was far from the minds of the nobility until quite late in the feudal period. For most of the landed aristocracy, wealth either was held or was used to maintain an entourage of servants and retainers, to fight battles, and, as markets grew, to live in opulence. In the feudal era, the quest for money was generally considered beneath the nobility. Indeed, the Catholic Church viewed usury—lending money with interest—to be a mortal sin.

Think About It

When you hear about someone "investing" their money, what does it mean to you?

If most of the wealthy weren't investing, and the expansion of the market required a huge infusion of capital in order to grow, where did this money come from? Some of it came from the expansion of trade as well as from new technologies and increased rates of productivity. In addition, as markets grew, some nobles—particularly in England—did turn their wealth into capital and become part of the expanding market economy. There was also an influx of capital from the rapid rise and expansion of colonialism at the beginning of the sixteenth century.

> Capital comes [into the world] dripping from head to foot, from every pore, with blood and dirt.
> —Karl Marx, Capital, Vol. 1, 1867

In a short span of time, primarily between the late fifteenth and eighteenth centuries, European powers expanded around the globe in competition for valuable resources, new markets, and a cheap labour force. The earliest colonial adventures brought huge sums of money into both England and continental Europe, and it was not long before the looting and plundering of non-European peoples and their resources acquired global proportions. In England, much of the wealth was used to develop a capitalist market, while in most of continental Europe, the new wealth was retained by a powerful monarchy. As a result, England became the main centre for industrial production at this time.

Some enterprising capitalists realized there was great wealth to be made by turning human beings into commodities, and soon the modern slave trade—from Africa to the New World—began in earnest. Slaves were also a cheap source of labour for the colonial powers in the Americas when Indigenous workers proved insufficient. At the cost of untold millions of lives, the total wealth of the European nations involved in colonization grew substantially. Indeed, whether in Europe or the colonies, wherever capitalism has taken hold it has had to first wrest people from their land, alter their traditional ways of life, destroy their social bonds, and leave most of them economically destitute.

Think About It
Many parts of the world are just now, in the early twenty-first century, becoming developed capitalist states. Would Marx's quote still apply? In what ways is developing capitalism today—for example, in India or China—being built by tearing people away from their land?

Advances in Technology and the Growth of the Labour Force
Early feudal society saw the development of many new technologies. In an attempt to increase profits, some merchants gradually began to expand control over the small, largely home-based units of craft production. By around the sixteenth century, many workers were drawn into what was at first referred to as the "manufactory" system, in which all the operations involved in a specific type of production took place in particular locations under the direction of the owner.

The large influx of capital into England and continental Europe would have meant little unless production expanded with it. Expansion required a massive increase in the number of workers. As already noted, dispossessed peasants who couldn't pay their rent were driven into urban centres to find some means of survival. A crucial push was also provided by the feudal lords themselves. Many lords, looking for new ways to increase their wealth, began to "enclose" the public commons—land that was collectively farmed by all peasants—as well as the forests on or around their estates, and turned them into private grazing land for their own sheep and cattle. This *enclosure movement,* as it came to be known, meant that peasants who had eked out a living no longer had access to the public lands on which they survived. Unable to subsist any longer on the land, large numbers were driven into the towns and cities.

As capitalism developed, workers needed to be disciplined to help increase productivity and profits. As a result, workers gradually came under the strict control of their employers. The shift away from small-scale "cottage" production only worsened the lives of the workers. Wages were so pitiful that whole families had to work to acquire enough simply for their survival. While classical feudalism had at times been a harsh system for peasants, they could at least be assured that, because of feudal obligations, they would be protected by their feudal lord and always be allowed to work their land. Now, freed from feudal bonds, they were also "free" to be potentially unemployed and without any means of subsistence.

The Industrial Revolution (as we now refer to this period in history) occurred, then, not simply because of the new technologies, but because there was a group of individuals with enough capital to purchase them, as well as an available labour force to work at them. With new technologies, and under pressure from the capitalists for expanding profits, labour productivity increased enormously. Most social scientists and historians agree that while capitalist elements begin to appear in the fifteenth century, it is only the period following the Industrial Revolution in the eighteenth century that can be definitively described as a capitalist mode of production.

Political Transformation in Europe and the Rise of Nation-States

If someone tells us they are Turkish, Finnish, or Nigerian, we readily understand that they come from the countries of Turkey, Finland, or Nigeria. However, people in feudal Europe did not think of themselves as belonging to a country. Most people lived in small villages attached to feudal estates, and their villages seldom had names. The language they spoke was often a local dialect that could not be understood even by neighbouring villagers. At most they saw themselves belonging to a tribe or clan. The notion that they belonged to some larger national group had little or no meaning for them.

The growth of the concept of nation-states is linked to several factors. As market economies began to grow and the traditional feudal relations began to decline, two groups began to expand their power: the monarch and the growing capitalist class. The former began to gain *political* power as that of the feudal lords began to weaken, while the capitalists gained *economic* power through their expanding wealth.

Both soon discovered their shared interests. The monarchs realized that their political power could be expanded via the wealth of the rapidly expanding capitalist class. Capitalists, frustrated with many constraints on trade and commerce, sought the protection of a strong leader who could make and enforce new laws limiting the power of the feudal lords and the local craft guilds. However, while the capitalist class and the monarchy formed temporary alliances of convenience, their basic goals differed. As we will see in Chapter 8, absolutist states (that is, those under the control of an all-powerful monarch) were not generally well suited to developed market economies.

However, in the short term, the capitalists benefited from a powerful sovereign at the head of a united kingdom, or **nation**. A nation is not simply a political entity; it also embodies the notion of a group of people living within a geographical boundary who share a common language, culture, and history.* The growth of nation-states in Europe gave momentum to the further expansion of trade and commerce, and colonialism was largely fuelled by competition for power between the heads of European states. Thus nation-states developed concurrently with capitalist economic relations.

At the same time, however, the new capitalist owning class increasingly resented the political power that continued to be held by the feudal nobility and restrictions on their profits. As a result, political transformation gradually spread across Europe to fit with the new capitalist economic relations. By the late eighteenth century the capitalist class had consolidated its power, and some form of republic or constitutional monarchy replaced most of the absolutist monarchies that had existed across Europe. Most importantly, once capitalist market relations developed, the whole world eventually came to be economically drawn into the ever-expanding system known as capitalism.

Changing World-View

Up to this point, we have been focusing on the objective material changes that gave rise to the new economic order called capitalism. But if we think dialectically, we must also pay attention to changing subjective conditions, including major transformations in religious and philosophical thought that began to spread across parts of Europe as the Enlightenment took hold. One of the key thinkers of the time was British philosopher John Locke (1632–1704). Among other things, Locke argued that people have inherent rights, such as the right to life, liberty, and property, which exist independent of the laws of any particular society. While we take these notions for granted today, they were very radical for a time when people were thought to be simply servants of God and their monarch. Locke's views on individual rights, as well as on democratic forms of government, were appealing to the new expanding bourgeois class and became a core element of the United States constitution after its War of Independence in 1776.

German sociologist Max Weber (1864–1920) felt that the origins of capitalism were closely linked to a new form of Christianity that spread across northern Europe starting around the fifteenth century. In *The Protestant*

---

* The question of what actually constitutes a nation and how more than one national group can live within a single state is complex. Canada has never totally resolved these issues, either with regard to the francophone population centred in Quebec or with the First Nations of our country.

Ethic and the Spirit of Capitalism, Weber suggested that Protestantism's new world-view was appealing to the growing class of capitalist entrepreneurs. The medieval Catholic Church saw the market as crass and usury as a sin; monastic life and doing good deeds were the things most highly valued. In contrast, Protestant churches attributed moral value to the rational pursuit of economic gain and saw hard work in the real world as a sign of grace. The sayings of American Benjamin Franklin (1706–1790), such as "Early to bed and early to rise makes a man healthy, wealthy, and wise" and "A penny saved is a penny earned," could be considered examples of the Protestant ethic, which valued planning and self-denial to achieve individual wealth. Today we refer to Weber's notion of the Protestant ethic as the "work ethic," and it is used to describe individuals of any religion or ethnic background. It must be remembered that this human attribute, highly valued in today's society, is not universal, but rather is tied to the socioeconomic formation we call capitalism.

What the Transition to Capitalism Teaches Us

The transition from feudalism to capitalism is an interesting case study of the process of major societal change. One of the most important lessons to be learned from this transition is that even societies that are relatively stagnant for long periods of time do change eventually, even if it takes hundreds of years. We can also see that change proceeds from the quantitative to the qualitative; that is, change within feudal societies occurred in numerous small ways until, finally, the sum total of many gradual changes led to the radical transformation of whole societies.

The class that had controlled feudal economies, as well as their political and ideological spheres, began to rot from the inside. The old feudal nobility came increasingly to be seen as amoral and unable to rule. It is as if the disintegration of an entire society is reflected in the decay of its ruling class.

Table 4.1 Comparison Between Two Different Class Societies

Feudalism	Capitalism
Slow social change	Constant and rapid social change
Simple commodity production: limited production for exchange	Capitalist commodity production: everything is a potential commodity
Workers retain some ownership or control of some means of production	Workers separated from ownership or control of the means of production
Limits to the appropriation of surplus	No limits to the appropriation of surplus
Surplus appropriated primarily via extra-economic forms of coercion	Surplus appropriated primarily via economic forms of coercion
Property and class relations a matter of tradition	Property and class relations a matter of legal contracts
Economic and political power identical	Economic and political power separated (although intertwined)

In opposition to the nobility was a new, forward-thinking class of capitalists that not only advanced technology and know-how but also began to have increasing moral authority within the old rotting system.

As feudalism transformed itself, the only thing the capitalist class lacked was numbers. This was ultimately resolved by drawing other disaffected sectors of feudal societies into the struggle for change. Indeed, many oppressed groups were swept up in and at times even led the reforms and revolutions that eventually spread across Europe and later into the colonies. However, once the old feudal nobility was defeated, the capitalist class began to assert its dominance, eventually gaining control of all aspects of the new order. By the mid-nineteenth century capitalism had gained ascendancy, and the modern industrial era had begun with the capitalist class firmly in control.

Living in the twenty-first century, with a long span of capitalism behind us, the majority of us probably think of it as the most natural and inevitable form of human society. However, our brief examination of the roots of capitalism helps us see that our form of economic organization has not existed throughout history; indeed it is a socioeconomic formation that has relatively recent origins.

The Development of Capitalism in Canada

What do changing conditions in Europe have to do with Canada? Obviously, the founding of colonies, first French and later English, in what subsequently became Canada was a direct result of the economic and technological changes that were overtaking Europe. But the growth and development of capitalism in Canada was not identical to the patterns seen in late feudal Europe.

Canada, of course, was not "discovered" by the Europeans. At the time of the European invasion there were more than fifty tribes and eleven distinct language groupings among the Indigenous peoples. However, for the European monarchs and the growing bourgeoisie, the North American continent was a place to secure their glory and their profits.

A land of abundant natural resources, from its beginnings, Canada was seen as little more than a source of raw material and a market for goods produced "back home." Canada has a history of subservience to two masters: at first it was France, but after the defeat of the French forces in 1760 Canada came under England's control. Canada's economy has always been highly dependent on resource extraction, at the expense of the development of a manufacturing sector. Canadians have often been described as "hewers of wood and drawers of water."

Industry did eventually develop, although later than in Europe and the United States. At the time of Confederation, half of Canada's population was in agriculture; by the beginning of the twentieth century Canada ranked seventh in industrial output among manufacturing countries of the world (Krahn et al. 2007, 9). Before Confederation, Halifax was a main centre of

Box 4.1 The Meaning of Progress

The transition from the medieval feudal period to the modern capitalist one was not simply about a changing economy. It was also a period in which radical new ways of understanding the world arose. We saw in Chapter 1 that a scientific world-view about both the physical and social world advanced at this time. Earlier in this chapter the new philosophical and religious world-views in this transition were addressed. Linked to all these various new ways of seeing the world is the notion of *progress*. Progress is the belief that the world moves forward via a series of inventions and discoveries that lead to perpetual improvement; in other words, society always advances from worse to better. As already noted, "improvement" is a defining concept of capitalism. It should not surprise us, then, that belief in progress went hand in hand with the growth of capitalism and new technologies of the industrial age.

Most of us accept the notion of progress without even thinking about it. We believe that new is better than old, and that the present is inevitably better than the past. Thus we see human history as an upward path from simple hunter-gatherer societies, through agrarianism, to supposedly superior modern industrial societies. And because our culture measures human progress primarily by technology, it just seems self-evident that we have progressed from our technologically deficient ancestors. The idea of progress is pervasive in the world today, especially in advertising, where everything is described as "revolutionary," "new," or "improved."

Was the shift from feudalism to capitalism in fact progress for humankind? In many obvious ways the answer is yes. Even Karl Marx—a product of his time and a believer in progress—thought capitalism was a great advance from the backward and narrow-minded societies that preceded it. And yet, if we think dialectically, things are not as straightforward as they seem. Improvements for some have been setbacks for others. The same twentieth century that gave us the polio vaccine and indoor plumbing has also given us weapons of mass destruction and industrial pollution. For all our advanced knowledge and technology—indeed at times as a result of it—we have created a world that now stands on the precipice, uncertain of its own future. We return to these complex questions in later chapters.

industrial production; after 1867, the areas around Montreal and Toronto became the industrial heartland of the country.

Of course, making sense of Canada as an economic, political, or social entity requires that we understand the peculiarities of its geography—most of our land is not easily habitable, and as a result, our relatively small population has spread out over vast distances not far from the U.S. border. Thus, although this book analyzes how Canadian society works, we must always keep in mind that we are a highly regionalized country. Issues that might seize one part of the country—for example, language legislation, the fishing rights of Indigenous peoples, or issues pertaining to the Canadian Wheat Board—are likely to be of little interest to another. Moreover, because the Canadian economy did not develop evenly across the country, regional disparities in economic growth and overall wealth have given rise to perpetual tensions between provinces and between regions.

The following are some new technologies of the twentieth century: the automobile; television; the computer; the cell phone. It is easy to discuss how we've benefited from them, but what has been the cost? Think in terms of consequences for both our physical and social worlds.

Capitalism Explained

Up to this point, you may have been thinking, "But what exactly *is* capitalism?" Most readers have heard the term before, but it is unlikely that you are completely clear on its actual meaning. **Capitalism**—the name given to the socioeconomic formation in which we now live—is, at its core, an economic system in which all production is subordinated to the needs of those who own the productive units. In a world dominated by the marketplace all things are potential commodities, including, as we will see, labour power itself.

Almost everyone today is dependent on the marketplace to acquire their means of life; as a result, the requirements of the capitalist market dominate our entire society and culture. It is therefore quite impossible to understand how our society works without first understanding how the capitalist economy works. However, this task is not as easy as we might think because capitalism differs in two key ways from previous socioeconomic formations. First, capitalism is an extremely complex and ever-changing system; second, unlike slave or feudal systems, the class structure of capitalism is very hard to see.

> Capitalism is neither a person nor an institution. It neither wills nor chooses. It is a logic at work through a mode of production: a blind, obstinate logic of accumulation.
> —*Michel Beaud,* A History of Capitalism 1500–1980

> The distinctive and dominant characteristic of the capitalist market is not opportunity or choice but, on the contrary, compulsion.
> —*Ellen Mieksins Wood,* The Origin of Capitalism

> The defining characteristic of capitalism is, first and foremost, the fact that most of the means of production are privately owned and controlled.
> —*Paul Phillips,* Inside Capitalism

A number of classical theorists wrote extensively about the nature of capitalist systems. One of the earliest was Scottish political economist and moral philosopher Adam Smith (1723–1790) in *The Wealth of Nations,* published in 1776. His most well-known argument was that a free market, while appearing to be chaotic and unpredictable, was actually guided by an "invisible hand" that made it work for the benefit of all. For Smith, the wealth and collective well-being of society was invariably produced in the marketplace as individuals pursued their own self-interest. Karl Marx, writing a century after Smith, disputed this argument. For Marx, the capitalist marketplace primarily benefited the owners of the largest productive units. Workers received only a small share of what they produced, and small business owners struggled hard to survive in the competitive marketplace.

Like feudalism before it, capitalism is a mode of production with private appropriation of surplus. As noted earlier in this chapter, there are two major classes. The appropriating class is generally referred to today as the capitalist class or simply the owning class; this class owns or controls the principal means of production, distribution, or exchange of goods and services. The producing class is generally referred to as the working class, or simply workers; they must work for a wage because they own no significant means of production. In economic terms, the owning class is often referred to as *capital*, while the working class is referred to as *labour*. Between these two major classes is another class, referred to as the **petite** (sometimes written as *petty*) **bourgeoisie**. This class is made up of small-business owners, independent farmers, craftspeople, and self-employed professionals—those who have a small amount of capital and may or may not employ a few workers, but who survive largely through their own labour.

Think About It

In Chapter 1 you were asked to think about which size of "fish" you thought you were. Now we can understand that the fish in the cartoon represent classes in capitalist societies. Which class do you now feel you are in? Has your answer changed from your answer to the question in Chapter 1?

It is important to note that classes in capitalist societies are not easy to see. In pre-capitalist societies, the appropriation of surplus by the owning class was direct and observable. Moreover, because the producing class handed over something to the appropriating class, either in the form of direct surplus or through some form of rent or tribute, it was clear who had the power and who was benefiting from the relationship. There were also usually markers of class difference—for example, styles of clothing or required acts of obeisance such as bowing—that clearly differentiated the classes.

In capitalist societies, class markers largely disappear and the power relationship becomes hidden. In fact, it now appears as if employers are actually giving something to workers (both the job and the wage) rather than taking something from them. The workers, in turn, appear to be freely entering into a fair exchange with employers.

Unseen is a relationship of dominance in which the class that owns and controls the means of production has the upper hand. In this way, capitalism is similar to all previous class societies. Certainly, most workers in capitalist societies are not in a relationship of servitude as in slave or feudal societies. Because workers in capitalist societies are not forced to work for any particular employer, the relationship appears to be a voluntary one. However, workers *are* forced to enter into a relationship with some employer; now, however, the coercive aspect takes on a primarily *economic* form. In other words, if workers don't sell their labour power for a wage, they won't normally be beaten or killed like slaves or serfs (although this does happen under certain circumstances). Rather, without work they will have no means of subsistence and will at best live a life of destitution. People can, in theory, start their own business if they don't want to work for someone else, but only a small proportion can do so.

Think About It
Why don't all dissatisfied and unemployed workers simply start their own businesses? What would happen if they all did?

Profit: The Driving Force of Capitalism

As we saw earlier in this chapter, the true capitalist is someone who moves beyond being a merchant. No longer interested in the simple buying and selling of commodities, capitalists are concerned with "investment," or what is also referred to as the *circulation of capital*. Capital is said to "circulate" because it enters the market with the sole purpose of coming back as an increased amount, which is realized as profits. Capitalists are primarily concerned with the *rate* of profit—that is, the amount of return they get on their initial investment. Capital must always keep circulating, and the faster this circulation occurs, the more can be reinvested. The larger the reinvestment, the greater the chances that even more profit will generated, in a never-ending process.

Because of the competitiveness within capitalist markets, the owners of businesses cannot just sit around waiting for commodities to be produced, sold in the marketplace, and later converted to profits. As a result, they try to speed up the cycle by borrowing money from financial institutions or by selling shares in their companies to quickly raise new capital. This money may be used to expand production, hire new workers, or buy new machinery. Although it appears that major corporations such as McDonald's, Microsoft, Google, and Toyota are producers of goods and services, this production is actually just a means to an end, which is the enlargement of profits.

The *short-term goal* of every capitalist is not simply profits, but the maximization of profits. Capitalists seek to maximize profits not because of personal greed (although any individual capitalist may indeed be very greedy), but because of the competitive nature of capitalist economies. However, despite the never-ending tension between capitalists competing against each other in the marketplace, they do share a similar *long-term goal*, which is the maintenance of the capitalist system itself.

> [A business] has no object in the world except to end up with more money than it started with. That is the essential characteristic of the entrepreneur economy.
> —economist John Maynard Keynes

The Hidden Source of Capitalist Profits

There is an old saying: "You can put yourself to work or your money to work. The trick in life is to put your money to work so that you don't have to put yourself to work." The notion that money is animate, that it "works" and "grows," is not new. In capitalist systems, it does seem that money has some magic quality. In reality, however, most wealth is not created in the marketplace, where it simply moves about, but rather is created in the sphere of production. The key producer of wealth is the worker.

Labour power—the sum total of a worker's physical and mental capacities that go into a particular work task—is a commodity that is purchased by the employer for one reason: workers add value to the business. They may add value by extracting raw materials from the ground, by converting them into new products that become commodities in the marketplace, or by some other contribution to the company such as design, marketing, or sales of a good or service.

For employers, the lower the purchase price of labour, the better able they are to secure profits. The price of labour power is, of course, referred to as a wage, although worker benefits must also be included. Thus we can see the structural basis for class struggle in capitalist societies. In order to maximize profits in a competitive marketplace, employers generally try to keep wages low, keep the number of workers down, and get employees to work as hard as possible. Workers, if able, will try to improve their wages and working conditions. (There have always been some enlightened employers who understand that satisfied workers are more committed workers, and hence they pay reasonable salaries and offer good working conditions.)

The process of private appropriation of surplus, then, occurs in capitalism just as it did in earlier class formations. However, in capitalist systems the process becomes indirect. The shareholders of the major corporations don't take home the actual products produced by the employees. Rather, the

---

Box 4.2 Who Creates Value?

In 2010, Jason Underwood, Chief Executive Officer (CEO) of Whiterock REIT (a real-estate development income trust) earned $4.8 million in compensation, an increase of 475 percent from the previous year. His base salary that year was $150,000, with the rest of his compensation based on various bonuses tied to the performance of the trust's unit price.

In an article in the *Globe and Mail* (May 25, 2011), Underwood justified his large salary by stating "I hope people understand that I have been paid well because I have created a lot of value for investors and if I did not perform I would be the lowest-paid executive in the industry," referring to his $150,000 base salary. But did Jason Underwood actually "create value" for his company?

Economist Jim Stanford had this to say in response: "This self-important shorthand is regularly invoked by business leaders to justify whatever it is they are doing. But do CEOs really 'create value,' even if the share price of whatever organization they are in charge of happened to increase in a certain time period? A more accurate and neutral statement would be that Mr. Underwood was in charge of this REIT during a year when the market value of its unit price increased. Does this mean he 'created value'? Of course not.

"The market value of those units could increase for all kinds of reasons that have nothing whatsoever to do with Mr. Underwood's talents....The only people in Mr. Underwood's industry who actually 'created value' are the workers who actually build and maintain the structures which his firm owns, operates, and markets. Needless to say, the compensation for these genuine value-creators did not increase by 475 percent last year."

Source: Adapted from Stanford 2011.

commodities produced (or services provided) are first sold in the marketplace for money that, after all expenses are paid, finds its way into the hands of the company's shareholders. In Marxist terms this new wealth that is acquired indirectly through the marketplace is referred to as **surplus value**. As in all class societies, in capitalism it is a producing class that creates wealth for the owning class.

Of course, most workers today are no longer direct surplus producers. Because of rapid advances in technology, fewer and fewer workers are producers of actual objects. Many of us are providers of knowledge or services that allow, in one way or another, for the surplus to be realized. Moreover, in recent decades there has been the growth of what is termed the *financialization* of capitalist economies, that is, their dominance by the financial sector. In the end, however, the principle remains the same: capitalists secure profits by paying out far less in wages than they secure, directly or indirectly, through the labour of workers.

The centrality of labour for the production of profit comes into high relief when workers go on strike. If the workers in a widget factory stop working, no widgets get produced. If no widgets get produced for some time, then no profits can be secured. Likewise, if professional basketball, hockey, or football players stop playing, little in the way of profits is made by the team owners. Whatever one might think of the high salaries of the players, it has to be acknowledged that it is the athletes, like the widget makers, who make money for the owners, not vice versa.

In order for class relations to be sustained, it is necessary for most people to believe that such relations are both natural and inevitable. For this reason, most of us have a hard time accepting that in capitalist societies workers may ultimately be more important than owners. This is because in a society where money determines value, those with the most money *appear* to be the most valuable. That the capitalist owning class is both deserving of its wealth and essential to our well-being are such strongly held notions that it is hard to think otherwise. Moreover, if so much wealth is—as Marx argued—created by workers, then questions arise as to why the majority of it seems to end up in the hands of the owners, not the workers.

The Rise of Monopoly Capitalism

Most of us have heard our economy described as a "free enterprise" system. **Free enterprise** occurs when no single buyer or seller can affect the price of a commodity by withdrawing their purchasing power or their product from the marketplace. However, most of the dominant sectors of the world economy have now undergone a process of **monopolization**, with the result that there are now so few companies in most sectors of the economy that in reality free-enterprise competition no longer exists. Monopolization does not mean that only one company controls an industry. If a small number of companies control a sector, then the free market effectively ceases to exist. In classical economic terms, this control is sometimes referred to as an *oligopoly*.

Both in Canada and internationally, the growing concentration and centralization of capital in the major economic sectors as a result of mergers and acquisitions has been increasing rapidly, and the size of mergers is enormous. In 2010 alone, the value of global mergers and acquisitions totaled US$2.4 trillion (Thomson-Reuters News Corp, 2011). The large shift away from making goods over the long term to simply making quick profits—as we will see below—was one key aspect of the economic crash of 2008 and beyond.

Think About It
Can you name some sectors of the Canadian economy that are highly monopolized?

The process of monopolization is part of a more generalized process referred to as the **concentration and centralization of capital**. *Concentration* refers to the fact that capital comes to be in fewer and fewer hands as a result of monopolization. *Centralization* means that capital is centred in a few core geographic areas both within countries and on a global scale. Within this loose structure, some regions and nation-states can be considered to be the *core*, while others are in the *periphery*. The core is made up of a small number of regions and nation-states that appropriate the majority of the world's wealth. The periphery is made up of the least economically developed countries or regions.

As a result of the concentration of capital, the owning class has become increasingly difficult to identify. Most ownership in Canada today is masked by the legal fiction known as the corporation, with many levels of management between the owner and the employee. But behind the corporation are real people. And despite the fact that most corporations are "public" (because they trade shares in public exchanges), there continue to be a few key individuals or families that control the major corporations, as we will see in Chapter 5. One of the valuable outcomes of the Occupy movement of 2011 was that it brought into public discourse the notion of a very small financial elite ("the 1%"), whose centre is Wall Street in New York City.

Think About It
Ask a number of working people if they know the individual or individuals who own the company they work for.

The Crisis of Overproduction
One of the strangest elements of capitalist economies—yet central to understanding how it works—is the irresolvable problem of overproduction. This

> Speculators may do no harm as bubbles on a steady stream of enterprise. But the position is serious when enterprise becomes the bubble on a whirlpool of speculation. When the capital development of a country becomes a by-product of the activities of a casino, the job is likely to be ill-done.
> —John Maynard Keynes, 1936

> The world is awash in capital.
> —Jacques Gordon, Lasalle Investment Management, 2006, less than two years before the global market crash

Box 4.3 What Is an Economic Bubble?

The nature of capitalist economies causes economic bubbles to occur from time to time. Put simply, bubbles are part of the crisis of overproduction and occur when too much capital is chasing too few investments. In simple supply-and-demand terms, if a particular commodity is suddenly seen as "valuable" and many want it, the price will increase, causing more people to think of it as valuable, hence increasing speculation as buyers outnumber sellers. The price of the particular commodity reaches absurdly high levels, far greater than its intrinsic value, and eventually the bubble bursts. This is usually followed by a sudden drop in the price of that particular commodity. We refer to this sudden drop as a *crash*.

This usage of the term originated in the 1711–1720 British South Sea Bubble. This was one of the earliest modern financial crises, in which the South Sea Company kept selling shares and people rushed to buy them although the stocks were essentially built on nothing real. Eventually the company collapsed and investors lost their money.

Sometimes a bubble involves not just a simple commodity or company, but rather an entire sector of the economy or even the stock market as a whole. In the late 1990s, with a major growth in Internet users, many start-up companies (known as "dot-coms") hoped to dominate the market and convinced investors to take a chance on them. In the end, few succeeded, and the dot-com bubble burst, sparking a mild economic recession in 2001. In 2008 and again in 2011, markets around the world tumbled.

In the United States after 2007, there was a "housing bubble" that burst. Many individuals were given extremely low-interest mortgages on houses they could not really afford. When interest rates rose, many could no longer make their mortgage payments and they lost their homes. Supply then outstripped demand and house prices in many parts of the U.S. fell drastically.

Although business schools have expanded, financial institutions are rolling in capital, and corporate leaders have seen their salaries skyrocket, no one seems able to predict when these bubbles will occur.

---

occurs because almost all production is directed to the profit maximization of each individual enterprise, and it is not coordinated. This is referred to as the **anarchy of production**.

Let us imagine what happens in the widget industry every year. Each company assesses the maximum number of widgets it thinks it might be able to sell to maximize profits. This year Company A will try to secure a slightly bigger share of the market than last year (perhaps with a new upscale widget or an advertising campaign to convince Canadians to buy its latest widget), and so it raises production somewhat. Companies B, C, D, and E all do the same. The final outcome is obvious. While some widget companies may indeed increase their market share, the sum total of widgets on the market far exceeds the total number of possible sales. Capitalist production thus leads inevitably to what is called the **crisis of overproduction**.

The first thing that is overproduced in capitalism, then, is goods. In some sectors, such as the fashion industry, where styles change rapidly, the unsold products will usually be discounted for quick sale and may even be sold at a loss. In other industries, such as the auto industry, other incentives such as low financing rates, free upgrades, or extended warranties may be offered. Why don't all companies simply lower the prices of their commodities to sell more? The problem is that lower prices can mean lower profits. Corporations can often make more profits by either destroying the excess or cutting back on production until surpluses are depleted.

Capitalists are well aware of the crisis of overproduction, and as far back as the nineteenth century they formed trusts, cartels, and syndicates in an attempt to coordinate production and avoid such crises. Another way capitalists have attempted to deal with the overproduction of products is to convince working people to buy more and more of them. While this seems self-evident today, it was a radical notion less than a century ago, when workers earned such low wages that they barely had enough to buy basic necessities. However, Henry Ford had a radical idea for his time. After developing the assembly line, he actually *raised* the wages of his workers. Ford was no friend of working people. Rather, he did this to raise his own profits, for not only did higher wages make them more reliable employees, it also allowed them to be future purchasers of his mass-produced products. The issue of mass consumerism is examined in more detail in Chapter 6.

Think About It
Have you ever had a job where your employer allowed you to purchase their product at discounted prices? What is the advantage to the employer?

In addition to a glut (or excess) of goods, capitalism inevitably has too many workers, which helps drive down the cost of purchasing labour power. Of course, the anarchy of production means that there may at times be worker shortages in some fields or in certain geographical locations, but overall there is always a surplus of workers. In 2011, well over 200 million people around the world lacked employment.

At the same time that the drive for ever-increasing profits creates a glut of goods and a glut of workers, we also see the creation of a glut of capital. This is a particularly strange phenomenon. On the surface, it seems absurd that capitalism could actually produce "too much" in the way of profits. However, with many investors looking for a rapid and high rate of return all over the globe, there are simply not enough places for all the capital to be reinvested. In mid-2011, it was reported that the top thousand non-financial companies were holding more than US$3.4 trillion in cash (McCracken and Foley 2011).

The crisis of overproduction is one of the main factors that gives rise to the economic cycles that occur within capitalist systems. These recurrent cycles of crisis, depression, recovery, and boom have occurred throughout the history of capitalist societies. While some crises in some countries may be relatively short-lived and not too severe, there are times in history when capitalism as a whole has gone into a major and prolonged crisis on a global scale. The most recent of these events began in 2008 and is still affecting economies around the world. We examine this crisis in more detail below.

The Financialization of the Economy

Money, of necessity, plays a major role in the marketplace. Not surprisingly, then, we find that money, now converted to capital in a capitalist marketplace, became increasingly important over the course of the twentieth century. Likewise, those who control and manipulate money—such as banks, insurance companies, brokerage houses, bond dealers, and investment companies—have taken on increasing importance. Because of the glut of capital and the increased competition that such a glut creates, investors search the globe for an ever larger and faster return on their investments. Large profits can often be made quickly in highly speculative areas such as the stock market, currency exchanges, or commodity markets.

The shift in all developed capitalist economies from production to finance, which has progressed since the 1970s, has been termed **financialization**. Financialization sees capitalists shift their interests from investing in the real economy—that part which produces actual goods and services—to what is termed the paper economy. Because these kinds of investments bring quicker returns, more and more investors shift to financial products. As a result, financial markets and financial institutions expand. By the late twentieth century, for example, there was so much trade in currency (i.e., the buying and selling of money itself) that global foreign exchange trade was more than ten times larger than the world's annual gross domestic product (GDP) (Singh 2000, 16). The United States, just prior to the start of the economic downturn of 2008, was the most financialized country in the world, with two dollars in financial assets for every dollar in tangible capital in the U.S. economy (Stanford 2008, 219).

Why does the shift to a financialized economy matter? Corporations involved in the real economy have traditionally sought economic stability, which allowed them to plan production for profit over extended periods of time. Financialization, in contrast, thrives on instability. The goal is to invest capital for the short term and extract maximum profit through slight changes in the stock market, commodity values, currency prices, or interest rates. The greater the instability of the financial markets the greater the opportunity to extract profits (Korten 1996, 199).

As part of the process of financialization, debt itself became a commodity for sale in the marketplace. As wealthy investors sought quicker and higher returns on their investments, the age of *securitization* quickly expanded (McNally 2011, 98–99). Securitization involved financial institutions taking many forms of debt—for example mortgages, student loans, and credit card debt—and repackaging them

> Increasingly, our economy is becoming divorced from reality. The activities which generate the highest monetary returns often have little or no real value.
> —John Dillon, Turning the Tide: Confronting the Money Traders

> The need for volatility [of a financialized economy] is contradictory, as too much instability could eventually bring the entire international financial system crashing down, a long-term consequence not desired by capital.
> —Joanne Naiman, How Societies Work, *previous edition, published in late 2007, just prior to the global economic downturn*

as a "security" that could be purchased by financial entities willing to take the risk. Banks and other financial institutions thus transferred their risks to the buyers of these debts; as a result they were much more likely to make loans that would previously have been seen as too risky.

We now know, as many predicted at the time, that this shift—one of the key factors leading to the economic crisis of 2008 and beyond—had extremely negative consequences for the entire global economy. At its core, this crisis can be linked to a global glut of capital. Financial entities offered quick returns and high profits, but were essentially built on little or nothing. Even traditionally conservative investment houses and banks got sucked into such products, which led to the collapse of Lehman Brothers, a prestigious Wall Street banking firm, and the near-collapse of many others.

Only massive government interventions, via loans and bailouts to the largest financial institutions, saved the capitalist world from self-destructing. Canada was less affected by this crisis primarily because of its tight rules governing the banking sector as well as having an economy still largely tied to resource extraction. However, Canada's overall economy has also become increasingly financialized, and our country is certainly not immune to the severe economic downturn that has touched most developed capitalist economies.

Social Production versus Private Ownership

We currently live in a society that emphasizes the individual. If we hear about a wealthy person, we usually look for what they *individually* did to acquire their wealth (i.e., they worked hard to build up their company; they got a great deal of education; they had a brilliant idea; they speculated cleverly in the stock market; they robbed a bank). Such a notion is a particularly capitalist one. In the feudal period, no one assumed that the feudal aristocracy had acquired their wealth as a result of some personal characteristic; it was simply accepted that wealth was unequally allocated, primarily on the basis of birth.

Because our society focuses on individuals, it is often forgotten that the production of wealth in capitalism is ultimately a social activity: it is produced by large groups of people working together in a highly complex division of labour. Indeed, capitalist production, when compared to the relatively small-scale peasant or craft production of agrarian societies, is the most complex production in history. Capitalist production continually expands to include more and more people in a worldwide network. Millions of people around the world are employed by the major corporations, and these corporations are increasingly interconnected.

And yet in capitalism, as in all class societies, the surplus is *privately* appropriated. In fact, we will see in later chapters that an ever-decreasing portion of the population is acquiring an ever-larger share of the surplus. Thus the product of social production is not placed at the disposal of all, but rather is appropriated by a small class of owners. Marx saw this as the basic contradiction of capitalism: the tension between the increasingly social nature of production and the increasingly private appropriation of the fruits of such production.

Moreover, capital must use a large portion of the surplus value in a very particular way: to further expand itself. In expanding, capital must search the globe for places to make ever-higher profits at an ever-faster pace. In this process, whether such self-expansion destroys human lives or the environment can never be the primary concern.

In Whose Interests?

If you take an economics course, or read the business section of any newspaper, you will hear about "the economy," "the markets," "productivity," and so on. All these terms are presumed to be neutral. If stock markets rise, we are led to believe this is a good thing, or if inflation increases as a result of higher wages, it is a bad thing. But what we are actually hearing about are *capitalist* markets, a *capitalist* economy, and *capitalist* needs. Within a single economy, some might be doing extremely well while others are suffering, and for exactly the same reasons.

It is commonly taken for granted—and reinforced by our media—that if big business is doing well, this must be good for everybody. On the surface, such a position seems self-evident. If corporations can secure ever-greater profits, so the argument goes, they will invest in economic expansion, the market will grow, jobs will be created, wages will rise, prices will drop, and so on. This tendency seemed to be a reality in the period between 1946 and the early 1970s. Even into the 1990s, a period in which these tendencies did not present themselves, arguments continued to be promoted that things had never been better and that "the market" was helping create a better life for everyone.

However, recent trends in Canada and the rest of the capitalist world have increasingly cast doubts on the legitimacy of such arguments. Between 1987 and 2004, the share of total GDP that went to corporate profits in Canada rose from 4 percent to 14 percent, while labour's share of national income fell from 56 percent to 49 percent (Fudge 2005). Moreover, jobs have sometimes been cut—and whole factories closed—specifically to increase corporate profits. Not only do companies no longer try to disguise this fact, they also are often directly rewarded for doing so. For example, despite fewer sales of motorcycles, Harley-Davidson saw its profits triple in 2010. How? It fired over one-fifth of its workforce (Schwartz 2010).

Such examples are clues that the interests of corporate owners do not seem to mesh with—and, indeed, often directly conflict with—the needs of workers. But this lack of commonality between big business and the average Canadian goes far beyond the workplace. The most extreme example would be in relation to war, which has been very profitable for many businesses over the last century. For example, while thousands of American and Canadian soldiers and hundreds of thousands of civilians or more have died in Afghanistan and Iraq over the past decade, many industries—including petroleum producers and security contractors such as Halliburton and Blackwater—have seen profits soar.

In the area of public health, research agendas are commonly linked to the interests of private companies seeking to increase profits. Put simply, sickness is more profitable than good health. While profits in the drug industry have soared in recent years, many diseases continue to kill millions of people because drugs to combat them make insufficient profits for the drug industry. Such diseases primarily affect people in the developing world who are too poor to pay for treatment. Of course, preventing diseases in the first place—via public health education, the elimination of pollutants, and improved standards of living—would be the best direction, but there's little profit to be made in that at all.

The Changing Face of Capitalism

Earlier in this chapter we saw that feudalism was a relatively rigid and inflexible socioeconomic formation. In contrast, capitalism over the last two centuries has proven to be an extremely flexible and adaptable system. Some capitalist countries are quite wealthy overall while others are very poor; some have democratic political forms while others are totally undemocratic; some are closely tied to traditional religions while others are secular (that is, not affiliated with a religion). But whatever the superficial appearance, almost all countries, in one way or another, are now tied to a single global capitalist economy.

Moreover, the dominant form of capitalism has changed over time. The period of the mid-nineteenth to the early twentieth century is often referred to as the stage of **laissez-faire capitalism**, when free enterprise still dominated, there were many small or medium-sized productive units, and there was only moderate state intervention to control the worst excesses of capital. However, the inevitable instability of the capitalist system led to a number of severe economic downturns, the most serious of which was the time from the Great Depression, which began after 1929, until World War II. Following the war, there were dramatic alterations to the developed capitalist economies. During this period, which continued until the early 1970s, governments played an increasing role in economic affairs, while the public sector and social safety net expanded. This form of capitalism is commonly referred to as the **welfare state** because governments developed policies that enhanced the welfare of most citizens rather than just the dominant class.

By the mid-1970s, however, the capitalist class found itself facing a number of serious difficulties. Extremely large corporate units had developed, and the competition was intense as they sought to increase their rate of profit. The welfare state gradually diminished in all capitalist societies and was replaced by a set of policies collectively referred to

> The need of a constantly expanding market for its products chases the bourgeoisie over the whole surface of the globe. It must nestle everywhere, settle everywhere, establish connections everywhere.
> —*Karl Marx and Friedrich Engels*, The Communist Manifesto, *1848*

as *neoliberalism*, which will be explained in detail in Chapter 9. In this period, more and more wealth was transferred to the largest corporations and the wealthiest individuals, while social spending by most governments continues to be drastically reduced. This assault on the welfare state must be seen as one of the major factors that gave rise to numerous protest movements in the United States in 2011. The first major protests began in Wisconsin at the beginning of that year when many public-sector workers there protested attempts by the state legislature to cut spending by restricting their collective bargaining rights.

Capitalism as a Global System

Many of us think that globalization is a recent trend. However, the quote from Marx and Engels, written over 150 years ago, gives us a clue that capital has always looked beyond its own national borders for new sources of profit. In the expanding global economy of the late nineteenth century, it was the European nations that competed for territories in Africa, Asia, Australia, and North and South America. Many of these colonies had already been utilized as military outposts, as trading centres, for the seizure of slaves, for the looting of gold and silver, and for European settlement.

However, with the advance of industrial capitalism, the world powers began to use their colonies in a different way. While Marx and Engels addressed the global nature of capitalism, it was several later analysts who drew attention to the process of **imperialism**. In this advanced stage of capitalism large monopolies came to control the economy. For change theorists, imperialism has always been part of developed capitalism because capital must continually expand, something that eventually reaches its limits when capital is confined to its own soil. Capitalism, therefore, has long had an element of force, which has always required both financial and military support from governments.

The imperialist stage of capitalist development began at the end of the nineteenth century. Following the Treaty of Berlin in 1885, signed by the major European powers and the United States, the whole African continent was divided up; by the start of the twentieth century only Ethiopia and Liberia remained as sovereign African states. The same process occurred in the Far East and Southeast Asia. In this way the European states established absolute power over their colonies around the world. Some of the countries that are today considered minor powers—such as Belgium, Portugal, and Spain—were once major players in the growing global economy.

As part of this process, industrialization was actively discouraged in the colonies. Instead they became exporters of natural resources, which were processed abroad and sold back to them as finished products at exorbitant prices. In most colonies, impoverished peasants were forced to work under the most horrific conditions, living lives marked by chronic hunger, bad housing, ill health, illiteracy, and political tyranny. The skills and knowledge of the small stratum of educated workers were constantly underutilized, and persistent racism kept many from obtaining jobs for which they were qualified.

Direct colonial rule gradually came to an end in the era following World War II. However, although the colonies became independent in theory, their economies were so grossly distorted and dependent on the imperialist powers that the majority could not come out from under their conditions of underdevelopment. Moreover, internal political instabilities, an impoverished or underpaid workforce susceptible to graft and corruption, as well as continued alliances between the imperialist powers and the local elites, meant little true independence or advancement for the majority of people in the developing world. In this way, the imperialist powers, led by the United States since the end of World War II, have—with few exceptions—retained effective domination over the poorest nations of the world.

Thus, although the term *globalization* has become popular in recent years, it is in reality nothing new. Most of us think that globalization today is about trade. However, the recent era of global expansion has taken on a number of distinctive characteristics, the most important of which is the rapid expansion of foreign direct investment (FDI). Canadian capital is now investing in many foreign countries, while at the same time international capital is investing in Canadian companies.

It is also important to note that the capitalist goal of maximizing profit has not led to the expansion of such investment equally around the globe. Instead, there has been a relocation of factories and businesses *within* the developed capitalist world, as well as an expansion of global capital to a select few areas, such as China, India, some parts of Latin America, and parts of Eastern Europe. Nonetheless, all economies, whether big or small, are linked to a single global structure dominated by global capital.

Think About It

Why do you think capitalist expansion has not developed equally around the world? What are capitalist enterprises looking for when they invest abroad?

Although capital has always sought profits beyond the narrow confines of any particular nation-state, a dramatic change occurred with the development of what are referred to as multinational enterprises (MNEs), or **transnational corporations (TNCs)**. It is mainly since the 1960s that TNCs have become a major force on the world scene. With the pressing need to always search out new sources of greater profits, major corporations are driven to look beyond their national boundaries for new markets, cheap labour, cheap raw materials, and governments sympathetic to the goals of capital.

By the beginning of this century, over half of the largest economies in the world were corporations; in other words, the major TNCs were larger than many nation-states. The majority of these conglomerates are based in what is often referred to as "the Triad"—the United States, Western Europe, and Japan. The combination of size and international networks gives transnational corporations tremendous power, and they are increasingly able to move capital to wherever return on investments can be maximized. Recent rapid advances in information and communication technologies make such moves both possible and necessary for the major players in the competitive global marketplace. Even the threat of such moves is often enough to allow the TNCs to put pressure on governments or trade unions to accede to their demands.

Power in Capitalist Societies

If you were asked who wields the most power in Canada, it's likely that you would say that it was the prime minister or the provincial premiers. However, while our political leaders certainly have more power than the average Canadian, their power is always closely connected to those who financially support them. In all capitalist societies, the owners of the largest productive units hold enormous amounts of power relative to the rest of us, and with the growing concentration of capital, this power is falling into fewer and fewer hands. In addition, the power of those who own or control the means of production can be linked to power in the sphere of ideas (also referred to as the *ideological* sphere). Indeed, the owning class could not maintain its position for long if it did not effectively control all three spheres within society: the economic, the political, and the ideological.

We have seen in this chapter that when we speak today about the owning class, we are referring not to the small business owner, but rather to the select few who own and control enormous amounts of capital worldwide via the entity of the corporation. Why should any of us care about this development? If we recall that ownership of the productive process gives societal power, then the concentration of ownership also means the growing concentration of power.

In a sense, the power of each class is a potential, and the degree to which each class uses its potential constitutes what was referred to earlier as the class struggle. This struggle can be envisaged as a game of tug of war: the more one class asserts its power to get its interests met, the less the other class gets its interests met. Hence the struggle between classes is structural, rather than personal.

Of course, class is not the only determinant of power within societies. In societies as large and complex as ours, many inequalities of power exist. Certain occupational categories—for example, doctors and lawyers—have more power than others. Men have more power than women. Certain ethnic or racial groups, for historical reasons, also have more power than others. Parents have more power than children. The list is endless.

Many sociologists have given primary attention to such inequalities of power, which we can say exist mainly at the proximal level. In our everyday lives it is certainly these power inequalities that we experience most directly. Women are beaten by men, children are abused by adults, workers are humiliated by managers, patients are mistreated by doctors, and so on. However, as the rest of this book demonstrates, the power of the dominant class, while much more invisible and distal than these other, more localized, forms of power, is also all-encompassing and much more consequential for the totality of our life experiences. From the minute we wake up until the minute we go to sleep, all of us, whether we know it or not, are under the sway of capital.

KEY POINTS

1. Capitalism developed out of the feudal system, beginning in England and gradually spreading to parts of Europe. The decline of feudalism is linked to many variables, which fed on and reinforced the others.

2. Capitalism has always been a world system to some extent, and Canada from the outset was economically and politically tied to a European power (first France, then England).

3. The transition from feudalism to capitalism teaches us that even the most rigid of socioeconomic formations can eventually decay and disappear. A clue that a social system is on the decline is the increasing inability of the dominant class to maintain its political and moral authority.

4. Capitalism is a mode of production with private ownership of the means of production. In capitalist societies, as compared to earlier class forma-tions, all production is subordinated to the imperatives of the market, and all things become potential commodities.

5. In pre-capitalist societies, the surplus was extracted through various forms of political, legal, and military coercion. In capitalism, the coercion takes on a mainly economic form.

6. The insatiable drive for profits on the part of the capitalist is a necessary condition of the capitalist system itself. Because of the competitive nature of capitalism, the goal of every capitalist must be not simply profits, but the maximization of profits.

7. The cost of purchasing labour power is always far less than the new value that the worker produces. From the Marxist perspective, this is the ultimate source of profits for the capitalist and of wealth for society as a whole. This source of wealth becomes totally obscured in capitalist societies.

8. The anarchy of production in capitalist societies leads inevitably to the crisis of overproduction, which produces a glut of goods, workers, and capital itself.

9. Financialization has become a major aspect of developed capitalist economies. One of the many consequences of this development is grow-ing economic instability.

10. There has been a growing contradiction between the increasingly social nature of production and the increasingly private appropriation of the fruits of such production. Those who own and control the productive proc-ess in capitalism have a particular set of interests that may not match the needs or goals of the rest of us.

11. Capitalism is a very flexible and adaptable system and can take many different forms.

12. Capitalism has, to some extent, always been a global system, looking beyond national borders for new sources of profit. In the last fifty years, transnational corporations have expanded in size and grown more powerful.

13. In capitalist societies, the power of those who own or control the means of production can also be linked to power in two other societal spheres: the sphere of ideas and the political sphere.

FURTHER READING

Foster, John Bellamy, and Fred Magdoff. 2009. *The Great Financial Crisis: Causes and Consequences.* New York: Monthly Review.
Two U.S. authors present a simple introduction to the creation of economic bubbles and the financialization of capitalist economies.

Frieden, Jeffry. 2006. *Global Capitalism: Its Fall and Rise in the Twentieth Century.* New York: W.W. Norton.
A comprehensive economic history of globalization from 1870 to the recent period.

Heller, Henry. 2011. *The Birth of Capitalism: A Twenty-First-Century Perspective.* Black Point, NS: Fernwood.
A recent contribution to the ongoing debate about the transition from feudalism to capitalism in Europe and elsewhere.

Kliman, Andrew. 2012. *The Failure of Capitalist Production: The Underlying Causes of the Great Recession.* London, UK: Pluto Press.
On the basis of an in-depth analysis of U.S. economic data, the author concludes that Marx's argument that the rate of profit tends to fall as capitalism progresses is, in fact, correct.

Marx, Karl, and Friedrich Engels. [1848] 2005. *The Communist Manifesto.* Edited by Phil Gasper. Chicago: Haymarket Books.
This edition includes the full text, commentaries, annotations with historical references, additional texts, and a glossary.

Rosenwein, Barbara H. 2009. *A Short History of the Middle Ages.* 3rd Ed. Toronto: University of Toronto Press.
A thorough overview of the period of medieval history from around 300 to 1500. Full of maps and photographs.

Stanford, Jim. 2008. *Economics for Everyone: A Short Guide to the Economics of Capitalism.* Black Point, NS and Ottawa, ON: Fernwood Publishing and the Canadian Centre for Policy Alternatives.
This is essential reading for those who want a beginner's guide to the economics of twenty-first century capitalism. The book covers both the economic and political spheres and offers some suggestions for change.

Wright, Ronald. 2004. *A Short History of Progress.* Toronto: Anansi.
Based on the CBC Massey Lecture series of the same name. Wright traces the history of our species from our beginnings to the present day. Will our arrogance soon lead to our extinction? This is the question Wright contemplates.

5 Analyzing Social Class

In This Chapter

- How is class different from socioeconomic status?
- Aren't most of us middle class?
- How are classes structured in capitalist societies?
- What is class consciousness?

If you were asked to make a list of ten words that you would use to describe yourself, do you think that you would include your class affiliation in your description? In earlier chapters we defined social class as a person's relationship to the means of production. However, such economic divisions between people are not easy for us to identify in our society. As a result we seldom identify others, or even ourselves, in terms of our class. Indeed, one of the most important elements of the Occupy movement, which began in 2011, was that its rallying cry, "We are the 99%," brought notions of class inequality into the public sphere for the first time in generations.

Usually we think of ourselves in terms of our gender, religion, sexual preference, race, ethnic group, occupational category, and so on. Sociologists would say that we focus on *status* categories rather than class categories. **Status** refers to any position held by people in society. It is normal to have many statuses concurrently—for example, woman, sister, daughter, student, employee, and so on. A status can either be *ascribed*, as in the case of sex or race, or *acquired*, such as level of education, occupation, or marital status. Status positions can be ranked in relation to each other by their privileges and obligations.

Prior to the rise of capitalism, class relations were highly visible. When the private appropriation of surplus first appeared and the division of labour expanded in agrarian societies, class categories were commonly defined in law and supported by religious beliefs and traditions. These categories were referred to as ranks, orders, stations, castes, or estates. In societies with such divisions, everyone knew their place and the place of others within these relatively rigid structures of inequality, which were noted through such symbols as official titles and different styles of dress. Positions were largely hereditary. Here is something to ponder: this whole book is an attempt to demonstrate that classes exist and that they have a major determining effect on your life. Although you are far more educated than any slave or feudal peasant, they didn't need an Occupy movement to convince most of them of such an obvious fact. This is one of the many contradictions of the society in which we live.

Although at an experiential level we tend not to "see" class in our society, it is nonetheless a key tool to help us make sense of society and our place in it. The concept of class helps us understand both the dynamics of power and some of the tensions that lead to social change.

The three major classes in capitalist societies—the *capitalists*, the *workers*, and the *petite bourgeoisie*—have been introduced in earlier chapters. However, the existence of another group, which Marx referred to as the **lumpenproletariat**, should also be noted. Because of the unplanned nature of capitalist economies, there is never full employment. As a result, there is an underclass that consists of the long-term unemployed, or those engaged in illegal activities, who are completely outside of production. For Marx, these were the individuals on the margins of every capitalist economy who have been used by the ruling class to oppose the working class. The lumpenproletariat should be distinguished from others—such as students, housewives, and the retired—who are outside of production, but who have not played this historical role. In some capitalist societies, although not in Canada, one may also find residual classes from the previous socioeconomic formation, such as an aristocracy or a peasant class.

Class and Socioeconomic Status: What's the Difference?

If you asked the average Canadian to describe social classes in Canada, it is likely that very few would speak in terms of the divisions noted above. Most often, people speak of an upper, middle, and lower class, with each class being thought of as linked either to income or to some combination of income, occupation, and education. Such differences between people are real, but are more accurately referred to as **socioeconomic status** (SES) rather than social class. Unfortunately, in much of the social sciences, as in our everyday understanding of social inequality, the concepts of social class and socioeconomic status are used interchangeably. This looseness has led to a rather muddied vision of the nature of structured inequality in capitalist societies and has diverted attention away from the true nature of power allocation within such societies.

In the late nineteenth century, the traditional conception of class was still a part of European social thought. The shift of emphasis away from a Marxist analysis of class in the social sciences more or less began with the work of German sociologist Max Weber. While Weber agreed with Marx that class was tied to the ownership or control of property, he felt that social inequality was multi-dimensional and not sufficiently explained by property relationships alone. For Weber, there were three dimensions of inequality:

class, which in Weber's analysis meant socioeconomic status or individual life chances; *status*, meaning the level of social prestige; and *party* (or power), which meant the degree of political influence. Following Weber, the ranking of individuals via status rather than using traditional class analysis gained popularity in social theory.

This tendency was particularly evident in North America. In the twentieth century, the social sciences grew in the United States, which was idealized as a classless society, or at least one where classes were minimized and equality was an achievable goal. In this context, American social science, including sociology after World War II, increasingly moved away from a focus on structured inequality as linked primarily to property relations; instead, it focused on status categories, most notably occupational status, or on levels of prestige.

This distinction is reflected in the fact that American sociologists commonly use the term *social stratification* when referring to social inequality. Strata are layers, and the term *social stratification* leads us to conceive of inequalities in social positions, or statuses, as ranked from top to bottom. To some extent, the concept of stratification and the theories connected with it serve as a direct counterpoint to Marxist class analysis, which sees inequality as tied to a struggle between opposing interests. There are no struggles between layers, just differences.

Think About It
What do you think most people mean when they talk about someone's "class background"?

There is no single order theory regarding social inequality; however, the order theories, or what—in this context—we might call *stratification theories,* do share some common elements. Stratification theories tend to focus on the complex division of labour in advanced industrial societies that leads to an inequality of power and income because of occupational status differences. Since in every society individuals and groups perform different tasks, stratification theorists see structured social inequality as inevitable. Generally speaking, classes are seen as groups of people who have similar rankings, usually on the basis of some combination of occupational status, income, and education.

In contrast, the Marxist approach sees class as being determined by a person's relation to production, that is, either through the selling of labour power or ownership of capital assets. Put more simply, Marxists ask whether a person makes their living through work or through ownership. In contrast to stratification theories, this determination remains constant over time and place. For example, a sociologist could use the identical Marxist definition of class to compare social class in Canada, Pakistan, Vietnam, or Bolivia. The same class categorization could also be used to compare classes in Canada today to the Canadian class structure in the eighteenth century. The only uncertainties occur at the very margins of each class—for example, whether a particular individual is haute (big) bourgeois or petite (small) bourgeois.

While there is by no means a shared Canadian perspective on social inequality, most sociologists in English-speaking Canada have traditionally fallen somewhere between the Marxist class model, which focuses on economic ownership, and the American stratification model, which focuses on occupational ranking. This duality is seen clearly in the writings of John Porter, whose classic work, *The Vertical Mosaic* (1965), became the basis for much subsequent Canadian sociology. On the one hand, Porter, like the stratification theorists, argues that "because there are no clear dividing lines, no one can be sure how many classes there are" and that "the... objective criteria of class are income, occupation, property ownership, and education" (1965, 9–10). On the other hand, in line with class analysis, one of the central themes of Porter's work is the concentration of power held by a relatively small, socially homogeneous group of individuals who sit on the boards of directors of major corporations.

It is important to note that *both* class and status differences exist within capitalist societies, and both must be taken into account in any social analysis. Some key statuses, such as race and gender, may even predominate in understanding certain social phenomena at particular moments in history. (These two key statuses are examined in depth in Chapters 11 and 12.) Moreover, there is an inter-relationship between class and socioeconomic status. For example, the ability to acquire a high-status occupation or a high-level education is, to a fair extent, correlated to one's class position. Thus, we should not ignore socioeconomic status but must appreciate that it is different from social class.

Canada: A Middle-Class Society?

When asked what class they are in, most Canadians will say they are "middle class," even if they might not be clear about what that means (see Box 5.1). A number of social analysts have argued that despite its many failings, capitalism has allowed many people to improve the conditions of their lives and become middle class.

In contrast, Marx and Engels argued that with the advancement of capitalism, society would split into two opposing classes. However, following World War II, particularly in North America, it seemed as if their predictions were completely wrong. Wages rose, and expanding numbers of families were able to achieve standards of living formerly thought to be unattainable. Many could buy their own home and a car; even a summer home, annual vacation, and what were previously considered luxury items became possible for an expanding number of families. More and more people were able to send their children to college or university. Those who critiqued Marxist arguments thought that Marx and Engels had failed to see the possibilities that capitalism provided for the attainment of a middle-class society.

How do we explain the expansion of the middle strata that occurred in the years that followed World War II? While such a group is regularly referred to as the "middle class," it is, in fact, not a class at all. Rather, the term reflects a reality that a fair number of people—including well-educated, well-paid workers and some small-business people—were able to achieve improved life chances and lifestyles distinct from those of workers in the early twentieth century. The term *middle class* is, in reality, a *status* category, connoting differences in education, occupation, income, and consumption patterns. Without a doubt, these middle strata did expand in the postwar period in Canada and most of the developed capitalist world.

There are a number of factors that explain this phenomenon (Teeple 2000, 26). First, following World War II, the economies of the capitalist world expanded rapidly. New technologies meant a decline in the proportion

---

Box 5.1 The Riddle of the Middle

It's like a bad riddle: almost everyone thinks they belong to it, but few can define what it is. Politicians claim to champion it, but it's increasingly difficult to determine what it actually wants. And, often, when we talk about it, we're really only referring to part of it—the part that doesn't really belong to it at all, but likes to think it does. What is it? It's the middle class.

The Canadian Centre for Policy Alternatives Growing Gap Project did extensive public opinion research to look at issues around income inequality and poverty—how it's experienced and how it's perceived. But something else was revealed: it doesn't matter if you make $25,000 or $150,000; everyone self-identifies as "middle class."

Now, obviously, the vast majority of Canadians understand there's a world of difference between life as experienced by someone living right around the poverty line and someone among the richest 5 percent of income earners. So how can both extremes possibly see themselves as part of the same class?

Is "middle class" simply a label that speaks to how people want to think of themselves and be perceived? Perhaps its real significance is as a term that de-stigmatizes both ends of the spectrum. It allows the well off to feel less pretentious and the working

poor feel less financially insecure.

We talk about the "disappearing middle class," but while disposable income is flatlining and decent jobs are vanishing, the middle class label isn't. On the contrary, it's being stretched like an elastic band to accommodate a huge range of people with very different lives and financial realities.

Constant use and acceptance of this term allows us to avoid addressing the persistent financial struggle experienced by too many, the accumulation of wealth by too few, and the difference in between. It provides us all with a convenient way to avoid the fact that far too many people constantly face the heartbreaking struggle between paying the rent or feeding the kids, while others bring in six figures and can top up their RRSPs each year quite comfortably.

Moreover, it relies on the illusion of economic commonality—even solidarity. Rather than political leaders addressing the vast disparities across the economic spectrum, we hear how their policies will benefit the "middle class" when even a cursory analysis reveals the real beneficiaries of many of these policies are those with much higher incomes (the very upper crust of the middle, so to speak).

Source: Adapted from Shaker 2011.

of manual workers (in the developed capitalist world, at least), with a corresponding increase in the number of scientists, technicians, and engineers, in addition to managerial, clerical, and administrative personnel. There was also a large expansion of the non-productive sectors, such as those involving the exchange and distribution of commodities, as well as an expansion of the public sector.

The changes in the composition of the working class were accompanied by overall improvements in wages and working conditions. More and more people worked in comfortable offices rather than in the sweatshops that had dominated early capitalism. More people worked with their heads than their hands. The material conditions of life improved for a fair proportion of the population as rising wages, buying on credit, an expansion of mass production, and a globalizing economy—and consequently lowered cost—made a large number of what were formerly luxury items available to the average worker. Many small-business people made millions in the rapidly expanding postwar economy. All of these developments gave the impression that the predictions of Marx and Engels were wrong.

Changes to the middle class began to occur by the mid-1970s. As a result of a number of altered economic conditions, which will be explained in subsequent chapters, the conditions that gave rise to an expanded "middle" gradually disappeared. At the same time, housing prices in many cities in Canada began to rise. The middle-class society—where large numbers of Canadians could achieve the "good life"—that many social analysts thought was an inevitable aspect of developed capitalism is today no longer in evidence. Both social scientists and many of the new social movements have noted increasing polarization in both wealth and income in many countries, including Canada, as we will see in Chapter 10.

Are these recent changes a temporary phenomenon or a general trend? While the "middle class" has by no means disappeared entirely, the predictions of Marx and Engels no longer seem as outrageous as they once did. Indeed, the usefulness of their concept of social class has grown, rather than diminished.

The Structure of Classes

In the last few chapters you have been introduced to the traditional Marxist concept of social class. To this point, this concept of class may have seemed fairly straightforward—one's class position is the result of one's relation to the means of production. However, class analysis is actually more complex than this, and therefore more detail is required. The following will help expand our understanding of social class:

Class categories are relational.

A class exists only insofar as another corresponding class exists. Within capitalist societies, there can be no bourgeoisie unless there is simultaneously a working class. That is because the existence of the owning class is dependent on its ability to appropriate the surplus value produced by the workers. Conversely, the working class exists because, under current economic relations, it must sell its labour power to the capitalists who "own" the jobs. Even the petite bourgeoisie can exist only insofar as they are connected to a market controlled by another class.

Classes are structurally in conflict.

As we have seen in earlier chapters, this conflict occurs because of the relationship of power wherever private appropriation of surplus exists. The more surplus that goes to one class, the less that goes to the other; the more one class has its needs met, the less the other class has its needs met. The problem is built into the structure of the private appropriation of surplus value and has nothing to do with personal feelings between people. The ongoing tension between the appropriating and producing class is referred to as *class conflict*.

Classes are not monolithic.

There are segments within particular classes (sometimes referred to as class *fractions* or class *strata*), and tensions can develop between the various sectors within a class. For example, in the working class, those who work in private industry may initially give support to government cutbacks, while public-sector workers may show more opposition to them. Or perhaps White male workers oppose equity programs that would assist women or racialized workers, fearing loss of their own jobs. However, while we must always note the distinctions between various strata, we must also keep in mind that all members of a particular class do share a common bond: those who appropriate surplus have a set of interests that is different from those who sell their labour power.

Classes change over time.

Classes can expand or contract in size, or their internal composition can change. For example, the small-business class has declined in the face of competition from large corporations. When studying the working class in Canada, it is important to note certain dramatic shifts that have occurred since World War II. These changes include the rapid increase in the percentage of women in the workforce, the shift from blue-collar to white-collar forms of employment, the expansion of the service sector, and the increase in the number of workers who have one or more part-time jobs. Thus, we must always study classes within a historical framework.

Class is linked to the allocation of power as well as to the allocation of material resources within a society.

As has already been noted, ownership or control of the means of production in any society gives one enormous control over one's own life and the lives of others, because productive activity is so central to human existence. The power of ownership, however, extends far beyond the productive sphere in any society, to power within the political and ideological spheres as well. This point is demonstrated in later chapters.

Classes must be seen in a global context.

We saw in the last chapter that capitalism in the twentieth century became global in structure, linking all nation-states to some degree in a single economy. While all countries, including Canada, retain their own distinct capitalist and working classes, no class system can be fully understood without linking it to broader global structures of inequality and power.

Class has both an objective and a subjective component.

One's class membership is determined by real attributes—that is, whether one survives through ownership (bourgeoisie), through work (working class), or through a combination of the two (petite bourgeoisie). Put differently, class is a material reality. However, classes have a subjective component as well. Humans are thinking social animals who try to make sense of the world in which we live. The term **class consciousness** refers to the understanding one has of one's place in the class structure and of the shared interests one has with others in the same place. Of course, not everyone in a class society has a high degree of class consciousness. Generally speaking, in societies where classes exist, class consciousness will be relatively high for the owning class but low for the rest. Otherwise, no class society would last for very long!

The Owning Class

Although most of us appreciate that there is inequality in Canada, our image of those "at the top" has traditionally come primarily from the mass media. Thus, we usually think only in terms of a few wealthy individuals, such as movie stars or professional athletes with large incomes, or perhaps a few well-known corporate heads such as Bill Gates. In addition, we tend to think of the rich with regard to what they can purchase, rather than the power some of them may hold over our lives. As noted earlier in this chapter, one of the most important elements of the Occupy movement was that it brought into public discourse the previously invisible few that control the global economy.

In Chapter 4 we saw that capitalism is a global economic system and that corporations became increasingly large and powerful in the last half of the twentieth century. But corporations are just legal fictions. Behind every corporation are real human beings who own and control them (as well as, of course, real people who work in them). Thus, although the term *corporate rule* is often used to describe the power of the major corporations, it must always be remembered that there is a small number of powerful individuals who are actually in control. Whether we are speaking of Canadian capital or global capital, those who control the economy tend to share a common set of interests and values.

Think About It

Can you name five of the most powerful members of the owning class in Canada? If not, why do you think you might be having such difficulty answering this question?

Many books have been written about the wealthiest and most powerful Canadians. Some are academic works, but a number were written by journalists. Few of these authors could be considered Marxists, and, indeed, the journalists in particular take great pains to distance themselves from a Marxist analysis. Rather than speaking of a bourgeoisie or owning class, these authors use terms such as "the elite" or "the establishment" to describe those at the top. And yet over the years there has been unanimous agreement among many writers that a small core of individuals wields an enormous amount of power in Canada (Porter 1965; Johnson 1972; Clement 1975; Newman 1975; Niosi 1981; Francis 1986; Fleming 1991; Newman 1998; Brownlee 2005). This is true at the international level as well (Sklar 1980; Korten 1996; Carroll 2010).

Because it is hard to get detailed and accurate information about those with great power and wealth, it is impossible to be precise about the exact size and composition of this class. The size is also dependent on how broadly or narrowly social scientists wish to cast their net. Certainly, there is a "core" controlling bourgeoisie that is very small. Porter's classic study (1965, 579) noted 907 individuals who together controlled, at the time of his study, the major corporations in Canada. Newman (1975, 186) spoke of under a thousand people, while Francis (1986) dealt with thirty-two families. Veltmeyer (1986, 30), drawing on a number of authors, maintained that the number was under 2000.

> In Canada today, there exists an economic elite that controls the country's major industrial, financial, and commercial companies and utilities.
> —Jamie Brownlee, Ruling Canada

> Every ruling class has wanted only this: all the rewards and none of the burdens. The operational code is: we have a lot; we can get more; we want it all.
> —Michael Parenti

> There's class warfare, all right, but it's my class, the rich class, that's making war, and we're winning.
> —Warren Buffett, ranked 3rd on Forbes World's Billionaires list of 2011

> I want my fair share and that's all of it.
> —Charles Koch, ranked 24th on Forbes World's Billionaires list of 2011

Connected to but somewhat distinct from the owning class is the stratum of extremely highly paid executives. These are people who hold key positions of authority, who are chief executive officers (CEOs), or who sit on the boards of major corporations. Although most of these individuals are technically employees, their wages, bonuses, and stock options have become so high in recent years that they have become part of the owning class rather than the working class. The pay of CEOs in Canada pales in comparison to that in the United States. The incomes of CEOs in the financial sector—as became widely known after the crash of 2008—have been particularly high. Besides huge incomes, most top executives also receive many additional benefits, including stock options worth millions of dollars, and negotiate large "golden parachutes" to be received when they leave their jobs.

The 1990s saw a transformation of the owning class in Canada. Prior to this decade, this class consisted primarily of what has been referred to as the "dynasties," the "old guard," or the Old Establishment—with family names such as Weston, Thomson, Bronfman, Eaton, Irving, Desmarais, McCain, and Webster. These men (and they were almost all men) shared not only the commonality of wealth, but also a convergence of interests, histories, and lifestyles. Most of these individuals were also linked through common backgrounds at private schools and summer camps, through shared social activities, through membership in private clubs, through intercorporate ownership, through interlocking directorships on corporate boards, and so on (Brownlee 2005). It is also worth noting that, despite the globalization of capitalism—discussed in future chapters—the network connecting members of Canada's corporate elite remains one of the most integrated in the world (Carroll 2010, 209).

In recent years, however, a number of new faces have been added to the list of the wealthiest Canadians. The appearance of this new group is largely the result of the rapidly growing global economy as well as the sudden expansion of new technology sectors of the economy. However, as Table 5.1 indicates, the "old guard" continues to hold five of the ten top spots in Canada with regard to wealth. Moreover, while this new establishment may not have quite the uniformity of shared family backgrounds, most of these corporate leaders were born into some wealth. Whatever their origins, the members of the owning class continue to be linked to each other through various corporate networks—both formal and informal—and share a set of common interests and values.

On the other hand, there remain distinctions within the bourgeoisie, and sometimes tensions can arise between what are referred to as *fractions*—or sub-groupings—within this class. Nonetheless, although occasional disagreements do break out between individuals, families, or sectors within the bourgeoisie, the people at the top in terms of wealth and power continue to share a common perspective and a common interest. Their overarching

Table 5.1 The Wealthiest People in Canada, 2011

Name	Main Businesses	Wealth/$billions
1. Thomson family	Media, info distribution	21.34
2. Galen Weston	Food, retail, real estate	8
3. Irving family	Oil, forestry, media	7.8
4. Rogers family	Cable TV, communications, media	5.94
5. James Pattison	Auto sales, food, media, entertainment	5.73
6. Saputo family	Food, real estate, transportation	4.28
7. Paul Desmarais	Financial services, media	4.27
8. Jeff Skoll	Internet, media	3.75
9. Fred and Ron Mannix	Mining, energy, real estate	3.44
10. Bernard Sherman	Pharmaceuticals	3.31

Source: *Canadian Business* Rich 100 2011.

goals are always the same: in the short term to maximize the rate of profit of the corporations they own or control, and in the long term to guarantee the maintenance of the system that allows them to privately appropriate wealth. Because their economic wealth and power allows them to exert pressure in the political sphere, as we will see in Chapter 8, they can be described as a *ruling class.*

It is sometimes argued that the notion of an owning class has become outmoded in an era when anyone can become an "owner" simply by purchasing stocks or mutual funds. However, despite the growth of mutual funds and other forms of stock ownership, the vast majority of shares of major companies remain in the hands of a small number of players. Even within this select group of individuals, the main means of subsistence for the majority continues to be through their work. Few individuals can survive on dividends alone, particularly in a time of economic upheaval.

It is also sometimes argued that the large amount of wealth transferred to the owning class is a result of their hard work. Some members of this class may indeed work hard; however, what differentiates this class from the rest of us is that it is their ownership or control of corporate assets, not their labour, which provides their wealth. If any of these individuals suddenly decides to give up working, their standard of living will not substantially decline.

We should also remember that wealth is actually created socially. It is the work of many thousands of people, drawn together in collective activity, which creates the surplus value in advanced capitalism that is then dispersed throughout the economy. Each one contributes a small share to the whole. Certainly it can be said that some, because of special skills or knowledge, contribute more than others. However, the huge amount of wealth that is transferred to the appropriating class is not the result of any particular individual attribute, but—as in the feudal era—simply a right that is given to them.

Class Consciousness in the Owning Class

As was noted earlier in this chapter, class has both an objective and a subjective component. Getting at the latter, which is referred to as *class consciousness,* is no easy matter. This is particularly true of the owning class, which values its privacy and has the power to maintain it. It is therefore not easy to provide extensive empirical data that indicate the degree of class consciousness in this class. More indirect sources must therefore be drawn upon.

One indicator of the degree of class consciousness of a particular class is the organizations it forms to protect its own class interests. In this regard, it seems that the owning class has a fairly high degree of class consciousness. From the earliest period of capitalism in Canada, business owners formed their own organizations, although they tended to be strictly regional or industry based. However, there are now a number of organizations that attempt to represent broader business interests: the Canadian Chamber of Commerce, the Alliance of Manufacturers and Exporters of Canada, the

Canadian Federation of Independent Business, the Canadian Council of Chief Executives, and le Conseil du patronat in Quebec.

The Canadian Council of Chief Executives (CCCE) constitutes the most powerful voice of big business in Canada. It began in 1976 as the Business Council on National Issues (BCNI), which was originally modelled on the Business Roundtable in the United States, a lobby group of about 200 corporate executives, although the BCNI eventually decided to become more public than the American group. Its aim, as stated by its original co-chair, was to "strengthen the voice of business on issues of national importance" (*Globe and Mail,* April 6, 1979). In January 2002, the BCNI changed its name to the Canadian Council of Chief Executives to reflect its increasing global orientation. Its aim is to promote the common interests of Canadian big business, both within Canada and internationally. This includes achieving a consensus within the corporate sector on major policy issues, influencing various levels of government, and swaying public opinion.

At the international level, there are also organizations of the most powerful circles of capital, where corporate leaders come together to discuss common concerns and plan future strategies. This is not surprising: as capitalist

---

Box 5.2 A Most Powerful Group You've Never Heard Of

In 1954, some of the most powerful men in the world met for the first time under the auspices of the Dutch Royal Crown and the Rockefeller family at the luxurious Hotel Bilderberg in the small Dutch town of Oosterbeek. At the end of the weekend they decided to meet once every year to exchange ideas and analyze international affairs. They named themselves the Bilderberg Group. Since then, they have gathered yearly somewhere in the world to try to decide the future of humanity. Among the select members of this private club are presidents of the International Monetary Fund, the World Bank, and U.S. Federal Reserve, heads of government, business executives, politicians, and bankers from all over the world.

The Bilderberg Group has been accused of identifying politicians who are friendly to big business and backing their runs for power. Former U.S. president Bill Clinton spoke at a Bilderberg conference a year before his election victory, as did British Prime Minister Tony Blair (CBC News online, June 13, 2006). Despite—or perhaps because of—its power, the press has never

been allowed to attend, no statements have ever been released on the attendees' conclusions, nor has any agenda for a meeting been made public (Estulin 2007, xiii–xiv).

The group has met three times in Canada, the last time in 2006, when it did get some media attention. As a result of the Internet and greater investigative abilities provided by new technologies, more is now known about this highly secretive group. Canadian attendees at the Bilderberg 2011 Forum were Mark Carney, Governor, Bank of Canada; Edmund Clark, President and CEO, TD Bank Financial Group; Frank McKenna, Deputy Chair, TD Bank Financial Group, and former premier of New Brunswick; James Orbinksi, Professor of Medicine and Political Science, University of Toronto; Robert Prichard, Chair, Torys LLP and former president of the University of Toronto; and Heather Reisman, Chair and CEO, Indigo Books & Music. Former prime ministers Paul Martin, Jean Chrétien, and Pierre Trudeau and current Prime Minister Stephen Harper have all attended a Bilderberg meeting at least once.

---

economies increasingly globalize, there has been a growing need for national elites to meet with each other and exchange views. One influential organization is the extremely secretive Bilderberg Group (see Box 5.2). One of the founders of this group stated that its aim was "to reduce differences of opinion and resolve conflicting trends and to further understanding… by… trying to find a common approach to major problems" (quoted in Korten 1996, 137).

Other key international organizations that bring together corporate leaders are the International Chamber of Commerce, the World Economic Forum—held once a year in Davos, Switzerland—the Trilateral Commission, and the World Business Council for Sustainable Development. All of these organizations are made up of prominent individuals from the developed capitalist nations, including Canada. The purpose of these organizations is similar to that of the CCCE but on a global scale: to formulate coordinated economic policies, influence governments, and affect public opinion, with the goal of advancing the interests of the TNCs. There are many interconnections between the key members of these various international organizations.

The existence of such groups is a clear indicator that those at the top—or at least those who represent them—are aware of their shared interests, understand the collective with whom they share these interests, and appreciate what positions or actions must be taken to protect their interests. These groups play a key role in allowing the various fractions of capital to express their differences within a relatively private setting and to come to a consensus on the best way to advance their common class interests.

Think About It
Have you ever heard of the Council on Foreign Relations, the Trilateral Commission, the Bilderberg Group, or the Canadian Council of Chief Executives? Why do you think we so seldom hear or read about these powerful organizations?

Such groups are also important to note since they give us a clue as to how the owning class is able to convert its economic power into political and ideological power. Supported by vast sums of money provided by member organizations, these groups are able to lobby governments—or help get them elected—as well as carry out independent advertising campaigns concerning important issues. The major corporations also fund several "think tanks" that publish supposedly "impartial" reports endorsing the views of the business elite. The two best known in Canada are the C.D. Howe Institute and the Fraser Institute.

What Is the Working Class?
While most social scientists generally agree that there is a small and identifiable owning class in capitalist societies (even if they use different terms to describe this powerful group), there is much more disagreement about the nature and composition of the working class. The traditional Marxist view

is that the working class is made up of all those who survive by earning a wage. However, among social scientists, even those who identify with the Marxist tradition, there has been a prolonged debate regarding the validity and utility of such a broad definition.

The reason for the split among analysts is rooted in the many real differences that exist among workers in advanced capitalist societies—differences in wages and working conditions, educational backgrounds, job autonomy, social status, control over the productive process and over other workers, and degree of class consciousness. There are also distinctions between those who work in the private sector and those who work for government, as well as between those whose work is related to the production of ideas and those whose work is connected to the production of goods.

Most social scientists agree that the working class includes "wage-workers who are engaged in the production of commodities, the extraction of natural resources, the production of food, the operation of the transportation network required for production and distribution, the construction industry, and the maintenance of energy and communication networks" (Veltmeyer 1986, 83). As a result of new technologies and increased productivity, the proportion of workers in these sectors has been declining both in Canada and globally. Workers in the service sector, clerical workers, and low- to mid-level government employees are also generally understood to be members of the working class. This latter group of workers, although not directly producing surplus value, certainly helps maintain a system in which such surplus value can continue to be produced and realized in the marketplace.

It is over the issue of whether a number of other categories of workers actually constitute part of the working class that the greatest debate occurs. The different lines of thought and the nature of the debates regarding what constitutes the working class need not concern us here. We may summarize by stating that some authors feel that the higher strata of working people constitute a distinct class, some argue that they should be considered as part of the petite bourgeoisie, while others argue that they cannot be defined in class terms at all.

One of the best-known arguments is that of Erik Olin Wright (1980), who asserted there was a distinct category, the "new middle class," consisting of certain occupational categories, such as managers and supervisors, small employers, and semi-autonomous employees who had some control over their work. Wright saw these people as having contradictory class locations, in that they shared characteristics of more than one class. Similarly, Clement and Myles (1994, 16) argued that the new middle class (or modern petite bourgeoisie) consists of those who exercise control over the labour power of others but do not have real economic ownership of the means of production and, as a result, must still sell their labour power, skills, or knowledge for a wage.

However, the separating out of groups of workers on the basis of what are essentially *status* differences diverts attention from class relationships and structures of power. Like other stratification approaches, it also draws attention to distinctions *between* groups of workers and away from their shared relationship to capital. It is therefore more analytically precise to describe the new middle class (with the exception of small employers, who remain the petite bourgeoisie) as a distinct fraction (or group) within a single class. This allows us to acknowledge the real status differences that exist between groups of workers, while simultaneously recognizing their common place in the relationship between classes.

For example, at first glance it appears that university professors are

---

Box 5.3 Temporary Workers in Canada: A Good or Bad Idea?

For decades, Canadian immigration policy—unlike that in most European countries—focused on attracting potential citizens, not workers. The temporary worker program began as a way to bring in high-skilled workers for specialized jobs, mainly in Alberta's oil industry, in addition to special programs for live-in caregivers and seasonal farm workers. However, in 2002, the Liberal government expanded it to allow employers to bring in a wide range of low-skilled foreign workers to work in the hospitality industry, food services, construction, and manufacturing.

To come to Canada, applicants need to obtain a work permit that is valid only for a specified job and length of time. There are no established limits on, or target levels for, the number of workers to be admitted under these programs. The number of temporary work permit applications rose from 91,270 in 2002 to 283,096 in 2010, an increase of more than 300 percent. In 2008, for the first time in history, more foreigners entered the country as temporary residents than as permanent immigrants.

Canada is not alone in relying on temporary residents to address some of its labour market requirements. There has been global growth in temporary worker programs in many Organisation for Economic Co-operation Development (OECD) countries. These programs are appealing because they enable countries to quickly address specific labour market needs without the increased costs associated with maintaining unemployed workers during a downturn. The costs associated with social and economic integration are also reduced. The benefits to employers are obvious: temporary foreign workers mean lower wages and benefits, no long-term commitments, no risk of unionization, a generally compliant workforce, and for multinationals the flexibility to transfer employees from country to country.

In late 2009, Auditor General Sheila Fraser issued a scathing report of Canadian government policies regarding temporary workers. The report noted that newcomers admitted to Canada might have to tolerate abuse, poor working conditions, and poor living conditions so as not to lose the opportunity to become permanent residents. "This creates risks to program integrity and could leave many foreign workers in a vulnerable position, particularly those who are physically or linguistically isolated from the general community or are unaware of their rights." At a news conference she noted that the failure of federal authorities to follow up on the genuineness of job offers for lower-skilled temporary workers means that work permits may be issued "for employers or jobs that do not exist."

During the 2011 election leaders' debate Prime Minister Harper responded to an expressed concern about the temporary worker program: "It benefits everybody. I don't know how anyone would be against it."

Source: Whittington 2009; Thomas 2010; Basen 2011.

not at all connected to factory workers. The former are generally well paid, are well educated, have traditionally had high levels of autonomy in their jobs, and are in a high-status occupation that is usually regarded as a profession. They work with ideas rather than objects and generally work in the public rather than the private sector. The low degree of class consciousness of this sector is reflected in the fact that the campus organizations of university professors are usually referred to as faculty associations rather than unions, and, indeed, many are still not certified bargaining units. Certainly, at the level of self-perception, few professors like to think of themselves as workers.

Yet something has happened to many university professors over the last forty years. As a result of massive cutbacks in funding to postsecondary education across Canada, which began in the 1970s, wages and research funds have, with some exceptions, not been keeping up with increasing workloads. Faculty have had to deal with expanding class sizes, more time spent on grant applications, deteriorating physical plants, and growing administrative control over their work. All of these developments have led to a general decline in faculty morale. Moreover, increasing use is being made of part-time and contract teachers who earn low wages, have heavy workloads, and have little or no job security. In other words, the university professor's job has come to have more and more similarity to that of a factory worker. In some cases, factory workers may actually earn higher wages. This trend is sometimes referred to as the process of **proletarianization**.

University professors are far from being the only sector to experience such changes. More and more of the formerly privileged sectors of the working class are discovering that, in the end, workers of all strata neither own nor control their jobs. Indeed, many formerly privileged workers—both in the public and private sectors—have found their jobs being eliminated in recent years. For those who have held on to their jobs, many experience increased workloads, lower wages, and high levels of stress. Thus, regardless of the privileges acquired by some workers at particular times, they all—except for top executives and the highest-paid stratum of workers—share an overarching set of material interests that distinguish them from the owning class.

For this reason, it is important to define all workers who survive by means of a wage as members of the working class, as long as we do not do so in a rigid, over-simplified, and non-historical fashion. Using this broad definition, working people constitute the vast majority of Canadians. Since the term *working class* is so strongly identified in our country with only those who wear hard hats and carry lunch pails, it is often easier to refer to this class as working people, wage workers, or simply workers. For the purposes of this book, we will use these terms interchangeably.

Having said that all wage workers share a common interest, it is important to remember that there are many ongoing stresses and strains between groups within this class. These are partly the result of real differences within the working class, partly the result of the forced competition between workers created by capitalism, and partly the result of the divide-and-rule tactics utilized by capital. These tensions within the working class are one of the major factors that have limited the ability of working people to unite and organize in their own interests. Thus, despite the fact that working people constitute a numerical majority in Canada and globally, they have been unable to attain the power that one might expect from their sheer numbers.

Class Consciousness in the Working Class

As noted earlier in the chapter, we would predict class consciousness in any class-based society to be relatively high within the owning class and relatively low in the producing class. We saw that, indeed, there is every indication of a relatively high degree of class consciousness among the owning class. What is the case for working people? At the present moment, the evidence supports the hypothesis that class consciousness among working people in Canada is very low. Few individuals even identify their interests with a collective of working people, let alone understand what those interests are or how to act in such a way as to protect those interests.

Think About It

Ask a number of working people you know—such as your parents, other relatives, or friends—what social class they think they are in. What do their answers tell you about class consciousness among working people today?

If class consciousness is, in part, connected to membership in organizations designed to protect the interests of the class, we should begin with a brief examination of the union movement, which is both a cause and a result of class consciousness. Few Canadians are aware of the history of this movement or of the many battles of workers to obtain the right to organize and bargain freely with their employers. Until 1872, unions were illegal in Canada. After that time, unionization was still extremely difficult, with many constraints from both employers and various levels of government.

A **labour union** is a group of workers who join together to bargain with an employer or group of employers with regard to wages, benefits, and working conditions. While most people assume that the primary reason workers join unions is to obtain higher wages, this is not always the case. Of course, most workers would like to feel that they are earning a fair wage for their work and want to obtain a sufficient wage that provides a decent life for themselves and their families. However, many workers turn to unions for a variety of reasons other than wages (see Box 5.4).

The first workers to organize were those engaged in crafts, such as weavers, printers, bakers, and so on. Workers in the resource and agricultural sectors fought a much harder battle to organize, particularly since the crafts workers generally saw unskilled workers as a threat and did not welcome them into their unions. Thus, at the beginning of the twentieth century it was the industrial unions, at least those in English Canada,

> No country has ever achieved widespread prosperity and created a large middle class without strong unions.
> —Bruce Campbell and Armine Yalnizyan

Box 5.4 How Unions Protect Our Human Rights

Unions are usually thought of as being about higher wages. It's true. Unions do produce higher wages for their members (and often, indirectly, for other workers as well). Unionized workers also get better benefits. Many people, including trade union members, see that as the end of the story. But unions do much more than this, and while wages and benefits are important, the other things unions do may be even more important.

Unions bring the rule of law and the rights that go with it into the workplace. Without a union, management can treat employees arbitrarily. With a union they cannot. They are constrained in their actions by the legal contract—the collective agreement—agreed to by the union (on behalf of its members) and the employer. That contract, the product of negotiations between union and employer, places limits on the potentially arbitrary exercise of power by employers and empowers union members to defend themselves against abuses in the workplace.

It is generally believed that employers don't like unions because they raise wages and improve benefits and working conditions. However, experience in the U.S. since World War II and in Canada in recent decades suggests that the decisive motivating force in employers' animosity to unions is that they lose the right to treat employees in an arbitrary fashion. Unions empower workers to protect themselves from abuse (unfair dismissal, discrimination, sexual assault, etc.).

The drive to destroy unions in North America has progressed furthest in the U.S., where union membership in 2010 was down to 10.9 percent, the lowest rate in more than seventy years. The union movement is stronger in Canada. However, in recent decades both the overall rate and the private-sector unionization rates have been declining.

Source: Adapted from Black and Silver 2011.

---

that were the most class conscious. At this time unions with clearly militant, socialist, and internationalist leanings—such as the Industrial Workers of the World (IWW) and the One Big Union (OBU)—were formed, and during the Great Depression of the 1930s workers and their unions became increasingly radical. However, union consciousness (fighting the employer in the workplace) did not necessarily translate into a broader understanding of class relations.

A decline in labour radicalism occurred following World War II. To a fair extent, this decline can be linked to the same conditions that saw the growth of the middle strata of workers with their improved living and working conditions, as well as to growing anti-communism, which resulted in the isolation of the most class-conscious workers and unions. It was not until the late 1960s that the union movement began to grow again—largely as a result of the expansion of the public sector. However, the degree of class consciousness within the union movement has remained low. Due to both internal and external pressures, union membership has stagnated in Canada, with 31.4 percent of Canadian non-agricultural workers belonging to unions in 2009, down from just over 35 percent in 1997. By province, unionization rates ranged from a low of 25 percent in Alberta to nearly 40 percent in Quebec (Human Resources and Skills Development Canada 2010).

Intensified globalization and the push of the corporate sector to create more "flexible" work arrangements have led to the decline of unions around the world. The increase in outsourcing, the decline of the manufacturing sector, and the use of contingent labour—all of which are discussed in Chapter 6—have all eroded workers' ability to organize themselves into collectives that can protect their interests.

Voting behaviour, public opinion polls, and the low degree of worker activism also indicate that there is little class consciousness among workers. This is perfectly logical in a society where classes exist. The maintenance of any class society requires that the class with economic power also exert its power in the ideological sphere—the sphere of ideas. Of course, we must also recall that all things change over time. In spite of the ideological power of the owning class, the degree of class consciousness of working people will ultimately be connected to the material conditions of their lives. Given the rapid erosion of conditions for many working people, class consciousness among workers will almost certainly increase in Canada in the future. The involvement of trade unions with the Occupy movement in 2011 was one indication that this is beginning to happen.

Think About It

In 2010, the unionization rate was 32.7 percent for women compared to only 30.4 percent for men. Can you come up with a hypothesis that might explain why rates of unionization are now higher for women than for men?

How Important Is the Variable of Social Class?

After the Russian Revolution in 1917, Marxist thought began to have an increasing appeal to many workers and intellectuals, who saw in it a means to struggle against the negative consequences of capitalism. In the period between the two world wars, communist parties around the world grew both in size and activism despite ongoing anti-communism, or "red baiting," as it is sometimes called. In addition, their consistent anti-fascism during World War II won communists many supporters, particularly in Western Europe. At the end of the war, the major capitalist world powers—dominated by the United States—quickly shifted their hostility away from their wartime enemies, Germany and Japan, to the Soviet Union. After 1946, what came to be known as the Cold War began in earnest. Although the United States is better known for its period of vicious assault on left-leaning citizens, the "red scare" occurred in Canada as well. Many people in government and universities lost their jobs for supposed "communist sympathies." In this context, it is not surprising that Marxist ideas more or less disappeared from the mainstream.

We should also be reminded that the 1950s and '60s was a time of tremendous economic growth in North America. Many of the predictions made by Marx were considered to be outmoded or even absurd. Moreover, after the horrors of Stalinism were revealed, many became disillusioned with the Marxist cause. At the same time, the period saw the rapid growth of the middle strata, whose children began to enter the expanding university sector by the mid-1960s. Many of these students had a conflicting attachment to capitalism: on the one hand, they read about (and, in some cases, experienced) forms of oppression (particularly sexism and racism); on the other hand, their socio-economic status made them relatively privileged within the capitalist order.

While many writers continued to be influenced by Marxism—particularly outside North America—critical theory shifted from the traditional premises of Marx to new, less class-based orientations. Two major interconnected transformations should be noted: the shift away from materialist analysis—that is, the focus on the real, material conditions of people's lives—to analyses that focused on subjective, individual feelings and ideas; and the shift away from class analysis to the study of status variables, oppression, and personal identity. In sociology, this shift is reflected in the advancement of what is referred to broadly as *postmodernism*. Simply put, postmodern theory generally opposes Marxist analysis because of its attempt to frame a universal (across history and around the globe) perspective. While these largely academic and esoteric analyses primarily affected academics and theoreticians rather than working people, the shift away from a Marxist orientation meant that class analysis was both less widely practised and less widely disseminated.

Traditional Marxism saw the working class at the centre of social transformations, primarily as a result of its potential economic power as the producer of surplus value, as well as its sheer numbers and organizational capacity. However, many critics of this approach felt that traditional Marxists were unfairly "privileging" the working class with regard to its central role in changing society. We should also recall that class has become increasingly invisible in developed capitalist societies. In its place, people have come to identify more strongly with those who share membership in various status groupings, such as gender, ethnicity, race, sexual preference, and even age.

However, a number of new social developments—including recent economic transformations, the gradual erosion of Canada's social safety net, political protests around the globe, and recurring global economic crises—are changing the dynamic between class and non-class analysis. Both workers and status groups such as women, gays and lesbians, the poor, people with disabilities, and racial minorities have seen many previous gains disappear. Moreover, many struggles have begun to overlap. For example, when nurses go on strike it is simultaneously a gender issue, a labour issue, and a health-care issue.

In order to protect their class interests, ordinary working people of all backgrounds would have to join together in increasing numbers. At the moment, class consciousness remains low in the working class, and for now structures of power appear to most of us to be eternal and unchangeable. However, as a result of the many global struggles for change that first appeared in 2011, the future direction of class struggle is unclear at the moment.

KEY POINTS

1. Although we tend to notice status differences rather than class differences, class is a central tool for understanding society and our place in it.

2. The class structure in Canada is made up of the two dominant classes, the owning class and the working class, plus two smaller classes, the petite bourgeoisie and the lumpenproletariat.

3. Class is often confused with socioeconomic status. The latter is a position in the hierarchy of inequality based on a combination of income, occupation, and education. Socioeconomic status is connected to, but distinct from, the traditional concept of class.

4. What is often termed the middle class is not a class at all; rather, it is a group of people with improved life chances and lifestyles distinct from traditional blue-collar workers.

5. We must always be careful not to be overly simplistic or mechanical in our approach to social class. It is important to note that classes are relational, classes are structurally in conflict, classes are not monolithic, classes change over time, class is linked to the allocation of both power and material resources, and class has both an objective and a subjective component.

6. There has been a split in sociology between stratification theorists, who put an emphasis on socioeconomic status, and Marxist-oriented theorists, who put an emphasis on inequality of ownership of productive property.

7. Substantial evidence supports the notion that there is a relatively small and powerful owning class in Canada. This class shares a common set of values, beliefs, and interests. The degree of class consciousness among the owning class appears to be fairly high.

8. There is a great deal of controversy in the social sciences regarding what constitutes the working class. In order to understand the shared interests of all workers, it is most useful to define the working class as all those people who survive by means of a wage.

9. It must always be noted that there are ongoing stresses and strains between fractions within the working class as a result of the many status differences between them. These divisions have limited the ability of working people to unite and organize in their interests.

10. There was a rapid expansion of the middle strata following World War II, giving the impression that Marx had erred in his predictions about capitalism. However, since the mid-1970s, the middle strata have been under attack across the developed capitalist world.

11. Class consciousness among the working class is relatively low in Canada, although the current global economic crisis may cause this to change.

FURTHER READING

Brownlee, Jamie. 2005. *Ruling Canada: Corporate Cohesion and Democracy.* Black Point, NS: Fernwood.
This is a detailed examination of the nature of the Canadian ruling class and the ways they are integrated.

Carroll, William K. 2010. *Corporate Power in a Globalizing World.* Don Mills, ON: Oxford University Press.
One of the foremost writers on the Canadian ruling class examines the links of power in a global setting.

Dobbin, Murray. 2003. *The Myth of the Good Corporate Citizen: Democracy Under the Rule of Big Business.* 2nd ed. Toronto: James Lorimer & Co.
The author explains the expansion of corporate power in a non-academic manner, linking economic power to ideological and political power as well

Kealey, Gregory S. 1995. *Workers and Canadian History.* Montreal/Kingston: McGill-Queen's Press.
An analysis of working class history in Canada that covers both theoretical debates and actual events.

Masson, Paul. 2010. *Live Working or Die Fighting: How the Working Class Went Global.* Chicago: Haymarket Books.
A non-academic examination of some historical workers' struggles, which describes real people trying to solve the complex issues of their time.

Porter, John. 1965. *The Vertical Mosaic: An Analysis of Social Class and Power in Canada.* Toronto: University of Toronto Press.
This book remains a central work in Canadian sociology. The range of material is vast and the methodology thorough. If nothing else, it must be recognized for its influence on the discipline.

Richardson, Ian, Andrew Kakabadse, and Nada Kakabadse. 2011. *Bilderberg People: Elite Power and Consensus in World Affairs.* London, UK: Routledge.
A thorough academic examination of this secretive organization.

Seabrook, Jeremy. 2002. *The No-Nonsense Guide to Caste, Class, and Social Hierarchy.* Toronto: Between the Lines.
There are many easy-to-read books in the No-Nonsense series. This one looks at social rankings, past and present.

6 Living in Capitalist Societies

In This Chapter
- What effect do transnational corporations have on our lives?
- How has the way we work been changing?
- How does capitalism in the twenty-first century affect small business?
- What is the culture of capitalism?

When was the last time you shopped at Wal-Mart? Chances are it was not long ago. Wal-Mart is the largest retail corporation in the world. If it were a sovereign nation, it would rank as the world's twenty-fifth largest country. It sells more DVDs, magazines, books, CDs, dog food, diapers, bicycles, toys, jewellery, and toothpaste than any other retailer. It is the largest private employer in the United States, Mexico, and Canada, and more people are employed by Wal-Mart than any other private company in the world.

This chapter expands on the nature of capitalism and its transformation in the twentieth century. Its goal is to help you understand that the distal sources of power—those individuals who own and control giant corporations like Wal-Mart—are becoming fewer in number yet more powerful on a global scale. The power of those who control capital—a force that so few see—goes far beyond the workplace, affecting everything we do, see, hear, or consume, everything we believe, and, indeed, everything we are.

In Chapter 4 we saw that capitalist economies changed in two very important ways in the twentieth century. First, an economy made up mainly of small, competing businesses was gradually replaced by one dominated by a few extremely large and powerful corporations. The second important development involved the globalization of capital. In order to maximize profits, the capitalist owning class had to seek new sources of profit throughout the world.

While most of us are quite sensitive to power exerted in the proximal sphere—such as that of our parents, teachers, or landlords—the power wielded by large transnational corporations is often too intangible or invisible for us to notice. Yet the size and power of these corporations means they have a major effect on many aspects of our lives. Let us return to Wal-

Mart. This company employs millions of people and subcontracts to a large number of other businesses that employ many people as well. It thus has a major determining effect on such things as wages, working conditions, and worker health and safety. Its large purchasing power affects farmers and food distributors, producers of plastics and paper products, and the transportation industry, among others. And the expansion of its suburban big-box stores not only affects competing retail stores but also has a dramatic impact on urban environments.

Isn't Bigger Better?

Most of us are aware that giant corporations exist. After all, we eat at their restaurants, use their products, wear their clothes, and work for their companies. However, few of us are concerned about the size and power of the transnational corporations, because—if we think of them at all—we tend to assume they are generally benefiting society as a whole. Surely, some of us might argue, if Wal-Mart, McDonald's, and Apple sell what we want or need, this is a good thing.

However, if we think dialectically, we can also see the dangers inherent in the growth of transnational corporations. As has become evident since the onset of the recent economic crisis, the creation of large global economic units also means that the entire economy can be put at risk when a small number of major businesses find themselves in crisis. As capital becomes increasingly international and the economy becomes more integrated, then the collapse of a major corporation can be a serious concern, even for the corporate sector itself. For example, the sudden and unexpected collapse of Lehman Brothers and some other investment firms in 2008 sent shock waves around the world as major banks, stock brokerages, and pension funds watched their investments disappear.

However, the biggest concern regarding large transnational corporations is their sheer global power. This power, as we will see in future chapters, allows them to assert dominance not simply in the economic sphere, but in the ideological and political spheres as well. No aspect of Canadian society or culture can now escape their influence. Corporations are, of necessity, interested in primarily one thing, which is maximizing profits. The disappearance of free enterprise in whole sectors of the economy may actually lead to higher prices, as a few companies effectively control the market. There are also concerns about ways one or two enterprises may come to dominate a whole geographic area. With a lack of economic diversity, the closing of one or two plants or businesses can set in motion the collapse of whole sectors or whole regions. Another concern about the growth of transnational corporations is with regard to how such growth affects the way we work in the twenty-first century.

The Restructuring of Work

Control Over Workers

The first major transformation of work occurred during the period we now refer to as the Industrial Revolution. Prior to the growth of the factory system, work (whether agricultural or craft production) was centred on the family unit and was under the control of the individual worker. New technologies and factories changed the way workers produced, as they were brought together into large productive units that were non-kin-based. At first the workers retained a fair degree of autonomy over the productive process, but in an effort to discipline workers and increase profits, employers increasingly gained control. This created tremendous social dislocation for new factory workers, and many fought to retain some control over their work.

In the early twentieth century, American engineer Frederick Winslow Taylor developed a new concept of worker control known as **scientific management**. Taylorism, as it was also known, spread rapidly across North America. Its aim was increased managerial control over the worker with the goal of maximizing worker output. At around the same time, Henry Ford developed the first automated production line, which further advanced, via technology, control over workers. The term **Fordism** is now used to refer to that period of capitalist development marked by intensive production, maximum use of machinery, and complex divisions of labour. Ford, as noted in Chapter 4, also introduced the notion of improving wages, which allowed his employees to buy the cars coming off the new assembly lines.

In the period following World War II, the North American economy expanded rapidly. This led to the availability of many jobs in such growth areas as manufacturing, construction, and transportation. At most, these jobs necessitated a high school education. As the economy expanded during this period, office jobs in both the private and the public sectors also increased dramatically. Increasing numbers of these jobs were unionized, providing good wages and reasonable job security. Although, of course, not everyone benefited from this booming economy, many workers at this time were able to buy a house, a car, and the other trappings of material comfort only dreamed about by their parents and were commonly able to do so on one income.

By the early 1970s major changes began to occur in the global economy. Competition between transnational corporations increased, as did the pressure to up their rate of profit. One major expense for employers is the cost of labour. Employers can try to save money in this area in a variety of ways, including reducing the number of workers, lowering the wages or benefits of workers, making employees work longer for the same or lower wages, or making them more productive during their hours of work.

> Rising unemployment was a very desirable way of reducing the strength of the working class.... What was engineered—in Marxist terms—was a crisis of capitalism which re-created a reserve army of labour, and has allowed the capitalists to make high profits ever since.
> —*Alan Budd, chief economic adviser to former British prime minister Margaret Thatcher, 1992*

The evidence indicates that all these techniques were utilized and are now widespread in the workplace. As a result, the way in which Canadians work has changed dramatically. Many analysts argue that these changes are linked to a shift from the Fordist model of production to what is referred to as **post-Fordism**. The post-Fordist stage involves new social and technical forms of work organization, with production linked to electronic information-based technologies. As a result of these technologies, the owning class now has both the need and the capacity for a much more flexible and productive labour force, as well as expanded global production and sales. There is no longer any notion of paying high wages to workers so they can buy the products they are creating. Some analysts argue that Wal-Mart—with many non-union part-time workers receiving low pay and few benefits—is the model for twenty-first-century capitalism (Lichtenstein 2006).

The shift to a post-Fordist model can be connected to a set of new management policies needed to improve profitability, which has been termed *lean production*. The shift to lean production has three aspects. First, there is an attempt to eliminate "waste" by moving to just-in-time production, minimal staffing levels, and greater worker productivity. Second, the workplace is restructured around a more differentiated workforce, with precarious forms of employment replacing many permanent jobs. Third, there is increased "management by stress," as a result of a declining workforce and threat of layoffs, in order to discipline the employees and get them to work harder (Sears 2000, 146).

In this context, employment has increasingly become polarized between "good jobs" and "bad jobs." A minority of the jobs are of the former type: they provide high income, non-wage benefits such as pension plans and employee-sponsored health insurance, relative security, and high levels of job satisfaction, flexibility, and autonomy. More jobs can be defined as "bad": they offer low income and few or no non-wage benefits, are not secure, are often part-time or seasonal, and provide relatively low levels of job satisfaction, flexibility, and autonomy.

Think About It

Do you have friends or family whose jobs have changed from "good" to "bad" in recent years? What effect does it have on the individual? When you think about employment after graduation, what job characteristics will you look for?

It is not hard to see how employers benefit from this process. Not only do they get workers who, in a highly competitive market, must sell their talents for the lowest possible price, but they also get to save on costs, such as pensions, medical and dental benefits, office equipment, and so on. In addition, new technologies and the shift to precarious employment have meant that workers are increasingly isolated from each other, making it more difficult for them to organize any collective response to their predicament.

All these changes have meant lower real wages, fewer benefits, and less job security for increasing numbers of workers.

The Growth of Precarious Labour

Prior to World War II, many workers in Canada lived with job insecurity and unstable wages. In addition, few received employee benefits such as pensions or health care. However, from the 1950s until the mid-1970s, the nature of work changed, and full-time, secure employment with decent pay and benefits became the standard.

Today, young people are once again being prepared for a world dominated by various forms of **precarious employment**. The world of work they are entering expects them to be "flexible" and "adaptable," and they are being advised to prepare to make a variety of occupational changes in their lives. Precarious employment includes those forms of work characterized by "limited social benefits and statutory entitlements, job insecurity, low wages, and high risks of ill health" (Vosko 2006, 11). Young people in particular, as well as women and immigrants, are disproportionately finding themselves in this type of work. Those with a combination of these variables are even more likely to find themselves in forms of precarious employment. In the twenty-five years that ended in 1975, precarious labour in Canada constituted at most 12 percent of formal employment; it now comprises at least a third of all jobs and probably more (Gonick 2011, 24).

Employers are increasingly replacing career employees with contingent workers, and whole sections of companies are being outsourced to other companies, often in other regions or countries. Outsourcing helps employers cut costs and have a fluid workforce to which they have few responsibilities. Employment agencies are now the largest employers in North America, and the global private employment agency industry has grown steadily since the mid-1990s, reaching a level of US$341 billion in 2007 (ILO Sectoral Activities Programme 2009, 11). Outsourcing is a new element in the development of a global capitalist economy and now includes both unskilled and knowledge-based workers. For example, nearly two-thirds of all Wal-Mart products are made in China. The rest mainly come from seventy other countries, including Pakistan, the Philippines, and Indonesia, countries noted for workers' rights abuses, official corruption, and active terrorist organizations (Sweeney 2006). Many companies are now shifting their entire accounting, engineering, research and development, or human resources departments to countries around the world where labour costs are lower.

Precarious employment means not only lower wages and less certain employment but also greater flexibility for the employer in hiring and work schedules. One study of contingent workers in Toronto (de Wolff 2000) also found a disturbing reality of discrimination on the basis of race, gender, and age. Temporary agency employers in particular can be selective about whom they hire and whom they place in assignments. In addition, many workers do not know their schedules in advance, must work split shifts, or are perpetually "on call." The reality for many people is juggling several jobs while trying to combine work and home life.

Because capitalist economies are unplanned and inevitably go through economic cycles, employers have always required some worker flexibility. In a boom period more workers may be needed to expand profits, while in the depression phase fewer workers are needed as production slows down. There is always a body of workers who move in and out of the labour force; these workers were referred to by Marx as the **reserve army of the unemployed**. The existence of unemployed people also helps increase the productivity of remaining workers, who are likely to work harder and moderate their wage demands for fear of layoffs. Thus the potential threat of unemployment is a way in which the owning class disciplines the working class.

While capital always needs a certain level of unemployment, in recent years the rate of unemployment and underemployment has increased across the capitalist world. While Canada's rate of unemployment is better than other parts of the world, including the United States, it was still over 7 percent in mid-2011, with the unemployment rate for young people aged fifteen to twenty-four years at over 14 percent (Statistics Canada 2011b). However, researchers have noted that unemployment figures would be much greater if we included all those who reported being unemployed for some part of the year (Shields et al. 2006). Including the underemployed—that is, people working in a job below their level of training and experience—would expand the figures even further.

Decline in Real Wages

Connected to changes in labour-market participation is the decline of workers' real wages (that is, wages after inflation is taken into account). The economic boom in Canada that followed World War II gave the impression that the standard of living for the majority of Canadians was on the rise. Certainly, the expansion of the economy, in conjunction with new social programs, did improve the lives of many Canadians. However, the entry of increasing numbers of women into the paid labour market made gains seem higher than they actually were, as two incomes gave many families a substantially increased family wage packet.

Today, the wages of workers in Canada are rising slowly and unevenly. From January 2009 to January 2010, real wages for Canadians rose only .1 percent (Weir 2010). On average, real wages for women increased by 11.6 percent in the twenty-year span between 1988 and 2008. While growth occurred in all age and wage groups, the most dramatic improvement was among women aged forty-five to forty-nine (+17.8 percent) and those at the higher end of the wage distribution (+16 percent). In contrast, the real wages of men edged up by only 1.3 percent between 1988 and 2008. In fact, on average, men aged thirty-five and over and those at the lower end of the wage distribution actually saw their real wages decline over this period (Statistics Canada 2011a). Overall, the number of low-wage workers has been growing: between 2000 and 2008, the proportion of minimum wage jobs grew from 4.7 percent to 5.2 percent of all jobs, and the number working at minimum wage grew by three-quarters of a million workers. In 2007, four out of ten minimum-wage jobs were held by people over the age of twenty-five years (Arundel and Associates 2009).

> The realm of freedom really begins only where labour determined by necessity and external expediency ends.... The reduction of the working day is the basic prerequisite.
> —Karl Marx, Capital, Vol. 3

> As individuals and as a society, we are paying a steep price for the time crunch. We're less healthy, both physically and mentally. We have less time for personal pleasures. And we're more dissatisfied with the quality of our lives.
> —Hon. Roy Romanow, former premier of Saskatchewan

> Productivity has at least doubled since 1970. We could have the same standard of living [as we did in 1970] with a four-hour [work] day.
> —Mark Leier, director of Labour Studies, Simon Fraser University, 2008

The Growing Intensity of Labour

In 2007, a Canadian Imperial Bank of Commerce teller launched a $600-million class-action lawsuit against her employer, alleging thousands of hours that went unpaid to her and her colleagues. This case reflects a growing trend by employers, because a major way to increase profits is to extend the working day without increasing wages. While many Canadians are working too few hours, others are working too many. Almost everyone is afraid of losing their jobs, and more and more employees are putting in excessive hours. Many have to work at two or more jobs to economically survive. Using Statistics Canada data, one author calculated that over 1.6 million Canadians each worked an average of 8.4 hours unpaid overtime per week in 2008, which resulted in approximately $286 million of lost income weekly, or over $21 billion per year (Perriera 2009).

Whatever the hours, for all those who work there is a growing intensity of labour, for profits can be improved if workers can be made to work harder within the same period of time. Even in the public sector, workers are made to do more because of cuts to the number of workers. On the assembly line this was originally referred to as "speed-up," because if the line were made to move faster, workers would have to work faster to keep up with the machinery. Today, the workers being subjected to speed-up are not primarily those on the assembly line. Computer technology allows workers of many types to be monitored and told to work faster. Even among the middle and upper echelons of management, there is an increase in the amount of work.

It is therefore not surprising that stress is also increasing because longer hours at the workplace lead to shorter hours with one's family. One study (Turcotte 2007) found that the average Canadian worker spent forty-five minutes less each workday with their family in 2005 than in 1986, a total of 195 hours a year—almost five forty-hour work weeks.

The deterioration of job quality is not bad for just individuals; it also has negative consequences for the broader community. If workers earn lower wages, have less job stability, work longer hours, or have to work at several jobs, this inevitably has an impact on families, the health-care system, the care of children and the elderly, and, as we will see below, overall social participation. Overwork can also lead to various forms of addiction, including, ironically, addiction to work itself (Menzies 2005, 79).

Are New Technologies the Problem?

In the 1950s and 1960s, technology represented a utopian future. The main problem by the end of the twentieth century, or so people were told, would be what to do with all their leisure time. Of course, reality has turned out quite differently. Many Canadians today are working harder and longer than ever before, while others are unemployed or underemployed. Why didn't technology prove to be the liberating force most people believed it would be? The answer lies in understanding who controls the technology and the purposes for which it is introduced.

As part of its drive to maximize profits, capital is compelled to constantly introduce new technologies into the workplace. If a company can be the first to introduce a new method of production or a new machine that will raise productivity, it will then have the competitive edge in the marketplace, at least for a time. This fact helps us understand how capitalism, more than any other socioeconomic formation that preceded it, has revolutionized technology. Undeniably, innovations in technology and knowledge have raised living standards, extended life expectancies, improved health, and so on. However, for capital, new technologies are introduced to increase profitability.

From the viewpoint of the employer, machines have a number of advantages over workers. For one thing, the productivity one can get from a worker is finite, since there are limits to human physical and mental capabilities. In contrast, there are no similar limits to the productivity that can be generated from machines or computers. Moreover, technology doesn't complain, doesn't need washroom breaks, doesn't form unions, and doesn't go out on strike.

Jobs that involve working primarily with one's hands are referred to as *blue-collar jobs*, because traditionally such labourers, predominantly males, wore darker shirts while they worked. Such jobs have been declining overall in Canada, particularly in manufacturing, as many of these jobs have been transferred to low-wage countries in the developing world. A quarter of a million manufacturing jobs were lost in 2008–09 alone. Total employment in the sector shrank back to its 1997 level of two million from an average of 2.3 million between 2002 and 2004 (Stanford 2011). Most of these lost jobs were "good" jobs in the sense that they provided workers with reasonable pay, benefits, and employment security.

White-collar jobs—that is, jobs where workers (again, originally male) traditionally wore suits, white shirts, and ties to work and where mental labour dominates—were also affected by the introduction of digital technologies several decades ago. Once-secure jobs in accounting, sales, and management began to decline as computer technologies allowed companies to transfer many jobs abroad. For those in professions such as medicine, law, education, and architecture, computer technology has meant that the individual's control over knowledge (and therefore their influence and power) has been declining (Teeple 2000, 70) while various on-the-job stresses have been increasing.

From the 1970s and onward, new technologies such as container ships, satellite communications, followed by computers and the Internet, rapidly changed the way business was done. While these new technologies certainly created jobs as well as eliminated them, the new jobs that were created did not necessarily match the skills of the workers who lost their jobs, nor were they necessarily in the same geographic location. Increasingly, the physical location of the worker has become irrelevant, with many competing in a global labour market for a job.

However, blaming technology for the changing nature of work leaves us with the notion that the transformations we see today are inevitable as societies progress. It is important, therefore, to repeat the point that technology could, in theory, allow for shorter working time, more leisure, and an improved quality of life for most workers. A shorter workday would also lead to the employment of more workers. Thus, the nature of work—its quality and its quantity—is both an economic and a political issue.

Worker Alienation

That work holds a special place in the lives of humans is reflected in the fact that we speak of it as "making a living." Work is the means by which humans live. But it serves not only to keep us alive; at a very deep psychological level, it also defines who we are, both to ourselves and to others. Moreover, work is not just something we do for a fixed number of hours a day. We think about our work, we bring it home with us, we even dream about it. Work is the central defining characteristic of human existence.

For most of human history, "work" and "life" were inseparable. Without electricity and timepieces, people of necessity lived by the rhythms of nature, and work was seen as tasks to be undertaken—for example, to build a hut, weave a mat, or gather nuts and berries. With the beginnings of social classes, work began to change, as an appropriating class began to control the surplus produced by others. Nonetheless, in the pre-capitalist period, most people still controlled their means of production and managed to retain a fair degree of control over the work process, however onerous the process may have been.

Capitalism, however, brought about a dramatic change in the relationship between humans and the work they did. This is because—for the first time in history—in capitalist societies most people who work are completely separated from the means of production, which is now owned and under the total control of the appropriating class. As a result, our capacity to labour (for the majority of us the defining characteristic of human existence) has been reduced to an object that can be bought and sold—that is, labour becomes a commodity.

Marx referred to the separation of workers from their labour, and all that this entails, as **alienation**. By alienation, Marx meant that workers in capitalism lose control over the work process, the product, and the surplus value they create. In capitalist societies another class decides what is to be produced and how it is to be produced, and decisions are made not to satisfy the needs of workers but to satisfy the needs of the capitalist owning class. Profit maximization is always the primary determining variable in the work process. Moreover, the majority of the surplus value that is created by workers is not controlled by them. Most of it is converted into profits for the owning class. Thus the act of working, according to Marx, actually reproduces the very class relations that oppress workers. This process dehumanizes work. Rather than having a purpose in its own right, work comes to be seen primarily as something that allows us to consume.

Think About It

The Marxist concept of alienation embodies the notion that the very things workers produce end up being used against them. Can you think of some examples that affirm this idea? Keep in mind that workers produce not only goods and services but also the surplus value that is converted into capitalist profits.

Utilizing this analysis, we can also see why for so many of us work is not only unsatisfying but also unsafe. In the seventeen-year period from 1993 to 2009, over 15,000 people lost their lives due to work-related causes, an average of 889 deaths per year (Canadian Centre for Occupational Health and Safety). Many workers are also injured on the job. In 2007, there were 18.8 work-related injuries per thousand employed individuals in Canada. Those working in manufacturing had the highest rate, at thirty-two cases per thousand employees (Human Resources and Skills Development Canada 2011b). This is not the result of a cruel and heartless owning class but rather of the need of capitalists to maintain their competitive edge. Safety costs money, and few capitalists are going to pursue it unless required to, usually by governments. Many countries in the developing world have become appealing places for capital investment, not only because of cheap labour, but also because of their governments' weak laws regarding worker safety and environmental standards.

It is not only unsafe workplaces but also the work itself that is killing many of us. Studies from Britain and Sweden on worker health found that job stress and lack of control seem to affect mortality rates and general health (Taylor 1993). Although many of us assume that it is those in positions of power who suffer most from stress and heavy workloads, the data seem to indicate otherwise. For example, a study of 10,000 British government employees found a gradual but clear increase in mortality from the top to the bottom of the job hierarchy. The Swedish study found heart disease most prevalent among those who saw their work as psychologically demanding but lacking in decision-making power.

At the same time, the lack of work is also destructive to our health. Unemployment can be linked to increased suicide rates, general physical or mental health problems, and greater use of health-care services (Jin et al. 1995). Even job insecurity can be correlated with declining health. A longitudinal study of government workers in Britain noted a relative decline in health standards in employees anticipating privatization and subsequent job insecurity (Sverke, Hellgren, and Näswall 2002). Thus Marx's theory of alienated labour seems to be borne out by empirical data. Humans suffer in a real material way as a result of powerlessness in the workplace.

Although few of us have actually read Marx's work on alienation, most of us understand it at a gut level, and most of us sense that somehow it is preferable to be our own boss than to have someone else in charge of our work lives. Most of us want to be in control of our labour, and, not surprisingly, small-business owners generally feel that the best thing about ownership is independence and control. However, life for most self-employed people in Canada today is not much rosier than for workers.

The Decline of Small Business and the Family Farm

Workers are not the only sector to be negatively affected by the capitalist accumulation of profits. Another major consequence of the process of monopolization has been the decline of the small-business sector in Canada. It is a popular myth in Canada that small business is the engine that drives the economy. However, the statistics indicate otherwise. In Canada and around the world a small number of major corporations now control the dominant economic sectors such as banking, insurance, automobile production, oil, and gas.

Unlike small business, the biggest of the corporations can afford to take losses for long periods of time until their competition is driven out of business. Moreover, most small businesses in Canada cannot compete with bigger corporations as a result of the fundamental nature of the goods and services they produce (Stanford 1999, 136). In addition, most smaller firms depend on sales to one of two markets: either the consumer purchases of individuals who already have jobs with other companies, or else purchases by those other companies of supplies and services used in their own operations. Most small businesses need some *other* employer to do something *first,*

> The thing that chokes us, believe or not, is the Internet. There are so many things that are accessible on the Internet that people can purchase for less than I can purchase from my distributor. Everybody thinks the Internet is this great thing that is happening to the world, but it is really, I think, killing a lot of small business. People that we talk to that are no longer in business say the same thing.
> —*small business owner, 2011*

> Everything is changing—the size of the farms are getting larger, more people are leaving the farm, the agricultural community is aging, and there is not a large number of young people taking up farming.
> —*Dave Marit, Saskatchewan Association of Rural Municipalities, 2008*

therefore, before they can sell their own product and create their own jobs. In this sense, most small businesses cannot "lead" the development of the broader economy. They can only follow it.

Thus, most small businesses have little in the way of independence. They exist solely at the behest of larger companies, who may cast them aside at any time for another company that offers a cheaper price or newer service. This is not to say that small business is irrelevant to the Canadian economy. While their aggregate volume may be low, small business continues to fill little corners of the capitalist marketplace, largely in market niches that are low profit or high risk. The few small businesses that become very successful are usually bought out by giant corporations that have let them take the big risks.

In sum, small business remains very small indeed. The vast majority of employer businesses (98 percent) have fewer than a hundred employees, 75 percent have fewer than ten employees and 55 percent have only one to four employees (Industry Canada 2008). During the economic downturn between October 2008 and October 2009, self-employment in Canada increased by more than 100,000, or 4.3 percent. However, the majority of these new self-employed were older workers (especially those at least fifty-five years of age), women, and "own-account" workers, i.e., those having no paid help (Statistics Canada 2010d). Many of these were likely workers who lost their jobs in the downturn. The self-employed generally have to pay for their own health, disability, dental, and pension plans and are not entitled to unemployment insurance. In addition, self-employed individuals often work longer hours than paid employees. In 2010, 31 percent of self-employed persons worked over fifty hours per week, compared with less than 4 percent of employees (Human Resources and Development Canada 2011a).

In particular, small commodity producers of food, Canada's farmers and small-boat fishers, have become a rapidly disappearing breed. In 1931, when the farm population count was first compiled, more than three million people were living on a farm—nearly 32 percent of the Canadian population at that time. Canada's farm population is now steadily declining in numbers, dropping by 6.2 percent since 2001 to just below 700,000 in 2006. It is not hard to understand why there are so few farmers today. Machinery has become too expensive, small farmers cannot compete with multinational agribusinesses, and changing weather conditions are making profits uncertain. As a result, many farmers and their children are being forced off the land. The stress of losing their farms has led to increased rates of alcoholism, broken marriages, and even suicide.

The number of Canadians who fish for a living has also declined drastically. Fishing industries on both the west and east coasts have been in crisis, with many fish-processing firms closing as a result of low fish prices, declining fish stocks, and overcapacity in the harvesting and processing sectors. Federal government regulations have also prohibited a number of fishing activities. The crisis has meant that many families, particularly in the Atlantic Provinces, where fishing has a long tradition and is often the only means of survival in small coastal communities, have been left totally dependent on inadequate government payments. More than 40,000 jobs were lost in Newfoundland alone as a result of the moratorium on cod fishing (Anderson 2003). The fishing that remains (particularly on the West Coast) is increasingly controlled by large foreign-owned corporations, and fish farming (rather than catching fish in the wild) has become more common. Formerly self-employed individuals often find that the only work available is as low-skilled, low-paid workers at these farms.

The decline of farming and fishing is obviously not spread randomly across the country and has had devastating effects for particular regions. Coastal communities, particularly in Newfoundland and Nova Scotia as well as some in British Columbia, have been seriously affected; rural areas of Saskatchewan have also been very hard hit. The loss of the family business has meant not just a change of employment for those who farmed or fished going back many generations; it has in many cases also meant the decline of communities and whole regions as young people no longer have a future near their families and must move to other parts of Canada to find work. In addition, increased dependence on food grown in other countries, or even regions, diminishes communities' food security.

Think About It

Do you ever check where the food you eat originated? Much of what we eat today is grown thousands of kilometres away in other countries. Why do so few of us ever think about this? Does it matter?

To this point, we have examined how those who work or those who own small businesses have been affected by the growth of transnational corporations. But the power of capital is so great that it not only affects particular groups or individuals in Canada, it also sets the framework for our entire culture.

The Culture of Capitalism

Chapter 3 introduced the core sociological concept of culture. Now that we understand the basics of how capitalism works, we can begin to examine how the culture we live in today is linked to the economic arrangements of our own society. People in capitalist societies, no less than in any other socioeconomic formation, have to eat, have a roof over their heads, and (in colder climates) have some clothing to keep them warm. They also need some love and affection, some sense of belonging to a community, and a reasonable degree of social stability. Within capitalist societies, however, all human needs are secondary to the needs of market.

Almost all of us will eventually enter the capitalist marketplace, as buyers or sellers of products or of labour power. However, we do not all enter this marketplace as equals. In the advanced capitalism of our era a small number of individuals have enormous amounts of wealth and power as a result of their control of immense amounts of capital. In turn, the interests and values of the capitalist owning class come to be the dominant ones within our society. In the process, everything is turned into a commodity, and everything is seen in terms of its marketability and profitability. What is defined as good in our society is increasingly linked to profit only.

In many ways, capitalism is a system in which the worst characteristics of our species—greed, individualism, crass materialism, selfishness—are encouraged and rewarded; in turn, such behaviours are defended as natural or inborn traits. For example, a whole school of thought about the economy—known as public choice theory—has argued that material greed is the single, natural, dominant motive underlying all human behaviour (Stretton and Orchard 1994). Not only is greed seen as inevitable in this argument, it is also seen as morally superior.

Regardless of our cultural background, most of us as children learn a common set of traditional values from our parents, our teachers, and our religious leaders: share your toys; do unto others as you would have them do unto you; honesty is the best policy; help those less fortunate than yourself. At the same time, however, it is clear that the society we live in frequently rewards the profiteers, the cheaters, and the greedy. How else do we explain that CEOs receive millions of dollars for increasing shareholder value by laying off workers, shutting down factories that have sustained local economies, polluting the environment, or causing a major economic downturn?

Capitalism is a system in which social value is determined by one's market value. Those who have great wealth or high-status jobs are seen as superior to those with lower incomes or low-status jobs. And some people—such as the elderly, people with disabilities, and the unemployed—are seen as having little or no value at all because they are either out of the market or peripheral to it. Indeed, where communities once collectively took responsibility for the care of their weakest members, now such individuals are considered to be a drain on societies.

The dominance of the corporate sector can be seen all around us. The largest buildings are those of the biggest corporations, and the tallest of those are usually the bank towers. Many banks, office buildings, and shopping malls, extravagantly decorated in marble and other expensive materials, seem to be edifices constructed to honour the god of money. Compare these buildings to our deteriorating public buildings. In addition, corporate branding has accelerated rapidly in the twenty-first century. Commercial advertising is everywhere in our lives, but few of us complain because most of us have never known anything different.

Think About It

For one day, walk around your city or town and count all the advertisements you see. Then look at the volume of ads you see on the Internet and on TV. Do these ads bother you? Why or why not?

The Culture of Consumerism

When you go out to shop for new clothes, what do you look for in a purchase? Price will probably be an important variable. But so will a thing called "fashion" or "style." Maybe you're more into technology than clothing. In today's world of electronics being new is even more important—when buying any new piece of technology, everyone wants the latest item. This process of creating things that always need to be replaced, referred to as *planned obsolescence*, is an essential part of the capitalist need to sell us ever more products. Indeed, most new electronic technology is not built to last. But few of us mind, because a newer "must have" model has just appeared on the scene.

At the end of the nineteenth century, social scientist Thorstein Veblen (1857–1929) was probably the first to analyze growing consumerism in American society, in *Theory of the Leisure Class* (1899). He is still remembered for coining the term *conspicuous consumption* to describe the tendency of an increasing number of people to buy things not out of need but rather to improve their social status. Since his time, consumerism has expanded exponentially. The twentieth century saw the creation of both societies of perpetual growth and an accompanying culture of consumer capitalism. In 1900, approximately $1.5 trillion was spent globally by public and private consumers. By 1975 it was estimated at $12 trillion. By 1998 it had reached $24 trillion, and it continues to grow (*CCPA Monitor*, March 2007, 3). Canada and the United States accounted for 31 percent of that amount although they only have 5 percent of the world's population (Anderssen 2007).

With the never-ending glut of goods on the market, corporations must perpetually convince us to

> Our enormously productive economy... demands that we make consumption our way of life, that we convert the buying and use of goods into rituals, that we seek our spiritual satisfaction, our ego satisfaction, in consumption.... We need things consumed, burned up, worn out, replaced, and discarded at an ever-increasing rate.
> —U.S. retail analyst Victor Lebow, 1955

> A friend attending a conference accompanied a group of Filipino women—all from rural areas of the Philippines—to the West Edmonton Mall. Twenty minutes into the tour the women burst into tears and pleaded with their hosts to get them out. The insanity, the grotesque over-stimulation of the place, no longer obvious to the Canadian women who had grown up with these monstrosities, was grimly apparent to the village activists. They were right. We should all burst into tears after twenty minutes in a giant mall—it would be a test of our mental and spiritual health.
> —Murray Dobbin

> If we are to preserve our orthodox economic system, it is time to empower Canadians to engineer an economy which relies less on immediate consumption, excessive leveraging, and hardship—one that commands a cultural shift more befitting of our resources and our experiences.
> —Anthony Ariganello, President and CEO, Certified General Accountants Association of Canada, 2011

Box 6.3 Our Love Affair with the Automobile

If there is a single consumer item that is central to understanding capitalism, it is the automobile. The car is far more than just a utilitarian object to get us from one place to another. In some ways it embodies the mythology of capitalism itself—the individual (usually male), alone and free, speeding along on the open road, in total control of a sleek, brand new piece of technology. This image is pervasive in the automobile advertisements we see.

In reality, of course, the automobile provides few of us with the speed, freedom, and independence depicted in these commercials. Most of us who drive actually spend hours a week on clogged superhighways and overcrowded city streets. We also spend years paying off the bank loan we took out to buy the car and incur large costs for maintenance, insurance, and parking. Indeed, Statistics Canada (2005) found that the common variable in households that spent more than they earned was the thousands of dollars a year expended on car purchases.

Mugyenyi and Engler (2011) humourously postulate that, from the viewpoint of a biologist, humans might be renamed *Homo automotivis*, the result of a century of people living with cars and capitalism. As the authors write: "Neither can survive without the other and both define themselves through the other... the car has economic, social, geographical, environmental, cultural and even religious dimensions" (13). The number of cars on the world's roads surpassed one billion in 2010, jumping from 980 million the previous year. Although China led the way in vehicle growth, with the number of cars on Chinese roads increasing by 27.5 percent, the United States still constitutes by far the largest vehicle population in the world, with 239.8 million cars. Even in times of social disruption, the automobile seems to play a key role, with burning automobiles now a central image for protests and riots around the world.

We can see the centrality of the car to our society by looking at our built environment. Cities have expanded far from the central core. For many of us a car is not a frivolity, but a sheer necessity: we need one to get to work, to visit friends, or simply to get a litre of milk. The design of our metropolitan areas and the lack of good public transportation that all can access is no accident. The power of the major automobile producers and the oil industry that literally fuels this industry is staggering. Of the top fifteen Fortune 500 Global Companies (2011), eight were petroleum companies and two were automobile companies (Toyota at #8 and Volkswagen at #13).

consume more and more. They spend billions of dollars a year persuading us that our lives will improve if we just buy their stuff. More and more of the people they target are children and youth. This is not surprising. One American study found that 55 percent of young people will keep on asking for something they want, even if their parents' initial answer is no (Klaffke 2003, 38).

Because many of us feel at least some sense of insecurity, it is not surprising that we are highly susceptible to advertising, even though most of us like to think otherwise. Those who cannot afford to buy these things are made to feel less worthy for lack of them; conversely, those who are able to purchase the most expensive commodities are looked up to and envied. However, recent data seems to indicate that once people have moved beyond having their basic material needs met, increased amounts of money and material goods do not seem to buy happiness (Toynbee 2003).

How do corporations get individuals to buy more and more when most workers are earning less and less? The answer is simple: the growth of personal debt. Increasing numbers of us are purchasing goods with money we haven't yet earned and are paying interest for the "privilege" of doing so. A 2010 study done by the Certified General Accountants Association of Canada concluded that Canadians are increasingly borrowing money for consumption rather than for wealth accumulation. And the amounts borrowed have been growing. At the end of 2010, household debt in Canada reached a record $1.41 trillion. If that was spread equally among all Canadians, each person would be carrying more than $41,740 in outstanding debt—an amount 2.5 times greater than in 1989 after adjusting for inflation and population growth. This figure ranked Canada first in terms of debt-to-financial assets ratio among twenty OECD countries.

That there might be alternatives to growing consumerism is an issue that is rarely addressed. And since we are not taught to understand who has power within our society, we are led to believe that current cultural changes are inevitable in the face of global developments and technological change. Discussions of possible alternatives to our current social arrangements are simply not on the agenda.

"We" versus "Me"

We usually don't think much about how our society works. It just does. Yet making any society work is actually quite complex. Societies are made up of individuals, each with their own feelings, wishes, needs, and desires. In order to survive, each individual has to make a compact with others—I will live with you because I can't survive without you. But by making this compact we are giving up some of our individuality.

The complex question of the relationship between the individual and the social world, and between individuals within the social world is the core of what sociologists study. In earlier chapters we briefly examined foraging and agrarian societies. In such societies, where life was a struggle for most people and survival depended on support from others, the "we" generally took priority over the "me." In Chapter 2 we saw that the ability of humans to live together was enhanced by the evolutionary development of empathy, which allowed individuals to imagine themselves in the place of the other. As societies grew in size and social divisions appeared, the ability to empathize became more complex.

As far back as the nineteenth century, social scientists and philosophers noticed that the growth of industrial societies was changing social relationships. A key development was the movement of large populations from tightly knit rural communities to newly industrializing urban areas. New structures of work also changed family and social interaction. In addition, industrial society was one of constant change rather than one centred on custom and tradition.

The movement of people into cities had a particularly strong effect on the way people connected with others. Cities had existed for centuries in many parts of the world, but for most of human history the majority of people lived far from cities or towns. In rural areas, human groups were connected to others primarily through kinship ties. Social rules were informal but adherence was expected; religious beliefs were a strong force binding people together. As people moved into cities, they were often separated from their extended families and forced to live physically close to total strangers. All these transformations were of interest to the growing field of sociology as it tried to create a science of society.

Marx noted that the growth of capitalist economies changed the way individuals were connected to each other and the larger social world. As workers were freed from their feudal bonds, they were also separated from their traditional connection to others and to a physical place. Their potential labour power became an atomized commodity for sale in the marketplace, now in competition with others who were also forced to sell their labour power to survive. Moreover, globalizing capitalism meant that people moved not only from rural areas to cities but also migrated to other regions or countries where their neighbours might have different cultural traditions and speak a different language.

Think About It
Are your parents immigrants from another country, or did they move from one region to another in Canada? If so, how did they try to avoid social isolation?

In the late nineteenth century, French sociologist Émile Durkheim provided one of the early sociological analyses of modern societies. Durkheim thought there were two forms of social cohesion. In pre-industrial societies, groups were held together by what he called **mechanical solidarity**. Such societies had a simple division of labour, and people were united by shared values and common social bonds. Industrialization and urbanization eroded such societies; their common consensus and moral integration were destroyed. How then, Durkheim wondered, was social order maintained? He felt that **organic solidarity** would develop in industrial societies and bind individuals together. With its complex division of labour and people performing highly specialized work tasks, he thought individuals would now be united by their interdependence (Durkheim [1893] 1933). Durkheim used the term "organic" to compare this interdependence to the ways organs in the human body are separate but connected.

Durkheim was an order theorist who thought that a newer form of social cohesion would simply replace an older form. Other social analysts were less optimistic. German sociologist Ferdinand Tönnies (1855–1936)

Box 6.4 Weddings Old and New

For most of human history, marriage had little to do with the individuals concerned. In traditional societies, marriage was about the creation of a new family, the bonding of different clans, and—once classes had developed—the passing down of property. Marriages focused on the coming together of families more than of individuals and were often arranged by parents. In a wedding in rural India in 2007, the groom arrived drunk, so the bride married his younger brother instead.

Clearly this would be unlikely to happen today in Canada, where weddings have taken on an entirely different meaning. In the advanced capitalism of the twenty-first century, weddings have become primarily extravagant shows of conspicuous consumption. The average Canadian couple now spends somewhere between $20,000 and $30,000 on a wedding, sometimes much more. Love has been commoditized into a diamond engagement ring, we "shower" the couple with expensive gifts—many of which they have pre-selected—and brides often spend thousands of dollars on a dress that will never be worn again. Weddings have become so large and complex that busy couples commonly hire a wedding planner to do the work for them. The goal for many—at least according to wedding guides—is to make their wedding "unique." The bride often sees this event as her special day, with the engagement period seen as a time of self-perfection to prepare for the wedding. The tension of all this is so great that stressed-out individuals may turn into "bridezillas" or "groomzillas."

We should not romanticize the traditional world of the "we." Too much "we" can mean a lack of individual rights and freedoms. For much of recent history, women have been forced into arranged marriages where they may be abused or even killed. But too much emphasis on the "me" is troubling as well, with some couples spending so much time planning their wedding that they forget to think about the impending marriage. Approximately one in three first marriages in Canada ends in divorce.

also addressed the transformation of societies and loss of social solidarity as large industrial cities began to replace small rural villages in Europe. He used the term **Gemeinschaft** ("commune" or "community") to describe traditional societies where social relationships were based on personal bonds of family or friendship that were held together by shared moral values usually tied to religion. In contrast, he used the term **Gesellschaft** ("association") to describe large urban societies where social bonds were eroded by the complex division of labour, individualism, and competitiveness. Tönnies was concerned about what the loss of traditional community meant to modern societies.

From the "Me Generation" to the "iGeneration"

Marx saw alienation as an inevitable aspect of living in capitalist societies. In the twentieth century, alienation—now taking on a broader meaning of an individual's loss of connection to community and other individuals—became a popular theme in fields as diverse as philosophy, psychoanalysis, and sociology. Social analysts were noticing that the growth of the "me" seemed to be having negative effects on both individuals and the society as a whole.

Following World War II, a number of American social analysts continued to focus on alienation, but its class component and connection to a capitalist economy were seldom discussed. Most authors now focused on what they saw as the increasing isolation of the individual from the broader social and political world. One author (Lasch 1979) described modern society as having a "culture of narcissism." *Narcissism* is the excessive preoccupation with oneself and a lack of empathy for others. The shift away from the collective was linked to the expansion of the middle strata, as well as their movement to the suburbs of major American cities. Philip Slater (1970, 7) described the growing emphasis on the "me" over the "we":

> It is easy to produce examples of the many ways in which Americans attempt to minimize, circumvent, or deny the interdependence upon which all human societies are based. We seek a private house, a private means of transportation, a private garden, a private laundry, self-service stores, and do-it-yourself skills of every kind.... Even within the family Americans are unique in their feeling that each member should have a separate room, and even a separate telephone, television, and car, when economically possible. We seek more and more privacy, and feel more and more alienated and lonely when we get it.

Slater was clearly referring to that sector of society with enough wealth to purchase the goods he describes. Nonetheless, his was a perceptive description of what would expand to a wide cross-section of the North American population. Keep in mind that he wrote these words before the advent of personal computers, cell phones, and other new technologies. With the growth of websites that allow for the downloading of music, TV shows, and films, even the social act of going to a movie, a music store, or a video rental shop is quickly disappearing.

Social theorists have expressed concern over the decline of both social activism and general social engagement. Robert Putnam's book *Bowling Alone: The Collapse and Revival of American Community* examined the erosion of what social scientists call **social capital**, that is, the social networks connecting individuals to each other that are based on reciprocity, shared norms, and trust. Drawing on a vast amount of data, he concluded that Americans—regardless of gender, race, age, or social background—have increasingly become disconnected from community life. According to Putnam (2000, 403), a solitary quest for private goods has replaced the shared pursuit of the public good. Of particular concern for Putnam was a growing generational divide by age, with those born after 1970 showing the greatest decrease in commitment to the wider community.

The baby boom generation, born between 1946 and 1964 in North America, was the first to be referred to as the "Me Generation." These were the children who grew up in the increasingly privatized world described by Slater. While their parents' generation had lived through depression and war, the baby boomers were raised in an era of growing material comfort, increasing access to postsecondary education, and an ever-expanding marketplace. However, this shift to a world of "me" over "we" has increased over the last thirty years.

One analyst has labelled the children of baby boomers, those born after 1970, as "Generation Me" (Twenge 2006), and data indicate they are increasingly self-involved and detached from broader social networks. This group still feels connected to family, friends, and co-workers. But the world they inhabit is more "me" oriented and less "we" oriented than ever. The popular culture of today glorifies the individual, embodied in the concept of "self." Young people are told to "be yourself," "respect yourself," "love yourself," "express yourself," "trust yourself," and "stand up for yourself." But according to Twenge, extensive U.S. data indicate that young people have higher rates of anxiety and depression than ever before.

On the one hand, young people are being told that if they only "believe in themselves" they can be anything they want. On the other hand, the changing world of work and the inherent nature of capitalism mean that many will not achieve their goals. Moreover, greater job insecurity, increasing debt, and less community involvement may leave young people feeling less and less committed to the broader society.

The term "iGeneration" has also been used by some writers to describe young people today; it is a play on words, meant to reflect not only the perceived self-involvement of young people, but also their increasing connection to privatized technologies. Most young people now spend a good part of every day by themselves, hooked into personal electronic gadgets; even when they connect to others, it is frequently via technologies such as cellphones or the Internet. Not long ago whole families sat together listening to radio programs or—somewhat later—watching family-oriented television shows, while generations of young people shared the fun of knowing all the lyrics to the latest song that topped the Hit Parade. Today almost everyone has their own private songlist, while films and television shows are frequently watched alone.

Putnam's book *Bowling Alone* was published shortly before the major expansion of social networking sites, and social scientists are just beginning to analyze the implications of this new means of connecting with others. Those who use these sites often have a wide circle of people identified as their friends. However, while their networks may be broader than those of their parents' generation, they may also be shallower. Many of these "friends"

As more and more people find themselves working at jobs that are in fact beneath their abilities, as leisure and sociability themselves take on the qualities of work, the posture of cynical detachment becomes the dominant style of everyday intercourse.
—*Christopher Lasch,* The Culture of Narcissism

The increase in narcissism in individuals is, we believe, just an outcome of a massive shift in culture toward a greater focus on self-admiration. Narcissism has spread through the generations like a particularly pernicious virus.
—*Jean Twenge and Keith Campbell,* The Narcissism Epidemic

Today, there's this perception that naming a child is almost like naming a product—there's this huge drive now to not be like anyone else.
—*Laura Wattenberg,* The Baby Name Wizard

may communicate only electronically from time to time, or they may occasionally organize a small group to go to a club or a social event. What is not yet well-researched is whether the expansion of social networking sites has had any effect on overall social or political engagement. Clearly, some young people are using it as a way to connect with others in movements for social and environmental change. However, it has also been suggested that the Internet in general is just another place for self-absorbed young people to document their every move and feeling (Smith 2006).

Think About It

Do you think that the analyses of American society described here apply equally to Canada? Do you think that new technologies and social networking sites have made young people more socially connected or less socially connected?

Conclusion

Durkheim's work on suicide ([1897] 1951) was one of the first to link the lack of social connectedness to negative personal outcomes. Rates of suicide, he discovered, were lower among married people, those with more tightly knit religious communities, and those with children; suicides were more frequent in times of rapid social change. Studies since that time have confirmed what Durkheim first noted, that social connectedness is a strong determinant of individual well-being. Social connections make us healthier: data from more than a dozen large studies demonstrate that socially disconnected individuals are two to five times more likely to die from all causes than those with close ties to family, friends, and community (Putnam 2000, 327). We also feel better when we help others. A number of recent studies have concluded that everything from gratitude to generosity is good for our mental and physical health (Agrell 2007).

It should not surprise us that social connections make us happier. Being human means being social, and people suffer a variety of mental stresses when they feel cut off from a supportive, cohesive community (Smail 1999). If, indeed, North Americans today are less socially engaged than in previous generations, it makes sense that we are seeing more and more instances of road rage, air rage, telephone rage, and even neighbour rage.

Young people are responding to this sense of detachment in various ways. Many are expanding their social networks via the Internet. Others continue to look for a sense of community and meaning through religion or by getting involved in volunteer work or social activism. Yet many young people are looking inward rather than outward. Gradually losing a sense of connection to communities, more are seeking a regular emotional or sensual "high" via gratification from alcohol, drugs, sex, gambling, or from the thrill of "extreme" sports. There is nothing wrong, of course, with feeling good or having fun. However, the potential addictiveness of such behaviours as well as the need to seek ever-increasing levels of excitement can be destructive to individuals, families, and communities. It also turns us away from any critical examination of our social world or formulating collective responses to changing social conditions.

The culture we live in today is a corporate culture, dominated by the values and needs of the transnational corporations. It is a culture of consumerism and narcissism, geared to getting us to buy more products while not challenging those with power. Some of us may be distressed by this state of affairs, while others may think that corporate expansion can only bring increasing prosperity and satisfaction. As already noted, humans act on the basis of their real material conditions. If people become disconnected from their economy, their political structures, or their social institutions, they will have little reason to sustain them and might actively oppose them. It is therefore not surprising that there has been a sudden resurgence of political activism among young people in many parts of the world. Society imposes itself on us, but at the same time we are the agents who both maintain and transform it. The rest of this book expands on the various ways in which the power of capital imposes itself on our society and the different ways in which ordinary people respond to it.

KEY POINTS

1. Although few of us pay attention to the power held by large transnational corporations, they have a major effect on our lives.

2. There has been a major restructuring of the Canadian workplace, with an increasing number of individuals in precarious forms of employment. As part of this restructuring, there has been a polarization of work into "good jobs" and "bad jobs," with more of the latter being created than the former.

3. The wages of Canadian workers have reflected this polarization. Some workers in the upper-income brackets have seen their wages soar, while the real wages of most workers have either stagnated or fallen.

4. Many workers are putting in longer hours, and most people are finding themselves working harder and faster.

5. The conditions of workers in Canada have eroded because of the increasing pressure on the capitalist owning class to up its rate of profit, not because new technologies have changed the way we work.

6. Marx felt that workers in capitalism experienced alienation, in that the capacity to labour is turned into a commodity that is bought and sold in the marketplace.

7. The concentration of production and capital has led to the decline of small business and small commodity producers of food.

8. Canadian culture must be understood within the current arrangement of classes, with the interests and values of the capitalist owning class becoming the dominant ones within our society.

9. Our culture is increasingly one of consumerism and narcissism.

10. Some social theorists, particularly in the United States, are concerned about the decline of both social activism and general social engagement.

11. Despite increasing amounts of wealth, people in developed capitalist societies do not seem to be happier. Social connections make us happier. People will suffer a variety of mental stresses when they feel cut off from a supportive, cohesive community.

FURTHER READING

Castells, Manuel. 2010. *The Rise of the Network Society.* 2nd ed. Maldon, ME: Blackwell.
This is the first of three volumes in which the author examines the many social, cultural, economic, political, and personal transformations arising out of the information technology revolution.

Graeber, David. 2011. *Debt: The First 5000 Years.* Brooklyn, NY: Melville House.
A British anthropologist examines the history and social role of debt.

Krahn, Harvey J., Graham S. Lowe, and Karen D. Hughes. 2011. *Work, Industry, and Canadian Society.* 6th ed. Toronto: Nelson.
A solid introduction to the basic issues pertaining to work and the workplace.

Menzies, Heather. 2005. *No Time: Stress and the Crisis of Modern Life.* Vancouver: Douglas & McIntyre.
A wide-ranging critique of how new technologies have made us "multi-taskers" who are overstressed and losing touch with our social world.

Mugyeni, Bianca, and Yves Engler. 2011. *Stop Signs: Cars and Capitalism on the Road to Economic, Social and Ecological Decay.* Vancouver and Black Point, NS: RED/Fernwood.
The authors argue that the automobile's ascendance is inextricably linked to capitalism and can be tied to corporate malfeasance, political intrigue, media manipulation, racism, academic corruption, Third World coups, environmental destruction, and war.

Patel, Raj. 2011. *The Value of Nothing: Why Everything Costs So Much More Than We Think.* Toronto: HarperCollins.
The author challenges the concept of *homo economicus,* commonly used in traditional economics, and in so doing offers a critique of modern capitalist economies.

Vosko, Leah F. (ed.) 2006. *Precarious Employment: Understanding Labour Market Insecurity in Canada.* Montreal and Kingston: McGill-Queen's University Press.
This is an interdisciplinary work covering various aspects of the new forms of employment in Canada. Also explored are possible responses to changed working conditions.

Worldwatch Institute. 2010. *State of the World 2010. Transforming Cultures: From Consumerism to Sustainability.* New York: W.W. Norton.
This book examines the rise and fall of consumer cultures and the need to move to a new culture of sustainability.

7 The Social Construction of Ideas and Knowledge

In This Chapter

- What is meant by the concept of ideology?
- What is liberalism, and why is it the dominant ideology in capitalist societies?
- How do the mass media reinforce current class relations in our society?
- What is the place of public education in Canada today?

Have you ever thought about how you know what you know? Or why you believe what you believe? It was noted in Chapter 1 that most of us think we exist in a world with certain self-evident "truths" or "facts." However, we have begun to see in this book that many things that most of us take to be true are in fact false, while there are many essential truths that we know nothing about at all. The beliefs and ideas we have in our heads arise out of the particular conditions at specific moments in history and can be linked to a particular set of relations of power. In order to appreciate how certain ideas come to dominate others, we must place them within those power relationships.

We refer to a body of assumptions, ideas, and values that combine into a coherent world-view as an **ideology**. Few of us have actually sat down to consciously construct our own ideological framework; rather, it has been built up over our lifetime. We acquire this package of beliefs and values through the process of socialization. The package is a more or less integrated one, rather than a hodgepodge of unconnected ideas, beliefs, and values. At a certain point, some ideas may be accepted simply because they fit within our already-existing ideological framework; conversely, ideas may be rejected because they would be out of place in this package. Moreover, every ideology has, at its core, the assumption that our group's beliefs and behaviours are morally grounded and superior to others' beliefs and behaviours.

How do we come to accept ideas as true? Sometimes we accept them because everyone else believes them. Humans are social animals, and few of us feel comfortable being different. Sometimes we accept ideas because we hear them from some authority figure we believe to be truthful, such as a parent, teacher, religious leader, or some "expert" in the media. Sometimes

> The ruling ideas of each age have always been the ideas of its ruling class.
> —*Karl Marx and Freidrich Engels*, The Communist Manifesto

> The power of global finance includes an extraordinary ability to create its own version of reality and persuade others to believe it.
> —*William Greider*, One World, Ready or Not

> It is difficult to get a man to understand something when his salary depends on not understanding it.
> —*American novelist Upton Sinclair, 1935*

we come to believe ideas simply because they provide an easy explanation for the realities of our lives. Whatever the basis for our beliefs, once our ideological framework is in place it will seem so objective and so obvious that it may be hard to dislodge. Only the views of others appear to have a bias. Ours appear as eternal truths.

All societies have a set of core beliefs and values. In pre-class societies, everyone within a community would generally share this common set of beliefs and values. The rise of classes meant greater societal complexity and opposing class interests. Although a core set of beliefs and values remained, people began to see things within differing frames of reference. A simplified example of this is portrayed in the fish cartoon presented in the first chapter: there we see three fish, each with its own place in the fish hierarchy, each with a different view on the moral order of the world.

But there is a troubling aspect to this cartoon. If, like the small fish, those at the bottom of the social order feel that the world is unjust, why do they continue to put up with it? Marx and Engels provide insight into this question by explaining that those with economic power in any society also have power over its ideas. If we apply this analysis to the fish cartoon, it is likely—for a time at least—that most small fish would come to believe that "the world is just."

In Canadian society this is exactly what happens. A few people appropriate the surplus produced by others, which leads to gross inequalities of wealth and power. While many of us do not benefit from such an economic arrangement, most of us come to support it. Indeed, the majority comes to see the entire social structure—with its particular institutions and values—as inevitable, probably even desirable. In this process, we also come to accept, without much questioning, many ideas that support the current social arrangements.

This chapter analyzes the dominant ideology of capitalism—liberalism—and two key agents of socialization that help sustain current class relations—the mass media and the schools. However, while people may be willing to accept myths for a time, social reality can be masked only for so long. Humans are not robots that passively accept received knowledge; as the contradictions within society become more and more evident, the demand for change increases and one or more counter-ideologies develops. In other words, at least some of the small fish will eventually notice that, indeed, "there is no justice in the world." This is what happened when the Occupy movement spread like wildfire across North America in late 2011. The notion that "we are the 99 %" quickly resonated with ordinary citizens who had never been politically active before.

Liberalism: "We" versus "Me" Revisited

Understanding our own ideological framework is not easy, for it requires that we step out of our own brains, figuratively speaking, in order to look at our thoughts and values from the viewpoint of a detached observer. The problem here is that, in every society, the dominant belief system is so deeply embedded in our minds, and so constantly reinforced, that it is hard to conceive of any alternative analysis.

It is important to note that something need not be true simply because most of us believe it. Throughout history, people have accepted and promoted ideas that have later proven to be false. If certain ideas or ways of seeing are widely accepted, there is little reason to challenge such assumptions. For example, if people are told by their parents, religious leaders, and teachers that the sun revolves around the earth, and if everyone around them also believes this to be the case, would there be any reason to challenge this notion? Would it even be a point of debate? What would people think of someone who disputed this position? (Of course, the fact that we now know that it is the earth that revolves around the sun is confirmation that reality cannot be masked forever.)

In class-based societies, it is inevitable that certain ideas will come to predominate over others. That is because the ruling class has a real interest in promoting and defending those ideas that best protect its interests and maintain the status quo. Given its economic power, this class also has the capacity to do so. The control that the ruling class has over a society's belief system is often referred to as **ideological hegemony**. This term, developed by Italian Antonio Gramsci (1891–1937), has embedded in it the notion that the dominant class maintains its power through a combination of coercion and persuasion. In other words, while force or the threat of it can be used to maintain the social order, class relations are more often sustained in the sphere of culture, or our everyday life. The ability of those with power to control the transmission of ideas means that the entire way we see the world—what we feel is "just natural" or "common sense"—is in fact socially constructed. The consequence of this hegemony is that we instantly dismiss alternative views and rarely question the basis for our own.

Within this framework for analysis, **liberalism** must be seen as the dominant ideology in all capitalist societies. Liberalism has many meanings—from the name of a Canadian political party to the notion of being open-minded on sexual matters. For this chapter we consider liberalism in its broadest philosophical sense. Put very simply, liberalism is a world-view that gives prominence to the "me" over the "we" in society.

Most theorists agree that modern liberalism developed through the sixteenth and seventeenth centuries and can be linked to the disintegration of the feudal system and the rise of Enlightenment theory in Europe and Great Britain. Some English writers closely identified with the early liberal tradition are John Locke, Adam Smith, Jeremy Bentham (1748–1832), Mary Wollstonecraft (1759–97), David Ricardo (1772–1823), and John Stuart Mill

(1806–73). Early liberalism was a criticism of the dominance and control of the feudal aristocracy. Its advocates promoted a new form of society that increased freedom and the rights of the individual. However, freedom, liberty, democracy, and equality were all conceived of within the broader framework of capitalist class relations, and the privileges and rights of the owning class were never in question. In the twentieth century, liberalism went through various transformations, but its basic doctrines remain unchanged.

Sometimes students ask if one or another aspect of society is "good" or "bad." If we recall the concept of dialectics, we can see that there is rarely a simple answer to such a question. We saw in earlier chapters that capitalism itself was simultaneously a step forward and a step backward for humans. Likewise, its ideological underpinning, liberalism, is too complex to simply designate as good or bad.

For example, while liberal notions of freedom and equality were first advanced by the bourgeoisie to promote their own interests, these notions were taken up as rallying cries by others. Within capitalist societies, liberal argumentation has been used to advocate equal rights for women, racial minorities, gays and lesbians, people with disabilities, the poor, and so on. If people are told that freedom and equality are worthy goals, they will increasingly demand them.

Most of us feel strongly about individual freedom, choice, and equality. As a result, it may be hard to grasp how closely these concepts fit with modern capitalist economies. Our modern notions of freedom and choice become clearer if we contrast them with some traditional notions, carried over from earlier agrarian-based societies, which continue to the present day. For example, most of you reading this book have accepted the religion of your parents without question; it is unlikely that you were allowed to freely choose your religion. In this example, individual freedom of choice (where the "me" comes first) is seen as less important than traditions or obligations to family and community (where the "we" comes first).

In traditional societies, the interests of the group (family, clan, tribe) generally took priority over the individual; in industrial capitalist societies, the interests of the individual, in theory at least, predominate over those of the collective. Some of you may be frustrated or angered by your family's persistent desire to match you up with a prospective mate or to require you to practise their religious precepts; your parents, on the other hand, may be horrified by your unwillingness to follow centuries-old traditions and bend to parental authority. While these struggles appear to be in the proximal realm, reflected mainly as relations between parents and children, they are actually aspects of the conflict between traditional ideologies tied to agrarian-based systems and liberal ideologies more suited to capitalist market economies. They are a struggle of values, one that emphasizes the "we" and the other that emphasizes the "me" of human societies. Indeed, some of the backlash against liberal values—as most clearly observed in the current global expansion of fundamentalist religions and of social conservatism—are a visible expression of people's unease with a world they see as having too much "me" and not enough "we."

Think About It

Consider some arguments you may have had with your parent(s) over the past few years. Can you reframe some of these disagreements into a broader struggle between "me" and "we"?

Liberalism and the Market

The liberal tradition not only accepts a market economy, it also sees the market as the model for all things, with sellers free to compete and buyers free to choose between these competing units. However, freedom of choice in this model goes far beyond the actual marketplace. For example, most of us value the ability to choose our political leaders, our occupations, our partners, our neighbourhoods, our music, and so on. Such choices were possible for only a few in pre-capitalist societies.

However, in the real world, few of us can actually take advantage of our freedoms because structured inequality continues to exist in capitalist societies. Although all of us have equality of *opportunity*, without equality of *condition* many of our rights and freedoms are absolutely meaningless. For example, we can all, theoretically, own a car; in reality, of course, we can own a car only if we have the financial capacity to do so. Moreover, all our choices can be made only from the items on offer, which means that we never have total freedom of choice. At the moment, for example, an electric car is not an option for most of us.

It should also be noted that there are many rights and freedoms that are not yet guaranteed in Canada because a capitalist economy *cannot* guarantee them: the right to a job; the right to decent and affordable housing; the right to sufficient food and clean drinking water; the right to an adequate standard of living; the right to a full education; the right to a healthy environment; the right to a safe workplace; and the right to be free of racism, sexism, homophobia, and other forms of social intolerance. Thus rights and freedoms are not abstract; they exist within particular socioeconomic formations, and they can change over time. Liberalism promotes the notions of freedom and individual rights, a social advance from earlier socioeconomic formations. However, such rights and freedoms are selective, framed as they are within the already existing class relations of capitalism. Moreover, the rights we have won can be taken away under certain conditions.

Liberalism and Ideas

Liberal notions of freedom and equality are also applied to the world of ideas. Within the liberal framework, competing ideas are seen as the equivalent of goods competing in a marketplace, with individuals having the freedom to choose from the marketplace of ideas. Just as liberals believe that a free market will produce the best goods, they also believe that a "market of ideas" will lead to the most rational and useful ideas. However, our freedom of choice with regard to ideas is largely illusory because not all ideas are presented equally or fairly. In the midst of a so-called information explosion, Canadians are facing a world in which the control over information is in fewer and fewer hands.

Whether it is the choice of shampoo, sociological theories, movies, or politicians, capitalism requires that we *believe* that we have true freedom of choice. But in all developed capitalist societies the choices we are offered are actually very narrow. For example, at any large grocery store one can find a countless array of breakfast cereals on the shelves. But most are produced by a few transnational corporations, and the variation in taste, nutrition, and cost is small. The situation is similar in the world of ideas. The Internet, hundreds of television channels, and huge bookstores full of a variety of books, magazines, and newspapers give us the impression that we have more ideas to choose from than ever before. Yet the variation in ideas, as with breakfast cereal, is, in fact, becoming smaller and smaller.

Think About It
Do you think the Internet has actually given us greater freedom of expression? Do you think it is a place that can actually challenge those with power, or is it simply a place where social activism is diverted?

Ideology, Culture, and Socialization
For sociologists, the process of socialization has traditionally been considered a central concept. This should not be surprising if we recall from Chapter 2 that sociology rejects the notion that human behaviour is biologically determined. Rather, sociologists argue that every member of our species—required to live in a social group—must learn (and relearn throughout life) the many complex components of culture from other human beings. It is important to note, however, that what we learn, primarily as children, is more than simply a body of information. The process of socialization affects not only what we know but also who we are.

In Chapter 6 we saw that culture cannot be separated from structures of power and economic relationships. The culture in which we live is a *capitalist* culture, with a set of beliefs, values, and material elements that can be understood only within a capitalist economy. Hence, when we speak of the process of socialization, we must also understand that it is occurring within a particular socioeconomic formation.

There are a number of important agents of socialization in all societies. These include the family, schools, religious institutions, peer groups, and the mass media. No one sat down with our parents or teachers to instruct them on the key norms, beliefs, and values that they are required to transmit to the next generation. As in all societies, the dominant beliefs and behaviours are so prevalent that most people simply accept them without question.

In the not too distant past, people understood little about their existence and looked to the supernatural for hope in a world that could often be unpredictable and cruel. Religious values framed the imagery of language, dance, music, art, and physical place. If we look around us today, what do we see? Everywhere we look—including educational institutions once thought to be outside of market relationships—we can see the logos of major corporations. Public buildings, cultural institutions, and even social and charitable events are named after corporations that in many cases have bought—with a tax-deductible donation—the right to promote their companies.

Billboards and outdoor advertisements are everywhere. Sports arenas and the athletes themselves are covered with corporate brands. And people actually pay for the "privilege" of being able to wear (and advertise) certain

---

Box 7.1 Look at What's Inside the Frame

How we interpret the world is largely determined by how the information that we hear or see is framed, that is, how words, metaphors, images, and topics are selected. *Framing* is a process in which communicators, either consciously or unconsciously, try to construct a point of view that encourages the facts of a situation to be interpreted by others in a particular manner (Kuypers 2009). For example, this book clearly has a particular frame of analysis that is focused on the class relations of society. This frame is probably quite noticeable to you because it is not a mainstream one and—as noted in Chapter 1—we are most likely to notice biases that are different from our own. Other sociologists may have different biases and will thus frame similar material in a somewhat alternative way.

Advertising agencies charge huge sums of money to private corporations, candidates running for office, and elected officials to frame their product—whether an item for sale or a government policy—in an appealing way. To use one example, many corporations have had to respond to charges by environmentalists that their products are polluting or that they are selling unhealthy products. But rather than actually changing, they have instead increasingly resorted to "greenwashing," that is, trying to make themselves and their products appear to be more environmentally friendly and healthy for consumption than they really are. One

major example in Canada has been the greenwashing of the Alberta tar sands, which have been rebranded as "oil sands" and reframed as "ethical oil," that is, contrasted to oil extracted in countries with repressive regimes. Another example of framing can be seen in government attempts to sell potentially unpopular policies (such as its support for the tar sands) or massive financial support for private industry by arguing that they create jobs. In contrast, when the government actually *cuts* jobs—for example, teachers, nurses, librarians, or postal workers—the framing is focused on unaffordability.

Another example of framing occurs regularly in the mainstream media with regard to political or social protest. These actions are frequently portrayed as disorganized and full of violent acts, with movements most certainly made up of "radicals" totally unlike the viewers. Inevitably, scenes of protest focus on broken windows or burning automobiles. Rarely are the specific issues made clear to the viewer; nor are they portrayed as legitimate, unless, of course, the protests are occurring in a country whose government is being opposed. And the role of police in either inciting violence by their actions or working as *agents provocateurs* inside social movements is rarely addressed.

The next time you watch/listen to a newscast or a commercial, see if you can detect how information is being framed.

corporate names. Everywhere we look we are being told that our entire culture "is brought to us" by the major corporations. Lost in this imagery is the reality that much of the wealth that the corporate sector "donates" has in fact been privately appropriated from those whose labour created it.

As noted in the previous chapter, children are learning this corporate-controlled culture at an earlier and earlier age. On a daily basis, children and young adults are bombarded with commercials trying to mould their needs and desires. Young people are a particularly appealing target, as companies want to instill product loyalty at the earliest age possible. Children speak the language of advertisers and demand the brands seen on TV, the Internet, or videos.

Everything is commoditized in capitalist societies, even rebellion, and young people who want to opt out of the dominant culture often do so through purchasing certain clothing styles or shoes. Much youthful rebellion has been co-opted by transnational corporations, repackaged, and sold back to young people looking for a collective with whom to identify. There is no clearer example in recent years than the hip-hop movement. Started in the Black ghettos of the United States by young people who felt marginalized economically, politically, and culturally, hip-hop was soon transformed into a multi-million-dollar mainstream industry producing music, videos, and clothing. When rioting occurred in England in 2011, many took not to the nearest street to protest but rather to the nearest upscale shop to see what they could take. Mass looting also happened during the Vancouver riots.

Think About It
Do you think it is possible to truly opt out of corporatized culture today?

Mass Communications in Canada

When you last got together with some friends, what did you talk about? Chances are good that you spent at least some of the time talking about a movie, TV series, YouTube video, or the latest woes of a Hollywood celebrity. It is clear that the various forms of mass communication are pervasive and important in the lives of young adults in the twenty-first century. Social scientists have noted that, given the sheer amount of time we all spend in contact with the various forms of mass communication in our society, we are all affected by them in a major way.

It was in the twentieth century that the mass media came to be the most important means of transmitting and maintaining the dominant ideology. The creation of new technologies allowed for the widespread dissemination of information, ideas, and values: new forms of communication, such as radio, television, and computers reached a "mass," or a large number, of unconnected individuals. At first, many intellectuals believed that the growth of the mass media would be beneficial to ordinary people, as it would expand their traditionally narrow world-views by giving them increased access to knowledge and a wider variety of perspectives.

By the second half of the century, some authors were beginning to challenge these assumptions, with a number of them arguing that the mass media are the primary means of transmitting the dominant ideology and that they play a key role in the legitimation of capitalist society. In *Manufacturing Consent: The Political Economy of the Mass Media* (1988), Edward Herman and Noam Chomsky argued that one of the main functions of the mass media is *propaganda*, or the promotion of the interests of those with economic and political power. Built into such arguments is the assumption that the mass media in capitalist societies are controlled by a small and integrated elite. This theme was first pursued in Canada by Harold Innis, who felt that varying forms of communication needed to be understood in terms of power relationships in societies (1964 [1951]). Sociologist John Porter further advanced this argument in *The Vertical Mosaic* (1965).

> The media not only give us information; they guide our very experiences. Our standards of credulity, our standards of reality, tend to be set by these media rather than by our own fragmentary experience.
> —sociologist C. Wright Mills, 1956

Ownership and Control of the Media

John Porter's research was the first to undertake a comprehensive study of media ownership in Canada. Using 1961 data, Porter concluded that the mass media were controlled by a small group of men who shared certain common characteristics. Most of them came from well-established families already connected to the publishing industry; they had graduated from private schools and belonged to exclusive social clubs; almost all had attended university; and all (in English-speaking Canada) belonged to the British charter group of Canadian society (1965, 483). Subsequent research by Wallace Clement (1975) confirmed that media ownership was indeed highly concentrated.

Since that time, the concentration of media-based capital has escalated, with only a few key players remaining in a complex web of interlocking ownership. This process is not restricted to Canada, although Canada has one of the most concentrated media markets in the world. It is a global phenomenon that is linked to a process known as **convergence**. Convergence refers to the merging of the technology and content of the telecommunications, entertainment, publishing, and broadcasting industries.

The process of convergence is linked to the growing vertical integration of ownership, in which a few giant corporations now control huge chunks of these rapidly integrating industries. Most media in Canada are owned by a small number of companies, the largest being CTVglobemedia, Rogers, Shaw, Astral, Postmedia, and Quebecor. Each of these companies holds a diverse mix of cable television, radio, newspaper, magazine, and/or Internet operations. Some smaller media companies also exist. Approximately two-thirds of Internet-access revenues go to the "big six": Bell, Telus, Shaw, Rogers, Quebecor, and Cogeco (Winseck 2011). The increasing concentration in ownership of ISPs (Internet service providers) and other aspects of the Internet

> Today the chief executive officers of the corporations that control most of what we read and see can fit into an ordinary living room. Almost without exception they are economic conservatives. They can, if they wish, use control of their newspapers, broadcast stations, magazines, books, and movies to promote their own corporate values to the exclusion of others.
> —Ben Bagdikian, The Media Monopoly

> Without exception the brave new technologies of the twentieth century eventually evolved into private behemoths… through which the flow and nature of content would be strictly controlled for reasons of commerce…. To understand the forces threatening the Internet as we know it, we must understand how information technologies give rise to industries, and industries to empires.
> —Tim Wu, The Master Switch: The Rise and Fall of Information Empires

> The mass media are class media.
> —Michael Parenti

will almost certainly stifle both free expression and future technical innovation (Wu 2010).

In the United States, six huge conglomerates—General Electric, Time Warner, Disney, Rupert Murdoch's News Corporation, Viacom, and CBS now own most of the newspapers, magazines, book publishers, radio and TV stations, and movie studios in that country, while control of the Internet rests primarily with Apple and Google. This enormous concentration of capital leads to obvious concerns about the true degree of choice that we actually have over media content as well as the freedom of individuals and groups to have their voices heard.

Most people assume that it is individuals such as the managers of the TV stations or the editors of newspapers who determine the content of various forms of mass media. However, the reality is that the owners of the media do retain their powers of control over content. Sometimes the control can be quite direct. More often, it can be maintained simply because the various levels of management are ultimately beholden to those who employ them. Few people want to get in trouble with their employer.

Owners and managers are not alone in the power to control what we see, hear, and read. Advertisers also exert much influence on media content, since advertising is the media's primary source of funding. Sometimes this economic power can be used to directly influence the content of the media: advertisers who feel that they or their product are badly represented can threaten to withdraw their advertising. However, such actions are rarely necessary. While there may be variations in the opinions of specific journalists or TV news commentators, the overarching orientation of newspapers, television, radio, and mainstream magazines is in support of the status quo.

In fact, we cannot understand the mass media without understanding the power of advertisers. With increasing affluence after World War II, corporations needed to find ever-growing markets for their new consumer goods. Advertisers played an important role in the shift from a "mass" market in the 1950s to a "segmented" one. Shows that brought families, friends, and neighbours across North America together around the TV screen in the 1950s were gradually replaced by shows of interest to specific groups whose members shared their socioeconomic status, gender, age, race, lifestyle, and so on. These shows were then used to sell products specifically targeted to these particular groups. Connected to this trend was the growth of market research, which provided essential data to advertisers about the purchasing habits of each particular segment (Cohen 2003, 292–344).

Today, most Internet users rely on free web services such as Google or Facebook. What few realize is that web advertisers are able to track what we do online in order to deliver targeted, attention-grabbing ads (Garfinkel 2011). Advertisers—by mining huge amounts of personal data from multiple sources—can obtain clues about where we live, where we work, what we buy, and which shows we watch, and then refine their ads accordingly. Smartphones can deliver ads based on our GPS-determined position, and may also be linked to the applications we've installed, whom we've called, and the contents of our address books. One author (Bakan 2011) is particularly concerned about marketing efforts that are designed to get young people addicted to social media and video games (many of which are extremely violent and highly sexualized). Both may separate children from their families and undermine their educational prospects. There is also concern—both in Canada and the United States—that new legislation will allow governments to tap into this information as well.

The main goal of the private media, like any other industry, is to maximize profits. Since their main source of profits is advertising revenue, the news and entertainment that accompany advertising serve as the means of getting people to read the ads or watch the commercials. Advertising does not simply try to sell us a product; it also tries to sell us a way of life. Put in the most general terms, advertising tries to convince us that material possessions will make us happy. This message begins early in life, and we are constantly bombarded by it.

A core theme of advertising is that of improvement. In Chapter 4 we saw that the notion of improvement goes back to the very beginnings of capitalism. Today the media promote primarily self-improvement. Television and magazines are now full of people who get a "makeover." And it is no longer just physical appearances, apparently, that need to be improved. We have shows to improve relationships, diets, and a whole TV channel about home improvement. All these shows teach us that we are not good enough the way we are. The underlying message is that our problems are rooted not in the broader society but in ourselves, and in most cases if we just buy stuff we will be happier people.

The heroes of our era are not, generally speaking, those who care for others, struggle to make the world a better place, or advance democracy and equality. Quite the contrary, ours has become the culture of the celebrity, a celebration of people who have no worth beyond their appearance or their fame. How else do we explain why many millions of people watched the wedding of Prince William to Kate Middleton in the summer of 2011 and subsequently lined the streets in Canada and elsewhere when they toured on their honeymoon?

The Myth of Objectivity

It was noted in Chapter 1 that there is no such thing as true neutrality or objectivity; as humans, all of us process information through our own pre-existing ideas or biases. The media, controlled by human beings, are no more neutral or unbiased than any other source of information. However, because media biases so often match our own and because these biases are so pervasive and constant, we seldom notice them. Nor are the biases of the media random. Despite supposed diversity, the media have consistently favoured management over labour, private enterprise over public ownership, males over females, officialdom over protesters, traditional politics over dissent, and so on (Parenti 1993, 8).

Newspapers have business sections but not labour sections, and business people—not union leaders—are considered experts on the economy. The invisibility of ordinary people is not limited to the news; television shows and movies seldom depict ordinary working people. Strangely, what is called "reality" television is not about reality at all, but rather about the depths to which people will sink in order to achieve some momentary fame or money. Such shows have become very popular and they are very inexpensive to produce. In contrast, practically no television, films, or magazines today offer viewers a critical analysis of their society or a sensitive and in-depth vision of people whose struggles are similar to theirs and who, together with others, have fought to improve their life conditions.

Much has also been written about gender stereotyping in the media. As far back as 1970, the Royal Commission on the Status of Women in Canada spoke out against the stereotyping of both sexes in the mass media. Since that time, the awareness of such issues has increased, and both women and men are certainly portrayed in a broader range of roles. However, all forms of the media continue to represent gender in ways that are often unrealistic or limited, while transgendered people are almost invisible.

> It is useful to remind ourselves that free expression is threatened not just blatantly by authoritarian governments and all those in the private sector who fear public exposure, but also more subtly by the handful of global media conglomerates that have reduced meaningful diversity of expression in much of the globe.
> —Gerald Caplan

> Media consolidation, the crushing pressure of the news cycle, and the drive to pander to salacious tastes in order to please advertisers, are rotting journalism from within. The promise of digital age innovation is being suffocated by a business model that treats news as a mere consumer product.
> —Michelle Chen

> For a democracy to succeed, the public needs sufficient information to make informed judgments on the important issues of the day.
> —John McManus

Images of racial minorities in the media are also troubling. When racialized people appear in the media, the image is often either a stereotyped or a negative one, or both. Some ethno-racial groups, such as South Asians, East Asians, and Arabs, are almost invisible in film and television, except when portrayed as the evil "other" or the humorous bumbling outsider. Indigenous people have also not been well served by the media and have generally been underrepresented—or represented in stereotypical ways—in Canadian television and films.

While most of us strongly oppose censorship, it is hard to oppose what you cannot see. With so few companies controlling the entire media and telecommunications industries, our choices become diminished. With regard to the news, much information that is essential to our understanding of the social world simply doesn't get revealed.

Some media analysts feel that news and entertainment have merged into what is sometimes referred to as "infotainment." More and more of what we see and read is celebrity-dominated, shallow, and devoid of substance. One author (Schechter 2007) feels that Chomsky and Herman's notion that those with power are "manufacturing consent" needs to be changed to "manufacturing indifference." As Schechter notes, the media owners want eyeballs for advertisers, not activists to promote change. Another author (Hedges 2009) argues that our societies are now "empires of illusion." In this illusory world, as noted above, we worship celebrities, while in the world of politics, argues Hedges, we vote for "a slogan, a smile, perceived sincerity, and attractiveness, along with the carefully crafted personal narrative of the candidate. It is the style and the story, not content and fact, that inform mass politics" (46), with people looking for a candidate who is "just like them."

Our ability to critically assess media content is limited by the fact that we often lack the background information to adequately understand the issues. For example, our ability to fully understand the current debate about environmental pollution requires that we understand both the corporate agenda and the particular economic framework in which it is taking place. Understanding current U.S. foreign policy requires knowledge of its long history of intervention in other countries around the world. However, such in-depth analyses are rarely provided. Rather, the electronic media in particular now rely on short sound bites, with instant analyses of issues provided by so-called experts. These commentators are often government spokespeople or, increasingly, other journalists. Moreover, since the media offer us information in highly disconnected form, we are often unable to put all the pieces together even when the

> There is almost no labour portrayed on TV and unions are almost never referenced. What's odd about the situation is that almost everyone who works in the TV industry belongs to a trade union and has benefited from advances made by the labour movement... too few TV shows deal in any realistic way with the workplace. People want fantasy and escape when they watch TV, but there are now so many channels and so many choices that there should be room for productions that say something—anything—about the truth of work.
> —John Doyle, Globe and Mail, Labour Day 2011

Box 7.2 What Is the Meaning of "Left" and "Right" in a Social Context?

Most of us have probably heard the terms "left-wing" and "right-wing" used to describe theories, people, social movements, and political parties. But if asked what these terms actually mean, few of us could likely come up with an answer.

The terms "left" and "right" first appeared during the French Revolution of 1789 when members of the new National Assembly sat on different sides, with supporters of the king to the president's right and supporters of the revolution to his left. Today the terms are generally used to explain political parties. Put very simply, the right wing is tied to the "big fish," that is, to people and theories supporting the interests of the dominant class; in contrast, the left generally supports the interests of the "small fish."

However, this is quite an oversimplification of the subtleties of these terms. First, while it is true that most "big fish"—the ruling class in capitalist societies—have no trouble supporting the interests of their own class, this is less likely to be the case for the "small fish." If, as this chapter argues, the dominant class in any society has control over its ideas, the small fish may be drawn into positions advanced by those with power, and thus feel that "the world is just."

In addition, we must also consider the situation for the "middle fish" in capitalist societies. Such people—particularly in times of social instability such as the current period—often feel torn, drawn to the interests of both classes. On the one hand, many of the "middle fish" support the system that has rewarded them with relatively high wages, high status, or the privileges of ownership. On the other hand, as was discussed in Chapter 5, many in the middle are feeling increasing stress from the economic instability of our times. Some of these individuals, in particular White males, may feel their share has been declining because others—women and immigrants, for example—have been getting a bigger share. For these individuals, the right-wing narrative can be appealing.

If there is a core difference—from a sociological perspective—between right-wing perspectives and left-wing perspectives, it is with regard to the complex relationship between the individual ("me") and the larger social world ("we"). The left, from the eighteenth century onward, realized that the power of the "small fish" existed only as a potential, by collectively uniting against the "big fish." Thus Marx called on workers of all countries to unite, and trade unions continue to emphasize worker solidarity. The value of internationalism—that people around the world share a common set of interests—also leads the left to support global struggles for peace and international solidarity movements.

The right wing, in contrast, places emphasis on the individual in capitalist societies, focusing on their rights and responsibilities. "Big government" is seen as being the opponent of individual freedoms, and the family is promoted as the basic unit of society. Government policies that advance minorities, provide pre-school care, or help the poor are opposed, while lower taxes, in the guise of "putting more money in the pockets of families" are promoted. Wars are seen as the inevitable outcome of the competition for scarce resources in an "us" versus "them" world.

The extreme concentration of media ownership, both in Canada and globally, has meant that there is little balance today in news reporting, with the right-wing perspective dominating. Indeed, whole television and radio stations are devoted to promoting the most extreme views from the right, particularly in the United States. Moreover, even though fewer of us listen to newscasts or read newspapers any longer, the right-wing narrative has entered the general discourse. For example, the term "taxpayer" is almost universally used to refer to what were formerly called "citizens."

These themes are explored further in later chapters.

information is available to us. Without an ability to really comprehend what is happening around the world, many of us simply tune out what appears to be nothing but bad news.

In this context, elections have become little more than political parties competing for the best advertising campaigns. Rather than offering in-depth analyses of real social problems, candidates—with the aid of major advertising agencies—increasingly offer slogans, repetitive but simple arguments, and often nasty or personal attacks against their opponents. Parties on the right of the political spectrum both in Canada and the United States have become especially good at "selling their product."

Think About It
Do you think the Internet has given us greater access to alternative views, or is it just so overloaded with information that we simply ignore most of it and cling to what we already believe to be true?

It is worth noting that those with dissenting viewpoints are not totally voiceless. There are many cultural workers who are critical of the status quo in one way or another, and who are able to promote their ideas via websites such as rabble.ca in Canada, small presses, alternative journals, and so on. A few individuals in Canada and the United States, having achieved some legitimacy, can even be seen or heard via the mainstream media. Nonetheless, the ability of alternative views to be heard in the face of increased monopolization of media ownership is a troubling issue for the democratic process.

> [Government] media and Internet policy and regulatory frameworks have encouraged the trends of concentration and conglomeration that has resulted in Canada having one of the most concentrated telecom, media, and Internet markets in the world.
> —*Shea Sinnott*

> The CBC [has never been] more important than today with the arrival of digital media. There is a fragmentation of all media, and we've gone from mass media to what I call "molecular media." One upshot is that increasingly any Canadian can be awash in any particular narrow point of view. They can listen to, read or watch the views they support or hold….we all may end up in self-reinforcing echo-chambers where all we hear is our own point of view.
> —*Don Tapscott*

The Role of the Government

The government of Canada has always intervened more directly in the mass communications industry than has the United States government. Such direct state involvement was seen as part of the nation-building process in this country. The Canadian Broadcasting Corporation (CBC) was created in 1936, with a mandate to help unite the country and provide an alternative to American radio. As a side benefit, public film and broadcasting organizations have also provided a service by producing material that does not necessarily turn a profit in the media marketplace.

The government has also directly intervened in the regulation of the broadcast media. This role, originally assigned to the CBC, later passed into the hands of the CRTC (the Canadian Radio-television and Telecommunications Commission). The CRTC has the power to issue, renew, or revoke broadcasting licences, as well as to set out conditions for Canadian broadcasting as a whole. Its role, in the main, has been to protect and encourage the development of Canadian culture in both French and English. In reality, the CRTC has frequently turned out to be little more than a body that legitimates current arrangements, rather than an entity that has any real power over the media or their owners (Lorimer and McNulty 1996, 236–37). In particular, the convergence of media ownership in Canada—with very few giant corporations controlling whole sectors—has not been challenged by the CRTC.

Historically the CBC and the CRTC have been a restraining force against a total incursion by the much larger American mass media. However, in recent years the government has been retreating from its protectionist role, as it has increasingly endorsed greater private-sector control of the media while gradually eroding support for public broadcasting. In 2007 the head of the CRTC announced a review of the CRTC itself by stating that the government "has directed us to accept market forces as the default and regulation as the exception" (Robertson 2007). The decline of government protection will almost certainly guarantee that Canadian culture—our stories, our history, our actors, our writers, our dancers, our music, and so on—will gradually be swallowed up by the much larger and wealthier U.S. entertainment industry. Since the Conservatives have come into power, millions of dollars in funding to the CBC have been cut. With decreased funding from the government, the public broadcaster will increasingly look to advertising as its funding source, making it more and more similar to other commercial broadcasters. At that point, it is likely that government funding to the CBC would end or be very minimal.

Think About It
Do you ever watch CBC television or listen to CBC radio? Would you care if the CBC disappeared? What can a public broadcaster provide that a commercial broadcaster might not? When was the last time you saw a Canadian film?

The Education System
Although most of us take public education for granted, it is actually a relatively recent phenomenon. For most of human history, the majority of people were taught life skills by their parents or their communities. Whether foraging or farming, the skills needed for survival did not require schooling. For the few who followed a trade, apprenticeship was the means of acquiring the requisite skills and knowledge. Wherever formalized learning did occur, it was accessible only to a small elite recruited almost totally from the upper strata.

The growth of mass compulsory education in the late nineteenth century must be connected to the development of capitalism. As industrialization advanced, people moved to cities to fill the factories hungry for workers.

At first the whole family—men, women, and children—worked for pitiful wages out of economic necessity. In Europe most of these people came from outlying rural areas; in Canada immigrants fleeing horrible conditions abroad filled most jobs.

The rapid advances in technology led to two important consequences. First, as technology advanced, a more educated and skilled workforce was required. Second, production needed fewer workers. A public education system developed to fit into these changing conditions. Some educational reformers feared that children, no longer needed in factories, would become troublemakers. Public schools were thus seen as a place to keep them busy. The new schools would also provide the next generation with the basic skills required by many employers. Even more importantly, schools could help the young develop certain characteristics—such as discipline, industriousness, docility, politeness, punctuality, and obedience to authority—that would make them good workers. The school system was also seen as a primary agent of socialization that would teach young people the values and norms of the dominant culture. This was particularly important in Canada, where so many were foreign born.

Since the late nineteenth century, there has been a gradual increase in the years of formal attendance at school. While an elementary-school education was once considered sufficient, students are now being told that postsecondary education is the minimum requirement to get a reasonably well-paid job. To some extent such a trend reflects the increasing complexity of technology, but it is also the result of the growing tendency toward **credentialism**. As the number of applicants expands, paper credentials are increasingly used as a means of limiting access into certain job categories, even if the particular credentials are of questionable utility in job performance. Many jobs that now require a university degree were formerly performed quite adequately by people out of high school; likewise, graduate degrees are often the minimum for jobs in which, only a short while ago, a B.A. was more than sufficient. It has also been argued that credentialism is primarily a means of justifying structured inequality, by linking social inequality to the individual's ability to attain a particular level of education (Bowles and Gintis 1976).

A growing problem is that of over-qualification. Young people are being urged to get postsecondary education, but upon graduation many are finding that they cannot get jobs suited to their qualifications. While job over-qualification can affect anyone, it is most likely to occur if you are an immigrant to Canada. Although 28 percent of Canadian-born workers aged twenty-five to fifty-four in 2008 had a higher level of education for their job than was normally required, about 42 percent of immigrants were over-qualified. This problem was most serious for university-educated immigrants who had landed within five years from when the survey was taken. Two-thirds of these individuals were working in jobs for which they were over-qualified (Statistics Canada 2009).

Moreover, while there has been an extensive expansion of education, particularly colleges and universities, in Canada in the last fifty years, not everyone has been able to take advantage of it. When the last census was taken, nearly a third of Canadians aged twenty-five to forty-four had not graduated from a postsecondary institution (Statistics Canada 2008a). Moreover, educational attainment is not random, but rather is linked to a number of variables. For example, studies have repeatedly shown that levels of educational aspiration and attainment are strongly correlated with the socioeconomic status of one's parents and, to a lesser extent, race and ethnicity. For biological determinists, such findings confirm the "natural" inferiority of certain groups. However, most sociologists argue that the cause of such inequalities lies within the social system rather than with the individual.

Education in the Twenty-First Century

The nature and functions of the education system have been explained by a variety of analytical frameworks. Of the order theories, the classic position is that of structural functionalism, most clearly exemplified by Talcott Parsons in an essay entitled "The School Class as a Social System: Some of Its Functions in American Society" (1961). For Parsons, the school performs two essential functions for the maintenance of an orderly and stable society: it socializes children, not only by teaching them a body of skills and knowledge, but also by transmitting the values and attitudes considered acceptable within society; and it sorts individuals through a grading system, preparing them for a differentiated labour market.

For functionalists, the school system is seen as neutral, with both the individual and the society benefiting in equal measure from the system of public education: society gets the various jobs filled by the most qualified personnel, while individuals get to achieve personal growth and development. In this sense, structural functionalism can be linked to liberal ideology, with public education seen as the tool that gives everyone a chance to compete in the capitalist marketplace and succeed both occupationally and personally.

In contrast to the order theories—with their notion of a neutral education system that exists to benefit both society and the individual—are the change theories. The various change theories agree with the order theories that socialization and sorting are the two key functions of education; however, in contrast to the order theories they recognize that societies have an unequal allocation of power, wealth, and prestige. In this context, the education system is a social institution that, in the main, helps sustain existing class relations.

Employers require workers, and workers of a specific type. At a more general level, the ruling class requires relative social stability and ideological acceptance of capitalist class relations. Given the power of this class, it should not be surprising that it pressures governments to ensure that schools meet *its* needs. That is not to say that schools act *only* on behalf of the dominant class, but rather that this class does have a broadly shared set of interests regarding public education and that it has the capacity to promote such interests.

As capital has globalized, the needs of the corporate sector vis-à-vis the education system have changed. According to Barlow and Robertson (1994, 79), North American corporations have had three goals as they increasingly intervene in public education:

> The first is to secure the ideological allegiance of young people to a free-market world-view on issues of the environment, corporate rights and the role of government. The second is to gain market access to the hearts and minds of young consumers and lucrative contracts in the education industry. The third is to transform schools into training centres producing a workforce suited to the needs of transnational corporations.

Many analysts have discussed the ways that our education system ultimately reinforces the status quo. In part, this is the result of the very structure of education—a person in authority presents what will be learned, offers it to students in narrowly framed units of knowledge, and then tests the student on what is learned. Students, then, generally "succeed" not by questioning authority, but by learning what is required. The same, of course, is true for teachers. In this context of general conformity, students seldom learn about the fundamental structure of our society or the relations of power, let alone how to challenge them.

Think About It

Did you or any of your friends ever get in trouble in school for challenging some authority figure?

Given this reality, it is obvious that most of us will come to see the world around us as natural and inevitable, rather than as something to be questioned or challenged. What has changed dramatically in recent years is the increasingly direct involvement of the corporate sector in education. In part this is a result of the capital glut discussed earlier in the book—as capital looks for new outlets for investment, corporations now see components of education (including food and janitorial services, electronic technologies, standardized testing, and building management) as possible sources of profit. Connected to this trend is increasing pressure to harmonize Canadian education with that in the United States, since private American educational services can now bid on Canadian contracts.

There is also an increasing desire on the part of business, both in Canada and globally, to be more directly involved in determining the content of education. Built into this goal is the philosophical belief that schooling should be more about skills training for specific jobs than about education that might provide critical-thinking skills and broader social awareness.

Increasing corporate involvement in education can also be seen at the postsecondary level. With government underfunding to postsecondary education a reality in Canada since the 1970s, universities and colleges have increasingly turned to corporations for donations of money and technology, as well as for research grants. In addition, the corporate elite has increasingly become directly involved in university governance, while a number of university CEOs or former CEOs have joined the corporate elite (Carroll 2010, 212).* As a result of these changes, the direction of research and education has increasingly shifted to fit corporate interests. Not surprisingly, business schools and technology programs have expanded massively while general arts and sciences programs have declined.

As government spending on public education has been cut, a number of worrying trends have appeared. First, there has been a slow but clear movement toward a two-tiered system of education, one for the well-to-do and one for everyone else. While private schools for the rich have always existed, the erosion of the public system has led more middle-income earners to look for alternatives. Although some have chosen private education, it is obviously a costly option. As middle-income parents increasingly move their children to private schools, their social commitment to public education declines, and public schools deteriorate even more. As public funds decrease, more and more public schools are shifting aspects of public education to the private sector.

At the postsecondary level, tuition fees for both undergraduate and graduate students in Canada escalated rapidly during the 1990s. Between the 1998–99 and the 2008–09 school years such increases moderated, but undergraduate students continued to see average increases of 4.4 percent. In contrast, inflation, as measured by the Consumer Price Index, rose at an annual average rate of only 2.3 percent in the same period (Statistics Canada 2008b). A four-year undergraduate course in Canada now costs about $60,000, with professional courses costing far more. Moreover, Canada is one of only three industrialized countries that do not have a national system of student grants. It is therefore not surprising that the average debt load for a student graduating from a four-year program has more than doubled since 1990, from around $12,000 to nearly $27,000, and increasing numbers of parents say they cannot afford to send their children to university (*Maclean's*, November 22, 2010, 86).

Think About It
How might the increasing cost of education affect the choices individuals make about what programs and courses they will take?

---

* For evidence of this linkage, revisit Box 5.2, on page 106, where a professor and former president at the University of Toronto—now head of an international law firm—are listed as attendees at the 2011 Bilderberg meeting.

Ideas and Power

Culture defines us as a species. Unlike other animals, humans must live together in social groups and learn their means of survival. Culture is not created in a vacuum; rather, it must always be understood in terms of the relationships of power within a given society. As we have seen in earlier chapters, it is the owning class that holds the majority of that power via its ownership and control of society's resources.

Wherever social inequality exists, the dominant class needs to legitimate both itself and the social system that gives it power. Most of us internalize the dominant norms, beliefs, and values of our society. Thus in the process of becoming human, we accept the existing structures of power. It is this power of ideology that allows the dominant class to maintain its rule. While outright force can always be used to control those who wish to challenge the structures of power, such actions can lead to increased instability and resentment. Ideological hegemony—the ability to control or dominate the belief system within any society—is a more subtle and effective means of maintaining power.

Within all advanced capitalist societies the mass media and the education system are two of the main agents of socialization that help maintain and reinforce class relations. These two social institutions are not simply the mouthpieces of the ruling class. However, while both continue to be contested domains within Canadian society, the power of economic ownership gives the dominant class an advantage because of its ability to control the content of these institutions, particularly the media. Moreover, the pervasive ideology of liberalism serves to reinforce the status quo without any direct intervention.

Neither the mass media nor the education system lacks critics. Yet much of the criticism is directed at these institutions as if they existed independently. As a result, we often fault them for failures of the broader society. This is particularly true of the education system, which we hope will give us true equality of opportunity by negating differences of birth, while at the same time providing the skills and knowledge necessary to find employment. When we (or our children) fail to get jobs, or when we see inequality persisting, it is easy to put the blame on our schools. However, the persistence of poverty and extremes of social inequality, as we will see in Chapter 10, are rooted in the economic system, not the schools. While the education system may be able to moderate the worst tendencies of capitalist economies, it can never eliminate them without some more drastic form of social change.

Likewise, the mass media are often blamed for promoting values detrimental to society. For example, violence in the media is often discussed. However, like the schools, the media are part of a broader social world. While they may, indeed, play their part in promoting violence, they are not, in and of themselves, the problem. We live in a world where violence is a fact of life. Moreover, violence sells in the marketplace. As long as the media remain largely in private hands, as funding to public television and film is slashed and as American media giants make increasing inroads in Canada, the ability of ordinary Canadians to affect media content will be limited.

The struggles about the education system and the mass media are ultimately struggles regarding democracy and power, for the bottom line in these debates is with regard to who should control our social institutions. The corporate agenda quite directly hands over increasing amounts of control to private enterprise. People who oppose this agenda dispute the argument that the marketplace can meet social needs. Such individuals and groups demand that the state fulfill its mandate of supporting public education as well as public broadcasting and film in addition to maintaining open access to digital media. It is likely that these struggles will continue in the near future.

KEY POINTS

1. Ideas do not develop in a vacuum; rather, they arise out of particular conditions at specific moments in history. The body of assumptions, ideas, and values that come together into a coherent world-view is referred to as an ideology.

2. Those who have economic power in a society are able to dominate the ideological sphere as well. This dominance is referred to as ideological hegemony.

3. Liberalism is the dominant ideology within capitalism. The liberal tradition sees the model for all things as the marketplace.

4. One of the main themes of liberalism is equality, conceived of as equality of opportunity. However, without equality of condition, equality of opportunity is limited.

5. Within the liberal framework, ideas are seen as goods competing in the marketplace. But ideas, like goods, are not equally represented in the marketplace. Thus there is the appearance of choice, when in reality there is little variation in the ideas most of us read or hear.

6. The education system and mass media are two of the major agents of socialization that transmit the dominant ideology.

7. In recent years there has been tremendous concentration of ownership of the mass media in Canada and around the globe. Media content is largely controlled by those with economic power.

8. The overall thrust of the mass media is in support of current social arrangements. Despite a variety of orientations, there is almost universal support for the private-enterprise system and the dominant ideology, liberalism.

9. The direct intervention of the state into areas of culture has always been widely accepted in Canada as a means of protecting Canadian media. However, this intervention is now declining; as a result, U.S. media domination will likely increase.

10. Both the order theories and the change theories agree that schools perform two major functions: they socialize children and they help sort individuals for the labour market. However, the various change theories argue that these functions help sustain existing class relations.

11. As globalization advances, the corporate sector has had an increased desire to be directly linked to education institutions. Big business has also gained a foothold in the college and university sector.

12. Current debates over education and the mass media must be understood as democratic struggles, in that they address the question of who should control various social institutions in Canada.

FURTHER READING

Côté, James, and Anton Allahar. 2011. *Lowering Higher Education: The Rise of Corporate Universities and the Fall of Liberal Education.* Toronto: University of Toronto Press.
The authors argue that the conversion of universities into training institutions has led to a number of troubling outcomes, including the decline of the humanities, social sciences, and natural sciences, as well as lowered standards and grade inflation.

Eagleton, Terry. 2007. *Ideology: An Introduction.* London: Verso.
This updated version of a classic work by a Marxist literary critic examines the many definitions of the term and traces the concept's complex history in contemporary society.

Edwardson, Ryan. 2008. *Canadian Content: Culture and the Quest for Nationhood.* Toronto: University of Toronto Press.
A detailed examination of the struggle of Canadians to define a national culture.

Hackett, Robert A., and William K. Carroll. 2006. *Remaking Media: The Struggle to Democratize Public Communication.* New York: Routledge.
Two Canadian sociologists examine the "democratic deficit" in the mainstream media and assess the ways alternative forms of media and new forms of activism might counter this problem.

Hedges, Chris. 2009. *Empire of Illusion: The End of Literacy and the Triumph of Spectacle.* Toronto: Knopf.
Written for a general audience, Hedges argues here that Americans are being diverted from confronting the serious political, economic, and moral issues of our time by a mass culture of celebrity and illusion.

McChesney, Robert W. 2008. *The Political Economy of Media: Enduring Issues, Emerging Dilemmas.* New York: Monthly Review.
One of the foremost analysts of media in the United States examines the monopolization of the media and its implications for democratic processes.

Sears, Alan. 2003. *Retooling the Mind Factory: Education in a Lean State.* Aurora, ON: Garamond.
A detailed examination of the links between current education reform and the neoliberal agenda.

Stephen, Peter. 2011. *About Canada: Media.* Black Point, NS: Fernwood.
A short critical examination of how our news and entertainment industry is struggling in the face of funding cuts, media concentration, and a generally hostile political environment. The author argues that the Canadian people must reclaim the media to enhance both democracy and our culture.

Wu, Tim. 2010. *The Master Switch: The Rise and Fall of Information Empires.* Toronto: Knopf.
Drawing on history, Wu—who created the term "net neutrality"—shows how corporate interests are attempting to seize control of the Internet and assesses what this might mean for the freedoms we now take for granted.

8 The Role of the State

In This Chapter

- What exactly is the *state*, and how does it differ from the concept of *government*?
- How does an understanding of social class help explain what states do?
- Do we live in a democracy?
- What is fascism?

Up to this point we have been talking about power that is rooted in the economic relationships of society, that is, in class relationships. But when most of us think of power in a society, we think of it in political terms rather than economic ones. As noted earlier in this book, if we were asked to name the most powerful person in Canada, it is likely that the majority of us would choose the prime minister. At one level, this is not incorrect—those who hold high positions in government do indeed have a great deal of power. However, as this chapter demonstrates, the power of our elected representatives can only be understood within capitalist class relations.

All advanced class societies have had some kind of state formation, although most were small and centred on a strong leader such as a king or emperor. The **state** is an organized political structure that carries out tasks required by more complex societies as their population and geographic size increase, as warfare and trade expand, and as social inequalities become more extreme. However, the state is more than a simple organizing structure; it is also a major means of social control. As Max Weber noted, the state has a monopoly on the legitimate use of violence ([1921] 1958, 78). Although we often use the term *state* interchangeably with the term *government*, the government is only one aspect of the state. The concept of the state is more inclusive and allows us to appreciate the element of force that is a key part of this social institution.

The state has not always been a part of every human society. While all societies require some means of maintaining social control or of handling relations with external groups, for most of human history this was done informally. In foraging societies, political power tended to be loosely organized, with a pattern of shifting leadership. Leaders used personal influence to encourage others to undertake activities, but there was no structural means of coercing anyone into following directions. With an increase in surplus and the subsequent unequal allocation of resources, increasingly formalized leadership developed. As agrarian societies with large surpluses and social classes developed, more formalized state structures arose. Along with the growth of the state apparatus, an ideology developed that supported and legitimized such a structure. In other words, most people came to see their state structure as inevitable and eternal.

The Separation of the Private and the Public Spheres

The capitalist state is different than earlier forms of the state. In agrarian societies, the owning class was in direct control of the state, which was used to appropriate surplus from the producers. For example, an emperor could accumulate wealth directly via various forms of tribute or taxation. In capitalist societies, in contrast, the owning class is separated from the state. The economic sphere is "privatized"—it comes under full and direct control of the dominant class. At the same time, the *social* activities formerly carried out directly by the owning class—that is, military, administrative, and legal functions—become transferred to the state, which is in the public sphere.

It is important to note that the separation of the private and public spheres in capitalist societies is only partial. The capitalist class gets to privately own and have control over most economic activity. This gives this class enormous power over the productive process because it has the capacity to organize and intensify production for its own immediate interests. However, the negative consequences of its activities—pollution, poverty, unemployment, and so on—are usually dealt with by governments. In reality, then, it is only the *benefits* of productive activity that are privatized in capitalist societies, while the *costs* are transferred to the public sphere. Moreover, as we will see throughout this chapter, the capitalist class would not be able to secure these benefits without the assistance of the state.

Understanding the Modern State: Two Views

In Canada today there are three levels of government. First there is the federal government, with its centre in Ottawa; second are the ten provincial and three territorial governments; third are the various municipal, or local, governments across the country. All of us connect to numerous components of all three levels on a daily basis. For example, on any given day we might listen to CBC radio on waking (federal government), have a glass of tap water and put out the garbage (municipal government), take a bus (municipal and provincial governments), renew our driver's licence (provincial government), buy an item and pay sales tax (provincial and federal governments), take courses at a university (provincial and federal governments), or visit a relative in the hospital (provincial and federal governments). Because of the huge amount of power that the various levels of government ultimately hold over our lives, it is important to take a closer look at exactly what the state is, how it functions, and on whose behalf it acts. A number of competing theoretical frameworks have tried to explain who controls the state and how it works. Two dominant analyses of the state—reflecting the order ("big fish") and the change ("small fish") frameworks, respectively—are the *pluralist approach* and the *class approach*.

Most of us don't think that we carry theoretical frameworks around in our head. And yet most of us, if asked to describe on whose behalf governments act, would likely respond with an approach known as **pluralism**. In the pluralist analysis, society consists of a variety of groups and associations with highly diverse and often conflicting interests. According to the pluralist analysis, no single group totally dominates political structures. A key function of the state, from this perspective, is *mediation* between the many different interest groups—workers, students, people with disabilities, First Nations, big business, small business, women, to name but a few—trying to get their needs met within a given society. Indeed, by balancing out the various interest groups, the state supposedly helps guarantee that order is maintained, while ensuring that the overall best interests of society as a whole are met.

From this point of view, the state has a high degree of autonomy, that is, the ability to act independently of any single pressure group. Pluralists recognize the greater power of big business relative to other interest groups but do not see this as a problem because of its important role in the economy. For pluralists, the state is a body that acts on behalf of society as a whole. Because it does not emphasize the element of social control, the pluralist approach usually speaks of "government" rather than "the state." The pluralist analysis of the state is the one most of us feel comfortable with, both because it fits with our already accepted notions of how societies work and because it does seem to match our own experience. On the surface, it appears that governments are, more or less, working on everyone's behalf. After all, while few of us may agree with everything our governments do, most of us feel we have benefited from the many services provided by the three levels of government, with our state-funded medical system being the most popular.* In addition, since all adult citizens get to vote in elections, we have the common-sense understanding that Canadians as a whole are choosing the individuals who sit in positions of power, and, therefore, it does seem that those individuals must by and large be representing our collective interests. The pluralist approach fits with the order theories: "The world is just."

The change theories do not support this commonly held view of the social world. Unlike the pluralist approach, which sees the Canadian state as essentially neutral, the class approach sees the state as an institution that acts primarily in the interests of the dominant class. Thus, in contrast to the pluralist notion of the state, the class approach sees the Canadian state

---

* While most of us think of our medical system as being fully funded by the Canadian government, many aspects of health care—including drugs, dental care, physiotherapy, eyeglasses, home nursing care and so on—are not normally covered. Moreover, in some provinces a monthly fee is paid.

as only partially autonomous, because the economic power of capital also gives it political power. Moreover, given the goals of the dominant class, having the state accede to its interests will mean the interests of others are not necessarily met.

Although nineteenth- and early twentieth-century class analysis initiated by Marx, Engels, and others provided a general theory of the capitalist state, the actual process was never clearly worked out. This issue was taken on in the second half of the twentieth century by a number of neo-Marxist social scientists who were interested in the relationship between the state and the economy. Nicos Poulantzas, James O'Connor, and Ralph Miliband initiated a debate that has continued to the present. Despite differences between various authors, all share a critique of the pluralist approach and a belief in the connection between the state and the appropriating class.

From the point of view of class analysis, the state carries out three interconnected functions on behalf of the dominant class, although the relative importance of each may vary in different socioeconomic formations and even at different historical moments within a specific society (O'Connor 1973, 6; Panitch 1977, 8):

1. *Accumulation function.* The state must try to create or maintain the conditions for profitable capital accumulation.
2. *Legitimation function.* The state must try to maintain social harmony, mostly by legitimating the current class structure and the right of the ruling class to rule.
3. *Coercion function.* The state, when necessary, must use force to repress subordinate individuals or classes on behalf of the dominant class.

The state is made up of a number of institutions, which can be classified into three categories: *repressive agencies*, which include the army and police, the judiciary, and the penal system; *government*, which includes the various administrative bodies, such as legislatures, parliaments, and councils, as well as the civil service; and *government-owned bodies*, which in Canada include such components as the education system, the health-care system, the postal service, and such "publicly owned" services as the CBC.

The rest of this chapter describes and analyzes the ways the Canadian state is linked to the capitalist owning class and, in the process, refutes the pluralist notion of a neutral state apparatus. Indeed, it is argued that the current activities of the various levels of the state in Canada—federal, provincial, and local—and their dramatic transformation in the last thirty or so years make no sense without understanding their class-based nature. The class perspective on the state immediately calls into question the strongly held notion that ours is a fully democratic society. Therefore, a preliminary discussion of the meaning of democracy is in order.

Democracy in Capitalist Societies

The argument that the various levels of the state act *primarily* in the interests of the appropriating class does not mean that it is the *only* group whose interests are being met. As the rest of this chapter argues, states act on behalf of the ruling class *in general*, but this does not mean that every individual activity of every level of state at every moment necessarily benefits the dominant class. First, we must be clear that the various individuals who are part of the state apparatuses are not under the total control of the ruling class. On a daily basis, they may make decisions for a wide variety of personal or political reasons. Thus human agency must always be taken into account when we analyze social institutions.

It must also be recalled that the capitalist owning class has two goals: its short-term interest is to maximize profits, while its long-term interest is to maintain the system that allows it to privately appropriate surplus value. If states *only* helped the owning class maximize its profits, the long-term stability of the entire capitalist system might be put at risk. Moreover, no political party would ever be voted back into office. Thus every state in capitalist societies must, to some degree, balance competing forces. One way of increasing stability has been the acceptance of democratic political forms.

The Meaning of Democracy

In its original Greek, *democracy* meant rule by the people. However, even within the Greek city-states that practised democratic forms, "the people" were a relatively small group, excluding women, slaves, and the foreign-born. Likewise, the *Magna Carta*, the great constitutional document of the feudal period, was a codification of the rights and privileges of the feudal lords, not the serfs. Democracy, then, is not an absolute; rather, it must be understood within particular social and historical conditions.

There are differing views about the relationship between the economic arrangement that we call capitalism and the political arrangement we call democracy. Some theorists feel that capitalism furthered the democratic process. In some senses this is true, as pre-capitalist societies tended to be dominated by authoritarian states closely linked to a small and very powerful ruling class. Notions such as human rights, equal opportunity, and elections of government representatives do not normally exist in such societies.

However, while there is no question that capitalist economies have advanced the process of democracy, they have done so in only a limited way. In capitalist societies, democracy has a very specific meaning, limited to the political sphere rather than to the economic one. Since economic property is "privately" owned, it remains outside the framework of democratic principles. Most of us accept, for example, that in capitalist societies only company owners should have the right to decide whether a particular

Box 8.1 Democracy Is About More Than Voting

Brigette DePape, a page in the Canadian Senate, came to the attention of the public on June 3, 2011, by silently holding up a sign that said "Stop Harper." Some may not agree with either her message or her action, but this young woman does raise interesting questions about the nature of the democratic process in Canada. What follows is a short extract from a longer essay she wrote, republished by rabble.ca (September 21, 2011):

Democracy is not just about voting every four years. We have been deceived to think that our responsibility to our communities ends at casting a ballot. The notion that democracy is limited to choosing a Member of Parliament who will then make decisions for us is preposterous when you think about it. Imagine if this was the case in your personal life: every four years you cast a ballot for the person who would make key decisions about your life including where you will live, whether you will have children, who your partner is, etc.

Would you trust them to know what was best for you and just let them make all the decisions? Of course not. We would not leave these important decisions to someone else, and we cannot leave the decisions about our country to politicians. We need to be active and engaged every day: asking questions, reacting and taking action. By taking to the streets, we become agents of democracy, rather than the subjects of a flawed system. We become a living, breathing force for change.

company should be able to close down, increase production, fire its workers, or move to another locale. While it is true that there are now many laws constraining corporations—for example, labour laws and environmental protection legislation—such laws were put in place only after a long struggle, and many of these constraints have actually deteriorated or disappeared in recent years.

Even within the political or "public" sphere of capitalist societies, democracy as defined in our society has a rather specific meaning. It pertains mainly to the electoral process whereby, at regular intervals, individuals get to select those who will represent them in some parliamentary-style body for a fixed period of time. Hence countries with massive poverty, extremes of rich and poor, and mass powerlessness are nonetheless called "democratic" simply because they hold elections from time to time. Just under 62 percent of Canadians voted in the 2011 federal election, up slightly from 2010. And although the Conservatives won a majority of seats in that election, they did so by obtaining only about 40 percent of those votes. In other words, approximately one in four Canadians actually cast a ballot for a Conservative candidate.

It should also be noted that even the basic assumptions about democractic process can be rescinded quickly in capitalist societies. For example, in late 2011 the Greek president, George Papandreau, was forced to resign after offering citizens of that country—with full support from his cabinet—a referendum on austerity measures being proposed by the European Union.

Both Papandreau, as well as the prime minister of Italy, who resigned at around the same time, were replaced by men with banking connections who had never held elected office.

Unlike in pre-capitalist societies, few members of the ruling class in Canada actually hold government positions. How, then, does the ruling class rule? One way is through financially backing those candidates during elections that support their goals. In Chapter 5 we also saw the important role played by lobbying groups for big business such as the Canadian Council of Chief Executives and think tanks such as the Fraser Institute. Such groups not only directly influence the decisions of governments, they also play an extremely important role in influencing public opinion. In addition there are a number of paid lobbying groups in Ottawa whose job it is to get the ear of the government on behalf of those who hire them. While they will certainly lobby on behalf of any interest group, it is obvious that only a small number of groups have enough money to pay for such lobbying activities.

Much lobbying is also done on an informal basis. While it is true that few elected government officials and even fewer civil servants are actually members of the bourgeoisie, many travel in social circles where they will regularly come into contact with such individuals or their representatives. Corporate leaders and government officials mingle regularly at social clubs, political fundraisers, charity events, and so on.

It should also be pointed out that those who have more powerful positions in the economy are always taken into consideration by the state simply because of such power. A key goal of the Canadian state is to advance the economy, and that economy is, by definition, a capitalist one. In other words, true democracy is always limited by the economic power of the ruling class. Capital owns the productive units; capital owns the jobs. Businesses can threaten to move to other cities, provinces, or countries if their needs are not met. No political party that wishes to stay in office risks alienating the class with economic power in any major way.

Representative democracy in capitalist societies by no means guarantees accountability from political leadership; nor does it guarantee that political

> Civil government, insofar as it is instituted for the security of property, is in reality instituted for the defence of the rich against the poor, or of those who have some property against those who have none at all.
> —economist Adam Smith, 1776

> Representative government means, chiefly, representation of business interests…. It seldom happens, if at all, that the government of a civilized nation will persist in a course of action detrimental or not ostensibly subservient to the interests of the more conspicuous body of the community's businessmen.
> —Thorstein Veblen, 1904

> As in England, [media baron] Rupert Murdoch and his managers have for many years had their way with the U.S. regulators and political players…. Sometimes Murdoch has succeeded through aggressive personal lobbying, sometimes with generous campaign contributions…. He plays both sides of every political divide. The point, always, is to assure that those with power are pro-business in general and pro-Murdoch (or, at the least, indebted to Murdoch) in particular.
> —journalist John Nichols, 2011

> Speculation in the 17th century was a crime. Speculators were hanged. Today they run the state and the financial markets.
> —Chris Hedges, 2011

> Since the fall of Communism, free markets and free people have been packaged as a single ideology that claims to be humanity's best and only defense against repeating a history filled with mass graves, killing fields and torture chambers. Yet in the Southern Cone...the contemporary religion of unfettered freed markets was predicated on the overthrow of democracy in country after country. And it did not bring peace but required the systematic murder of tens of thousands and the torture of between 100,000 and 150,000 people.
> —*Naomi Klein*, The Shock Doctrine: The Rise of Disaster Capitalism

parties, once elected, will adhere to their own party policies. Indeed, it is becoming increasingly common for politicians to run on a specific platform and then either ignore or actually contradict their promises after they are elected. As a result, many Canadians have become cynical about politicians and the electoral process, and as already noted, many citizens—particularly the more powerless—do not even bother to vote. This, of course, gives increased power to the upper strata, which tends to vote in larger numbers, further eroding democracy.

The Need for Democratic Forms

In any discussion of democracy in capitalist society, an obvious question arises. If class analysis is correct, why doesn't the ruling class in capitalist societies simply maintain their power in the manner of slave or feudal socioeconomic formations; that is, why is there democracy at all?

Unlike agrarian societies, which have fairly homogeneous ruling classes, the upper class in commercial societies is highly diverse and segmented. Democratic forms, in which political parties compete within a narrow framework of electoral representation, allow differing sectors of the dominant class to compete with each other with little risk of destabilizing the entire system. In addition, democracy as we know it allows working people to feel a commitment to the very system that structurally disempowers them. Thus the tensions both within and between classes are reduced within the framework of representative democracy.

The reduction of such tensions is important if the capitalist market is to function. Wage and price fluctuations, strikes and protests, arbitrary government decisions, constantly changing regulations, and so on make it difficult for businesses to secure their profits. The owning class likes stability, and parliamentary or representative democracies seem to work best at providing such stability.

Limits to Democracy

Although the dominant class in capitalist societies prefers a democratic political form, there is no automatic relationship between democracy, even in its limited meaning of the electoral process, and capitalism. The central component of democracy that we usually take for granted—one person, one vote—has not always existed in capitalist societies. For example, the right to vote in Canada was only gradually extended. Prior to 1918, this right was generally limited to White males who were British subjects, and several provinces required literacy tests for prospective voters. Women in Quebec did not receive the right to vote in provincial elections until 1940;

in British Columbia persons of an "oriental or Hindu" background were disenfranchised until 1945, while Japanese in that province could not vote until 1948. Status Indians were first able to vote in federal elections in 1960.

Moreover, electoral democracy has not existed in a large number of developing countries around the world. Although the ruling class generally prefers some democratic form of capitalist rule, this is possible only under certain conditions. As Naomi Klein argued in *The Shock Doctrine* (2007), from the perspective of the owning class, there are times when a more repressive form of rule is preferable to democracy. This point will be addressed in more detail later in this chapter.

Thus the ruling class in capitalist societies maintains its power through what can be described as "carrot and stick" tactics.* In order to maintain social stability, ordinary people (in the developed world at least) are offered the "carrot" of representative democracy, civil rights, and some social welfare. When that fails, and people increasingly demand greater democracy or a larger share of the social surplus, then the "stick" of the repressive state apparatus is there to restrain them. This is the coercion function of the state, which is examined in more detail later in this chapter. But first we should examine the key role the state plays in promoting the economic interests of capital.

The Accumulation Function of the State

It is often presumed that the state plays little or no role in capitalist economic matters. In fact, direct government intervention in economies is often thought of, incorrectly, as socialism. It therefore may come as a surprise to learn that governments in every capitalist society are actively involved in their economies. Indeed, the market economy of capitalism actually *requires* such involvement.

The state is the regulator of capitalism. It sets the rules regarding economic activities, and in the long run those rules always favour capital. Moreover, because capitalist economies are unplanned and therefore subject to instability and crises, most people—even those in the ruling class—count on the state to limit its worst excesses, particularly those that might lead to major economic downturns. This was clearly seen after the economic crash of 2008, when the U.S. government, via the Federal Reserve, quickly provided trillions of dollars in bailout funds to a number of financial institutions that were deemed "too big to fail" (see Box 8.2).

Some might wonder why, in a capitalist economy, all economic activities aren't carried out

> It is beyond dispute that the development of capitalist enterprise has always been crucially dependent on significant state intervention.
> —*Harry Shutt*, The Trouble With Capitalism
>
> The rich and powerful turn to the government to help them whenever they can, while needy individuals get little social protection.
> —*economist Joseph Steiglitz*
>
> There is little doubt that the concentration of financial wealth in Canada is also leading to a concentration of political influence.
> —*economist Jim Stanford*

---

* The term "carrot and stick" means offering a reward (a carrot) while simultaneously threatening a punishment (being hit with a stick). This is how donkeys were traditionally made to pull carts.

by the private sector. Many activities have been undertaken by the state because, while they may be necessary for industry, they simply are not profitable enough for the private sector to run on its own (for example, the post office). Other enterprises have traditionally been owned or controlled by the state because they were seen as part of the public good and were therefore expected to be outside the marketplace (for example, the public education system and hospitals). Often the reason for public ownership was a combination of both.

Money Coming In: The Tax System

If there's one thing everybody loves to hate these days, it's taxes. What are taxes? Taxes are the mandatory payments people and businesses make to the three levels of government. Since states generate little wealth on their own, they must appropriate a portion of the socially created surplus value to carry out various activities. One part of these revenues is used to sustain the various components of the state itself (the civil service, police and military, judiciary, and so on). The rest is used for a variety of purposes, ranging from road and bridge construction to education and support for the arts. While, in theory, the state both collects and distributes moneys for the benefit of all Canadians, various levels of the state in Canada have consistently favoured corporations and the wealthiest Canadians.

Think About It

Although money collected from our taxes helps pay for such important things as health care, education, roads, libraries, and so on, most people today see taxation in a very negative light. It wasn't always this way. Why do you think this is now the case?

Governments take in money in a variety of ways, such as various direct forms of taxation, licensing fees, excise and customs duties, fines and penalties, and user fees, to name but a few. In Canada, different levels of government have access to different means of acquiring funds. Taxation can be described as either progressive or regressive. **Progressive taxation** occurs when citizens are taxed on the basis of their ability to pay. In a fully progressive taxation system, the more wealth or income one has, the more taxes one pays. With **regressive taxation** there is no connection between the amount of wealth or income one has and the tax one pays. Most people assume that Canada has a relatively progressive system of taxation. In reality, Canada's system of taxation has been, at best, only mildly progressive, and all levels of government have been moving to increasingly regressive forms of taxation. A 2011 report on inequality by the Organisation for Economic Co-Operation and Development noted that "taxes and benefits reduce inequality less in Canada than in most OECD countries" (OECD 2011).

The most progressive form of taxation in Canada, introduced in 1917, is that of taxation on corporate and personal income. Both federal and provincial governments use this form of taxation as a source of revenue.

However, while it is certainly more progressive than other forms of taxation—because, in theory, the more you earn the more you pay—the income tax system is by no means fully progressive. While supposedly taxing people and corporations in proportion to their incomes, there are so many allowable deductions and tax credits that the degree to which income tax can be described as truly progressive is limited. Of course, all Canadians are legally entitled to such deductions and tax credits, and some specifically benefit low-income earners. However, most credits and deductions—such as those allowed for investments, retirement savings plans, charitable donations, childcare expenses, and political party contributions—require an initial outlay of money, which lower-income earners lack.

As a result, primarily higher-income earners are able to benefit from credits and deductions. In addition, the federal corporate tax rate has been dropping. While corporations made 52 percent more profit in 2009 than in 2000, they paid almost 20 percent less in federal/provincial income tax (MacDonald 2011a, 2). These on-going cuts mean that the corporate tax rate will have dropped from over 20 percent in 2007 to 12.3 percent when they are full phased in by 2015. A large amount of tax cuts has gone to financial institutions. The value of various tax preferences and recent tax cuts—exemption from the federal GST, cuts to federal and provincial corporate income tax, and preferential tax rates for capital gains and stock options—totals approximately $11 billion a year for Canada's financial sector and is projected to reach $15 billion a year in 2014 (Sanger 2011, 4). In addition, approximately $1.4 billion in tax breaks and incentives went to the oil and gas industry in 2011 (Gue 2011).

It should also be noted that increasing numbers of Canadians are investing in countries with secrecy laws and may not be paying any taxes on the profits from such investments. About 20 percent of Canadian investment, valued at an estimated $100 billion, now goes through offshore centres (Murphy 2011) that are being used for profit laundering and so on so that taxes can be minimized.

> The bargain that Canadian governments made to provide Canada's largest companies with massive tax breaks in return for the promise of jobs and prosperity has not materialized. These companies are the ones that should be showing the best job creation results from corporate tax cuts because they get the biggest benefit. Instead, the most tangible result of those cuts is that corporate profits are up, government deficits are also up and Canada's biggest companies are laughing all the way to the bank.
> —David MacDonald, Canadian Centre for Policy Alternatives, 2011

> The growing share of income going to top earners means that this group now has a greater capacity to pay taxes. In this context governments may re-examine the redistributive role of taxation to ensure that wealthier individuals contribute their fair share of the tax burden.
> — OECD report, 2011

> Not since the Gilded Age plutocracy of a century ago has there been such a near-consensus as there is today in North America on the need to raise taxes on the rich.... We can have a discussion [about this] peaceably in school auditoriums across the country. Or we can have it in the streets. But there will be a reckoning, because the status quo is untenable.
> —David Olive, Toronto Star, September 2011, one week prior to the beginning of the Occupy Wall Street movement

Also worth noting is the size of corporate tax deferrals. While individuals are expected to pay their taxes in full at the end of each taxation year (or pay a substantial penalty), corporations are allowed to defer a large chunk of their taxes without interest. Although in theory these taxes have to be paid eventually, the reality is that when taxes are deferred, they are deferred indefinitely. As far back as 1980, the total amount of tax deferrals that had accumulated in corporate accounts was $24.5 billion, more than the entire federal deficit at that time (*Canadian Business*, January 1985).

There are many other ways that the various levels of government acquire revenue, all of them regressive. Taxes at the point of consumption (that is, sales tax) are increasingly being utilized by the federal and provincial governments. Since the tax is determined by the cost of the item rather than the ability of the individual to pay, sales taxes are clearly regressive. Likewise, property tax, the main tax employed by municipal governments, is not progressive for a variety of reasons—primarily, as with sales tax, because it is not linked to the income or wealth of the property owner. In recent years the federal and provincial levels of government have increasingly cut back on their **transfer payments** to municipalities, while at the same time downloading more functions onto them. This has meant that local governments, which carry an increasing burden for the cost of such necessities as education, welfare, policing, and public transportation, have been financially strapped and forced to cut back on social services.

Although not technically taxation, an increasingly popular way for governments to raise funds is via what can collectively be referred to as hidden taxes. For example, the fees one pays to use a government service is such a hidden tax. These include such things as public transportation fares, entrance fees to public museums and galleries, tuition fees, licence fees, and toll roads. Since this form of taxation appears as an optional fee for a service, it might be argued that one need not pay for the service if one so chooses. However, many user-pay services are essential to most citizens (public transportation being an obvious example). Such user-pay schemes are regressive because, once again, they are unrelated to the user's ability to pay. Hidden taxes are actually a double tax: having already paid taxes to support various government services, individuals are asked to pay again when they use a particular service. Obviously, lower-income earners are hardest hit by such schemes, and many end up excluded from some of these services. Lotteries, video lottery terminals, and gambling casinos constitute a rapidly increasing source of funds for the state. Overall revenues from gambling grew from $130 per Canadian over age eighteen in 1992 to $520 in 2008 (Marshall 2010). This is a particularly regressive way for governments to raise funds. While more high-income households are involved in gambling than poorer ones, those with low incomes spend a greater proportion of their incomes on gambling (Carey 2003). Although gambling is voluntary, this makes it no less regressive. Lotteries and other forms of gambling also serve the function of directing people to personal rather than collective solutions to structural problems.

Before leaving the issue of taxes, it is important to point out certain kinds of wealth in Canada that are not taxed at all. For example, Canada is one of only three advanced industrial nations to lack any inheritance taxes or taxes on net wealth. Even a modest inheritance or wealth transfer tax on the largest estates could add billions of dollars to government coffers.

Not surprisingly, as corporations and the very rich have seen their taxes decline relative to others, middle and lower income earners have had to absorb some of the losses. In other words, our entire system of taxation has become increasingly regressive. In the 1980s and onward, as middle- and lower-income Canadians faced a heavier tax burden—at the same time that wages stagnated—increasing numbers of them became sympathetic to the call for lower taxes. Once government funds shrank as a result of declining taxation, it was only a matter of time until governments claimed there was "just not enough money" to provide required public services. Indeed, some change theorists have argued that the main goal of tax cuts was primarily about justifying a dramatic shift in government priorities, as we will see in the next chapter.

Think About It

At the same time that governments were making our tax system more regressive, government officials and candidates in elections consistently started referring to us as "taxpayers." What is the difference between being a citizen and a taxpayer? Who is more empathetic to others, a citizen or a taxpayer?

Money Going Out: The Growth of Corporate Welfare

In recent years many Canadians have become hostile to people on social assistance because they mistakenly think that these individuals may be getting "something for nothing." In reality, social welfare is paid for by municipal governments and is only a very small part of their total budgets. In *Louder Voices: The Corporate Welfare Bums* (1972), David Lewis correctly pointed out that the real welfare recipients in Canada have not been those on various forms of social assistance, but rather the major corporations. Between 1982 and 2006, $18.4 *billion* in various forms of direct government assistance to corporations was authorized by the federal government. Of that amount, 39 percent ($7.1 billion) is classified as repayable. Less than 20 percent, or $1.3 billion, has actually been paid back (Canadian Taxpayers Federation 2007, 12).

In all capitalist societies, the state provides major financial support to its corporations. Therefore, support for "corporate welfare" is not limited to any one political party. If we examine policies at both the federal and provincial levels, all major political parties in Canada—including Lewis's own New Democratic Party—have allocated grants, loans, and tax concessions to those at the top. In theory, or so we are told, governments do this

The dominant narrative of the recent period has been one of reduced government interference in our lives, with the supposed goal of putting more money in the pockets of individuals and families as taxes are cut. In the United States, this has been the rallying cry of the Tea Party, and in Canada, the voice of political conservatism. What is little known, however, is that most of the groups calling for tax cuts are financially backed by the wealthiest capitalists, who have no trouble taking reams of money from their governments, either directly or through tax benefits.

During the election debate of 2011, Prime Minister Stephen Harper said: "If you raise taxes, you will hurt growth, hurt jobs and hurt revenue." But less money coming in means less going out. Federal spending as a proportion of GDP has been shrinking steadily, from 21 percent in 1983 to 13 percent in 2009. In 2001, all levels of government in Canada were spending about 49 percent of their GDP. By 2009, that had dropped to 38.5 percent, a loss of $152 billion in services annually (Russell 2010).

Whether it is "money coming in" to governments or "money going out" via various benefits, the data make clear that the key beneficiaries of shifts in government policy over the last forty years have primarily been the very rich. As we will see in Chapter 10, these reforms have led to an extreme polarization of wealth in our country.

In late 2011, the first-ever audit of the United States Federal Reserve—a quasi-private agency that is essentially the U.S. government's bank—revealed that it had made $16 trillion in secret bank bailouts between late 2007 and mid-2010. Overall, the greatest borrowing was done by a small number of institutions, including Citigroup, Morgan Stanley, and Bank of America. Banks based in countries outside the United States also received money (Cardinale 2011).

The question that must be asked is why governments keep telling us there's just no money in their coffers for health care, social spending, public education, pensions, and other social needs, but there always seems to be money available for those at the very top. If we think dialectically, we can also ponder the concerns of some mainstream economists that the capitalist world is heading down a dangerous path as a result of this massive shift of wealth, creating both economic and social instability. We will return to this issue in the final chapter.

because these corporations will create jobs. However, the data demonstrate that many corporations have received substantial sums of money even as they were losing money or actually reducing the number of jobs. If the true aim of governments were about job creation, they would be pouring money into the public sector, where labour-intensive fields such as health care, education, or social services would create many more jobs than in, for example, the biotechnology or aerospace sectors, which are among the major recipients of federal funds.

According to one analyst, the main role of governments in relation to the economy is to provide a favourable fiscal and monetary climate for capital to secure and increase its profits (Panitch 1977, 14). This involves a number of tasks, including underwriting the private risks of production by providing companies with grants, loans, subsidies, tax breaks, and so on. Governments also provide technical infrastructure for capitalist development—including state ownership and state construction of railroads, harbours, canals, power-generating plants, airports, and highways—when the costs or risks for capital are too high to undertake themselves. As well, both provincial and federal levels of government in recent years have regularly funded global trade missions to directly sell Canadian products to foreign buyers. Less obvious are the ways that governments create capitalist labour markets via control of land policy and immigration policy, and the way governments absorb the social costs of capitalist production, via such activities as environmental clean-up, welfare services, and health care.

Moreover, while the Canadian government continues to fund social programs, the proportion of the budget allocated to these expenses has been dropping. In 2007, Canada allocated just 16.9 percent of its GDP to citizen support through its social spending, ranking it twenty-third out of thirty-four OECD countries. One year later, it was ranked twenty-seventh in terms of infant mortality; in 1983 it had been ranked tenth (oecd.org). We revisit the issue of cuts to social spending in Chapter 9.

Money to the Military

World War II saw the development of a symbiotic relationship between government and the arms industry, which has continued to the present day. Dwight D. Eisenhower, then president of the United States, coined the term *military-industrial complex* to describe this relationship. In essence, the interests of the top military—to obtain the latest technology and equipment—and the interests of the corporate sector—to maximize profits—were merged. In the centre was the state apparatus, which, in effect, wore two hats. Not only did it set policy for both budget allocation for military spending and political decisions with regard to military activity, it was also the direct purchaser of military-related goods and services from private corporations. Moreover, the state, as we have already discussed, was not a neutral body: it consistently favoured capital.

While Canada has long had the image of being a peacekeeper, in recent years the federal government has vastly increased military spending. In the fiscal year 2010–11, military spending was nearly $23 billion, which is 61 percent—or $8.4 billion per year—higher than it was in 1998–99. Among twenty-eight NATO members, Canada is the sixth largest military spender, trailing only the United States, the United Kingdom, France, Germany, and Italy, all of which have much larger populations and economies (Robinson 2011).

Meanwhile Canada has actually *reduced* its commitment to global peacekeeping efforts. Canada now contributes just fifty-six military personnel to U.N. peacekeeping operations, making it sixtieth on the list of 102 military contributors. Our contribution in spending terms is equally tiny. Between 2001 and 2010, Canada contributed an average of $11.4 million per year. For 2010/11, the amount was just under $8 million (Robinson 2011)

Production for military use is big business, with global military spending estimated to have been $1.6 trillion in 2010 (Stockholm International Peace Research Institute). It is also a highly monopolized sector of business, with

> The magnitude of the means of violence and social control is unprecedented. Computerized wars, drones, bunker-buster bombs, star wars, and so forth, have changed the face of warfare. Warfare has become normalized and sanitized for those not directly at the receiving end of armed aggression.
> —sociologist William I. Robinson

very few corporations controlling the entire industry. One of the largest of these, U.S.-based United Technologies, owns Pratt & Whitney Canada, the second largest recipient of government funding between 1982 and 2009. It is worth noting that Pratt & Whitney has its own "vice-president of government affairs."

Unlike products such as clothing or household appliances, which are produced before they are sold in the marketplace, military hardware is manufactured only after contracts have been secured. As a result, there are no unsold products, and no wastage occurs. Moreover, companies often don't even have to compete for government contracts. The percentage of all military contracts in Canada that were classified as "noncompetitive" (meaning that the government didn't solicit multiple bids) doubled over two years, between 2004 and 2006, to 40 percent (Staples 2006). At the urging of military leaders, governments are often convinced to buy the latest technology, whether or not it is needed. Such technology, of course, rapidly becomes obsolete and must constantly be replaced.

Because such industries bring immediate commercial benefits, governments often become promoters of trade in military goods with other countries. For example, the Canadian government has sponsored trade missions, engaged in direct-marketing efforts, and modified legislation that would have limited some questionable overseas arms sales. It is estimated that Canada now exports between $5 and $7 billion in military and so-called "security" products per year. While much of this goes to the United States, Canada also has permitted military sales to repressive, undemocratic regimes (Sanders 2011).

Thus the Canadian government is tied to the global military-industrial complex in a number of ways. First, it sets government policy about participating in global conflicts, such as the war in Afghanistan, which increase our country's need for more military machinery; second, it purchases products produced by the major corporations for military use; third, the government gives large loans and grants to producers of military hardware and technology; fourth, money from the Canadian Pension Plan is now used for military purposes. In late 2003, the CPP had over $2.6 billion invested in military contractors. Almost a third of that was invested in sixty-five U.S. military corporations (Sanders 2004).

While the benefits of such policies to the owners of companies producing goods for military use are obvious, the costs to the rest of us are less evident. Of course, there is the clear moral concern that a substantial portion of our manufacturing base produces weapons of destruction that are increasingly being used in military conflicts around the world. It is also of some concern that governments, having spent large amounts on military expenditures, must continually look for uses to justify such expenses. But in straight economic terms, production for military use is also problematic. Such production is actually more capital-intensive than labour-intensive, which means that relatively few jobs are created for each dollar invested. Moreover, because it is either largely produced for export or stockpiled by the Canadian government, military hardware does not generate much of a spin-off effect to other Canadian industries. Thus excessive military spending does not benefit the average Canadian; rather, it is a key way in which the accumulation function of the state acts in the interests of the corporate owning class.

Coercion: The Repressive State Apparatus

When we are small, we learn to go to a police officer if we are in trouble, since the police are there to "serve and protect." Certainly, most of us would want to be protected from those who might want to physically harm us or do damage to our personal property. However, while in theory the police exist to benefit every Canadian, the reality is that their primary role has always been to serve and protect those with wealth and power. This role is not the result of some insidious or evil plot on the part of police officers but rather is a necessary part of all class-based societies. The state ultimately decides what is legal and what is a crime; determines, via the judiciary, who is innocent and who is guilty; and hands out the punishment for those found guilty. All advanced capitalist societies accept—at least in theory—the notion of the **rule of law**, a formally determined set of rules or principles that applies to all within its jurisdiction. In theory, then, the coercive component of the state is neutral and unconnected to class relationships. Whether you are rich or poor, unemployed or an employer, a corporation or a communist, all are supposedly equal under the law. In reality, however, class relationships impose themselves on the repressive apparatuses as they do in other spheres of the state. Indeed, the ruling class could not retain its rule without support from the coercive element of the state.

Although all societies have rules of behaviour and punishments for violations, it is only with the development of class societies that these rules come to be formalized as laws. Since agents of the state write the laws, it should not be surprising that most laws in any society will protect the interests of those in power. In all class societies, the majority of laws are linked to rights of property. In theory, the forms of property in law are not necessarily distinguished; that is, economic property and property for personal use are generally treated in the same way. In practice, however, those who own and control economic property are treated distinctively.

We saw in Chapter 7 that corporations are treated in law as if they are human beings in some ways, yet are privileged in other ways. For example, according to the Heart and Stroke Foundation, there are more than 37,000 smoking-related deaths in Canada each year. It goes without saying that any individual who killed that number of Canadians would be considered a mass murderer. Yet in 1995 the Supreme Court of Canada decided that the

Box 8.3 The Growth of the Prison Industry

The national crime rate has been falling steadily for the past twenty years, and in 2010 reached its lowest level since 1973. The homicide rate fell by 10 percent to a level not seen since 1966. Overall, the violent Crime Severity Index declined 6 percent in 2010, the fourth consecutive annual decrease, while the non-violent Crime Severity Index fell 6 percent in 2010, the seventh consecutive decline (Statistics Canada 2011c). Nonetheless, since the Harper government took power in 2006, the cost of the federal prison system has skyrocketed. When the Conservatives came to power, the system cost nearly $1.6 billion per year. Budget projections for 2013–14 are $3.147 billion, almost double that amount.

Building new prisons and expanding existing facilities are one reason costs are rising. Many of the new prisons are likely to be privately run. In addition, the cost for each prisoner is increasing. According to Correctional Service Canada's *2010–2011 Report on Plans and Priorities*, the cost for a male inmate in prison rose from $88,067 per year in 2006 to $109,699 in 2009. Since the Conservatives came to power, nearly six thousand more employees have been hired. The government's "crime-fighting agenda" has meant that inmates are now getting longer mandatory minimum sentences, having less chance of release, and are being kept under tighter security conditions. More are being kept in solitary confinement and are being kept there for longer periods of time, which necessitates more work for guards. Health-care costs of prisoners are also rising, particularly due to an outbreak of Hepatitis C across the prison system (Davis 2011).

In 2007–08, Aboriginal adults accounted for 22 percent of admissions to sentenced custody although they represented only 3 percent of the Canadian population. More than one in five new admissions to federal corrections is now a person of Aboriginal descent. Among women offenders, one in three federally sentenced women is Aboriginal (Therien 2011).

A report issued in 2009 by two experts correctly predicted that the Conservative government was planning to bring in an American-style prison system that would cost billions of taxpayer dollars and do little to improve public safety (Jackson and Stewart 2009). Unfortunately, crime control is fast becoming an entrenched industry and a political tool to address social problems such as addictions, mental health, broken families, poverty, and social exclusion.

tobacco industry's constitutional rights of free expression had been denied when tobacco advertising was banned in Canada. Thus corporations are treated as individuals with regard to their so-called rights, but not with regard to the consequences of their activities. Moreover, the state must pay the bill for all smoking-related health costs, family benefits to survivors, and so on.

Although in theory everyone is treated equally before the law, it is primarily those with money and influence who can get the best lawyers and present the strongest cases. Indeed, at all stages of the justice system—who gets arrested, who gets charged, who gets probation, who gets convicted, and how long the sentence is—socioeconomic status, in addition to the variables of race and gender, plays a role (Samuelson 1995; Brannigan 1984). An apt title of a popular book on the criminal justice system in the United States is *The Rich Get Richer and the Poor Get Prison* (Reiman and Leighton 2009). This issue is examined in more detail in Chapter 10. It should also be noted that in every society, including Canada, the police and other members of the repressive state apparatus are almost immune from prosecution regarding criminal acts carried out in the course of their occupational activities.

The repressive state apparatus also keeps watch over the behaviour of the population. It may come as a surprise that Canada has a long history of spying on its citizens. While every country has some form of spy agency, the activities of Canada's secret police have always been more secretive than most (Kinsman et al. 2000, 2). In theory, the purpose of citizen surveillance is to protect the state and its citizens from any threat. In reality, the RCMP, and later CSIS (the Canadian Security and Intelligence Service), has deemed anyone who even mildly challenges the status quo—because of either political or personal activities—to be a potential threat to the state. In 2007 it was revealed that during the 1970s Canadians were also spied on by agents of a foreign country, the U.S. Central Intelligence Agency.

Over the last century national security surveillance in Canada has included spying on trade unions, left-wing political groups, Quebec sovereigntists, First Nations people, peace activists, gays and lesbians, feminists, consumer housewives' associations, high school students, university students and professors, Black community activists, and immigrants. Files have been kept on hundreds of thousands of Canadians, very few of whom could actually be considered a threat to national security. In 2011, newly released documents revealed that extensive files were kept on Tommy Douglas, former premier of Saskatchewan and usually considered the "father of medicare" in Canada. In 2004, he was voted "The Greatest Canadian" via a nation-wide poll on CBC television.

Think About It

Why do few of us seem to care about governments spying on us, the living conditions of prisoners, or the general growth of the repressive state apparatus? Try to think in terms of how we construct a world of "us" and "them."

The issue of the state being able to spy on its citizens has become even more worrying in recent years as a result of new technologies. For example, many cities in Canada are currently expanding use of closed circuit television cameras (CCTC) on city streets. These cameras have been used extensively in Great Britain since 1994, and on a typical day, someone may be captured by cameras as many as 300 times. Many question their large cost, their invasion of privacy, and their limited ability to reduce crime. Others are concerned about the creation of a new "security-industrial complex," that is, the joining together of private data and technology companies with the repressive state apparatus, supposedly in the

> Though we tend to take it for granted, privacy—the right to control access to ourselves and to personal information about us—is at the very core of our lives. It is a fundamental human right precisely because it is an innate human need, an essential condition of our freedom, our dignity and our sense of well-being.
> —George Radwanski, The Privacy Commission of Canada, Annual Report to Parliament, 2001–02

pursuit of criminals and terrorists. Few of us are aware that every time we use a cellphone, computer, or a debit or credit card, we leave a record; our profile can be purchased by anyone for a small price. If a car or cell phone has a GPS system, it is easy to track its movements at all times. And by using Facebook and Twitter, we obviously transfer our private lives to the public domain, in spite of supposed "privacy rules." But few of us seem at all concerned about the growing ability of both corporations and the state to monitor our lives.

The law and the courts are another means of constraining dissent, and the judicial system in Canada has repeatedly been used to punish those who have opposed the ruling class or simply the status quo. Police have commonly been used to harass strikers, attack protesters, and—as under-cover agents—undermine legitimate dissent. In 1970, the Liberal cabinet of Pierre Trudeau—without seeking the approval of Parliament or even its own party ranks—invoked the War Measures Act, a powerful piece of legislation that removed the civil rights of all Canadians, to deal with a sup-posed "apprehended insurrection" by the Front de libération du Québec (FLQ). Evidence was later presented that the hardcore of the FLQ consisted of only a few dozen members, including a number of RCMP infiltrators. Of the more than 450 detained under the War Measures Act, few were ever charged with any offence (Finkel et al. 1993, 528).

A number of analysts have noted the recent advance of this process, referred to as the *criminalization of dissent*. While the repressive apparatus of the state has always been used to control those who oppose the existing power structure, the tendency to repress and criminalize dissenting voices has been increasing in Canada and around the world. This trend was first observed in Canada in 1997, when the RCMP used pepper spray to suppress a small group of peaceful protesters in Vancouver. The protesters, mostly students, were opposing the repressive policies of the then president of Indonesia, who was visiting Canada for an international meeting. Since that time, observers have noted that the RCMP, as well as provincial and municipal police forces, have all increased their repression of legitimate dissent.

The process of criminalizing dissent took a giant leap forward at the end of 2001, when the Canadian government, in line with many governments around the world, passed extremely repressive and anti-democratic legisla-tion in the wake of the attacks on the World Trade Center and the Pentagon in September of that year. Although the new legislation was passed allegedly to protect Canadians from the risks of terrorism, most analysts agreed that pre-existing Canadian law would have been more than sufficient to deal with a real threat. The fear of many civil libertarians and lawyers special-izing in criminal law has been that this legislation gave widely expanded powers to the repressive state apparatus, while restricting the civil rights of all Canadians (Daniels et al. 2001). One particular concern has been that the definition of what constitutes terrorism is so vague, and its sweep so broad, that it can potentially include certain forms of legitimate dissent.

Since 2001 successive Canadian governments have devoted an additional $92 billion to security expenditures over what would have been spent had budgets grown in line with pre-9/11 levels. A new "national security establishment" has been created that includes the departments of National Defence, Foreign Affairs and International Trade, Public Safety, and Justice, as well as the RCMP, the Canadian Security and Intelligence Service, and the Canadian Border Services Agency (Macdonald 2011).

Think About It
Did you know that one of the few people to ever be granted honorary citizenship in Canada, Nelson Mandela, spent twenty-eight years in a South African jail for terrorist activities as a member of the African National Congress? Have you considered that any Canadian today who actively supports liberation movements similar to the ANC in the 1970s could be charged under Canada's anti-terrorism legislation?

For most of us, these changes have little relevance to our lives. Indeed, most Canadians probably support strong anti-terrorist legislation, since few will ever be directly affected by it and since people want to feel assured that the government is protecting our security. But whenever expanded powers are given to the repressive state apparatus, all citizens should be concerned. Any one of us can be arrested unexpectedly or charged with a crime. Perhaps it is a case of mistaken identity, being in the wrong place at the wrong time, or having a friend or relative suspected of criminal activities. Such a possibility increases if we have physical characteristics or national origins that identify us with groups more often thought in these times to be "terrorists."

Forcing governments to be transparent and accountable to their constituents is an essential part of the democratic process, because it minimizes the possibility that individuals will act outside the law. Most people working in government agencies would rather go about their business without having to be accountable to citizens for everything they do or every dollar they spend. This is not necessarily because they are up to something evil, but simply because it takes more time and effort to be certain that every elected government official or public employee is acting within the law and according to accepted policies.

It is therefore worrying that Canada has seen an erosion of freedom of information in recent years. The 2011 National Freedom of Information Audit undertaken by Newspapers Canada found that federal departments and Crown corporations, in particular, made a mockery of the principle of freedom of information by delivering reams of unreadable documents in response to FOI requests. As the author of the study noted: "Attempts to access records to hold governments accountable become bogged down in long delays, demands for prohibitive fees and bureaucratic intransigence. Transparency has been far more elusive than the promise of FOI legislation would suggest" (Vallance-Jones 2011, 5). On a broader scale, attempts by the website WikiLeaks to expose a variety of secret government agendas from around the world via the release of documents has been met with the most extreme attempts to shut down the site and severely punish the activists behind it.

History has shown that governments—even those that may be relatively democratic—under certain conditions may arbitrarily move to more repressive forms of rule. Germany under the Third Reich was an extreme example of this process. As a result, any legislation that gives more power to the repressive state apparatus, even if that power isn't immediately evident, should be of concern to all. Dissent is an essential requirement of a democratic society, and without it any country will have moved toward becoming a police state.

What Is Fascism?

Fascism is one of those words that most of us have seen or heard on numerous occasions but could probably not define. At best, we might be able to link it historically to the governments of Germany, Italy, and Spain that came into power prior to World War II. Perhaps we might see it simply as some kind of dictatorship or autocratic rule. While both these points are partially correct, they are far from giving us the full picture of either the meaning or history of fascism. That is because most of us understand fascism as a political form but do not link it to a particular economic arrangement. However, fascism cannot be understood without linking it to capitalist economies. Stalin's regime in the Soviet Union may have been repressive but it was not fascist (Paxton 2004, 212). And although George W. Bush claimed to be fighting "Islamofascism" in the Middle East, groups such as al-Qaeda do not fit the classic definition.

Fascist organizations develop long before actually taking state power. Often they appear to be on the fringes of legitimacy, but at certain historical moments they win substantial financial and moral support from those with wealth and power who fear for their future in times of social instability.

Fascism is essentially capitalism in its most repressive, undemocratic, and militaristic form. Although the personal lives of ordinary citizens are strictly controlled and there is an obsession with crime and punishment, large corporations are able to operate in relative freedom and gain increasing control over the economy. Put simply, fascist societies are capitalist economies within a police state. As an ideology, fascism emphasizes a strong leader and a strong state, while opposing human rights, democracy, pacifism, and collectivism. It is often embedded with a notion of racial or ethnic superiority and is linked to some form of intense nationalism; it promotes fear—particularly of the "other"—in the general population. The term *fascism* derives from *i fasci di combattimento*, a movement led by Benito Mussolini that grew following World War I in Italy.

We saw earlier in this chapter that the owning class in capitalist societies prefers to rule when possible via a liberal democratic state form. However, there are times in history when this class, for various reasons, has forged alliances with fascist and other right-wing movements. This was the case in Italy in the early 1920s, as it was at that time in many other countries, including Germany. When the fascists took state power in these countries—which they were able to do as a result of large-scale financial support from the wealthy and powerful—organized labour was crushed, opposition parties and independent publications were outlawed, and most civil liberties disappeared. Hundreds of thousands of opponents were imprisoned, tortured, or murdered, and in Nazi Germany millions of innocent people were sent to the gas chambers.

> The liberty of a democracy is not safe if the people tolerate the growth of a private power to a point where it becomes stronger than the democratic state itself. That, in its essence, is fascism—ownership of government by an individual, by a group, or by any other controlling private power.
> —Franklin D. Roosevelt, President of the United States, 1938

> Fascism should rightly be called corporatism as it is a merger of state and corporate power.
> —Benito Mussolini, Italian head of state, 1922–1943

> Whatever fascist leaders say, fascism has never been opposed to capitalism.
> —Frank Cunningham, Understanding Marxism

Charles Higham (1983) uncovered evidence that it was not simply German capital that supported Hitler, but capital from major American corporations as well. These included General Motors, General Electric, Ford, and Standard Oil, among others. These U.S. corporations continued to provide support to Hitler right through World War II, when Germany was ostensibly America's enemy.

Fascism, while most often connected to Italy and Germany, can actually occur in any capitalist society under certain conditions. Fascism does not develop overnight. Rather, there is a gradual shift from a democratic to an undemocratic form of governance, with the growth of fascist beliefs and values. It usually expands during times of economic and social turbulence.

Fascist movements always present themselves as peoples' movements. Although fascism is ultimately of benefit to the ruling class, fascist political movements cannot take power without support from a wide section of the middle strata. As noted in an earlier chapter, at certain moments in history, these people—the "middle fish"—feel squeezed economically and are frightened by rapid social change or groups they see as outsiders in their midst. The underclass, the lumpenproletariat, may also be drawn into such groups. Fascist movements give people a sense of belonging, of moral certitude in uncertain times, and of protection against supposed "enemies" that have infiltrated their communities. It plays on the fear we so often have of "the other," and it promotes a simple and often appealing narrative of "us" versus "them."

The document issued by Anders Breivik in Norway in 2011, after his attack that killed seventy-six people, made clear his fascist orientation. But while this story made international news at the time, many more incidents around the world have been getting less attention. The combination of high unemployment and widespread migration (both legal and illegal) from parts of Africa and Asia has led to the recent growth of fascist groups in many parts of Europe. Just prior to the Norwegian attack, youths in Greece rampaged through a heavily immigrant neighbourhood in broad daylight, knifing and beating foreigners. Athens has since suffered a spate of hate attacks. In the previous year, the leader of a neo-Nazi group won a seat on Athens' city council.

Following the events of September 11, 2001, a number of analysts in the United States have argued that their country has been slowly shifting to a fascist form. Certainly, the rule of law in that country has increasingly been eroded; patriotism and militarism have escalated; more citizens are being spied on; and the repression of dissent has increased, among other things. Since the Conservative Party came into power in Canada—and certainly since winning of a parliamentary majority in 2011—there have been similar troubling shifts.

This chapter has demonstrated that our common-sense understanding of the state—the pluralist view that our governments act in the interests of all citizens—is not borne out by a detailed examination of state activities. While the three levels of government in Canada certainly do many things that benefit the average citizen, the overarching role of the state is to protect the interests of the capitalist ruling class. In the next chapter we will see how many of the benefits that Canadians have been able to win from their governments over the years are now being eroded. We will see how this process—happening across the developed capitalist world—must be linked to the recent transformations of capitalist economies in the era of globalization.

KEY POINTS

1. State structures arose with the growth of surplus and the consequent development of classes and exploitation.

2. In capitalist societies, the economic and political spheres come to be separated. The appropriating class gains enormous control over the productive process, while the state is assigned the social, or public, activities formerly carried out directly by the owning class.

3. A number of frameworks explain how states function. The main approach within the order theories is pluralism, while the change theories emphasize the class approach.

4. Pluralism sees the key function of the state as one of mediation, while class analysis sees the state carrying out the accumulation, coercion, and legitimation functions on behalf of the dominant class.

5. While capitalist societies, in general, have been more democratic than pre-capitalist societies, capitalist democracy is, at best, a limited form that must always be understood within the specific class relations of power.

6. Capitalist economies require active intervention from the state.

7. In recent years, there has been a dramatic shift by all levels of government in Canada to more regressive forms of taxation.

8. All levels of government in Canada, regardless of political affiliation, have provided a large degree of financial support—directly or indirectly—to major corporations.

9. The Canadian government supports the military-industrial complex more substantially than many people realize.

10. All capitalist states have a coercion function. No ruling class could retain its power without the ability to resort to the coercive component of the state when necessary.

11. Although all Canadians are, in theory, equal before the law, corporations are not held responsible for criminal activities in the same way as individuals. Moreover, those with money and influence are advantaged within the criminal justice system.

12. There has been a recent increase in the criminalization of dissent in Canada.

13. Capitalism in its most repressive, undemocratic, and militaristic form is referred to as fascism. Any capitalist society can shift to a fascist form under certain conditions.

Engler, Yves. 2009. *The Black Book of Canadian Foreign Policy.* Vancouver and Black Point, NS: RED/Fernwood.

Engler exposes the myth of Canada as a "peacekeeping" nation, showing how our governments have long supported the imperial powers, first Great Britain and later the U.S., and have promoted corporate interests around the world.

Glasbeek, Harry. 2002. *Wealth by Stealth: Corporate Crime, Corporate Law and the Perversion of Democracy.* Toronto: Between the Lines.

This work explains how owners and investors can legally hide behind corporations, enabling them to carry out heinous acts on the general population with impunity.

Kinsman, Gary, Dieter K. Buse, and Mercedes Steedman, eds. 2000. *Whose National Security? Canadian State Surveillance and the Creation of Enemies.* Toronto: Between the Lines.

This book provides a variety of articles detailing the long history of surveillance activities of the Canadian government, which has regularly and extensively spied on any citizen deemed to be a security threat.

Mallea, Paula. 2011. *Fearmonger: Stephen Harper's Tough on Crime Agenda.* Toronto: James Lorimer & Co.

The author, a criminal lawyer, argues that the new "tough on crime" agenda will cost a fortune but will do nothing to lessen crime. Indeed, it will actually expand the role of organized crime.

Roper, Brian S. 2011. *The History of Democracy: A Marxist Interpretation.* London, UK: Pluto Press.

An overview of the concept of democracy, from early Athenian and Roman times to the present. Alternatives to present forms of representative democracy are offered.

Parenti, Michael. 2010. *Democracy for the Few.* 9th ed. Belmont, CA: Wadsworth.

Although the data are American, Parenti's book is a highly relevant and readable examination of the link between economic ownership and political power.

Price, Stuart. 2011. *Worst-Case Scenario: Governance, Mediation and the Security Regime.* London, UK: Zed Books.

The author examines the myths and mechanisms used to advance the repressive state apparatus in recent years.

Sewell, John. 2010. *Police in Canada: The Real Story.* Toronto: James Lorimer.

A critical examination of policing in Canada by a former Toronto mayor.

9 Neoliberalism and Globalization

In This Chapter

- What is meant by the term *welfare state*?
- What is neoliberalism, and how did it lead to the decline of the welfare state?
- What is the relationship between nation-states and global institutions such as the World Trade Organization and the United Nations?
- What are some of the tensions that have resulted from the process of globalization?

Since early 2008, the developed capitalist world has found itself in a state of extreme economic turbulence. Most explanations for this situation—given the enormous control that the conservative elements now have over the media—are highly simplistic, putting the focus of the blame on the excessive spending of governments. However, the root of the problem is never addressed, and the narrative remains one-dimensional, focusing not on government spending to support the capitalist class but rather on spending that has been of benefit to the average citizen, such as health care, social services, and public services in general. The argument was made in the previous chapter that the state is a class-based institution, generally giving priority to the interests of the class with economic power. But if we think dialectically, we will realize that the three levels of government in Canada often do things that are of benefit to the rest of us. It is therefore important to take a closer look at the reasons for the rise in government social supports in Canada following World War II, and why such supports began to decline in the 1970s and beyond.

The Erosion of the Commons

Despite the fact that we live in a capitalist society—one in which the concept of private ownership of property is central—there are still a great many areas of life that have remained in the public domain. These areas have traditionally been considered out of bounds for private ownership or trade because they have been accepted as collective property, existing for everyone to share as they have for millennia. These elements are sometimes referred to as the **commons**.

This term, as noted in Chapter 4, was used in feudal Europe to describe the public grazing lands shared by all until the feudal aristocracy enclosed them in the eighteenth century to secure personal profits. However, this term has been revived in recent years. Today, the commons includes such natural elements as the air we breathe, the water we drink, the oceans, and the genetic matter of living things. It also includes our public spaces, our shared languages and culture, our informal community support systems, and modern technological developments such as the broadcast spectrum and the Internet.

As capitalism advanced, some components of the commons transferred to private ownership. In many parts of the world, the commonly held lands of Indigenous peoples were stolen from them and transferred to private individuals or companies. In spite of this trend, many peoples around the world remained outside of capitalist development and continued to survive through communal sharing of land and other natural resources.

Even in the developed capitalist world, many elements of society remained in the public domain and were socially valued. Governments of all levels in Canada built bridges, roads, tunnels, harbours, government buildings, public schools, libraries, water filtration plants, and so on. Many of these public works projects are renowned today as major architectural accomplishments of their time. In addition, many parks, beaches, and other Crown lands were kept from private development. The commons also includes activities undertaken by various levels of the state to serve the public good, such as health care, education, and sewage and water treatment, as well as care of the elderly, the poor, the unemployed, and so on.

Think About It

Graffiti artist Banksy has argued that it is corporate advertising that defaces our buildings and buses, while graffiti artists are actually trying to respond to these ads. Do you think that graffiti art is an attack on the commons, or, as Banksy argues, are they subversive political statements about the erosion of public spaces?

After the 1970s, the privatization and commodification of the commons became a major component of government policies, as we will see later in this chapter. Many Crown corporations—such as Air Canada, CN Rail, and PetroCanada—were sold to private companies at very low prices, and the management of some public corporations and spaces was also handed over to private companies. Many other aspects of the commons formerly thought of as unacceptable for private ownership or trade have now been transferred into the capitalist marketplace, and since 2008 this trend—occurring both within Canada and across the globe—has rapidly escalated.

The Growth of the Welfare State

There was a short period during the second half of the twentieth century when it seemed as if the commons—particularly with respect to its social aspects—was expanding and that governments were taking the interests of their citizens more seriously. It was a time of relative economic stability and improved living conditions for many in the developed capitalist world. For these reasons the period between approximately 1945 and 1973 is sometimes referred to as the "golden age of capitalism" even though it was far from "golden" for everybody. Nonetheless, the global economy expanded dramatically. The transnational corporation appeared on the scene and grew in size and dominance. The most powerful of the TNCs were based in the United States, although Germany and Japan became key players as well. The power of these new economic giants went far beyond the merely economic. With mass production and the global expansion of consumer goods came the spread of American advertising and American culture, and culturally related products from the United States (such as films, television shows, and popular music) became their largest area of export. Economic globalization led to cultural globalization.

During this period, what is commonly referred to as the *welfare state* expanded rapidly, with the Canadian government taking a greater role as a provider and protector of citizen well-being and security. To provide such benefits in a welfare state, the surplus value produced by workers is transferred to the state in the form of taxes and then given back to workers, not in the form of money, but through the provision of social necessities such as health care, education, unemployment insurance, old-age pensions, and so on. The state provides these services to us collectively rather than us having to purchase them in the private marketplace. The advantages for citizens are twofold. First, the state can generally provide services at a lower cost because of both its large size and its lack of a profit motive. (The obvious comparison here would be between the public health-care system in Canada and the much more costly U.S. system.) Second, a universal system maximizes fairness. The major cost of government services is paid from income taxes, which, as was explained in the previous chapter, is the fairest way that governments can acquire funds.

Because we currently live in a period where taxes are portrayed in an extremely negative light, we seldom ponder the value of government services, not only socially but also financially. If we receive something as part of a government benefit then we don't have to pay for it out of our real wages. Thus, it can be worthwhile to pay taxes to the government if the major part of it is returned to us in the form of needed services.

Think About It
Can you think of anything that is not currently part of what is provided by the government in Canada that might be worth having? (Here's one to get you started: free postsecondary education and grants for all qualified students.)

The obvious question that must be asked here is why the capitalist owning class—if the analysis of the previous chapter is correct—would suddenly have agreed to having a larger share of government funds transferred back to the workers, rather than continuing to resist any expansion of the welfare state as they did in the early twentieth century.

To make sense of this change of heart on the part of capital, it is important to understand the context in which it occurred. We must also recall that the owning class has both long-term and short-term goals. While the short-term goal is profit maximization, the long-term goal is maintenance of the system that allows it to secure its profits. It is this long-term goal that is of particular importance here. There were a number of serious problems that capitalists faced following World War II. One serious concern was the expansion and consolidation of the socialist world. Suddenly, the capitalist part of the world had to face the reality that the other (now expanded) part was trying to build a social system not dominated by capital. In a sense, the capitalist owning class had to prove that "its" system was the better of the two, and expanding the welfare state was one means of legitimating capitalist rule.

In addition, workers in the capitalist world were putting pressure on governments to help them. Many had just fought in defence of their country and now thought their country owed them something in return. Even those who hadn't actually gone overseas had suffered through a long depression and then lived through the deprivations of a wartime economy. Citizens had high expectations of their governments. Employers, on the other hand, needed these individuals—relatively "de-politicized" and eager to work—to fill the jobs in a rapidly expanding postwar economy. In this context, the capitalist owning class and organized sector of the working class reached what has been termed an "accord."

The main underpinning of this accord was an agreement that the state would act as a mediator in the struggle between capital and labour. Corporate leaders agreed—grudgingly and in a limited way—to recognize greater rights for workers and citizens and to accept the labour movement's demands for higher wages, collective bargaining rights, and an increase in social benefits. The labour movement, in return, agreed to accept the control of employers over production and investment, to confine class struggle primarily to collective bargaining in the workplace, and to isolate or expel radicals from their midst. They also agreed to work toward social reforms *within* capitalist political and economic structures instead of struggling for any type of more radical alteration of the capitalist system.

Organized labour saw this accord as a great victory. In the ten years following World War II, union membership in Canada rose from 24.2 percent of the non-agricultural workforce to 33.7 percent. Fringe benefits—including pensions, paid holidays, shorter workweeks, sick pay, and disability benefits—became more common for workers. The low unemployment rates through the 1950s and 1960s also gave workers more power because of their ability to negotiate improved wages and working conditions with their employers. However, as a result of the accord, unions became more mainstream and less radical.

At the same time that the state took a greater role in regulating workers, it also increasingly regulated capital. The notion of state regulation, known as **Keynesianism**, after British economist John Maynard Keynes (1883–1946), led to greater state intervention in the economy. Keynes was no socialist; after the crisis of the Great Depression in the 1930s, he and other economists argued that increased state intervention in capitalist economies was necessary to protect them from their own excesses, to control for the inevitable crisis of overproduction, and to reduce the instability created by capitalist business cycles. Following World War II, the owning class was more willing to agree to a Keynesian welfare state. The booming economy and growing productivity resulting from new technologies meant that profits could rise even as workers were able to get a bigger share of the social surplus. Indeed, the social safety net, creating healthier and happier workers, could actually help raise productivity.

Of course, every country has its own unique history, and the degree to which each country adopted Keynesian policies and expanded the welfare state varies. Europe, particularly the Scandinavian countries, saw a much-expanded social safety net, while the United States scarcely developed a safety net at all. While it is impossible here to detail all the reasons for the differences, the political strength of the working class in each of these countries was certainly a key variable in its ability to win social supports from the state.

Neoliberalism and the Decline of the Welfare State

Unfortunately, greater government intervention in the economy could not permanently eliminate the contradictions of capitalist economies. By the mid-1970s, the so-called golden age came to a rapid end as capitalism entered a permanent state of economic crisis. As a result, the ruling class tried ever harder to increase the rate of profit by introducing new technologies, downsizing corporations, merging, seeking additional benefits from national governments, and advancing globalization. New computer-based and digital technologies gave many TNCs increasing geographical flexibility and the ability to truly globalize—that is, to move capital to those global sites with the most favourable conditions for profitability. There was also a major transformation of capitalist economies, as increasing profits were sought not through production of goods and services as in the past, but rather by—to put it simply—manipulating money. This complex process—as noted in Chapter 4—is often encapsulated in the term *financialization,* and at both the government and corporate levels it involved taking on massive amounts of debt. The leader in taking on debt, ironically, was the financial sector itself (McNally 2011, 86).

In this context, the accord between corporate employers and organized labour collapsed. During this period, most capitalist governments shifted away from Keynesian policies to a new set of economic and political policies that were more favourable to the needs of major corporations. The combination of increasing rates of unemployment, stagnating wages, and growing global competition weakened the ability of workers to respond to the power of capital.

This new set of policies is referred to as **neoliberalism**. Neoliberalism is the rejection of the Keynesian welfare state and its replacement with free-market doctrines and practices. It is, in essence, the political side of the economic transformations discussed in Chapter 6, the alteration of political structures to fit the needs of global capital. The current period of global competition requires that capital institute an all-out assault on workers and ordinary people to protect its own interests.

The term *neoliberalism* links this approach to classical liberalism, such as that of Jeremy Bentham and John Stuart Mill, which saw government's role as minimal, the market as the central determinant of social values, and the individual as the core unit of society. When she was prime minister of Great Britain, Margaret Thatcher went so far as to state that "there is no such thing as society. There are individual men and women and there are families." However, although neoliberalism expressed strong opposition to government intervention, it was, ironically, national governments that advanced the neoliberal agenda. According to one author (McQuaig 1992, 13), the underlying goal of this agenda was straightforward: it was simply a massive transfer of wealth and power to the corporate sector.

For the average Canadian, this has meant a rapid decline in social benefits. Total government social spending in Canada puts it in the lower end of OECD countries. Indeed, if one excludes health care, it would rank close to the bottom. Canada now also ranks last among developed nations in spending on early childhood development (Rushowy 2007). As government supports have declined, particularly for the economically disadvantaged, there has been a widening gap between the rich and poor, as we will see in the next chapter.

There are a number of distinct but interconnected components to neoliberalism, which have been enforced around the world via what have been termed **structural adjustment policies**. These policies were implemented by the World Bank and the International Monetary Fund. Their purpose—in theory to help poorer nations advance their economies and to create a single global market—has in reality been to increase the private accumulation of capital on a global scale.

It is impossible in the short space of this chapter to give a detailed picture of all the elements that constitute the many inter-related aspects of the neoliberal agenda. However, a few key policy components of this process are important to note (see Box 9.1). In addition to the general elements of neoliberalism that can be seen in all advanced capitalist countries, there are also a few that are specific to Canada. First, our economy and military have increasingly become tied to those of the United States and

Box 9.1 Elements of Neoliberalism

- *"Free trade," global trading blocs, and international treaties.* As capital internationalizes, it requires economic rules and regulations that are international as well. Although often called "trade rules," they are really about the free movement of capital. Any legislation that gives protection to specific countries or individuals is weakened or eliminated.

- *Privatization.* Privatization involves selling off various aspects of the commons to the corporate sector as it seeks new sources for investment. This is particularly true in the areas of health and education, where billions of dollars can be made from for-profit services. Governments don't always fully privatize a sector but, rather, create public-private partnerships, or P3s. At their core, P3s allow corporations to make large profits while governments absorb most of the financial risks.

- *Deregulation.* Rules and regulations that were created to protect citizens or limit the rights of corporations are either eroded or cancelled. This includes legislation that protects workers, the environment, and national industries.

- *Decline in government benefits.* Government funding to many social programs is cut drastically. This includes spending on health care, education, old-age pensions, and various forms of social assistance such as welfare. It can also include cuts to public support for the arts. Eligibility for many benefits is severely tightened and the universality of certain programs is eliminated.

- *Shift from government support to charities.* Help for the poor and the sick as well as support for education and the arts are increasingly via voluntary, tax-deductible "gifts" rather than via government supports.

- *Tax reforms.* Changes to taxation are instituted that primarily benefit the rich and large corporations. Governments increasingly turn to regressive forms of taxation (such as sales tax and user-pay schemes) while cutting income tax, the most progressive form of taxation.

- *Attack on labour.* Legislation protecting workers and the workplace—for example, union rights, minimum wages, employment standards, and worker health and safety—is weakened or removed entirely.

- *Decline in democracy and civil rights.* Sweeping new legislation is created that gives vastly expanded powers to the repressive state apparatus, while legislation that protects the individual from arbitrary measures on the part of the state is weakened. Police become less accountable, while access to information about government activities declines. Funding cuts are made to human rights organizations, legal aid services, and groups defending the rights of the disadvantaged.

- *Decrease in the size and scope of the state.* As all the processes noted above occur, the size of the state sector declines. Any state function that does not further the ability of corporations to secure their profits is seen as "waste." As a result, governments reduce the number of agencies, and the number of workers in the public sector declines. The exception is the repressive state apparatus—including the police and prison system—which expands.

Source: McBride and Shields 1997; Teeple 2000.

its interests, while our sovereignty in all spheres has declined; second, the relationship between the provinces and the federal state has changed. More independence has been given to the provinces, allowing them to advance their own neoliberal agendas, while a few key federal powers—specifically those that enhance corporate interests—have been strengthened (McBride and Shields 1997).

While the elements of neoliberalism are separated out for the purposes of analysis, it should be made clear they are all are interconnected. To pick one example, with regard to postsecondary education, both the federal and provincial governments made massive funding cuts through the 1990s. As universities and colleges faced reduced funding, universities now increasingly rely on corporate and individual donations. In addition, tuition fees at most Canadian universities skyrocketed, while postsecondary institutions began to spend increasing amounts of time and money on private fundraising. Postsecondary education increasingly became market-driven, with most universities and colleges now advertising to attract students and research dollars. Faculty members now spend more and more time writing research proposals because there is less money to go around, and find themselves working harder in an increasingly competitive environment.

While neoliberalism meets the needs of the corporate sector *in general*, there can be occasional disputes and differences between different sectors of capital on specific issues. As a result of tensions between different sectors of capital, neoliberalism has not advanced in a straightforward and simplistic manner.

Canadians find themselves in a particularly difficult position regarding this agenda. On the one hand, since Canada borders the United States and is its biggest trading partner, there is strong pressure to adopt these policies as the economies of the two countries become harmonized. On the other hand, as a result of its distinct geography and history, Canada has always had greater dependency on state intervention as well as values that supported such intervention. Thus there is an ongoing tension between the traditional expectations Canadians have about the role of their governments and the new assumptions of a minimalist state that are part of the neoliberal agenda. However, few countries have been able to resist the global drive toward neoliberalism; whether they want to or not, most have increasingly adapted to the needs of the corporate ruling class.

Think About It

Do you think Canadians have a different attitude than Americans to changes brought about by the neoliberal agenda?

Selling the Corporate Agenda to Canadians

Despite the fact that the state's role is to advance a corporate agenda, the welfare state that expanded in the so-called golden age of capitalism certainly did provide many benefits to ordinary Canadians. How does the state subsequently cut back on such things as unemployment insurance, health care, public education, workers' rights, and care for disadvantaged groups? Why didn't more Canadians protest these cuts? If people are going to accept an erosion of their standard of living and an attack on those things they hold dear, they must be convinced that such cuts are being done in the name of a higher good and that everyone will ultimately benefit from such activities.

Starting in the mid-1970s, Canadians were bombarded with various messages from business and government leaders, as well as corporate-supported think tanks such as the C.D. Howe Institute and the Fraser Institute. The framing of messages was very one-sided and persistent. In the Trudeau era, the main issue was the high wages of workers that were supposedly the root cause of inflation. By the 1980s, the key issue became huge government deficits, which Canadians were told were going to destroy the future for young Canadians. Along with the deficit scare came the attack on public services, which people came to believe were inefficiently run by lazy and overpaid civil servants, followed by an intensive and prolonged campaign to promote tax cuts. All of these campaigns had a specific goal: to lower the expectations of Canadians about what the state could do for them.

Many myths were advanced to sell this negative view of the state to Canadians. One of the biggest myths, still being advanced to this day, was that the Canadian government had been spending too much on social benefits. The data simply do not bear this out. As noted in the previous chapter, Canada allocates less for social spending than most developed capitalist countries (OECD 2009). Moreover, Canada's largely public health-care system actually costs far less and is more effective than the privately run system in the United States. According to the OECD, Canada spent US$4,363 per capita on health care in 2009, while the U.S. spent $7,960. As well, in Canada, 100 percent of the population has some form of health-care coverage, compared to only 85 percent in the U.S.

The intense and constant promotion of the neoliberal agenda must be understood as part of the ideological hegemony of the dominant class in capitalist societies. It is not that Canadians are too dimwitted to understand their real interests. Rather, if people are repeatedly told by supposed "experts" that something is true, they are apt to believe it, at least in the short run, particularly if the issues are complex and the alternative view is not readily available. Moreover, with many people facing longer work hours, more stress, and stagnating wages, there is simply no time in their lives to be involved in political activities.

Globalization and the Changing Role of the State

The rapid expansion of globalization has forced social scientists to rethink the role of the nation-state in developed capitalist societies. In the past, the Canadian state has traditionally played an important role in nation building, in mediating squabbles between and within classes, in moderating the worst excesses of capital, and in promoting the specific interests of Canadian-based corporations. Social scientists are now debating the extent to which the state will be able to continue to play this type of role. Some theorists feel that the power of nation-states will weaken; others feel that nation-states will align themselves more closely with international capital, so that their role will change rather than decline.

In order to make sense of the changing role of the state, we should recall that, as explained in Chapter 4, the capitalist owning class has always had the need to expand beyond its own national borders. Capital moves around the globe to maximize profits, and those who own and control it turn to governments to help in that quest. Economic domination requires political and military domination, so capitalists turn to their governments for support. As capital expands around the world in an attempt to increase the rate of profit, the most dominant nation-states gain control over the economies of other nation-states. This is why it is more accurate to speak of the process as *imperialism* rather than using the benign concept of globalization. In the eighteenth and nineteenth centuries, England and the countries of Western Europe became the dominant imperial powers as they colonized many countries around the world. Direct colonial rule ended in the second half of the twentieth century, but most nations remained economically dependent on the larger players in the global economy.

Thus globalization is not a recent phenomenon, nor is it an inevitable process resulting from the expansion of trade. What has changed in the past half-century is that new technologies have allowed capital to move around the world in greater volumes and at faster speeds than ever before. While England and the Western European states were the dominant imperial powers in the nineteenth and early twentieth centuries, the United States became the pre-eminent imperial power, or empire, following World War II.

We saw in the last chapter that two key functions of the state are those of accumulation and coercion. As capital becomes increasingly global, both of these functions must be redirected to a certain extent from nation-states to organizations that are themselves global in scale. With regard to the accumulation function, a number of such bodies play a central role in advancing the needs of global capital. With regard to the repression function, the United States military has become the world's police officer. Both of these points require some understanding of the key role played by the United States, beginning in the second half of the twentieth century.

The United States as Global Superpower

From the period following World War II until the fall of the Berlin Wall in 1989, the world spoke of two contending superpowers, the United States and the Soviet Union. However, after the fall of the Berlin Wall and the subsequent break-up of the Soviet Union, it became clear that the Soviet Union had never been a match—economically, politically, or militarily—for the United States. In reality, the last half of the twentieth century was dominated by only one global superpower, and that power has continued into the twenty-first century, although some analysts are questioning how much longer this will last.

Prior to World War II, corporations usually turned to their governments for economic and military support as they expanded globally. However, the competition between these nations as each promoted their own spheres of influence inevitably led to outcomes—including internal economic problems and international wars—that were destructive not only to human life and property but also capital itself. Following World War II, corporations realized that they needed to reach an accord with each other so that the global capitalist economy could continue to expand without nation-based corporations destroying each other in the competitive marketplace. This New World Order, as it came to be called, was dominated by the United States.

At first, the United States government mainly represented U.S. capitalist interests. However, as corporations gradually merged to form transnational corporations, the U.S. government increasingly came to represent capital as a whole as well. Global capital now shared a common set of interests that went beyond narrow national interests, and the key goal was to create a single world economy of competing corporations (Teeple 2000, 54). The government of the United States played a central role in creating global structures that would advance that goal.

The Role of Global Institutions

In Chapter 5 we saw the ways capital tries to coordinate its activities through such organizations as the Council on Foreign Relations, the Bilderberg Group, and the Trilateral Commission. As was noted in that chapter, these organizations are not the outcome of some "secret plot" on the part of those with power, but rather reflect their need to act collectively on the basis of their shared class interests.

The post–World War II period saw the creation of a number of international agencies—dominated by the United States—that reflected the desire of capital to create global political, economic, and military structures as well as policies. On the military side, the United States became the dominant force in the North Atlantic Treaty Organization (NATO), formed in 1949 as the international agency to coordinate military operations of the North American and European powers. On the political side, the United Nations was created as an umbrella organization to help coordinate the activities of nation-states. While in theory it was a democratic body representing all nations of the world, in reality its structure gave dominance to the United States. Moreover, the U.N. was financially dependent on the United States, as were most of its member nations. The global economic dominance of the United States thus came to be reflected in its global political and military dominance as well.

On the economic side, a number of global agencies and institutions were created in the second half of the twentieth century. Recommendations from the Council on Foreign Relations led to the Bretton Woods conference in 1944, at which the World Bank and the International Monetary Fund (IMF) were created. Their goal was to help stabilize and integrate world economies, to develop programs that would allow for greater capital investment in the less-developed countries, and to create an international monetary system that would improve global capital flow. In recent years, both the World

Bank and the IMF have played a key role in imposing structural adjustment programs on the less-developed countries, as well as recommending austerity programs for several countries in Europe in 2011.

The World Trade Organization

Throughout this book we have talked about power existing in both the proximal (nearby) realm and the distal (distant) realm. One of the most powerful organizations in the distal realm in recent years has been the World Trade Organization (WTO). The WTO was established in 1995 as an international body that would effectively set the rules for global trade and investment. While few of us know much about this organization, it has had an enormous influence on our communities and our everyday lives.

Currently, over 150 countries, including Canada, are members. However, the real decision-making power lies primarily with the United States, the European Union, and Japan. The WTO is the administrator of a number of treaties that govern world trade, including the General Agreement on Tariffs and Trade (GATT), the General Agreement on Trade in Agriculture, and the General Agreement on Trade in Services (GATS). The WTO is in some ways the world's highest judicial and legislative body, with the powers of an international state. Its agenda is very clear—to open the entire world to the TNCs so that they can maximize profits, without constraints from laws or procedures of nation-states that might put limits on corporate goals. Not only is the WTO closely linked to a number of big-business coalitions, but also in many cases the WTO rules have actually been written directly by global corporations themselves.

While the World Trade Organization is clearly an effort on the part of big business to reconfigure world economies to its benefit, the competition between various groups—particularly companies within nations—continues. Large corporations still press their national governments to support them in the increasingly competitive global marketplace at the same time as governments are feeling the pressure to endorse free trade and the promotion of a variety of global bodies. Thus while the creation of various international agencies has helped minimize the worst effects of capitalist economies, including global wars, for more than sixty years, the underlying contradictions now seem to be escalating once again.

Moreover, despite the creation of a global entity to deal with trade issues, individual countries still jockey to maintain the interests of their own corporations. The United States has always had a strong isolationist tendency, and this has continued into the twenty-first century. Its ideology has always emphasized what is referred to as American *exceptionalism,* that somehow the United States is unique among the nations of the world. In this context, it is not surprising that the U.S. government refused to sign the Kyoto Protocol on climate change, refused to sign the treaty banning anti-personnel mines, rejected the Comprehensive Nuclear Test Ban Treaty, and unilaterally withdrew from the Anti-Ballistic Missile Treaty, which it had signed in 1972. It also refused to become part of the International World

Court and voted in the U.N. General Assembly to oppose limitations on both biological warfare and weapons in space.

However, although it has maintained its independence with regard to its economic and political policies, the United States became more international in its global military activities. Although such activities escalated rapidly after 9/11, the strategies for advancing such activities were first proposed many decades earlier. In 2003 the United States, with only a few allies and without support from the U.N. Security Council, began the war in Iraq. More recently, the United States has continued its military activities, often in coordination with international bodies such as the United Nations or NATO. But most analysts recognize that such activities—for example against Muammar Gaddafi in Libya in 2011—were essentially under the control of the U.S. military.

The United States as Global Police Officer

As noted throughout this chapter, the second half of the twentieth century saw the rapid expansion of the global economy, primarily to meet the needs of capital. Transnational corporations arose and rapidly expanded both in size and geographical reach, while international agencies were created to oversee and structure the new economic order. At the same time, however, some kind of repressive apparatus was required to guarantee that the creation of a global economy open to the needs of capital would go according to plan. This role was increasingly carried out by the U.S. military, with direct support from the U.S. Central Intelligence Agency (CIA) via a number of covert activities.

While we often hear that people around the world hate the United States because they oppose its freedoms, this is rarely the case. Unfortunately, the history of U.S. foreign interventions in the twentieth century has left a sad legacy in many countries. Leaders who have been assassinated with U.S. complicity since World War II include Mohammed Mosaddegh in Iran (1953), Abdul Karim Kassem in Iraq (1963), Patrice Lumumba in the Republic of the Congo (1961), and Salvador Allende in Chile (1973). From 1945 until today, the U.S. government has been involved in numerous

> From the halls of Montezuma,
> to the shores of Tripoli,
> We will fight our country's battles,
> on the land as on the sea;
> First to fight for right and freedom,
> and to keep our honor clean:
> We are proud to claim the title of
> United States Marines.
>
> Our flag's unfurled to every breeze
> from dawn to setting sun;
> We have fought in every clime and
> place where we could take a gun;
> In the snow of far off northern lands
> and in sunny tropic scenes;
> You will find us always on the job,
> the United States Marines.
> —*official song of the U.S. Marine Corps, written over 100 years ago*

> I spent 33 years and four months in active military service and during that period I spent most of my time as a high class muscle man for Big Business, for Wall Street and the bankers.... I helped make Mexico safe for American oil interests. I helped make Haiti and Cuba a decent place for the National City Bank. I helped in the raping of half a dozen Central American republics for the benefit of Wall Street. I helped purify Nicaragua.... I brought light to the Dominican Republic for the American sugar interests. I helped make Honduras right for the American fruit companies. In China I helped see to it that Standard Oil went on its way unmolested.
> —*Major-General Smedley Butler, U.S. Marine Corps, 1933*

attempts to overthrow foreign governments and to crush people's movements that have opposed their repressive regimes. In most cases it succeeded. In the process, millions of people have lost their lives and at least that many have suffered untold agonies and prolonged social dislocation. Since 2000, the United States military has intervened in Yemen, Macedonia, Afghanistan, the Philippines, Iraq, Haiti, Somalia, and Libya.

What is the goal of these actions? One author (Blum 2000, 13–14) argues that there are four key imperatives driving U.S. foreign policy:

- opening the world to transnational corporations, particularly U.S.-based ones;
- justifying and increasing the size of government military spending necessary to sustain the profitability of defense contractors;
- preventing the rise of any society that might serve as a model for economic independence by wanting to opt out of the global capitalist economy; and
- preventing the rise of any other government that might challenge U.S. economic, political, or military global dominance.

In advancing these imperatives, the United States has helped replace elected governments in many countries with repressive regimes and often supported or trained some unsavoury characters, including Saddam Hussein and Osama bin Laden. However, some analysts wonder if the U.S. has now entered an irreversible period of "imperial overstretch." As sociologist John Conway notes (2011), despite the fact that the U.S. armed forces are spread all over the globe and consume almost half of total world military expenditures, its recent military successes have been few. It achieved nothing in Iraq, and the prolonged military intervention in Afghanistan has in reality done little either to improve the lives of Afghani people or to protect the world from terrorism.

Moreover, the huge cost of these actions has played a major role in leading the United States into a major economic crisis. As one author (Mooers 2006, 4) notes, "Its superiority in firepower vastly exceeds its economic supremacy." In other words, the United States is no longer at the head of the global economy, and countries such as China—which holds $1.1 trillion of U.S. debt—and India are expanding rapidly. In addition, its growing need for natural resources can be seen, in part, in the desire of the United States to gain control of the major oil-producing regions of the world. With declining economic power, overwhelming military might has become the only way for the United States to protect global capitalist interests. The result is a permanent state of warfare.

Think About It
Why do you think we learn so little about the history of U.S. intervention in countries around the world? If we do hear of certain interventions undertaken by the United States, how are they portrayed?

Why have Americans and their allies, including Canada, accepted the huge cost—both in human and financial terms—of such a highly militarized society? Why has there been so little response to the global corporate agenda in North America? Why do so few of us even know about this agenda? The answer to these questions requires us again to remember the key role of ideology in sustaining structures of power.

We must start with something very simple: no government—whatever its political orientation—is going to justify its policies by announcing that it is doing something most people would find unacceptable. For example, no government will ever say: "We are going to war because we want to control the natural resources of that country," or "We are helping our transnational corporations expand." It is not hard to understand that when a government prepares a population to send its young people to their possible death, at great financial cost, it must always be done in the name of good, not evil.

Every government—including our own—justifies its push to war and conquest with positive values such as overthrowing dictators, bringing rights and freedoms to the country in question, or promoting the glory of a higher power. Earlier European and British imperial conquests were justified in part because they were said to be bringing superior Western civilization and religion to inferior populations. In the period following World War II, successive U.S. governments and the media promoted the notion of a world communist conspiracy in order to justify aggressive international policies. As late as 1987, just a few years prior to the fall of the Berlin Wall and the subsequent collapse of the Soviet Union, 60 percent of Americans agreed with the statement that there was an international communist conspiracy that was attempting to rule the world (Blum 1998, 12). Blum describes the way North Americans thought of this supposed communist conspiracy:

> A great damnation has been unleashed upon the world, possibly by the devil himself, but in the form of people; people not motivated by the same needs, fears, emotions, and personal morality that govern others of the species, but people engaged in an extremely clever, monolithic, interna-

At least 35,000 people worldwide have been convicted as terrorists in the decade since the Sept. 11 attacks on the United States. But while some bombed hotels or blew up buses, others were put behind bars for waving a political sign or blogging about a protest.... The Associated Press documented a surge in prosecutions under new or toughened anti-terror laws, often passed at the urging and with the funding of the West.... The sheer volume of convictions, along with almost 120,000 arrests, shows how a keen global awareness of terrorism has seeped into societies, and how the war against it is shifting to the courts. But it also suggests that dozens of countries are using the fight against terrorism to curb political dissent. The actual numbers undoubtedly run higher because some countries refused to provide information.
—*Martha Mendoza, Associated Press, 2011*

[After 9/11 in many countries] the approach was "the stronger the counter-terror laws, the better for the security of the world." But that was a serious mistake. Nowadays people are realizing the abuse and even the actual use of counter-terror laws is bad for human rights and also bad for actually stopping terrorism.
—*Finnish law professor Martin Sheinin*

tional conspiracy dedicated to taking over the world and enslaving it; for reasons not always clear perhaps, but evil needs no motivation save evil itself.

Now, re-read this quote, but instead of thinking of it as a description of how we viewed communism in the past, think of it as a description of how we view global terrorism today. Surprisingly, the description fits exactly.

With the socialist world in disarray, the United States needed a new enemy that would allow it to continue—indeed expand—its global activities on behalf of capital, and "terrorism" became the new code word for this enemy. That is not to say that there are no terrorists in the world. However, the term is used in particular ways for particular ideological outcomes. For example, the term terrorism excludes any acts of governments and their military that are able to inflict large-scale terror on civilians. It also excludes economic terrorism, such as trade embargoes, which may restrict food, medicines, and other necessities from reaching a population. Moreover, some terrorists seem more acceptable than others. For example, Luis Posada Carriles was convicted of planting the bomb on an Air Cubana flight in 1976 that took the lives of seventy-three passengers, and he was also likely responsible for the 1997 bombing at a Cuban hotel that killed an Italian tourist. He escaped from prison in Venezuela in the 1980s, and in 2005 he made his way to the United States. A U.S. immigration judge refused to extradite him to Venezuela on the grounds that he might be tortured there.

While the United States remains the world's foremost "global police officer," other countries—including Canada—have played important supporting roles. For example, Canada's military was a significant participant in the 2004 U.S.-led "regime change" in Haiti that forced President Jean Bertrand Aristide into exile (Engler 2009). The Canadian military was also an essential part of the "war on terrorism" in Afghanistan, which allowed the U.S. military to focus on Iraq. Both the Liberals and Conservatives justified Canadian participation in this war—and its concurrent escalation of military spending—by arguing that they were trying to help the people of Afghanistan. However, most analysts agree that conditions have seriously worsened for the Afghan people since 2001. Meanwhile, military spending has risen under the Harper government as Canada became more closely aligned with the United States. Canada will spend close to $23 billion on its military forces in fiscal year 2010–11, a figure 26 percent higher than in 1989–90 and 61 percent—or $8.4 billion per year—higher than it was in 1998–99 (Robinson 2011, figures adjusted for inflation). Like Canadian military spending, global military spending is now higher than it was during the Cold War. The largest spender by far is the United States, accounting for almost half of all military spending. No other country even comes close to the U.S. in terms of actual dollars spent.

Globalization: Growing Tensions

As the world is increasingly being integrated both economically and culturally as a result of globalization, there is a simultaneous tendency of countries in various parts of the world to experience growing internal tensions. Some of these tensions have led to long and protracted civil wars, "ethnic cleansing" of minorities, and the breaking up of nation-states into smaller units. Some countries have become what are referred to as *failed states*. Failed states can no longer perform basic functions such as education, security, and governance, usually as a result of violence or extreme poverty. Their failure can be the result of internal factors or intentional destabilization from foreign governments. When we look at the entire globe, it seems, then, that the world is both coming together and breaking apart at the same time. Both of these opposing tendencies can be linked to the rise of capitalism and its development into a global entity.

The concept of the nation-state is relatively new. Prior to the industrial era, most people lived in small communities, identifying primarily with their family, clan, or tribe. Groups of individuals who lived together usually shared the same language, religion, cultural traditions, and history. With the growth of capitalism and the nation-state, diverse groups of people had to be forged into a somewhat artificial entity called a "nation." In order for governments to create a loyal population, they actually had to create the nation, with citizens now being pressed to share a common language, history, and culture. War often played an important role in binding populations together, uniting diverse peoples and groups against a common enemy. The narrative of "us" versus "them" has repeated itself through all of modern history.

Canada provides an interesting example of how nation-states were forged from groups with extremely different histories, languages, and cultures that were not easily brought together. Two competing European peoples colonized Canada, with one of these groups defeated in war by another. Both played a role in conquering the Indigenous population. These historic residues left lingering tensions. In many parts of the world, as a result of war or conquest, national boundaries were arbitrarily drawn or re-drawn, and some cultural and linguistic groups suddenly found themselves living as minority populations in one or more nation-states.

Often, then, it was not particularly easy to bring together the various cultural groups within a single country, and underlying tensions remained. Usually the economic, political, and intellectual elite consisted mainly of one dominant ethnic, linguistic, or racial group. Under certain conditions, those with power used divide-and-rule policies in combination with every attempt to encourage traditionalism, tribalism, and superstition to divide and weaken the oppressed masses of the population. Many of the hostilities of the twentieth century and onward are rooted in the attempts of the ruling elite or the European colonizers to play one nationality, tribe, or religion against another—Tamil against Sinhalese in Ceylon (now Sri Lanka), Hindu against Muslim in India, Tutsi against Hutu in East Africa, and so on.

Another factor leading to increasing tensions around the world has been the large-scale migration of populations. As capitalism expands globally it creates "push-pull" conditions that lead naturally to the migration of populations. Sometimes this movement is within a country, as people who can no longer survive by agricultural labour are pushed into cities, where they hope to find work in expanding industries. In other cases, the migration is between countries, as people seek to better their conditions of life. In the case of Canada, aside from the Indigenous peoples, almost all of us are relatively recent immigrants or descendants of immigrants, going back less than a few hundred years.

Sometimes migration is forced upon people against their will. Probably the largest involuntary migration of people resulted from the slave trade, with untold millions of Africans forcibly transported to the Western hemisphere. Today in many parts of the world, millions of people are refugees or internally displaced persons who have had to leave their homes as a result of civil wars or natural disasters. Climate change is also having negative effects on food production in a number of regions, forcing people to migrate elsewhere. Meanwhile, many of the world's poor become victims of human trafficking and effectively become slaves against their will. One component of failed states is the massive movement of people, which creates major humanitarian crises.

While employers may benefit from the large influx of immigrants and temporary workers willing to take any job for relatively low pay, working people may have mixed feelings about the next wave of newcomers to their country. Not only are temporary workers often used by employers to drive down the cost of labour, but they have at times also been used to break strikes. Rather than blaming employers for using immigrants in this way, it is more common for people to blame the victim, seeing immigrants as the cause of a country's ills. Whether it is rising unemployment, rising crime rates, or a decline in traditional values, new waves of immigrants have often been turned into scapegoats to explain a variety of social problems.

Think About It

Ask family members and friends (even if they were once immigrants themselves) what they think about immigrants now coming to Canada. To what extent should immigrants be forced to adapt to Canadian ways?

Rapid social change brought on by the spread of global capitalism has also had negative consequences for the less-developed parts of the world. Here locals often view the inundation of modern Western values and culture as a serious problem. The fear of some people that their ancient traditions and religious beliefs are disappearing often gives rise to radical religious or nationalist movements. Ironically, some of these organizations and some of their leaders have received support from the United States, which saw them as a preferable alternative to local left-wing political movements that might have threatened the interests of global capital.

In sum, while the expansion of globalization draws increasing numbers of diverse populations together via a shared economy, culture, and governance, there is a simultaneous growth of tensions that pit groups of people against one another. These tensions have frequently led to the death or dislocation of large numbers of people. Once again we can see the ways in which capital seeks stability to carry out its activities, but in seeking to secure its profits, the outcome has often been instability.

Where Is Neoliberalism Headed?

The entire post-World War II period can be seen as a delicate and prolonged attempt to create a world that would be friendly and open to the advances of global capital. From the point of view of the ruling class, there have been innumerable successes. For the rest of us, the outcomes have been mixed. While many of us have certainly benefited from the development of a global capitalist economy, the costs have been high. Neoliberalism, the growth of the security state, increased militarism, and expanding global economic instability are just some of the negative consequences of globalization.

In Chapter 1 the concept of dialectics was introduced. If we think dialectically about what is currently happening around the world, we realize that it is possible that the neoliberal corporate agenda may be leading to the very opposite of what capital has been seeking. The major part of the twentieth century saw the state playing a larger and larger role in capitalist economies, primarily to guarantee their stability. If neoliberalism continues unabated; if the TNCs continue to increase their global power at the expense of national governments and people's needs; if public expenditures continue to be reduced with the consequent reduction in social benefits to working people; if environmental degradation and climate change are allowed to continue; if increasing numbers of people migrate as a result of starvation or ecological disasters; if capital can maintain its rule only through increasing repression and war—then the long-term viability of capitalist economies must be cast into doubt. We return to this complex issue in the final chapter of the book.

KEY POINTS

1. Although the state is a class-based social institution, all levels of government in Canada have provided many rights and benefits to ordinary Canadians.

2. Even though capitalism promotes the concept of private property, many elements of society remained in the public domain until recently. The public domain is often referred to as the commons.

3. The welfare state grew after World War II, as the capitalist owning class and the organized sector of the working class achieved an "accord" that was mediated by the state.

4. The decline of social reform began in the 1970s as capitalism entered a permanent state of economic crisis, and the accord between capital and labour began to collapse.

5. By the 1980s, most capitalist governments around the world began to shift to policies more sympathetic to the needs of the corporate sector. The package of changes is commonly referred to as neoliberalism.

6. From the mid-1970s on, Canadians were bombarded with a number of myths meant to convince them to accept fewer social benefits from all levels of government.

7. The nature and role of nation-states has been changing with the advance of a globally integrated capitalist economy, but social scientists are still debating where these changes are headed.

8. The United States has become the leading force—economically, politically, and militarily—in an increasingly integrated global capitalist economy. There is now some question of how long this dominance will continue.

9. In order to allow a single world economy of competing corporations to function properly, a number of global agencies and institutions were created in the last half of the twentieth century.

10. There is an increasing tension between the global dominance of the United States, with its propensity to act unilaterally in its own interests, and the need for countries to work together to advance the development of an integrated global economy.

11. The U.S. military has increasingly played the role of "global police officer" in order to ensure the creation of a global capitalist economy dominated by its own corporate sector.

12. Although there has been an increasing integration of people around the world, there has concurrently been an increase in tensions between groups of people, both within countries and between countries.

FURTHER READING

Butler, Smedley. 2010. *War Is a Racket: The Profit Motive Behind Warfare.* World Library Classics.

Originally published in 1935, this short book was written by a major general in the U.S. Marine Corps. Butler spoke widely about war profiteering and U.S. military adventurism, and from 1935–37 was a spokesperson for the American League Against War and Fascism.

Klein, Naomi. 2007. *The Shock Doctrine: The Rise of Disaster Capitalism.* Toronto: Knopf.

Canadian journalist Klein argues that neoliberalism thrives on wars, terror attacks, natural catastrophes, poverty, trade sanctions, market crashes, and other economic, financial, and political disasters.

Harmon, Chris. 2009. *Zombie Capitalism: Global Crisis and the Relevance of Marx.* Chicago: Haymarket Books.

This work applies Marx and Engels' work to the modern era, demonstrating—as the title notes—the continued relevance of Marxist analysis.

Harvey, David. 2007. *A Brief History of Neoliberalism.* London: Oxford University Press.

A concise history of the roots of neoliberalism, the reasons for its global spread, and the prospects for more socially just alternatives.

Lilley, Sasha. 2011. *Capitalism and Its Discontents: Conversations with Radical Thinkers in a Time of Tumult.* Oakland, CA, and Black Point, NS: PM and Fernwood.

These short pieces from various authors cover material in a manner that is highly accessible to readers.

McBride, Stephen, and Heather Whiteside. 2011. *Private Affluence, Public Austerity: Economic Crisis and Democratic Malaise in Canada.* Black Point, NS: Fernwood.

A timely examination of neoliberalism, the economic crisis, and the decline of democracy in Canada.

McNally, David. 2011. *Global Slump: The Economics and Politics of Crisis and Resistance.* Oakland, CA, and Black Point, NS: PM and Fernwood.

A thorough and up-to-date analysis of the world financial meltdown from a Marxist perspective, including some discussion of the possibilities of resistance to the crisis.

Parenti, Michael. 2011. *The Face of Imperialism.* Boulder, CO: Paradigm.

This short, easy-to-read book introduces readers to the concepts of imperialism and empire, explaining the role of the United States as the world's current global imperial power

Peck, Janice. 2008. *The Age of Oprah: Cultural Icon for the Neoliberal Era.* St. Paul, MN: Paradigm.

A fascinating examination of the intersection of U.S. political economy with culture over the past thirty years. It explains how the underpinning of neoliberalism was packaged and sold, not by the dominant class but rather by media stars.

Wood, Ellen. 2005. *Empire of Capital.* London, UK: Verso.

An examination of past empires in order to understand the present.

10 Inequality of Wealth and Income

In This Chapter

- Why is the gap between rich and poor growing in Canada and globally?
- How easy is it to move up the ladder of success in our country?
- What is the extent of poverty, and who are the poor in Canada?
- Is it true that "the poor will always be with us"?

Of all the topics students study in introductory sociology courses, probably the most emotionally difficult and controversial are those regarding various forms of social inequality. It is not that students are surprised about inequalities, either in Canada or globally. One doesn't have to take a course in sociology to realize that there are gross inequalities of wealth and status in our society. Rather, the debates regarding social inequality arise from disagreements about both its causes and its possible solutions.

While social inequality has obvious consequences for those who fall at the lower end of the economic scale, what is less obvious is that we *all* feel its affects. The work of Wilkinson and Pickett (2010) demonstrates that a variety of health and social problems—including mental illness, life expectancy and infant mortality, obesity, children's educational performance, homicides, and levels of trust—can all be linked to the degrees of inequality. The key variable is not the *absolute* economic level of a particular country, but rather the level of inequality within it. The higher the level of inequality within a society, the more these social problems occur.

Because social inequality affects so many aspects of our lives, it should not be surprising that it is a topic that dominates the discipline of sociology. Sociologists generally focus on the extent of such inequalities, whether inequalities are expanding or shrinking, and why inequalities seem to exist in every modern society. Order theorists have proposed a number of explanations for the existence of social inequality. Two approaches noted earlier in this book are the biological determinist arguments, discussed in Chapter 2 (and further discussed in Chapters 11 and 12), and the functionalist approach, which is explained in more detail in this chapter. While very different in content, both these theoretical frameworks conclude that social inequality is inevitable.

In contrast are the change theories, which link inequalities of wealth and income to the economic structure and class relationships. Change theorists accept that there will always be differences of ability among people. However, for these theorists the more important issue is how inequalities become structured in particular ways at certain times in history. Change theorists tend to emphasize the linkage of various forms of modern social inequality to the capitalist economic system, as well as to the structures and beliefs that arise within that system. Some of these theorists have also looked at the ways in which the recent expansion of globalization and neoliberalism has increased the divide between the haves and have-nots, both in Canada and around the world.

Because our society puts so much emphasis on the individual, it should not be surprising that most of us connect inequalities of wealth and power not to structural arrangements but, rather, to individual characteristics. Conversely, of course, inability to succeed is seen to be the result of some failure on the part of the individual. Without knowing it, most of us adhere to liberal notions of inequality. Liberalism, as we saw in Chapter 7, is the underpinning of almost all belief systems within capitalist societies.

Think About It

Why do you think most of us really *want* to believe that income and wealth inequality are the result of individual differences rather than being rooted in the nature of capitalist societies themselves?

The eighteenth and nineteenth centuries witnessed rapid social change, with the rigid feudal order gradually replaced by the new capitalist economic order. Throughout the feudal era, social inequalities were generally seen as the inevitable working out of God's plan; they required no explanation and certainly were not open to change. The growth of markets and of capitalist productive relations gave rise to a new way of thinking about social inequality. The new and expanding bourgeois class promoted the argument that anyone should be able to attain wealth, prestige, and power. The market, rather than an accident of birth, should determine one's place in the system of inequality, with equality of opportunity for all. The bourgeoisie, of course, was not opposed to structured inequality, but rather to their own exclusion from the highest ranks within such a system. Soon other people who saw themselves as marginalized or oppressed took up the rallying cry of the justice and equality that were key aspects of Enlightenment thought.

The essence of liberalism is fairness, in the particular sense of equal ability to compete. Life itself is seen as a marketplace in which all individuals get to compete for places in the status hierarchy. If we imagine all humans as competing in "the race of life," liberal ideology sees equality when everyone gets a chance to "run" in this imaginary race in the hopes of achieving wealth, prestige, and power. As everyone knows, there are always winners and losers in a race. Thus within liberal ideology, structured inequality is acceptable as long as the "race" for positions in society appears to be a reasonably fair one.

Change theorists, in contrast, argue that the "race of life" under the conditions of capitalism can never truly be fair. Like the "small fish" of the cartoon in Chapter 1, they feel that in capitalist societies "There is no justice in the world." These theorists do not advocate—as is often assumed—for total equality of *outcome*, that is, a world where everyone's social position and financial rewards would be exactly the same. These theorists agree that inequalities are necessary in any society, to reflect different levels of individual contribution and effort.

Rather, change theorists focus on equality of *opportunity*. For these theorists, true equality of opportunity is not possible in capitalist societies because a small number of individuals—those with great wealth and power—effectively control the competition between individuals, just as they control the competition between economic units. As a result, the race of life is set up in such a way as to prevent most people from winning. For

---

Box 10.1 Winners and Losers: A Core Capitalist Notion

Our society is so dominated by competition that it is hard for us to accept that it is specific to capitalist societies. While there may be some genetic component connected to our desire to compete, and while other societal forms certainly had competitive elements in them, capitalism is unique in having competition between individuals and groups as a core cultural value. In today's world we are surrounded by competition. Businesses—even the largest transnational corporations—constantly compete for markets, investors, raw materials, and so on. The political arena is also a hotbed of competition, with candidates and political parties spending more and more money to win our vote.

At the individual level, competition begins when we enter the school system, if not before. We get graded by our teachers and pass or fail our year. More and more school systems across Canada have introduced province-wide tests at the elementary level so that the schools themselves can be graded. By the time students leave high school they have begun to be sorted into winners and losers. Of course, this process continues in university, as students compete for grades, scholarships, bursaries, and

internships. Schools increasingly compete with each other to get top students, professors, research dollars, and donations. Once students graduate, they enter the work world, where they compete with each other for jobs and promotions.

In our spare time, most of us are at some point involved in competitive activities. This can range from sports—where there are always winners and losers—to electronic games and various forms of gambling. Some of the most popular television shows involve competition of one sort or another, from dancing to entrepreneurs pitching business ideas. Increasing numbers of awards are given out annually for the best films, books, music, plays, architecture, entrepreneurs, and so on. There is a "top ten" of the week for nearly everything, and you can even rate your professor. Whether the winners are actually any better than the losers is ultimately irrelevant.

Most of us do believe in fairness and do care about those less fortunate than ourselves. However—given our culture of competition—it is not surprising that most of us accept the idea that winners and losers are just a natural part of life.

---

change theorists, liberalism actually masks structural inequality because it gives the impression that everyone gets a reasonably fair chance to run the race. With this assumption, any failure to achieve wealth, prestige, or power appears be the fault of the individual.

Thus liberalism—like capitalism itself—is full of contradictions. On the one hand, it draws us toward such admirable goals as equality, democracy, and individual human rights and freedoms; on the other hand, liberalism helps mask the structural basis that sets limits on these very aspirations.

Symbolic Markers of Social Inequality

Humans are pre-eminently a symbol-creating species, and we have always symbolically represented difference, either between individuals or between groups. Once social classes came into existence, it became important for those who owned the means of production to distinguish themselves publicly from the masses that did not. With their control of the surplus, vast sums could be spent on clothing, housing, and other indicators of their place in the status hierarchy. In today's society—where most people live in large, anonymous cities and their place in such a hierarchy is unknown—the external markers of one's status become particularly important. Such markers are referred to by sociologists as **status symbols**. They refer not only to one's housing and manner of dress, but also to speech, mannerisms, hobbies, food preferences, favourite alcoholic beverages, and so on.

Such markers are socially created and can change over time and place. Indeed, in advanced capitalist societies, where cheap imitations of the symbols of wealth can be mass-produced very quickly, status symbols, particularly in the area of fashion and style, are constantly changing. Somehow people come to understand these shared meanings.

Think About It

It has been said that the automobile is the preeminent status symbol of capitalist society. Do you agree? Can you think of something you bought in the past month primarily because this item would impress others?

Many books and articles have been written detailing the lifestyles of various status groups, particularly those at the top. Such analyses are very much in line with the early theoretical work of Thorstein Veblen, an American economist who wrote about the patterns of what he termed "conspicuous consumption" of the "leisure class" (Veblen [1899] 1994). Veblen and other social analysts have argued that wealth comes to be reflected in something far more complex than simply social position, something we generally label "style" or "taste." Demonstrating to others one's place in the status hierarchy required, according to Veblen, both leisure and the consumption

> Blessed with riches and possibilities far beyond anything imagined by ancestors... modern populations have nonetheless shown a remarkable capacity to feel that neither who they are nor what they have is quite enough.
> —*Alain de Botton*, Status Anxiety

of conspicuous goods. Writing at the turn of the twentieth century, Veblen could have had no idea how accurate his analysis would prove. Today, mass advertising convinces us to buy more and more products that serve no purpose other than as status symbols.

More recently, a wide-ranging work by British writer Alain de Botton examined status anxiety over several thousand years. Botton was particularly interested in the high degree of such anxiety in today's society. Why, for example, do the very wealthy feel so insecure that they continue to accumulate totally unnecessary and ridiculously expensive material objects? Like Veblen, Botton feels that humans need affirmation from others, and in today's society wealth and material objects are the things that are valued (Botton 2004, 7).

Analyses such as those of Botton and Veblen are useful in explaining how human behaviour can be understood only by examining both our objective conditions and our subjective interpretations of these conditions. In other words, economic inequality always becomes embedded with cultural meaning. However, if we are not careful, such studies can direct our attention exclusively toward status differences and distinctive patterns of consumption and away from the key issue of class relations and inequality of power. We must always recall, therefore, that the underlying basis for structured inequality is more than style. Unequal allocation of our society's resources is the result of the private appropriation of surplus value.

Inequality: The Growing Gap

There are two key ways of measuring social inequality. The most common way is to measure differences in **income**, that is, the money that is acquired through wages, salaries, or various forms of government assistance. Social scientists can also study differences in **wealth**, which comprises all assets—including real estate holdings and money in bank accounts, stocks, bonds, and so on—minus debts. Most studies of social inequality tend to focus on income for the simple reason that data on income are more readily available. However, examining income alone ignores the fact that a small number of people can legally acquire huge amounts of wealth, not through their labour but via a surplus produced by the labour of others. Wealth, therefore, is more clearly a measure of true economic power and command over a country's resources (McQuaig 1999, 134).

There are few people in Canada who would argue for a society where there is no inequality of income or wealth whatsoever. The issues that interest most of us are whether inequality is moderate or extreme, and whether the gap between those at the top and those at the bottom is growing or shrinking. Recent data indicate—for both income and wealth—that the inequality gap in Canada has been growing over the last thirty years.

From the 1980s onward, all levels of government in Canada asked citizens to participate in a great social experiment. As we saw in Chapter 9, the shift away from the welfare state and toward a more free-market economy was promoted. Canadians were told that if the economy were allowed to expand, freed from government constraints, all citizens would benefit.

However, the data do not indicate improved incomes for all Canadians. Rather, what we see is a growing gap between the rich and everyone else. Between 1976 and 2009 the earnings gap between the lowest 20 percent and the top 20 percent of earners grew from $92,300 to $177,500, showing that income growth has been distributed unequally (Conference Board of Canada 2011). While we might assume that the top 10 percent has seen their incomes soar as a result of harder work, the data indicate exactly the opposite: everybody *except* the richest 10 percent of families has seen their work time in the paid workforce increase (Yalnizyan 2007, 21). Between 1997 and 2007, top CEOs in Canada saw their salaries increase by 444 percent (Mohammed and Hood 2009). In 1999 there were only twenty-three billionaires on the *Canadian Business* Rich 100 list; by 2010, the number had risen to fifty-eight (Potter 2011). In terms of accumulated financial wealth, the figures are even more dramatic. By the end of 2009, 3.8 percent of Canadian households controlled $1.78 trillion of financial wealth, or 67 percent of the total. This extreme inequality is unprecedented in Canadian history (Yalnizyan 2010).

A worrying trend is the growing generational gap in income. Of course, younger workers traditionally earn less, on average, than older workers. However, the 2000 census indicated that younger workers seemed to be on a consistently lower earnings track than older, more experienced workers. For men, this divide occurred at the age of forty, while the dividing line for women was the age of thirty (Statistics Canada 2003, 10). This trend is continuing, and it now seems that younger workers start their careers earning less than their counterparts who started work thirty years earlier and make slower progress for at least the first ten years of their working lives. Moreover, the proportion of youth in part-time jobs has risen, while many start work as volunteers or in a mentoring program without any income at all.

> Wealth begets power, which begets more wealth.
> —economist Joseph Steiglitz
>
> As a result of the increasing concentration of income and wealth at the top during the last few decades, the United States, Britain, and Canada have become extremely unequal societies.
> —Linda McQuaig and Neil Brooks, The Trouble With Billionaires
>
> The World is dividing into two blocs—the Plutonomy and the rest. The U.S., U.K., and Canada are the key Plutonomies—economies powered by the wealthy. We project that the plutonomies will likely see even more income inequality, disproportionately feeding off a further rise in the profit share in their economies, capitalist-friendly governments, more technology-driven productivity, and globalization.
> —Citigroup document, 2006
>
> The rich are getting richer, the poor aren't going anywhere and there are fewer people in the middle to mediate the two extremes. We ignore these trends at our collective peril.
> —Armine Yalnizyan, The Rich and the Rest of Us

According to a Government of Canada report (2010), recent immigrants are also more vulnerable to low income than other Canadians. Immigrants who arrived in Canada from 2000 to 2005 and were in economic families had a low-income rate of 32.6 percent in 2005, while those who were unattached had a low-income rate of 58 percent. An earlier study (Statistics Canada 2003, 12–13) showed that even after ten years in the country, immigrants still earned less than the average income earned by Canadian-born workers. This inequality persisted whether they worked in a high-skilled or a low-skilled occupation.

The economic downturn after 2008 served to expand this gap, particularly in countries like the United States that were hardest hit. Indeed, despite its core ideological belief in "the American Dream"—that the circumstance of your birth will not determine your life chances—the United States today has extremes of wealth and poverty and a decreasing chance of social mobility. The United States is now one of the most unequal of the economically advanced societies in the world (Wilkinson and Pickett, 2010).

Explaining Social Inequality

While pre-capitalist societies are relatively "closed" class systems, with economic inequalities based on heredity, modern societies are generally thought of as "open" societies, where one's class or status is based on merit. A society where advancement is based on individual ability or achievement is commonly referred to as a **meritocracy**. Without knowing it, most of us believe Canada is such a society. In a recent questionnaire, a sample of Canadians was asked what qualities they felt were essential or important to "get ahead" in society. Over three-quarters of respondents felt that a good education, hard work, and ambition were key variables. Coming from a wealthy family, as well as one's gender and race were least likely to be seen as essential or very important. Only 13.4 percent of those asked thought coming from a wealthy family was important to get ahead (Jedwab 2010).

Order theories generally see capitalist societies as meritocracies. One of the predominant order theories is that of functionalism. Functionalism (or structural functionalism), a theoretical framework that has been discussed in several chapters in this book, tries to explain how certain components of a society serve particular functions. It starts with the assumption that there are no sharp cleavages, such as classes, within a society, but rather there are simply differences of ranking or privilege. With regard to inequality, functionalists argue that since social stratification is so prevalent in various types of society, it must serve an essential social function.

In the second half of the last century, functionalist explanations of social inequality attained some prominence in North America. Such explanations essentially tried to demonstrate the value of structured inequality, primarily by showing how inequality guaranteed that the "top jobs" would be filled by individuals most qualified to fill them. Of all the functionalist analyses of structured inequality, the best known is probably that of Kingsley Davis and

Wilber E. Moore (1945). The Davis-Moore thesis, as it came to be known, sparked a great debate among sociologists at the time. While it is now largely rejected by sociologists, it continues to reflect the common-sense view that assumes that societies such as ours are meritocracies.

Davis and Moore looked at the division of labour to explain inequality. They argued that the unequal allocation of societal rewards, both material and social, is both universal and functionally necessary in all societies, since there has to be some motivation to get individuals in a society to fill the most important and difficult occupations. Some jobs require exceptional talent, while others require a long and costly training process. Thus the unequal rewards of the occupational structure ensure that all jobs that are "functionally necessary" for society are filled.

The functionalist analysis ends up being a circular one. In our society, where wealth determines value, salaries are assumed to be connected to job importance, whether or not this is actually the case. Those occupations that receive high salaries come to be *seen* as the most important jobs. This becomes particularly clear when we look at jobs that have historically been deemed to be "women's work." These positions—such as childcare worker, nurse, and social worker—have consistently been undervalued and underpaid, even though many require a high level of training and all are, without a doubt, functionally important. By ignoring the fact that both financial rewards and access to job opportunities develop within an already-existing structural inequality, functionalists turn cause and effect on their heads.

In contrast to the functionalist argument, class analysis argues that a true meritocracy is not possible within current social arrangements. This approach stresses the privileges held by those at the top of the social hierarchy, who are able to obtain the best education for their children in addition to making the important social connections that help them get the right jobs. These individuals also have easier access to money—through inheritance, family trusts, or loans—that help them get a head start. From this point of view, one's structural position is as much a determinant of success as, if not more than, any inherent capabilities one might have. Moreover, within the current arrangements of capitalist societies, certain status groups—the poor, recent immigrants, Indigenous people, women, people with disabilities, and racialized groups—have consistently been disadvantaged. Thus everyone does not have an equal opportunity to achieve wealth and power. Those born into privilege have a distinct advantage over those who lack it.

How do we explain the expansion of inequality in North America since the 1970s? Clearly many variables are at play, most of which can be linked to the rise of neoliberalism and the growth of globalization, as detailed in the previous chapter. If you re-visit the list in that chapter describing the elements that constitute the neoliberal agenda (Box 9.1), most of them— including privatization, deregulation, tax reforms, and government cuts to social programs—have led to a growth in social inequality. One key element is certainly the attack on labour that led to the decline of unions. For example, Western and Rosenfeld (2011) argue that the decline of unions in the United States accounts for one fifth to one third of the growth in men's earning inequality there.

There are a number of reasons why unions help reduce inequality. First, unions raise wages among less-educated and blue-collar workers. Second, collective bargaining standardizes wages within firms and industries. Thus, even non-union workers benefit from raises given to unionized workers, because employers often raise wages to prevent unionization. Third, unions in general promote norms of equity, struggling for fairness for low-wage workers while opposing the injustice of unchecked earnings of managers and owners. Lastly, unions bring workers together, raising their class consciousness and making them part of a political force for change. As unions have declined and their political influence has weakened, policymakers have fewer reasons to support unions or otherwise equalize economic rewards.

It should also be pointed out that wages are determined, in large measure, in the marketplace. In capitalism, as we have seen, there is not equality within this marketplace. For corporate owners, some jobs are of marginal interest to them, while others are highly valued. For example, few of the top-earning jobs in Canada are in the helping professions or the arts. Moreover, as noted earlier in this book, those in the very highest circles of corporate power can pay themselves outrageously high incomes and bonuses simply because they have the ability to do so. In recent years corporate compensation packages in Canada have grown enormously. In 1995, the average pay of Canada's fifty highest paid CEOs was $2.66 million, eighty-five times the pay of the average worker. In 2009, the average pay of the fifty highest paid CEOs was 219 times the pay of the average worker (Mackenzie 2011). Paul Desmarais, CEO of Power Corp, made more than $5 million in 1995; in 2007, it had risen to more than $29 million (Mohamed and Hood 2009).

Thus, for change theorists, while a hierarchy of inequality with rewards based strictly on merit is possible in theory, the nature of capitalism severely limits this possibility. The interests of the dominant class are to maximize profits and to maintain, in the long run, a system that will allow it to continue to do so. Financial compensation for work performed is not the result of some collective society-wide decision-making process, nor does it reflect either the quality of the work performed or its value to society.

The Degree of Social Mobility in Canada

The degree to which we will tolerate economic inequality of any kind in our society must to a fair extent be related to how we feel about our ability to move from a position with few rewards to one with greater rewards. Obviously, we may be willing to tolerate even major inequalities as long as we feel that we, or our children, will have a chance to move up the status hierarchy. It is important, therefore, that we examine the data regarding social mobility in Canada.

"*Actually, Lou, I think it was more than just my being in the right place at the right time. I think it was my being the right race, the right religion, the right sex, the right socioeconomic group, having the right accent, the right clothes, going to the right schools...*"

"Rags to riches" stories have always been part of North American (mythology, and people are generally fascinated by them. Such stories are appealing because, of course, if someone else can start with nothing and make it to the top, then so can we. Social scientists examine whether such stories are the exception or the rule. In order to answer that question, they study patterns of **social mobility**, or movement of people from one social position to another. Sociologists are interested in two forms of mobility: *intragenerational mobility*, which is the status change that occurs within an individual's lifetime, and *intergenerational mobility*, or changes between the occupational status of parent and child.

Such studies, both in Canada and internationally, indicate that mobility is certainly possible within capitalist systems, and mobility in Canada has historically been greater than in other countries. On the other hand, research in all capitalist countries has repeatedly indicated that achievement is not based on merit alone. People with some wealth and privilege are able to pass on their advantages to their offspring. Ascribed statuses such as gender, race, ethnicity, and national origin also affect the degree of occupational mobility.

In addition, it should be noted that most occupational movement is very modest. Only a small percentage of Canadians experience rags-to-riches mobility, and even fewer fall to the bottom from lofty heights. Thus the very top and the very bottom of the status hierarchy remain relatively closed, and most occupational mobility is mainly small movements in the middle. A Statistics Canada study (Corak and Heisz 1996) confirmed this finding.

Box 10.2 Planning for Your Retirement?

For most of you reading this book, the last thing on your mind is how you will live after retirement. When you get a job after graduation, it's unlikely that you'll even consider whether it offers you a pension.

Most young people assume they will automatically receive some kind of pension from the Canadian government after they retire. The government does administer a number of different pensions and benefits for older people. However, the amount that most people over the age of sixty-five receive is not substantial. In 2010 the maximum Canada Pension Plan (CPP) amount was $934.17 per month, although most people do not qualify for the maximum. There is also Old Age Security (OAS), which has a maximum of $524.23 per month if you've lived in Canada for forty years after you've turned eighteen. Some of the OAS can be "clawed back" by the government depending on your retirement income. Clearly, even those who receive the maximum amount of retirement income from government benefits are not financially secure, particularly if they live alone.

Most unionized workers also receive some type of private pension (which they partially contribute to during their working years) because their union negotiated this as part of their benefits package. In 2008, 38 percent of the labour force was covered by a registered pension plan (RPP), down from 45 percent in 1992 (Statistics Canada 2010f). However, many companies have recently ceased offering plans where a pension related to earnings and years of service is guaranteed. In its place, new hires are put into plans where retirement income depends on investment returns and no particular amount is assured. Moreover, most workers with registered pensions are in the public sector. These workers and their pensions are now falsely being blamed for the government's excessive spending, so it is likely that these pensions will diminish or disappear over the next decade.

For those without any pension plan or for those who wish to top up their occupational plan, there is always the option of private investment. Canadians have increasingly been told to plan for their retirements by investing in Registered Retirement Savings Plans, and the Canadian government encourages such private investment by allowing citizens to deduct the cost of RRSP purchases from their incomes, thus reducing their taxes. Not surprisingly, even with that incentive little more than a third of those eligible actually put money into an RRSP, with a median annual contribution in 2008 of $2,700. By the time of retirement, this will "buy" most Canadians a monthly pension of about $175.

In 2011 the Canadian Payroll Association released a study showing that 40 percent of Canadians are now planning on putting off retirement because they are struggling just to make ends meet. When asked how much they felt they would need to retire, almost two-thirds felt that they would need more than $750,000, with those between eighteen and thirty-four feeling they would need a million dollars or more.

The study tracked 400,000 men between the ages of sixteen and nineteen from 1982 to 1993. This study concluded that, while there is a good deal of movement on the income scale, the richest and poorest tend to inherit their income levels from their fathers. According to one of the authors, "You are three times more likely as a young man to move from rags to rags than rags to riches. And moving from riches to riches is the most likely of all" (quoted in the *Globe and Mail*, January 26, 1996, A1).

Think About It:
Ask older members of your family or your older friends how they are planning for their retirement.

Education and Meritocracy

At the core of our liberal belief in the existence of a meritocracy is the assumption that our education system will help to overcome ascribed status barriers and be the key to social mobility. Certainly the data do show that a university education is correlated with higher wealth and income on average, regardless of one's ascribed status. However, averages can mask particular cases. For example, one study of census data (Block 2010) concluded that racialized individuals in Ontario were far more likely to live in poverty, to face barriers to Ontario's workplaces, and even after they get a job are more likely to earn less than the rest of Ontarians.

The unemployment rate for racialized workers in Ontario in 2005—three years before the economic crisis hit—was 8.7 percent, compared to 5.8 percent for the rest of Ontarians. Racialized women made 53.4 cents for every dollar made by non-racialized men. Census data for first-generation racialized individuals aged twenty-five to forty-four who had a university education showed that they earned less than non-racialized immigrants of the same age and educational attainment. This research gives us a hint that the education system in Canada alone cannot eliminate existing inequalities.

Order and change theories agree that a key function of the education system is "sorting," as it channels young people into the different jobs required by society. However, the order theories generally see the process as a relatively straightforward one in which everyone competes within an educational structure that provides equality of opportunity. Change theories, on the other hand, see the school system as generally reproducing inequalities that already

> As early as preschool, children have a sense that certain students get their needs met more often than others, and that certain students get attention more often than others. Middle-class students are constantly asking for attention in a way that working-class students are not. So, even when the teachers are really trying hard to talk to everyone, they get interrupted a lot by the middle-class children and their attention is diverted.
> —Jessi Streib, "Class in the Preschool Classroom"

> As presently constituted, the educational system favours the already privileged, and screens out the already disadvantaged. Rather than defeating stratification, formal education is a cause of persisting and increasingly rigid stratification.
> —Dennis Forcese, The Canadian Class Structure

exist. Those with wealth, power, and prestige have an unfair advantage in pursuing success, and in most cases the school system simply serves to justify and maintain the already-existing inequalities.

The maintenance of inequalities comes about in a number of complex ways. Many students—particularly racialized individuals and those from lower socioeconomic backgrounds—are "streamed" into lower-level programs. In addition, exclusionary curricula, texts, and teacher-student interactions, as well as the overall culture of the school system, alienate many young people. Students (and parents) who do not see the school as their own are less likely to feel committed to it. Marginalization can create feelings of self-doubt and shame, which can interfere with both learning and motivation.

By the time we enter elementary school, economic inequalities have already had an effect. One study from the United States, for example, found that students from lower-income families entering kindergarten already had significantly lower cognitive skills than their more advantaged counterparts (Lee and Burkham 2002). Schools can do only so much to eliminate existing inequality of condition. As one study notes about children from low-income families, they are "less healthy, have less access to skill-building activities, have more destructive habits and behaviours, live more stressful lives, and are subject to more humiliation" (Ross et al. 2000, 2).

A Statistics Canada study (Frenette 2007) found that only 31 percent of those in the bottom 25 percent of the income distribution attend university, compared to 50 percent of young people in the top 25 percent. The study concluded that many factors influenced the probability of going to university. Those that mattered most were standardized test scores, high school marks, parental education, parental expectations, high school quality, and financial constraints. Youths from well-to-do families ranked higher on all these variables.

It would be unfair and inaccurate to attribute total failure to public education with regard to providing the key to social mobility. Certainly, more women, racial and ethnic minorities, and economically disadvantaged individuals are attending postsecondary institutions than was the case thirty years ago. However, it is unclear whether the patterns of the last thirty years will continue into the next thirty. Governments have massively reduced funding to education, while corporations have been gaining a more direct foothold in the education system. As noted in Chapter 7, dramatic changes to education seem to be leading increasingly to a two-tiered system—one for the privileged and one for everyone else. Such changes include the expansion of private schools, more "back to the basics" curricula, cuts to equity and anti-racism programs, more parental fundraising for individual schools, and an increase in formalized streaming and standardized testing. While all Canadians are affected by such changes, the most seriously affected are those at the lowest levels of income in Canada.

Poverty in Canada

What is meant by the term *poverty*? On the one hand, the question seems absurd—poverty is when you're poor! However, both social scientists and government bureaucrats require a more precise and empirical measure of poverty. The question is no mere academic matter, since the definition may affect who qualifies for various forms of government assistance targeted at the poor, or how humane (or how fiscally responsible, depending on the values being emphasized) a particular government appears.

There are two different ways of defining poverty. The first is referred to as *absolute poverty*. Using this approach, only those who are not getting their most basic daily needs met—that is, who are not able to acquire a minimum of nutrition, basic shelter, and adequate clothing—would be defined as poor. From this point of view, favoured by corporate think tanks such as the Fraser Institute, there are relatively few poor people in Canada. The second approach, which sees poverty more as a form of social exclusion, is referred to as *relative poverty*. In this case, those whose incomes are far less than the average in their locale are deemed to be poor, even if they are above the barest subsistence level. Using this relative definition, a much greater number of Canadians live in poverty.

There is no official Canadian government definition of poverty. The Statistics Canada annual survey of incomes probably comes closest to being such a measure, although it now has three different measures related to low income.* The best known and most commonly used measure of poverty in Canada is based on a set of low-income cut-offs (LICOs), below which people are said to live in "straitened circumstances." The LICO, a compromise between measures of absolute and relative poverty, determines a threshold below which families spend a disproportionate share of their income on food, clothing, and shelter. The threshold is calculated on the basis of what other Canadians are spending on their basic necessities and varies according to family size and geography.

The second measure, called the low-income measure (LIM), is a simple calculation that draws the line at half the median income in Canada. While not well known or used by social services or academics, this mainly statistical definition allows comparisons with other countries that often use this measure to express their rates of low income. The third Statistics Canada measure of low income is based on an absolute "market basket measure" (MBM) to define poverty. A shopping basket of basic life necessities has been developed, and those with incomes prohibiting them or their family from acquiring all the necessities in the basket are defined as low income.

Each of these measures produces different results. In 2009, the number

---

* It should be pointed out that data from Statistics Canada exclude those living in the Yukon, Nunavut, and Northwest Territories, as well as those in homes for the aged or prisons, and Indigenous people on reserves. Thus, the Statistics Canada data necessarily underestimate the full extent of poverty in Canada.

of Canadians living in low income was 3.2 million (9.6 percent of the population) as measured by the LICO, 3.5 million (10.6 percent) as measured by the MBM, and 4.4 million (13.3 percent) as measured by the LIM (Conference Board of Canada 2011).

The fact that there are three quite different measures of low income is a clear indicator that defining poverty is not as easy as it first appears. The definition is made even more complex in Canada because social assistance is provided primarily by provincial or local governments rather than by the federal government, although the federal government shares some of the costs of these programs via transfer payments from the one level to another level of government. The cut-off lines for social assistance vary from locality to locality. The current evidence, including the numbers of the homeless and of welfare recipients using food banks, indicates that the income provided by social assistance is inadequate to allow most families to get by.

It should also be noted that many people not officially defined as poor are also barely able to meet their basic needs. Such people, who do not get government assistance and who may even consider themselves middle class, are living from paycheque to paycheque, with no money put away for the future. The study undertaken by the Canadian Payroll Association (2011) found that 57 percent of respondents said they would be in financial difficulty if their paycheque were delayed even one week. The numbers were even higher for younger Canadians aged eighteen to thirty-four (63 percent) and single parents (74 percent). Some people survive by having several jobs. Paying for a university education is out of the question; a sudden illness, rise in mortgage rates, or unexpected emergency could push them over the brink into serious poverty. Many young people with low-income part-time jobs and large student debt loads are increasingly forced to live with their parents even after graduation. They may not think of themselves as poor because they see their low income as a temporary phenomenon.

The rapid growth of debt in Canada has also placed many Canadians in highly vulnerable economic conditions. Household debt reached a new high of $1.41 trillion in 2009 (Certified General Accountants Association of Canada 2010). The wealth of many Canadians is now tied up in housing, bought by taking out large mortgages. If, as happened in the United States after 2008, the economy collapses and there is consequent job loss, many middle-income families will find themselves in crisis.

Think About It
Obviously, few of us plan to be poor. Can you think of a number of unexpected occurrences that might push you into poverty at some point in your life?

Who Are the Poor in Canada?

At one time, those at greatest risk for poverty were the elderly. However, the age group now most likely to be poor is children. Although in 1989 the House of Commons passed a resolution to end child poverty by 2000, more than 18.4 percent were still living in poverty that year, up slightly from 1990. Despite being one of the richest countries in the world, more than one in seven Canadian children still lives in poverty. At 15.1 percent, Canada's child poverty rate ranks it thirteenth out of seventeen OECD countries (Conference Board of Canada 2010). Children and youth are 38 percent of food bank users in Canada although they are only 20 percent of the population (Campaign 2000, 2010).

Overall, racialized groups (most notably recent immigrants), Aboriginal people, and people with disabilities have much higher rates of poverty than the national average. In 2006, the median income for Aboriginal people was $18,962, 30 percent lower than the $27,097 median income for the rest of Canadians (Wilson and MacDonald 2010). The introduction of the Canada Pension Plan in 1965 virtually wiped out poverty among those over sixty-five. Seniors earning less than half Canada's median income fell from 36.9 percent in 1971 to just 3.9 percent in 1995. However, reflecting the stock market crash and stagnating government pensions, senior poverty climbed back up to 11.5 percent in 2009 (Conference Board of Canada 2011). Women in all categories are at greater risk for poverty than men, but it is particularly serious in lone-parent families headed by women. If there is a single factor that reduces the chances of ending up poor, it is having two wage earners in the family.

> When I feed the poor, they call me a saint. When I ask why they are poor, they call me a communist.
> —Brazilian Bishop Dom Helder Camara

> Thousands of accumulated studies have come to the same basic conclusion: The incidence of poverty is a severe—if not the most severe—threat to the health and quality of life of individuals, communities, and societies in wealthy industrialized societies such as Canada.
> —Dennis Raphael

> The challenge that we face lies not so much in finding ways to tackle poverty. The deeper and more difficult test lies in finding ways to reduce the widespread indifference to this deep and enduring problem.
> —Sherri Torjman, Caledon Institute of Social Policy

And while a large number of poor lack postsecondary education, the data do not support the fact that people are poor simply as a result of low educational levels. For example, a recent study found that in 2006, 18 percent of university-educated adults and 23 percent of college-educated adults aged twenty-five to sixty-four in Ontario earned less than half the national median employment income, $16,917 before taxes and transfers (Zeman, McMullen, and Broucker 2010).

Inequality and poverty are not new. What is of concern today is that the growing gap is making it harder for particular groups of "have-nots" to move permanently out of their state.

Why Does Poverty Exist?

The data in the previous section give us a clue that poverty, at least in part, is connected to a number of structural realities that go beyond personal inadequacies. An obvious source of poverty is low wages. Close to half of low-income Canadians work, yet remain poor. One in four workers earns $10 an hour or less. In 2009, the median annual wage after taxes for women

Box 10.3 How We Blame the Victim

In an introductory sociology class, students were asked to write a short response to the question "Why do we want to believe that street people asking for money are to blame for their own misfortune?" However, many students couldn't look inward at their own way of seeing poverty; instead, they simply explained why such individuals were indeed the cause of their own misfortune. Below are some sample responses. Notice the recurring themes of personal choice and that anyone can succeed if they want to:

- "I believe that if you are strong you can accomplish anything you desire."
- "There are opportunities out there, it is only a matter of taking advantage of it and take the first step."
- "I believe that the homeless are the cause of their own misfortune simply because they choose to live that way. We live in a country where we are taken care of by the government. Therefore there should be no reason, other than choosing to live like that, should someone be on the street."
- "If they really try to find work they can find at least some work to do. Even if they don't have education, still they can work somewhere, where you don't actually need any qualification."
- "Because they had the right to make their own choices, that's why they're in the circumstance of living on the streets."
- "How could one let themselves stoop to that level? One would not allow themselves to reach that social status, simple as getting a minimum wage job..."
- "The society that we live in today gives a chance to everyone to work and study. It is up to us to try and survive through these circumstances."
- "We want to believe that it is their own fault because it IS their own fault. They don't want to work and rather sit on the sidewalk and ask for money."

These students were not mean or heartless. Why do you think so many showed no empathy but rather blamed the poor for their own situations? Next time you see a street person, imagine that they are a relative or a friend. Stop and talk to them for a few minutes, perhaps asking them what happened that has put them in a situation where they have to ask strangers for money.

---

was $31,900 (Statistics Canada 2011a), which means that half of all women in Canada earned less than that. Another major source of poverty is the inevitable existence of unemployment. Without work, many must live on the margins of society. In addition, many workers, particularly women, cannot find affordable childcare and are therefore unable to work.

Poverty can be linked to the increase in precarious forms of employment, inadequate minimum wages, wage discrimination against recent immigrants, racial minorities, and women, as well as massive cuts to unemployment insurance—now referred to as Employment Insurance (EI). These cuts, introduced in the 1990s, drastically reduced eligibility to the point where only four in ten unemployed now qualify for benefits. Others exhausted their benefits before finding new work (Torjman 2011).

Declining rates of unionization, the decline of well-paid public-sector jobs, and the growing inability of Canadians to secure adequate incomes from fishing or farming must also be noted. In 2005, before the economic downturn, over two million Canadian families had a net worth of less than five thousand dollars; over a third of those had negative net worth (Statistics Canada 2010f).

However, few of us see structural realities as the causes of poverty. Instead we focus on certain inherent characteristics of those who are poor—their supposed laziness, lack of education, lack of ambition, and so on (see Box 10.3). Such an approach reflects the ideology known as "blaming the victim," first delineated by American author William Ryan in 1971.

Ryan compared this ideology with the views of biological determinists, who see social inequality as the result of natural differences. In contrast to biological determinism, the emphasis in the blaming-the-victim ideology is on environmental or cultural causation, and the analysis is couched in terms that may even display deep concern for the victim and a sincere commitment to reform. However, in the final analysis, the approaches of the biological determinists and the victim blamers end up in the same place.

In recent years, the term *poor-bashing* has been used to describe the process first noted by Ryan. It is not just others who blame the poor. What is particularly troubling about this process is that it is often the poor who blame themselves for their condition. With low self-esteem, the poor often turn to self-destructive coping mechanisms such as smoking, alcohol abuse, or substance abuse. With the poor internalizing the blame, it often becomes more difficult for them to get out of poverty.

Blaming the victim allows us to feel pity for the poor, while assuming that it is these individuals who must be changed if poverty is to be reduced. Across Canada the expansion of neoliberalism also saw the return of a nineteenth-century notion—the "deserving" and the "undeserving" poor. For those deemed by governments to be deserving—such as children, people with disabilities, and the elderly—a bare minimum of social assistance is provided. For all the rest, the state provides practically nothing. Help for the poor is provided on a "case by case" basis via charitable or religious organizations, with the onus being on the poor to prove they are deserving. In major cities across Canada, many of the poor—such as panhandlers and the homeless—have increasingly been criminalized.

Why the Growing Gap Affects All of Us

William Ryan notes that a major component of blaming the victim is the separating out and identification of a particular population of victims as a special group different from the rest of us. In his terms (1971, 9), we define

> Canada's Charter of Rights and Freedoms guarantees every Canadian security of the person. People who live in poverty do not have security of the person. If they live in hunger, their health and their lives are at risk. If they are homeless, they do not have physical or mental security. Poverty means that people do not enjoy their basic human rights.
> —*Free the Children Canada*

> Failure to tackle the poverty and exclusion facing millions of families and their children is not only socially reprehensible, but it will also weigh heavily on countries' capacity to sustain economic growth in years to come.
> —*OECD Policy Brief*

> Eradicating poverty is not only an ethical responsibility, but it also makes good economic sense.
> —*Canada Without Poverty/Canada Sans Pauvreté*

such people as "the Different Ones," who are perceived as "less competent, less skilled, less knowing—in short, less human." This attitude can be seen in the comments of students in Box 10.3. Of course, this tendency is not unique to current victim-blamers. Throughout history, the dehumanization of particular groups of people has been used to justify their abuse, maltreatment, enslavement, or even extermination. To return to a point made throughout this book, humans have the propensity to create a world of "us" and "them." The current demonization of the poor in Canada is part of a process that has allowed us to tolerate, and even actively support, government cuts affecting the most vulnerable in our society.

It is therefore important to point out that the economically disadvantaged are not different from us; they *are* us. At a psychological level, this is something that few want to hear. We want to believe that poverty is the result of a personal failing that, of course, we ourselves lack. Students in particular want to believe they cannot be poor. After all, they are laying out a large sum of money for tuition, something most have been told is an investment in their future—a protection against ending up as a "have-not." However, the reality is that any of us (or our relatives and friends) may at some time in our lives find ourselves just a paycheque or a divorce away from poverty, particularly if we are women.

Poverty means far more than simply the lack of money. It affects all aspects of an individual's life; it is linked to a number of variables, including mortality rates. People in the poorest income group in Canada can expect to have more children die before their first birthday, have more ill health throughout their lifetime, have more years of illness so severe it inhibits major activities, and die at an earlier age. These patterns are consistent with those in other developed capitalist countries.

It is important to note that international data indicate that the key variable to determining one's outcome in life seems to be the distribution of income within a society rather than the attainment of a particular amount of income. For example, Sweden, Norway, and the Netherlands—which have more equitable income distribution—also have the highest average life expectancies, while the United States—with its extremes of wealth and poverty—has the second-lowest average life expectancy among developed countries (Wilkinson and Pickett 2010). If we begin to see that poverty is a structural rather than an individual problem, then it becomes easier to understand how the existence of poverty affects us all.

In straight capitalist terms, poverty costs us all a lot of money. The costs of poverty come in two forms: lost output and diverted output. Lost output is connected to the fact that the poor represent, in economic terms, unutilized or underutilized resources. Not only are many of them not producing goods and services, but also with low incomes they are unable to purchase a variety of goods and services. Diverted output means that poverty adds costs to the economy that would not be required if poverty did not exist. These costs include additional demands on the health-care system; substantial costs for government to administer a wide variety of public welfare and assistance programs; large amounts of voluntary labour to assist the poor that could be put to more productive use; increased expenditures to protect individuals and property, as well as additional demands on the entire criminal justice system; and additional costs to the education system in its attempts to deal with children living in poverty. One study estimated that homelessness alone costs Canadians between $4.5 and $6 billion annually (Laird 2007).

It is also worth noting that there is evidence that inequality played a role in the U.S. financial crashes of both 1929 and 2008 (Wilkinson and Pickett 2010, 296–97). This is because inequality leads to increases in debt, as noted earlier in this chapter. Rising property prices made investment in property highly appealing for many at all income levels, although those with the lowest incomes could only do so by taking out dangerously high mortgages. The housing bubble grew bigger and bigger, and as we now know, when the bubble burst many people suffered.

The growing gap between rich and poor also leads to a decline of social solidarity, an essential component of civil society. In the United States, with its greater extremes of wealth and poverty, the middle and upper strata are increasingly moving into walled communities with security gates to keep the "unwanted element" out of sight and out of mind. Such communities can also be found in Canada. Greater equality means a more vibrant, socially integrated society.

… And the Poor Get Prison

As noted in the previous chapter, the entire criminal justice system—from what behaviours are defined as illegal to who gets incarcerated—favours the privileged and works against those at the bottom of the socioeconomic scale. Given the high poverty rates of Indigenous people in Canada, it should not be surprising that they are highly over-represented in the prison population. As noted in the previous chapter, Aboriginal adults accounted for 22 percent of admissions to sentenced custody in 2007–08 although they represented only 3 percent of the Canadian population; in Saskatchewan alone, where Aboriginal people make up 11 percent of the population, they constituted 81 percent of new prison admissions (Himelfarb 2011). One in three federally sentenced women is Aboriginal (Therien 2011).

It might be thought that the extent of poverty is of no interest to those in power. However, the poor and long-term unemployed may be seen as a threat to the stability of the capitalist system. They are not being well served by the current economic arrangement; in fact, they have every reason to oppose it. In addition, the poor make capitalism look bad to the rest of us. As the rich grow richer, many of Canada's largest cities are full of homeless people, making the extremes of wealth and poverty highly visible. In a more concrete way, the poor are more likely to commit petty crimes of property and make the middle classes afraid to visit areas

> Getting tough on crime often means getting tough on the poor, the troubled and the excluded...and this tough-on-criminals beast just gets hungrier the more we feed it.
> —Alex Himelfarb

where they congregate. Since poverty as a whole is not going away, it is now the poor themselves who are being made to go away.

This is not to say that those in prison are innocent (although some certainly are). Rather, it is to argue that the entire criminal justice system works against the poor, guaranteeing that many end up in prison. It is also worth noting that the United States, with one of the greatest extremes of wealth and poverty in the world, also leads the world in the number of prisons and imprisonment. In the United States, the number of people in prison quadrupled in just over twenty years, from approximately 500,000 in 1980 to more than two million in 2000. In 2008–09, its incarceration rate was 753 per 100,000 of national population (United States Bureau of Justice Statistics). Many of those in jail have been found guilty of minor drug offences, and a large number are either Black or Hispanic. As the Conservative government in Canada further advances its "tough on crime" approach to dealing with poverty, we can expect that our incarceration rate will move closer to that of the United States. When the Conservatives came to power in 2005, Canada's federal corrections system cost nearly $1.6 billion per year, but the projected cost for 2011–12 has increased to $2.98 billion per year. This represents a budget increase of over 80 percent (Davis 2011).

The current criminal justice system serves many positive functions for those with wealth and power within our system. First, our attention is directed away from failures of our social system and our inequitable distribution of wealth to the poor, who we fear may kidnap our children, break into our houses, and so on. During elections, many find a "law and order" platform very appealing. Second, it convinces the middle strata that the poor are deserving of their condition and that they are *not* "just like us." Third, it demobilizes the poor as a potential political force. Fourth, it brings down unemployment rates, as those in prison are not counted as part of the unemployed.

In addition, following the U.S. model, increasing numbers of prisoners in Canada are being exploited as cheap labour. Federal prisoners are currently making office furniture, textiles, and farm products, as well as doing printing and data entry work. Prison labour can be very profitable: wages can be extremely low because governments cover costs of food, housing, clothing, and shelter. There is also a growing trend—begun in the United States but now happening in Canada as well—to privatize prisons, creating what has been called a "prison-industrial complex." Thus, prisons are becoming a growth industry, and crime does pay—to the shareholders of companies that run private prisons.

Think About It
Listen to or watch newscasts over several days. How many stories are about crime? Why do you think these stories are so pervasive? What effect does this have on our view of the world?

Can Poverty Be Eradicated?

Because we see inequalities as linked solely to individuals, we lose sight of the fact that an unrestrained marketplace will inevitably lead to extremes of wealth and poverty. While the corporate elite secures ever-greater personal wealth, the majority is left to face the possibility of unemployment or underemployment, low wages, and inadequate social supports.

Moreover, capital will flow where it can get the best return on its investment. In the long term, the production of luxury items can generate greater profits than the production of necessities, because greater mark-ups can be attached to the price of the former. If capital flows out of the production of necessities, then, as a result of supply and demand, the price of necessities will rise. As the prices of these commodities rise, a certain percentage of the population will simply not have the "extra" money to pay for the increase. Such individuals will no longer be able to afford the necessities of life.

An example can be seen in the housing market. Governments at all levels have been letting market dynamics provide for housing needs—they have provided little publicly funded social housing, and all provinces have abolished or weakened rent regulation. When rents escalated rapidly in many Canadian cities, some people absorbed the extra cost by skimping on other expenses. However, for some, any increase was too much: they simply could not afford the increase, because they had no "extra" to draw on. As a result, some people were driven into homelessness. In 2007 there was a core of about 150,000 homeless people across Canada (Laird 2007). Others, not quite so badly off, obtained their rent money by cutting into their food budget. The highest rate of food bank use (867,948 individuals) since 1997 was reported in 2010.

The persistence of poverty must also be connected to the growing constraints that the corporate sector has placed on governments regarding any attempts to either redistribute wealth (for example, via taxation) or provide adequate social supports to the poor. Many social analysts have noted that one of the main functions of the welfare state (as described in Chapter 8) was to reduce inequality through a variety of social policies. It is not surprising, then, that the neoliberal policies that led to an erosion of the welfare state have also led to an increased disparity between rich and poor. Without the government to moderate the worst excesses of an unrestrained market, we are seeing a return to the unfettered capitalism of the nineteenth and early twentieth centuries.

While the total elimination of poverty may not be possible in any capitalist society, it is certainly possible to moderate it, if governments have the political will to do so (see Box 10.4). There are other actions that our government could undertake to make a more equitable society. One report concluded that federal and provincial tax credit programs for postsecondary students, valued at $1.8 billion annually, are not helping the neediest students. In fact, the entire system of tuition and education credits primarily benefits those from high-income families, who are more likely to attend

Box 10.4 Let's Not Blame the Victim: Government Actions Can Reduce Poverty

In 2011, the Caledon Institute for Public Policy proposed a number of concrete ways that the federal government could reduce poverty:

- Raise the Canada Child Tax Benefit from its current maximum $3,436 to $5,000 per child. Such an increase would raise the cost of the program from $13 billion to $17 billion a year. To make up this difference, abolish the flawed Universal Child Care Benefit and non-refundable child tax credit.
- Enhance the Working Income Tax Benefit for low- and modest-income earners. The maximum annual payment in 2011 is $944 for a single worker and $1,714 for a family. While this has improved in recent years, many working poor still do not qualify so further improvements are needed.
- Modernize Canada's social security system to meet the demands of a changing economy and society, starting with support for the unemployed. Maximum weekly benefits should rise to the pre-recession level of $570, representing 70 percent of insurable earnings, up from the current 55 percent. Ottawa should also create a new program that pays temporary benefits to jobless workers with low incomes who cannot qualify for EI, including the self-employed.

- Ensure that having a disability does not equal being poor. Our current disability income system leaves more than a half-million Canadians with severe disabilities on welfare and in deep poverty. A basic income plan should replace welfare for most working-age persons with severe disabilities, while provincial/territorial savings should be reinvested in disability supports.
- Support caregivers to people with disabilities. An estimated five million Canadians provide care for family members suffering from physical, cognitive or mental health conditions. To ease the financial burden on caregivers, the government should reform disability income, enhance work-related leave, and provide additional compensation for disability supports.
- Make good on the pledge to work with First Nations leaders to improve education on reserves and bolster high-school completion rates.
- Overhaul Canada's retirement income system. A two-fold reform is needed: Increasing the Guaranteed Income Supplement for poor seniors and strengthening the Canada Pension Plan. CPP reform alone would mean a real difference of around $4,500 a year to the average Canadian senior.

Source: Adapted from Battle, Torjman, and Mendelson 2011.

university (Church 2007). A much more effective approach to help less affluent families would be to give the same amount of money directly to students in the form of grants.

In addition, governments could improve market incomes by requiring employers to give workers a living wage, enhancing the ability of workers to organize unions, and granting part-time workers equal rights and benefits. Governments could also help increase the number of "good" jobs by, for example, expanding public-sector employment, rewarding those employers who provide well-paying full-time employment, and legislating a shorter work week. They could help families meet their basic needs by developing a national childcare program, increasing social and cooperative housing, expanding public transportation systems, and ensuring that all Canadians have equal access to health care and education. There is no lack of money to undertake these programs, and a return to a more progressive tax system would provide the financial means to build a more equitable and sustainable society. Even the OECD has called on the Canadian government to reform its tax and benefit policies to assist low-income groups (OECD 2011). Unfortunately, the notion that taxation is inherently bad is so widespread in North America today that no political party wants to risk losing votes by raising taxes.

Inequality on a Global Scale

Until this point, we have largely been discussing unequal allocation of resources and power within Canada. However, inequality also exists on a global scale. All of us are aware that there are countries in the world where life is much harder and the standard of living much lower than in Canada. These countries are referred to as underdeveloped, developing, the Third World,* or the South. The United Nations uses the term "less developed countries" (LDCs). Such countries share a number of common traits, including low per-capita income, high rates of unemployment, a large gap between rich and poor, unrepresentative governments, increasing populations, rural-based economies, and a high level of political instability

The explanations for the existence of inequality between countries mirror those for inequality within Canadian society. Hence, the biological determinists see the underdevelopment of some nations as proof that certain groups of people—notably those with dark skin—are biologically inferior. In contrast, the various liberal theories see global inequality as the result of some inherent disadvantage that keeps certain countries from fairly competing in the "race of life." While ostensibly neutral, such theories end up blaming the victim; that is, the causes of underdevelopment are linked to various tendencies within these countries. Such failings include overpopulation, corruption and nepotism, traditional cultural values, low achievement motivation, underdeveloped markets, low levels of technology, and so on. From the liberal perspective, if underdeveloped countries can be given help in overcoming such problems, they will move along the path to development and wealth.

Change theories, in contrast, focus on the

> Instead of reducing and flattening economic distinctions, globalisation has made them sharper.
> —Richard Florida
>
> The globalisation of poverty is unprecedented in world history. This poverty is not, however, the consequence of a "scarcity" of human and material resources. Rather it is the result of a system of global oversupply predicated on unemployment and the worldwide minimization of labour costs.
> —Michel Chossudovsky, The Globalisation of Poverty

---

* This term first appeared in the 1960s. It was used to distinguish the majority of countries in the world that were neither part of the developed capitalist West (the First World) nor the Soviet Bloc countries of the East (the Second World).

structural basis for global inequality. In this analysis, developed and under-developed countries are not compared to each other, but rather are seen as being in a relationship of structural inequality. Countries suffer from "underdevelopment" because of the massive export of surplus value from their countries to the developed world, which deprives them of the benefit of their natural resources and labour (Rodney 1972, 22). As Chossudovsky's quote notes, gross inequalities on a global scale result from the ongoing needs of the corporate sector. Just as inequalities *within* countries must be understood as relationships of power and domination, so must inequalities *between* countries be seen that way.

Change theorists argue that the problems noted by liberals are the *result*, not the *cause*, of underdevelopment. We have already seen that capitalism grew as a result of European expansionism. In this competitive process, the European nations seized territories in Africa, Asia, Australia, and North and South America. By the end of the nineteenth century, the European states had established total control over their territories, and the era of imperialism had begun.

The colonial powers were also active behind the scenes within the colonies to secure their political and economic control. First, they undertook to gain support from the most conservative elements in these societies. These included feudal landlords and royalty, traders who were often agents for foreign companies, and, at first, the small group of educated individuals drawn from the local population. At the same time, divide-and-rule policies—in combination with every attempt to encourage traditionalism, tribalism, and superstition—were used to divide and weaken the oppressed masses of the population.

The end of direct colonial rule did not change the situation of the less developed countries in any way, as their economies had become extremely distorted and dependent on the imperialist powers. Moreover, internal political instabilities, an impoverished or underpaid workforce susceptible to graft and corruption, as well as continued alliances between the imperialist powers and the local elites, meant little true independence or advancement for the majority of people in the Third World. Thus the imperialist powers, led by the United States in the second half of the twentieth century, retained effective domination over the poorest nations of the world through political, economic, social, military, and technical means.

The economies of the less developed countries, particularly those in Africa, have continued to stagnate, in large measure because of massive debt loads. A total of forty-eight nations, more than two-thirds of them in Africa, were classified by the U.N. as least developed countries (LDCs) in 2011 (U.N. General Assembly Economic and Social Council). The rating was based on several criteria, including per capita gross national income of less than $905. The U.N. report noted that despite some progress, the gap between LDCs and the rest of the world has been widening. The bottom line for the debt-ridden poorest nations is that, to pay off their debts, they are now exporting more wealth than they receive from abroad. Moreover, it was estimated that some 64 million more people would be living in extreme poverty in 2010 because of the economic crisis of 2008–09 (World Bank 2010), a crisis that was created in the economically developed countries.

Just as there has been an increase in the gap between the "haves" and "have-nots" within capitalist countries, there has also been an increasing gap between the "have" and "have-not" countries, and economic conditions in the less developed countries continue to be bleak. Although a small number of the LDCs, such as China and India, have seen their overall economies grow as a result of an integrating world economy, globalization and trade liberalization have not improved the lives of the majority of people around the globe. Moreover, in countries such as China a rapidly developing economy has led to a massive growth in disparity between the rich and poor *within* that country, particularly a disparity between rural and urban populations. It should also be noted that the poor countries are most vulnerable to growing environmental risks resulting from extreme weather conditions caused by climate change. In 2011, as a result of both natural disaster (extreme draught) and economic conditions (extreme poverty), Somalians were forced deal with the worst crisis in sixty years by fleeing to refugee camps in Kenya and Ethiopia. Parts of neighbouring Kenya, Ethiopia, and Djibouti were also suffering from severe food insecurity. At that time, over 12 million people throughout the Horn of Africa were in need of lifesaving assistance.

Imperialism—the more precise term for what is commonly known as globalization—is not, in the end, a relationship between nations. Rather, it is the same unequal class relations found within capitalist economies but on an international scale. Working people in the developed capitalist world are not the beneficiaries of imperialism. While some small amount of the total wealth taken from the developing world may return to some workers in the form of higher wages, cheaper goods, or better working conditions, the ultimate beneficiary is the capitalist owning class. Thus all inequalities of wealth and income—whether within countries or between them—must be understood within a particular set of class relations.

KEY POINTS

1. Because we live in a society that puts so much emphasis on the individual, we usually connect social inequalities to individual characteristics rather than to structural arrangements.

2. Humans have always symbolically represented differences between groups or individuals. In capitalist societies, mass advertising convinces us to buy products that serve as symbols of high status.

3. Liberalism, the dominant ideology of capitalism, stresses fairness and equality of opportunity but actually masks structural inequality.

4. Functionalist theories argue that unequal allocation of societal rewards is both universal and necessary in all societies. Change theorists, on the other hand, argue that structured inequality unfairly advantages those at the top, while the majority do not benefit from such arrangements. From the class perspective a true meritocracy cannot exist in capitalist societies.

5. Movement from one social position to another is referred to as social mobility. While some upward mobility is possible in Canada, most mobility is occupational, relatively modest, and occurs within the "mass middle."

6. Although education is assumed to be the primary agent of social equalization, in reality it more or less sustains the already-existing inequalities of socioeconomic status, race, and gender. In today's economic climate, it is likely that such inequalities will increase.

7. There is no single definition of poverty in Canada, although Statistics Canada creates low-income cut-offs (LICOs); individuals and families below these cut-offs are said to be in "straitened circumstances." Social assistance is provided mainly by the provinces, and cut-off lines are fairly arbitrary.

8. Poverty is not equally distributed across all groups in Canada. Racialized groups (most notably recent immigrants), Indigenous people, and people with disabilities have much higher rates of poverty than the national average. Poverty rates are also higher than average among female-headed lone-parent families with dependent children.

9. The ideology referred to as "blaming the victim" directs our attention to the poor and their particular environments as the cause of poverty. In reality, poverty is the inevitable result of the economic arrangements within capitalist societies.

10. It is possible for governments to reduce the degree of social inequality in Canada.

11. Inequality also exists on a global scale. Like inequality within nation-states, global inequality must be understood within particular class relations.

FURTHER READING

Abdel-Shehid, Gamal, and Nathan Kalman-Lamb. 2011. *Out of Left Field: Social Inequality and Sports.* Black Point, NS: Fernwood.
An examination of the effects of colonialism and capitalist inequalities on high-performance sport, both globally and locally.

Albanese, Patrizia. 2009. *Child Poverty in Canada.* Toronto: Oxford University Press.
This work looks at definitions of child poverty, its impacts, current data, and possible solutions.

Cobb, Clifford, and Phillipe Diaz. 2009. *Why Global Poverty? A Companion Guide to the Film "The End of Poverty?"* NY: Robert Schalkenbach Foundation.
This book offers a wide variety of interviews done for the film and includes the entire transcript of the film as well.

Dwyer, Augusta. 2011. *Broke but Unbroken: Grassroots Social Movements and Their Radical Solutions to Poverty.* Black Point, NS: Fernwood Publishing.
A journalist looks at participatory democracy among the poor in four countries—Brazil, Indonesia, India, and Argentina, and how the disadvantaged in these countries are struggling to solve their own problems.

McQuaig, Linda, and Neil Brooks. 2010. *The Trouble With Billionaires.* Toronto: Penguin Group Canada.
The authors focus on the consequences of inequality not—as is usually done—by looking at those at the bottom, but rather those at the top of the socioeconomic scale. Suggestions for change are offered.

Reiman, Jeffrey, and Paul Leighton. 2009. *The Rich Get Richer and the Poor Get Prison: Ideology, Class, and Criminal Justice.* 9th ed. Saddle River, NJ: Prentice-Hall.
A critical examination of the criminal justice system in the United States, the country with the highest incarceration rate in the world.

Wilkinson, Richard, and Kate Pickett. 2010. *The Spirit Level: Why Equality is Better for Everyone.* London, UK: Penguin Books.
Essential reading on the topic of inequality, with much international data provided. The authors show how—as the title indicates—we all pay a price for social inequality. Up-to-date material can be found on the website <equalitytrust.org.uk>.

Yalnizyan, Armine. 2007. *The Rich and the Rest of Us: The Changing Face of Canada's Growing Gap.* Ottawa: Canadian Centre for Policy Alternatives.
A brief overview of the growing economic disparity in Canada. The CCPA regularly produces studies and reports that provide up-to-date information on a wide variety of topics. Their website is <policyalternatives.ca>.

11 Race and Ethnicity

In This Chapter
- What is racism, and what are its roots?
- Do racism and other forms of social intolerance exist in Canada?
- How do various social theories explain the persistence of racism?
- What is the outlook for the future?

There are many differences between human beings, but only some seem to be socially significant. One difference that is consistently noted in our society is that of gender. Another is race and ethnicity. With regard to race and ethnicity, the very categories of analysis have been hotly debated, and there is no consistency in their usage. For example, people of Jewish origin have variously been described as a race, ethnic group, nation, religion, or people. Moreover, individuals often have their own interpretations of how they see themselves and others. Thus it can be said that issues of race and ethnicity are perhaps the most complex in the social sciences. Such debates give us a clue that we are dealing with social categories, rather than self-evident biological ones.

Let's begin with the concept of race. All humans belong to a single species, *Homo sapiens*, which likely evolved in Africa millions of years ago. Over time, some members of our species, isolated within particular gene pools, developed certain distinctive physical characteristics. Such characteristics were likely the result of natural selection: for example, while dark skins would provide benefits in hot climates, such as better protection from the sun, lighter skins would be advantageous in moderate and cold climates, allowing for more absorption of vitamin D. However, over time people moved about and came into contact with new gene pools. This process advanced in the modern period, as new modes of transportation developed. As a result, there are no genetically "pure" races, and modern-day distinctions between people are more cultural than physical. Nonetheless, humans continue to try to prove the biological reality of "race."

The concept of race first appeared in the English language around 500 years ago. However, it was not until the eighteenth century that the term began to refer to a category of people with shared physical or biological characteristics. The scientific categorization of people into races was the result of two interconnected developments: the expansion of capitalism with its imperial domination of non-European peoples, and the growth of science, particularly, in the nineteenth century, the field of physical anthropology.

Exactly how many races are there? One scientist in the eighteenth century suggested that there were four: Europeans, Asiatics, Africans, and American Indians. This categorization was based on skin colour and the subjective assessment of behavioural differences. In 1781, a German physiologist, Johann Friedrich Blumenbach, proposed a categorization based on head or skull shape. By the nineteenth century, physical anthropologists became seized with the question of categorizing people into racial categories, and new divisions and subdivisions appeared as new populations became known. While such research was supposedly neutral, it was occurring in a particular social context in which it was assumed that some racial groups were innately superior or inferior to others. This context helps us understand that the obsession with race is a social phenomenon particular to a specific time and place.

Think About It
The next time you're sitting in a classroom, consider the following: have you ever paid attention to which students in the class are left-handed? Blue-eyed? Wearing glasses? Short? Compare this to the way we notice skin colour or other physical characteristics linked to racial difference.

What Is Racism?

From a strictly genetic standpoint, it can be said that there is no such category as a race. The genetic variation between two people described as being of the same "race" may actually be larger than between two people described as being of different races. Nonetheless, certain individuals with particular physiological characteristics have been disadvantaged, in spite of the fact that race has no scientific validity. Race, therefore, is important as a social, rather than a physiological, reality. In this context, **race** can be defined as a category of people who share certain common physical traits deemed to be socially significant. Many sociologists now prefer to speak of **racialized groups** because this term highlights the social process by which certain groups of people are singled out for unequal treatment on the basis of real or imagined physical characteristics (Li 1990, 7). Race, then, should be distinguished from **ethnicity**. Ethnic groups are distinguished by socially selected *cultural* traits, rather than physical ones. These cultural traits may include language, religion, ideology, ancestry, or historical symbols.

In reality, of course, there is some overlap between the two concepts of race and ethnicity. Some groups that may share common physical traits and may be defined socially as a race may also share distinctive cultural traits. On the other hand, some European ethnic groups have been racialized at certain times in Canada's history. For example, Ukrainian immigrants at the turn of the century were considered "racially" suited for the difficult work of pioneer farming on the prairies, while Italian immigrants were brought into Canada in the postwar era in part because they were considered "racially" suited to the difficult and dirty work in the construction industry (Satzewich 1999, 323).

However, the most commonly racialized groups today are those with darker skins. The Employment Equity Act of 1986 used the term *visible minority* to describe "persons other than Aboriginal peoples, who are non-Caucasian in race and non-White in colour." The following groups are considered visible minorities: Chinese, South Asians, Blacks, Arabs and West Asians, Filipino, Southeast Asians, Latin Americans, Japanese, Koreans, and Pacific Islanders. The 1996 census was the first to ask Canadians if they felt they were members of one of these groups.

As noted in Chapter 3, social groups and cultures tend to evaluate themselves and their way of life favourably in relation to others. This tendency is referred to as *ethnocentrism*. In and of itself, ethnocentrism is not a negative social characteristic, but rather reflects group solidarity. Indeed, its absence can be a sign of social disintegration, as when a chronically disadvantaged and oppressed group thinks so little of itself that individuals see the culture of outsiders as superior to their own.

Under certain conditions, ethnocentrism becomes more virulent and hateful, taking on a quality of hostility, aggression, and antagonism toward non-members of a particular group. If this hostility is directed toward people on the basis of their membership in a particular ethnic group—for example, Greeks, Irish, or Ukrainians—it is referred to as **ethnic chauvinism**. If it is directed toward people with particular physical characteristics—such as skin colour, eye shape, or hair texture—it is referred to as **racism**. The term **anti-Semitism** is used to refer to hostility directed specifically at those who are of Jewish origin, while **Islamophobia** is a relatively recent term that refers to hostility directed at Muslims and their religion, Islam.

Two more terms are worth noting here. **Prejudice** is an attitude of dislike or hostility toward individuals on the basis of their membership in particular groups. On the other hand, **discrimination** refers to the denial of equal treatment or opportunities to these same social groups. While these two phenomena are usually connected, they can be distinguished from each other. Some people might be highly prejudiced, but unable to discriminate because they have no structural means of doing so. On the other hand, others might find themselves in a position where they must discriminate, although they are not in fact prejudiced (for example, a restaurant worker might be told not to serve Black customers). Discrimination is generally the more serious of the two processes since it inevitably hurts the victim's life chances, such as getting a job or finding a place to live. However, because prejudice can also lead to hurtful acts—including those of a violent nature—it too can have negative consequences for the victim.

The lack of clarity of terminology has often led to imprecision of analysis. For example, race and ethnicity are often used interchangeably or combined into the term "minority group." Prejudice and discrimination are sometimes used interchangeably, and antagonisms toward a variety of social groups are commonly described as forms of racism. In part, this confusion of terms reflects the fact that the consequences of ethnic chauvinism, anti-Semitism, Islamophobia, and racism are often similar, and the existence of one can at times mean the existence of the other. In addition, while criticism of theocratic nation-states that privilege their religious majorities—such as Israel or Iran—may be interpreted by some as forms of anti-Semitism or Islamophobia, these should rather be seen as criticism of government policies, not of the religious groups themselves.

Racism, unlike other forms of social intolerance, is always linked to real or perceived physiological traits. As Bolaria and Li (1988, 18) note: "It is the combination of physical traits and social attributes that makes racial oppression unique. Since the permanence of physical features is unquestionable, racial minorities carry a social stigma along with their experience of oppression that becomes indistinguishable from their physical appearances." Most importantly, racism differs from other forms of social intolerance because it is rooted in very specific historical and economic conditions.

> We speak so blithely about "race" and yet the concept is as unstable as water.... To speak personally, I am tan-tinted, and of African and Aboriginal and European heritage, and grew up "Black" in Nova Scotia. Yet, in South Carolina, a woman declared I was Filipino, or Chinese; in Quebec, a man swore I was Arab; in Ontario, another man presumed I was Portuguese. To some, I am African (but pallid); to others, Caucasian (but swarthy); to still others, Asian (but with curly hair). I am "Black"—but can pass easily for "Cuban" or, post-9/11, "Middle Eastern," and my loud "Yankee" laughter gets me thrown out of restaurants.
> —George Elliot Clarke, Canadian poet and novelist

Think About It
Sometimes we confuse responses to racism with racism itself. For example, racialized groups are sometimes accused of being racist because they don't associate with the dominant group. At your high school, did kids from racialized groups hang out together? If so, can you think of some social reasons why you/they might have done this?

In recent years, many analysts have begun to address the issue of *White privilege*. Of course, there is no real biological "White" person, and many actually have darker skin colours than individuals from racialized groups. "White," however, is more than descriptive; it also has positive linguistic connotations as it is a colour usually connected to cleanliness, purity, and even holiness. It has been argued that being perceived as White guarantees various social advantages that most people in this category take for granted:

> White people can count on certain things: they are not routinely intercepted by police while going about their business.... vacancies do not suddenly disappear when they seek housing; their bad behaviour is seen in individual terms rather than as a reflection of their group identity; they are not regularly asked to explain "the White view of

Some years ago I was standing in a check-out line at a local store. The line was moving very slowly, and I complained to the woman in front of me that they needed to hire more staff. The woman told me she didn't mind the wait. "I like that woman at the cash," she said, "she's Black, but she's very nice."

How we categorize others—how we decide who will be part of "us" and who will be considered "them"—is largely framed by those with power. However, once these categories are created, we use them without thinking too much about it. Because most of those with power in Canada have historically been European, it should not be surprising that "us" is often assumed to be people of European ancestry, while "them" refers to any non-Europeans.

With regard to the comment made to me by the woman at the check-out line, what is disturbing is not just the underlying racism, but also her assumption that she could say what she did to a total stranger—in her mind we both shared a category different from the woman at the cash, since we were both White.

The assumption that White is normal—a kind of default category—is so much part of our culture that we rarely notice it. For example, we rarely hear comments such as "I heard a great band the other night—the lead singer is this amazing White guy" or "A new corner store just opened up in the neighbourhood that's run by a nice White family." Even among non-racialized people who profess to be "colour-blind," race is a category that we all note, and people who are not White are still considered to be the different ones.

things" or to speak on behalf of their "race"; they regularly see people like themselves represented in media, in professions, and in positions of authority; they do not need to make special efforts to find children's literature, dolls or toys that feature people who look like themselves;… they are not routinely followed by store clerks watching that they do not steal; they do not need to wonder if the obstacles they face are based on racism or if their appearance will count against them if they seek legal or medical aid. (Sorenson 2003, 47–48)

Whether we acknowledge it or not, our social world is divided along racial lines. Those with light skins are considered Canadians, while those with racialized characteristics—even if their family has been in Canada for generations—are still considered "outsiders" (see Box 11.1).

The Roots of Racism

There is a great deal of debate about the origins of racism. The debates generally centre on whether the various forms of social intolerance prior to the capitalist era can be defined as racism. It is argued here that racism as we know it is a relatively recent phenomenon, and its emergence as a systematic world-view developed with the rise of capitalism and its global expansion.

It was common for foraging peoples to define themselves as "chosen people." However, outsiders could achieve acceptance by simply acquiring a kinship tie, whether real or symbolic. During the period of antiquity, slavery was based on capture in war rather than on any particular physical characteristics. There is no evidence of racism among the ancient Egyptians, Babylonians, or Persians. The Greeks viewed all outsiders as barbarians, inferior as a result of cultural and linguistic, rather than physical, differences; those who acquired Greek culture, particularly its language, were welcomed into Greek society. Among the Romans, distinction was based on citizenship, which was extended to all people defined as "free" throughout the empire, regardless of physical traits. Slaves were not distinguished by their physical characteristics (Cox 1970, 322–23).

> With the British leading the way, European capitalism invaded Ireland, the Americas, Asia and Africa, exhibiting a barbarity and cruelty that is almost incomprehensible.... In the process, a colonial system and an ideology of modern racism were constructed—abominations that continue to haunt the world in which we live.
> —*David McNally*, A Better World Is Possible

In many parts of medieval Europe, the fundamental distinction between people was that of Christian and non-Christian. Anti-Semitism was persistent and widespread because of its basis in the Christian dogma of the period, rather than any specific physical traits attributed to Jews. Likewise, the expansion of the Islamic world into Europe during the Middle Ages can be linked to economic and religious goals, rather than any racist assumptions. Of course, people in the pre-capitalist period could observe physical distinctions between peoples. However, nowhere did such differences become central or even important in defining particular social institutions or social structures.

The beginnings of racism can be traced to the expansion of European economies—first under a mercantilist and later an industrial capitalist system. This early globalization by the imperial capitalist powers, dominated by Britain, was primarily into countries where people had skin colours different from those of Europeans. Imperialism could then be morally justified by arguing that those affected were somehow inferior and that the Europeans were actually there to help them. This argument came to be known as the "White man's burden"—the title of British poet Rudyard Kipling's poem published in 1899 regarding the U.S. conquest of the Philippines—which refers to the conquered as "new-caught sullen peoples/Half-devil and half-child." In the name of "civilizing the heathen," racialized groups around the globe were robbed of their resources and their cultures and forced to work in the mines, fields, and forests to create great wealth for rich Europeans. This wealth became the economic basis for the development of capitalism.

It is impossible here to give full attention to the horrors that were inflicted on racialized people around the globe at this time. Everywhere the European colonists settled, from the Americas to India, from Africa to Asia, Indigenous populations suffered untold miseries. Populations were decimated by a combination of mass murder, disease, and maltreatment; some peoples—such as the Beothuk of Newfoundland and the Tasmanians of Australia—were completely eradicated. This period also saw the widespread reintroduction of the social institution of slavery. Slavery was the result not of racism, but rather of the economic requirements of the exploiters; however, once slavery developed, a complex belief system developed to maintain it.

The first forced labourers in the New World were actually the Indigenous populations of the Spanish, English, and French colonies. However, their numbers were never adequate and their sustained resistance led to perpetual uprisings. Thus the enslavement of these populations came at a very high social and economic cost. As the Anglo-American colonies expanded, the planter class needed a larger and more secure source of cheap labour. At first, many bonded or indentured workers were brought from the mother country. When the numbers of such workers also proved insufficient, plantation owners sought a new source of labour. Millions of workers brought from Africa—kidnapped and transported for sale to the New World—proved most suitable, not because of their race, but because they were abundant and they were cheap.

The British and Europeans certainly believed that darker-skinned peoples were uncivilized and distinctly inferior to themselves. In the mid-eighteenth century, however, an additional notion began to appear: racial minorities, primarily Blacks, were no longer seen as simply culturally or socially inferior to Europeans; they gradually came to also be considered *biologically* inferior, not fully human (Miles 1989, 28–30).

Prior to the eighteenth century, it was rare for European-Americans to refer to themselves as "White." Usually they thought of themselves in terms of their country of origin or with reference to their religion. As the concept grew of Blacks as biological inferiors, the concept of "Whiteness," with its natural superiority, grew as well. This rigid separation of Blacks and Whites proved very useful to plantation owners. In the classic divide-and-rule fashion, the slave-owning class encouraged White workers to identify with their White masters, rather than their Black fellow workers. By giving certain privileges and the perception of a shared "Whiteness" to poor British and European labourers, they could minimize the class identification of these people with Black slaves, and thus lower the risk of a successful rebellion (McNally 2002, 113–24).

Within the economic reality of colonialism and slavery, racism as an ideology grew and flourished, reaching its full development in the latter half of the nineteenth century, ironically just at the time that the formal institution of slavery was coming to an end. The belief in the "natural" inferiority of Blacks was now reinforced by the pseudo-science of the biological determinists.

Why would such an ideology advance just at the time when slavery was ending? Unlike all class societies that preceded it, capitalism was the first socioeconomic formation that, in theory, did away with the privileges of birth. And yet social inequality and classes still existed. Since capitalism did provide a degree of upward mobility, there had to be some ideological justification for the failure of most people to move upward in the social hierarchy. What better explanation than the social Darwinist notions that some were naturally superior to others? Notions of racial inferiority, which were a basic element of social Darwinist thought, thus constitute a major component in the ideological underpinning of all modern capitalist societies.

In Chapter 2, both the prevalence and invalidity of biological determinist arguments were noted. It was pointed out that biological determinism sees the hierarchical arrangements of society—in which some receive more power and wealth than others—as simply a reflection of innate differences between people. Biological determinist arguments have been used to justify the unequal treatment of women, the poor, immigrants, and—most persistently—racial minorities. For well over a hundred years, some social scientists have tried to prove that there is a hierarchy of races and that Blacks in particular form a "natural" underclass. Yet legitimate biological, behavioural, and social scientists, using universally replicable data, have repeatedly discredited such attempts. Nonetheless, many Canadians continue to believe that certain groups constitute a natural underclass.

> It always amazes me when people express surprise that there might be a "race problem" in Canada, or when they attribute the "problem" to a minority of prejudiced individuals. Racism is, and always has been, one of the bedrock institutions of Canadian society, embedded in the very fabric of our thinking, our personality.
> —Adrienne Shadd

A History of Racism in Canada

Some Canadians like to believe that, in comparison to the United States, Canada is a country with little history of overt racism. Others believe that racism exists, but that it is a relatively recent phenomenon linked to modern immigration patterns. In reality, racism in Canada has a long and sordid past. This history begins with the subjugation of the First Nations, a tale that is nothing less than one of state-directed cultural genocide, domination, and control (Frideres 1988).

Indigenous Peoples

The first British and French colonists made contact with Indigenous people[*] primarily to exploit their labour power in the fur trade. They were paid pitifully low prices for their pelts or given worthless objects in trade; at the same time, alcohol was introduced into their societies. The Hudson's Bay Company eventually gained monopoly control over the fur trade and, in the process, made First Nations totally dependent on them for survival. Despite

---

[*] Since racial categories are social rather than biological entities, the terminology used to describe them is also a social creation. Because of structured inequality, the terminology used by others may not reflect the self-definition of the oppressed group. As a result, there is no totally satisfactory terminology when speaking collectively of Indigenous peoples of Canada. In this book, the terms *Aboriginal people*, *Indigenous people*, and *First Nations people* are used. The term *Indians* refers specifically to those defined by the federal government as status Indians under the Indian Act.

the evidence of the destructive effects of alcohol on these societies, company traders commonly bartered alcohol for furs. Indigenous peoples received none of the huge wealth they created for the Hudson's Bay Company; rather, large numbers of them perished from famine or were ravaged by diseases introduced by the Europeans.

As the fur trade declined and agriculture expanded, the colonists, no longer needing the labour of Indigenous peoples, now sought the increasingly valuable lands inhabited by them. After Confederation, the Canadian government used various means to gain control over Indigenous lands. In the end, assimilation was seen as best, for it was thought that if First Nations could be absorbed into the broader population, there could be no land claims. The tool used to promote this end was the Indian Act of 1876. Although there have been some subsequent changes to this act, it set a framework of domination over First Nations that continues to the present day.

The Indian Act was sweeping legislation that controlled every aspect of the lives of Indigenous people. It also laid out who would be bound by the act: Indigenous people enrolled in the register of the Department of Indian Affairs were (and continue to be) defined as "status Indians." (The groups not included under the act are non-status Indians, Métis, and Inuit.) Under the terms of the original act, status Indians were prohibited from owning land, from voting, and from purchasing or consuming alcohol, and they were forcibly segregated on reserves. Although the reserves were generally in areas long occupied by various bands, they were much smaller than previous First Nations territory, were often poorly suited for farming or other economic activity, and could not be disposed of without permission from the federal government.

Traditional First Nations governments were eventually replaced by band councils that had little real power or influence. Amendments to the act in 1884 prohibited Indians from engaging in certain traditional cultural activities, such as the potlatch and sun dance. The goal of the legislation was to encourage assimilation through contact with White "civilization"—through such institutions as missionary-run residential schools—while concurrently dissolving First Nations culture and political structures.

Altogether, over 160,000 children were forcibly removed from their families and communities and spent many years getting inferior education in an environment of neglect and disease, as well as one of physical, sexual, and emotional abuse. Many never saw their families again. Even when children were reunited with their families, they were divided by language and culture, the schools having forbidden all things Indian. In thousands of cases, children died at the schools and never returned home. The last federally operated residential school closed in 1990.

Residential schools deprived children of healthy parental role models and weakened the community and family structure upon which their traditional life was built. The legacy of these schools has been profound.

Many survivors of these schools display a constellation of symptoms similar to those of post-traumatic stress disorder. Some argue that the residential school policies were part of an overall pattern of genocide, because the government was consciously attempting to eradicate Indigenous people as a cultural group.

Government policies over the years were largely contradictory. Indigenous people were simultaneously segregated from the dominant culture while being expected to integrate into it. They were often unable to continue their traditional means of subsistence, but were not allowed to draw on the resources or services of White settler communities. Meanwhile, the provincial and federal governments gradually acquired massive tracts of valuable First Nations lands, often through expropriation, which sometimes required the forcible resettlement of Indigenous communities. Thus, the Indigenous peoples of Canada saw the theft of both their resources and their culture. At the same time, they were marginalized from the dominant economy and its culture and were forced to become dependent on the Canadian state.

That marginalization continues up to the present. More than three centuries of prejudice and discrimination against the First Nations of Canada have left a scandalous legacy. Although there has been some improvement in the last twenty-five years, massive inequities remain. As noted in the previous chapter, the median income for Aboriginal people in 2006 was 30 percent lower than the $27,097 median income for the rest of Canadians (Wilson and MacDonald 2010). In 2009, the average employment rate for Aboriginal people was 57 percent, compared with 61.8 percent for non-Aboriginal people. Between 2008 and 2009, the employment rate for off-reserve Aboriginal youth between fifteen and

I want to get rid of the Indian problem. Our object is to continue until there is not a single Indian in Canada that has not been absorbed. They are a weird and waning race... ready to break out at any moment in savage dances; in wild and desperate orgies.
—Duncan Campbell Scott, Deputy Superintendent General of Indian Affairs, 1913–32

I quite often hear from the Indians that they do not want to send their children to school as it is a place where they are sent to die.
—W.M. Graham, Indian Commissioner for Saskatchewan, 1925

To the approximately 80,000 living former students, and all family members and communities, the Government of Canada now recognizes that it was wrong to forcibly remove children from their homes and we apologize for having done this. We now recognize that it was wrong to separate children from rich and vibrant cultures and traditions, that it created a void in many lives and communities, and we apologize for having done this. We now recognize that, in separating children from their families, we undermined the ability of many to adequately parent their own children and sowed the seeds for generations to follow, and we apologize for having done this. We now recognize that, far too often, these institutions gave rise to abuse or neglect and were inadequately controlled, and we apologize for failing to protect you. Not only did you suffer these abuses as children, but as you became parents, you were powerless to protect your own children from suffering the same experience, and for this we are sorry.
—Prime Minister Stephen Harper, June 11, 2008, in the House of Commons. (This was the first time in Canadian history that a sitting prime minister apologized for these atrocities.)

twenty-four fell by 6.8 percentage points, compared with a decline of 4.2 percentage points among non-Aboriginal youth (Statistics Canada 2011b).

A larger proportion of First Nations people live in over-crowded homes than do non-Aboriginal people in Canada (11 versus 3 percent) as well as in homes in need of major repairs (23 versus 7 percent). And according to self-reported information from the 2009 General Social Survey (GSS), Aboriginal people were two times more likely than non-Aboriginal people to experience a violent victimization such as an assault, sexual assault, or robbery (Statistics Canada 2011d). High rates of poverty, unemployment, and poor housing lead to many other negative outcomes, including ill health, lower life expectancy, and higher rates of infant mortality and youth suicide.

Blacks in Canada

Ironically, the commonality that brings people of colour together is not their shared cultural or biological origins but, rather, their experience of racism (Bolaria and Li 1988, 18). This is particularly true with regard to Blacks. On the one hand, utilizing concepts such as "African-Canadians" or "Blacks" masks the vast range of differences—in culture, length of time in Canada, national origin, socioeconomic status, and so on—within these categories. On the other hand, such terminology is required to point out their shared experiences as the victims of racism.

African-Canadians have had a long presence in Canada. The first Black slaves were brought to Canada by the French in the seventeenth century. Although the kind of agricultural production in Canada did not lend itself to the widespread use of slave labour, the practice of slavery continued. Approximately 10 percent of Loyalists who came to British North America after the American Revolution were Black. The Black population of Canada subsequently increased as many runaway slaves from the United States found their way north on the Underground Railroad. In 1860, the Anti-Slavery Society estimated there were 60,000 Blacks in Canada (Walker 1980, 56).

Far from finding Canada a refuge, Blacks faced overt prejudice and discrimination and were tolerated mostly as a source of cheap labour. They were restricted in their ownership of property as well as their ability to educate their children. Both Ontario and Nova Scotia legislated racially separate schools. Indeed, segregated schools continued in Nova Scotia until the 1960s. Racism was both pervasive and public and could be seen not only in schools but also in government, the media, the judiciary, the workplace, and elsewhere in society.

Such racism continues into the twenty-first century. At the time of the 2006 census, Blacks constituted the third-largest visible minority group in Canada, with the majority centred in Toronto. Discrimination against Blacks in the labour force continues to be a reality. An analysis of census data found that Blacks experience lower employment rates and employment income and higher unemployment rates regardless of educational level. As one author (Mensah 2002, 129) notes, "The unabashed racial discrimination in the job market impacts Blacks more than any other form of bigotry." Overall, Blacks are more likely than other visible minorities to feel discriminated against or treated unfairly because of their ethnicity, culture, race, skin colour, language, accent, or religion (Milan and Tran 2004, 7).

Immigration from the Nineteenth to the Twenty-First Century

While a wide variety of immigrants have historically met with discriminatory treatment on their arrival in Canada, those who faced the greatest hostility in the late nineteenth and early twentieth centuries were from China, Japan, and India. As many as 14,000 Chinese men were brought to this country in the late nineteenth century to build the Canadian Pacific Railway. The work was arduous and dangerous, the living conditions appalling, and the wages pathetic. The men were not allowed to bring their families, nor were they allowed to establish relations with White women. Many died from malnutrition, disease, and construction accidents. When the railway was completed in 1885 and their labour was no longer needed, politicians tried to force the Chinese to leave Canada. Some did return to China; of those who remained, most lived in British Columbia.

To discourage further Chinese immigration, in 1886 the federal government imposed a "head tax" of $50 on every Chinese immigrant; by 1904 it had risen to $500, which was equivalent to a year's wages for steady work. In 1923, the Chinese Immigration Act (also referred to as the Chinese Exclusion Act) was passed, which virtually ended Chinese immigration. Meanwhile, the Chinese in Canada faced blatant discrimination. They could not serve in public office or on juries, could not vote in provincial or municipal elections, and were barred from the higher-paying professions. As a result, most ended up in small businesses, restaurants, or laundries.

The Japanese in Canada faced similar hostility. Like the Chinese, they encountered economic exploitation and job restrictions and were not allowed to vote. Their schools and housing were segregated, and they were not allowed access to many public places. One of the most shameful examples of racism in Canadian history was the treatment of the Japanese during World War II. After the bombing of Pearl Harbor in 1941, the federal government gave the order to detain all Japanese Canadians living within a hundred miles of the Pacific Coast. In early 1942, more than 20,000 people—including more than half who had been born in Canada—were forced from their homes and transferred to camps in Alberta, Manitoba, and the B.C. interior. Meanwhile, the federal government sold all their property at a fraction of its value. No comparable actions were taken against German or Italian Canadians, although Canada was also at war with Germany and Italy at the time. In 1946, with the war over, the federal government tried to deport 10,000 Japanese, but a large public outcry forced them to back down.

The third group that endured racial discrimination in immigration policy during this period was from India. Although only a small number of Indians had settled in British Columbia by the early twentieth century, this did not stop the press in that province from attacking what was referred to as a "Hindu invasion." Like the Chinese and Japanese, those of Indian origin were exploited economically, denied the franchise, and restricted from certain occupations and property ownership. In 1908, the government implemented the Continuous Passage Act, which made immigration from India virtually impossible. The argument used to justify the exclusion of immigrants from China, Japan, and India was their inability to assimilate; underlying such arguments was the assumption that such individuals were both different and inferior.

Anti-Semitism was also part of Canada's early history. Most Jewish immigration came after 1880, when hundreds of thousands of Jewish refugees fled the virulent anti-Semitism of Eastern Europe. Having been denied the right to own land in Europe they were unfamiliar with farming, and most ended up in larger urban centres, either as workers in the expanding sweatshops or, if they were more fortunate, as owners of small businesses. Anti-Semitism was widespread: Jews were prevented from working in certain occupations, and there were quotas limiting the number of Jewish students allowed to enroll at universities. Jews fortunate enough to find their way into the professions often had to hide their identities. Signs that said "No Jews or Dogs Allowed" or "Christians Only" could be seen in various clubs, resorts, and vacation areas. Canada has a shameful record in regard to providing sanctuary for Jewish refugees from Europe in the 1930s and 1940s (Abella and Troper 1982).

Following World War II, there was some lessening of clearly discriminatory immigration policies in Canada and a decline in overt racial and ethnic discrimination. In part, this was due to the growth of international human rights legislation following the war, as well as the struggles of various groups to end discriminatory practices. The changing economic conditions of the time also helped push such struggles forward. The 1950s and 1960s were times of economic growth in Canada, which led to a rapid expansion in the need for workers; at the same time, improved conditions in postwar Europe led to a decline in immigration from the formerly "preferred" groups of northern Europe. To fill the void, the government loosened its policy with regard to immigrants from non-European countries.

While overt forms of racism and discrimination became in some ways less acceptable, they by no means disappeared. From the 1970s onward, hostilities toward immigrants and racialized groups increased. For example, South Asian immigrants in a number of cities were the victims of vandalism and assaults. Blacks continued to face job and housing discrimination, as well as unfair treatment in the criminal justice system, and "racial profiling" by police of both Blacks and Indigenous people has become a major controversy in many Canadian cities.

Since the events of September 11, 2001, there has been increasing hostility toward Muslims. This hostility is not new. It has been a feature of European societies since the eighth century and took on a particular form after the expansion of European imperialism into predominantly Muslim countries. The term *Islamophobia* developed in the 1990s, because at that

Box 11.2 Islamophobia in Canada

On July 22, 2011, a lone gunman in Norway killed seventy-seven people. Within hours, the media were awash with analyses of who did it and why. More than a few in the United States and elsewhere declared that the perpetrator was clearly an Islamic terrorist, even though there was no evidence to support this hypothesis. Hours later it became clear that not only was the thirty-two-year-old attacker *not* a Muslim, he was in fact Anders Breivik, a Christian fundamentalist and a virulent *anti*-Muslim, who ranted in his 1500-page manifesto against Muslim immigration to Europe and vowed revenge on those "indigenous Europeans" whom he deemed had betrayed their heritage.

Since the attacks in the United States on September 11, 2001, one particular aspect of Islamophobia has taken hold in many parts of the world including Canada—the belief that Islam is a violent, aggressive religion that is supportive of terrorism around the world. This line of argument is not restricted to extremists such as Breivik. Government leaders such as David Cameron in England and Barack Obama in the United States have advanced notions of "Islamic extremism." In Canada, the Conservative government cancelled funding to the Canadian Arab Federation in 2009, asserting (without any supportive evidence) that it was a supporter of terrorist organizations in the Middle East. In late 2011 Prime Minister Harper stated in an interview with CBC's Peter Mansbridge

that the greatest threat to Canada since 9/11 is "still Islamicism" and that the threat "exists all over the world" (CBC News online September 6, 2011).

The current attack on Muslims in Canada is a repeat of an age-old narrative used by those with power, where certain groups are promoted as the "others" who do not have beliefs or values in common with "us" and are threats to "our" way of life. And because many (although not all) of those who practise the Muslim faith have darker skins, there is also a strong aspect of racism inherent in it. Indeed, other racialized groups such as Sikhs have falsely been attacked for being Muslims.

There are currently fewer than one million Muslims in Canada, less than 3 percent of the population. Yet the narrative of an Islamic threat is widespread in the media. For example, an article in the *National Post* (Lewis 2011) entitled "Number of Muslims in Canada expected to triple over next 20 years" promoted the notion that there would be a surge of foreigners in our midst, some of whom, according to one analyst, "come here with the intention of destroying the social fabric of the country." At the end of the online version of this article was the following: " Editor's note: Comments have been shut down on this posting. Too many postings used racist language and unsubstantiated accusations to allow comments to continue."

---

time there was an increase in the negative treatment of Muslim immigrants in a number of European countries. After 9/11 and the U.S. government's response to it, Islamophobia became widespread (see Box 11.2).

This brief overview of Canadian history suggests that racism involves more than simply the personal biases of individuals. Rather, what we begin to see is a pattern of **institutional racism** (also referred to as systemic racism), in which whole social institutions—such as education, the judiciary, the media, and so on—are embedded with racist ideologies and help sustain them. Moreover, the history of racism and other forms of social intolerance in Canada points out the central role played by the various levels of the state. Not only have governments repeatedly turned a blind eye to waves of social intolerance, they have at times been the perpetrators of such actions.

Liberalism: Focusing on Culture

Liberalism is one of the many order theories that try to explain why racial inequality exists. The central variables of social analysis from the perspective of liberalism are values, attitudes, and cultural differences. The liberal perspective does not ignore structural inequities; rather, it argues that structural inequities are a result of cultural problems.

Such arguments are pervasive within the social sciences. In contrast to those theories that focus on the psychological bases for prejudice, sociologists have tended to focus on racism and other forms of discrimination in the cultural sphere. In the period that followed World War II, most North American sociologists saw social intolerance as a temporary phenomenon that would disappear as various groups assimilated over time into the broader culture. This approach, commonly referred to as **assimilationism**, starts with the assumption that industrial societies—which tend to promote individual freedom and initiative—will naturally discourage discrimination. From this point of view, since modern societies tend to promote equality, the persistence of racism must be the result of certain groups clinging to traditional values, attitudes, and beliefs.

Similar to, but distinct from, the assimilationists are those theorists who focus on the cultural or psychological characteristics of the oppressed groups. Perhaps the best known of these early theories was that of Oscar Lewis (1966), who advocated a "culture of poverty" approach to explain social inequality. Lewis, an American anthropologist, felt that living in poverty creates a culture imbued with a number of characteristics, including a low level of social organization, hostility toward representatives of the broader society, and feelings of despair, dependence, and inferiority. It is this culture of poverty, according to Lewis, that keeps certain groups from attaining economic success.

In Canada, such arguments have been used to explain the condition of Indigenous people. One author (Nagler 1972), for example, believed that a century of life on the reserves, with its forced idleness and isolation, helped create a culture of poverty that left Native people ill-prepared to adapt to urban living. From this point of view, the basic value system of Indigenous people conflicts with the values dominant in North American society, such as "the value of punctuality, saving, future orientation and the work ethic" (134). The conflict between these two value systems, according to this author, keeps Indigenous people from assimilating or attaining equality.

One of the main problems with such arguments is that they confuse cause with effect: the values and cultural orientations of particular groups are seen to be the source of the problem, rather than the result of it. (Perhaps, for example, high rates of poverty and unemployment among Indigenous people have led to a poor work ethic, orientation to the future, or ability to save money.) As such, the assimilationist and culture-of-poverty theorists end up blaming the victims for their own oppression. As was noted in Chapter 10, theories that focus on the victims of social problems draw attention away from the structural bases of such problems. The solution to these problems, then, is seen as being some alteration of the victim's attitudes or behaviour, rather than any necessary change in the social structure itself.

More recent liberal theories acknowledge the existence of institutional racism and direct attention away from the victims toward the broader society. While such approaches no longer focus on those oppressed by racism, liberal theories continue to see racism as a cultural problem rooted in values, beliefs, and attitudes. Language and discourse are the means by which these cultural elements are transmitted, and the various social institutions become embedded with racist ideology. The solution, therefore, is directed at eliminating racial prejudice, which is seen to be the basis for discrimination.

The Class Perspective: The Structural Basis of Racism

Unlike the liberal perspective, which focuses on the cultural roots of social intolerance, the Marxist or class perspective looks at the material basis for such behaviour and beliefs. Class analysis accepts the notion that racism is sustained by a body of ideas. However, Marxists try to explain how such ideas come to be pervasive in our society and why they are so resistant to change. The class perspective, unlike liberalism, focuses first and foremost on structures of power.

Extra Profits from Discrimination

From the Marxist perspective, the capitalist owning class benefits from racial inequality in a number of ways. First, and most directly, the underpayment of racialized groups is a major source of extra profits for those who employ them. Moreover, underpayment of one sector of the labour market serves to keep all wages down. Members of these groups (as well as recent immigrant groups) also constitute an important part of the reserve army of the unemployed, first described in Chapter 6. A greater percentage of racial minorities not only are unemployed but also are underemployed or work part-time. These groups exert a downward pressure on wages.

Data indicate that Whites earn more than racialized minorities. Indeed, one author (Galabuzi 2006) speaks of Canada as having a system of economic *apartheid*, a term used to define the institutionalized system of racism in South Africa from the 1960s to the early 1990s. Using Statistics Canada income figures from 1996 to 1998, Galabuzi concludes that racialized groups in Canada tend to do less well than Whites in

> Racialized Canadians encounter a persistent colour code that blocks them from the best paying jobs our country has to offer.... The Census data [from 2006] makes clear: Between 2000 and 2005, during the one of the best economic growth periods for Canada, racialized workers contributed to that economic growth but they didn't enjoy the benefits.
> —*Sheila Block and Grace-Edward Galabuzi, Canada's Colour Coded Labour Market*

income, employment, and poverty levels. Among the worst off are visible-minority women, immigrant women, and Aboriginal women. More recent data confirm that racialized minorities continue to do less well than Whites in terms of income.

There is no single explanation for the persistence of lower wage rates for racial minorities. In the past, it could be linked to such easily identifiable realities as government immigration policies, hiring restrictions, and other legalized forms of racism. While such overt forms of racism are generally unacceptable today in Canada, more subtle forms of discrimination in the labour market continue. Many companies have also excluded racial minorities by demanding "Canadian experience," by disallowing foreign credentials, or by using excessively narrow job recruitment channels. Data from the 2001 census indicate that while the earnings of immigrants used to improve with length of time in Canada, immigrants now continue to have lower wages than Canadian-born workers even after ten years in the country. Moreover, the racialized employment gap persists among both low- and high-income earners and among those with both low and high educational attainment. This gap lessens only in unionized workplaces (Galabuzi 2006, 91–119).

The Ideology of Racism

Racism provides more than short-term economic benefits for capital. We should recall that capital has two goals: in the short term, profit maximization; in the long term, the maintenance of a system that allows it to achieve its short-term goal. As an ideology, racism goes beyond the immediate function of enhancing profitability. Racism and other forms of ethnic hostility also serve to separate workers in the classic divide-and-rule pattern, as was noted earlier in this chapter. The more that various racial and ethnic groups are pitted against each other, the less likely it is that they will be able to unite in a common struggle to oppose those with power. In addition, if racial minorities become scapegoats, they can direct attention away from the real bases for social problems.

However, to say that capital benefits in general from racism is not to deny that individual capitalists or companies may work toward eroding racism. There are many reasons—hiring more qualified workers, hiring workers that reflect the diversity of their customers, or simply personal values—why individual employers may work against discrimination in the workplace.

Conversely, one cannot assume that all workers oppose racism. Indeed, White workers have often been the perpetrators of racist actions. In the early twentieth century, racist attitudes permeated the whole trade union movement, both in Canada and in the United States, and many unions barred specific minorities from becoming members. The unions justified their opposition to certain groups by the fact that employers frequently hired racial minorities or recent immigrants at lower wage rates and used them to bust unions or to break strikes. The perpetuation of racism did give many White workers a certain short-term advantage in wages, job security, working conditions, and promotions. In the end, however, racism among workers actually eroded their conditions and played into the hands of the employers.

At the moment, many working people are susceptible to racism and ethnic chauvinism. People are not innately cruel or prejudiced; however, since capitalism turns workers into commodities who must sell their labour in the market, it makes workers rivals who must compete against one another. In a world where jobs constitute a scarce resource, there are many people who are open to arguments that would exclude certain groups from direct competition for these resources. In bad economic times, as jobs become even scarcer, racism and other forms of group hostility generally increase. Educational opportunities and affordable housing are also scarce resources in capitalist societies. Competition for these resources in the face of government cutbacks and declining wages can set the stage for increased social intolerance. In 2010, *Maclean's* annual university ranking edition included an article asking whether Canadian universities were becoming "too Asian." The rapid rise of rabid Islamophobic, anti-immigrant sentiments in many parts of Europe and Great Britain can also in part be linked to the erosion of economic conditions for many workers there.

In addition, working people feeling the negative effects of a competitive, individualistic capitalist workplace may be looking for some sense of community. As a result, many may turn to their ethnic, religious, or racial group for solidarity. While this can certainly be a positive response, there is a danger that, under certain conditions, such solidarity can turn to anger or hatred against those who are "outsiders." Again—as has been seen in Europe—such hostility is likely to increase in bad economic times, as globalizing tendencies make people feel increasingly powerless, as fear and frustration grow, and as people look for easy explanations for their deteriorating conditions. In such circumstances, people can become susceptible to arguments that place them above some other supposedly naturally inferior minority.

Think About It

Do you think racism and other forms of social intolerance are increasing or decreasing in Canada? Have you personally encountered such acts? If you are not Canadian-born, would you say social intolerance is worse or better than where you lived previously?

The Struggle for Racial Equality: How Far Have We Come?

Given the history of racism in Canada, it does appear that there has been a major advance in the struggle for racial equality in recent years. Certainly, it is now the exception for a public figure to openly make a racial or ethnic slur, something that was quite common only fifty years ago. Blacks and other racialized groups are gradually gaining visibility on television and in

> The colour of justice in Canada is White.
> —*David Tanovich*, The Colour of Justice

other media. Racism within the school system has been acknowledged, and, while there are variations across the country, anti-racist education has been gaining ground. Since the report of the Royal Commission on Equality in Employment (1984), there has been some equity legislation passed federally.

On the other hand, it can also be argued that the struggle for racial equality has not come very far. There is substantial evidence that racism is widespread in the criminal justice system (Tanovich 2006). Our popular culture remains permeated with racist images and negative stereotypes. Racialized groups, especially recent immigrants, continue to face discrimination in housing and employment, and hate groups, now using the Internet as a means of promoting their ideologies, continue to exist across the country.

While the federal and provincial levels of government have given lip service to fighting racism, their actions have been limited and of a very specific nature. It is true that the Canadian government has ratified the United Nations International Convention on the Elimination of All Forms of Racial Discrimination, and we have a Charter of Rights and Freedoms that outlaws discrimination on the basis of—among other things—race, ethnic origin, colour, and religion. In addition, the federal government, all provinces, and the territories have human rights codes, and most have human rights commissions to administer the codes.

However, there has been much criticism of the overall approach to discriminatory practices in Canada. The onus is generally on the victims of discrimination to pursue charges, either through human rights commissions or, in the case of alleged Charter violations, through the courts. The adversarial nature of the process; the cost in time, money, and effort; the prolonged delays; and the stringent requirements for the complaint system have together made official challenges to discrimination an unrealistic option for most people. Most importantly, current government legislation focuses on individual acts of discrimination, rather than on broader and more pervasive forms of institutional racism. Individual rights, rather than collective rights, are emphasized.

The federal government adopted the Employment Equity Act in 1986, which applies to approximately 1,250 federally regulated companies. Employers designated under the act are required to submit an employment equity plan annually, which sets out goals and timetables for hiring persons from designated groups (women, racial minorities, Indigenous people, and people with disabilities); the ultimate goal is ostensibly that the workforce should eventually reflect the diversity within the broader Canadian population. However, the act has proven to be ineffectual in bringing about real change (Henry et al. 2000, 344). It contains no penalties for failure to implement programs, no criteria for measuring success, and no provisions for enforcement, except with regard to failure to comply with the reporting documents. Even more revealing, the federal government has exempted itself from the provisions of the act.

The area where the federal government has shown itself to be most proactive is in the sphere of multiculturalism, as it actively promotes ethnic diversity in many spheres. Multiculturalism as government policy was first introduced by Prime Minister Pierre Trudeau in 1971 and in 1988 became enshrined in the federal Multiculturalism Act. While it certainly was an advance in that it did recognize ethnic diversity within Canada, its emphasis has been on promoting cultural traditions rather than the eradication of systemic racism and other forms of discrimination. Multicultural policies, like liberalism in general, transform complex political and economic problems—including the relationship between Canada's two charter groups, the English and the French, in addition to the historic oppression of Indigenous people—into mere cultural and linguistic differences. By so doing, multiculturalism has drawn attention away from inequities of power and the root causes of differences within the Canadian mosaic.

The First Nations Struggle

For more than a century, Canadian government policy has left Indigenous people with little structural power. Moreover, the pervasiveness of institutional racism against Indigenous people, the devaluation of their culture, the limited opportunities for economic development, the legacy of residential schools, and the persistence of widespread racial stereotypes have all had a debilitating effect on Aboriginal self-worth and their ability to struggle against the conditions of their lives. Nonetheless, there are some pockets of resistance across the country from time to time.

Changing the conditions for Indigenous people in any major way requires that they be given true control over their lives and the ability to obtain their fair share of Canada's wealth. This requires the settling of land claims and provision of a stable land base as a starting point. But even that first step has not been achieved by most First Nations, and large areas of Canada continue to be the subject of Indigenous land claims. Such claims are based either on traditional use and occupancy of the land or on assertions that the Canadian government did not fulfill historical treaty obligations.

Starting in 2004, many Indigenous organizations came together with provincial, territorial, and federal governments and hammered out the Kelowna Accord, which would provide $5.1-billion in funding over ten years for education, health, housing, and economic opportunities. However, a federal election was called shortly after the accord was signed, before a budget could be passed that would have allocated the funding. The Conservative Party won the election of 2006 and shortly thereafter cancelled the accord. The new budget allocated a fraction of the money that would have gone to First Nations people under the Kelowna Accord. In 2008, the federal government set up the Specific Claims Tribunal Act, with the aim of providing timely settlements to land claims. However, in 2011 the government made a number of "take it or leave it" financial settlements to a number of bands, and there was concern that these would undermine legitimate ongoing land claims (Minsky 2011).

Box 11.3 The Save the Fraser Declaration

On December 1, 2010, sixty-one First Nations in British Columbia signed the Save the Fraser Declaration; one year later, that number expanded to 130. Such a united political opposition by First Nations is quite unprecedented in Canadian history. The Declaration read as follows:

WE THE UNDERSIGNED INDIGENOUS NATIONS OF THE FRASER RIVER WATERSHED DECLARE:

We have inhabited and governed our territories within the Fraser watershed, according to our laws and traditions, since time immemorial. Our relationship with the watershed is ancient and profound, and our inherent Title and Rights and legal authority over these lands and waters have never been relinquished through treaty or war.

Water is life for our peoples and for all living things that depend on it. The Fraser River and its tributaries are our lifeline.

A threat to the Fraser and its headwaters is a threat to all who depend on its health. We will not allow our fish, animals, plants, people and ways of life to be placed at risk.

We have come together to protect these lands and waters from a grave threat: the Enbridge Northern Gateway Pipelines project. This project, which would link the Tar Sands to Asia through our territories and the headwaters of this great river, and the federal process to approve it, violate our laws, traditions, values and our inherent rights as Indigenous Peoples under international law. We are united to exercise our inherent Title, Rights and responsibility to ourselves, our ancestors, our descendants and to the people of the world, to defend these lands and waters. Our laws require that we do this.

Therefore, in upholding our ancestral laws, Title, Rights and responsibilities, we declare: We will not allow the proposed Enbridge Northern Gateway Pipelines, or similar Tar Sands projects, to cross our lands, territories and watersheds, or the ocean migration routes of Fraser River salmon.

We are adamant and resolved in this declaration, made according to our Indigenous laws and authority. We call on all who would place our lands and waters at risk—we have suffered enough, we will protect our watersheds, and we will not tolerate this great threat to us all and to all future generations.

The various levels of government do not seem to be particularly interested in resolving many of the land claims. There is even some suspicion that they may actually be trying to co-opt, divide, and depoliticize the leadership of the First Nations. This is not surprising, since much of the land under dispute is now quite valuable and often occupied by others. Moreover, major corporations covet the resources on First Nations lands and generally oppose any settlements that give the First Nations increased control over these lands. In response, First Nations in some regions are taking matters into their own hands and uniting to oppose corporate and government attempts to undermine their rights and the sanctity of their lands and way of life (see Box 11.3).

The Outlook for the Future

A recurring theme throughout this book is that capitalist societies are full of contradictions. Such contradictions are reflected in the area of racial inequality. On the one hand, capitalism emphasizes the free movement of capital and labour. In this sense, both the struggle for economic advantage (i.e., for employers to get the best worker for the job, regardless of physical or cultural characteristics) and the ideology of liberalism ought to lead to an erosion of racism. Likewise, the shift toward democracy and multiculturalism should play a role in lessening racial inequality.

There is some evidence to indicate that racial and ethnic prejudice in Canada has moderated in recent years, certainly when compared to the first half of the twentieth century. Nonetheless, racism and other forms of social intolerance persist in all advanced capitalist societies. In spite of changing attitudes and values, many minorities in Canada continue to face prejudice and discrimination. As noted in Chapter 5, the "bad" jobs available in the restructured capitalist economy disproportionately go to, among others, certain racialized groups and immigrants. Moreover, recent cuts to public education and social services have the most negative consequences for those who are already disadvantaged. Also worrying are trends already seen in many parts of Europe as well as parts of the United States. With a continuing economic crisis that leads to high unemployment, fewer job opportunities, and low wages, many—as has been the case so often in modern history—go after the "foreigners" in their midst rather than those with power.

As long as jobs, educational opportunities, and affordable housing constitute a scarce resource, people and groups will be forced to compete against each other in the marketplace. In such a context, employment equity programs and other government initiatives that might limit structural racism are likely to face a backlash. Moreover, in our increasingly globalized world—where people move to improve their lives or to reunite with family members—many feel threatened and are susceptible to the simple narrative provided by racist ideologies.

This chapter has argued that the persistence of racism can be understood only within the broader framework of capitalist class relations. As American writers Baran and Sweezy (1966, 271) note, "It was capitalism, with its enthronement of greed and privilege, which created the race problem and made it the ugly thing it is today. It is the very same system which resists and thwarts every effort at a solution."

KEY POINTS

1. From a strictly genetic standpoint, there is no such thing as race. The concept of race, therefore, reflects a social rather than a physiological reality.

2. Racism, while connected to other forms of social intolerance such as ethnic chauvinism, anti-Semitism, and Islamophobia must be seen as distinct from them.

3. Prejudice is the holding of biased beliefs toward individuals on the basis of their membership in particular groups. Discrimination is the denial of equal treatment or opportunities to these same social groups. Discrimination generally has more serious consequences for the victim than does prejudice.

4. Racism as we know it began to develop after 1492, as the European powers began their global expansion and competition. Racism grew and flourished within the economic conditions of colonialism and slavery.

5. At the same time that slavery was disappearing, biological determinist arguments about racial inferiority became increasingly popular. Racism reached its full development by the end of the nineteenth century.

6. Canada has a long history of state-supported racism, particularly against First Nations people.

7. Liberalism sees the cause of racial inequality as rooted in values, attitudes, and cultural differences. In contrast, class analysis focuses on the material basis for such ideas, that is, the way they are rooted in our society's economic and political structures.

8. From the Marxist perspective, racism continues because the dominant class in capitalism benefits from its existence.

9. While there have certainly been some advances in the struggle against racism, there is substantial evidence to indicate that racism remains pervasive in Canadian social institutions. The anti-racist policies of the government are very weak.

10. The struggle for self-government and for the settlement of long-standing land claims remains central for First Nations people.

11. There is some evidence that Canadians have become more tolerant of racial and ethnic minorities. On the other hand, the capitalist structure has limited economic and social advances for racialized groups.

FURTHER READING

Boyko, John. 1995. *Last Steps to Freedom: The Evolution of Canadian Racism.* Winnipeg: Watson & Dwyer.
This book asks readers to face their racist past by offering short pieces regarding past discrimination against six groups in Canada.

Davis, Lynn, ed. 2010. *Alliances: Re/Envisioning Indigenous-non-Indigenous Relationships.* Toronto: University of Toronto Press.
The various authors in this book examine the complex dynamics between Indigenous and non-Indigenous individuals as they work together in the struggle for social change.

Henry, Frances and Carol Tator, eds. 2009. *Racism in the Canadian University: Demanding Social Justice, Inclusion, and Equity.* Toronto: University of Toronto Press.
An examination of the prevalence of institutional racism in our universities and the equally prevalent denial of its existence on campuses across the country.

Ighodaro, MacDonald E. 2006. *Living the Experience: Migration, Exclusion, and Anti-Racist Practice.* Black Point, NS: Fernwood.
An examination of the issues faced by refugees, immigrants, and other racialized minorities, both in Canada and around the world.

Mensah, Joseph. 2010. *Black Canadians: History, Experiences, Social Conditions.* Revised Edition. Black Point, NS: Fernwood.
This book provides both a brief history of Blacks in Canada and an overview of current issues and controversies.

Milloy, John S. 1999. *A National Crime: The Canadian Government and the Residential School System, 1879–1986.* Winnipeg: University of Manitoba Press.
This book uncovers the full extent of the government's complicity for nearly a century in destroying the lives and cultures of Indigenous people.

Satzewich, Vic. 2011. *Racism in Canada.* Don Mills, ON: Oxford University Press.
A short and accessible book that examines a variety of issues pertaining to Canadian racism, past and present.

12 Gender Issues

In This Chapter
- To what extent does gender inequality exist in Canada?
- What are the theoretical explanations for its persistence?
- When did gender inequality begin?
- What are some key gender issues in Canada today?

When a child is born, one of the first things we want to know is its sex. Indeed, many of us now want to know the sex of our child before it is born. Clearly, then, the status categories of male and female are central to our lives. While humans hold many statuses at any given moment, gender constitutes such an elemental status—its recognition begins so early, its socialization is so intense, and its imposition on all components of our lives is so total—that we could term gender a *core status*.

One of the foremost analysts of human behaviour in the twentieth century was Sigmund Freud. Freud believed that anatomy was destiny: he argued that women's lack of the male sex organ inevitably led to certain negative behavioural consequences for them. But Freud was far from being the first, or the only, man to believe in the natural inferiority of women. Indeed, as far back as Aristotle one can find philosophical justifications for women's inequality. A century after Freud we continue to speak of men and women as "the opposite sex," while pop psychologist John Gray, the author of *Men Are from Mars, Women Are from Venus*, tells us that the two sexes "think, feel, perceive, react, respond, love, need, and appreciate differently" (1993, 5).

Around the world, *gender difference* has been used to justify *gender inequality*. This chapter will examine both the beliefs we have about gender difference and the consequences of these beliefs regarding gender inequality. It should be noted that, technically speaking, the word *sex* refers to the physiological categories of male and female, while the term *gender* refers to the socially created categories of masculine and feminine. However, in recent years gender has come to encompass both meanings. Some social scientists argue that this

> What are little girls made of?
> Sugar and spice and everything nice,
> That's what little girls are made of.
> What are little boys made of?
> Snakes and snails and puppy dogs' tails,
> That's what little boys are made of.
> —*nursery rhyme*

is reasonable, since in reality it is impossible to separate the physiological from the cultural.

Gender Inequality in the Twenty-First Century

In 1970, the Royal Commission on the Status of Women in Canada tabled a report that contained 167 recommendations. Canadians were beginning to acknowledge that in the workplace, the home, the justice system, religious institutions, and everyday life, women and men were not equal. On the surface, it may appear that the issue of gender inequality is no longer relevant. Certainly, since 1970 there have been many advances for women in Canada. They have entered the paid labour force in large numbers, with their participation rate now very close to that of men, and women today can make many personal choices that were considered radical only forty years ago. However, while Canadian women now have equality protection in the Charter of Rights and Freedoms, it is clear that full gender equality does not yet exist:

- In 2009, Canadian women earned an average total income of $31,100 compared to the average total income for men of $45,200 (Statistics Canada 2011b).
- Women accounted for 56 percent of those who graduated from university in 1992; by 2007, the female share had risen to 61 percent (Statistics Canada 2010a). However, even women who successfully complete a program at the postsecondary level continue to earn far less than the men with the same type of educational attainment. In 1998, the average annual earnings for women with postsecondary education was 61 percent of men's earnings; by 2007 that figure had risen only slightly to 63 percent (Statistics Canada 2010g).
- Women have lower career expectations than men, anticipating smaller paycheques and longer waits for promotions. One study found that women predict their starting salaries to be 14 percent less than what men forecast, and this gap in wage expectations widens over their careers, with women anticipating their earnings to be 18 percent less than men's after five years on the job. Gender gaps in salary expectation and career advancement were widest among students planning to enter male-dominated fields such as science and engineering and narrowest for those preparing for female-dominated or neutral fields such as arts and science. (Boesveld 2011).
- In Canada today there are still men's jobs and women's jobs. In 2009, over half of women were found in two occupational groups: sales and services; and business, finance, and administration (Statistics Canada 2010g).
- Of 547 top officer jobs in Canada's hundred largest publicly traded companies in 2010, only thirty-six were held by women. Only five of Canada's top twenty-five companies had a woman at their most senior levels (Rosenzweig & Company 2011).

- One recent study found that women with MBAs from top business schools around the world earned an average of $4,600 less as a starting salary than men with the same credentials. Women also were less likely to move into leadership roles than men, were less likely to be promoted, and were three times as likely to have lost their jobs due to downsizing as men (Catalyst 2010).

- Only 3 percent of decision-making positions in the media (film, TV, newspapers, radio, online, etc.) are held by women. Fewer than 25 percent of newspaper "op-ed" articles are penned by women, and, of the 250 top-grossing films of 2009, only 16 percent had a woman in a key creative role as producer, director, cinematographer, writer, or editor (Monk 2011).

- Despite the fact that increasing numbers of women are in the paid labour force, they continue to do the majority of unpaid housework, home maintenance, childcare, and care of the elderly. In 2006, women in Canada spent approximately 248 minutes per day in unpaid work compared to 146 for men (Miranda 2011).

- While both men and women experience spousal violence, women are more likely to experience more serious forms of violence as well as repeated violence. In 2009, the rate of spousal homicide against women was about three times higher than that for men (Statistics Canada 2011c).

Everywhere we look, we can see the concrete manifestations of gender inequality. Far fewer women than men run for and are elected to public office. For example, after the 2011 federal election, only 25 percent of those elected to sit in the House of Commons were women. Indeed, Canada now ranks fiftieth on the world scale of women's participation in politics, trailing Pakistan, Bolivia, and the United Arab Emirates (Ward 2010). Although women can now be ordained in some religious faiths, few are headed by women, and many still promote women's place as being inside the home as wife and mother. Traditional female roles are still widely promoted in the media; in the pop music industry male artists are given more radio time than their sales figures would support (Harris, 2011). Meanwhile women remain among the poorest people in Canada. Senior women, women in lone-parent families, women with disabilities, and Indigenous women all experience significant poverty.

Think About It

Spend a day observing the gendered world around you. Watch for differing behaviours of men and women on public transportation, at school, or in your family. See how men and women are portrayed in the films, videos, or TV shows you watch. What differences do you observe? What are the similarities?

In other parts of the world conditions for women are far worse than in Canada. Of the nearly two billion people living in poverty, the majority are women, as are the majority of illiterate adults. Women still face many health dangers—including death from childbirth, illegal abortions, and HIV/AIDs—while the global preference for sons over daughters remains widespread. In some parts of the world brutal mass rape has become a common part of modern warfare, in some cases in an attempt to make women pregnant as a form of ethnic domination. In addition, while some countries have extended anti-discrimination provisions to include sexual orientation, homosexuality remains illegal in many countries, and sexual minorities—both men and women—continue to face unfair arrest, persecution, torture, or even death.

Is Biology Destiny?

Gender inequality is often assumed to be the result of gender difference. Biological determinists, as we have seen throughout this book, argue that certain biological differences inevitably lead to inequality. And yet how different are the sexes? If we carefully examine a group of women and men, their similarities far outweigh their differences. Even more surprising, while most of us assume that there are two clear gender categories—an unambiguous classification based on obvious biological distinctions—a number of traditional societies in fact have three or four gender categories (Martin and Voorhies 1975, 84–107). Such diversity reminds us once more that biology is always invested with cultural meaning.

One of the major focuses of research on male-female differences has been on intelligence and brain function. This perspective saw women as lacking the intellectual capacity to compete as equals with men. In the nineteenth century, the research into intelligence was mechanical and crude, usually comparing brain sizes and weights of men and women.

As noted earlier in the book, analyses that emphasize biological or genetic differences to explain social inequalities are very popular, particularly in the mass media. Such arguments are also now commonly used to explain the existence of homosexuality. Even many within the gay and lesbian community subscribe to this view. Yet there is no clear scientific evidence that homosexuality is "caused" exclusively by either hormones or genes. While same-gender eroticism and different-gender eroticism have always existed in every society, specific behaviours and attitudes about them have varied widely (Kinsman 2001, 214–5). This is another example of the way biology is filtered through culture.

The question of physiological difference between the sexes requires closer examination. Social scientists are agreed that there are a few real physiological differences between males and females—chromosomes, gonads, internal and external reproductive organs, hormones, and secondary sex characteristics. Women lactate and menstruate. However, there is no clear dichotomy between the

> In the most intelligent races, as among the Parisians, there are a large number of women whose brains are closer in size to those of gorillas than to the most developed male brains. This inferiority is so obvious that no one can contest it for a moment; only its degree is worth discussion.
> —Gustave Le Bon, 1879

Box 12.1 The Issue of Sexual Diversity

Humans have a tendency to think in binary ways, part of our predisposition to want relatively simple narratives. Thus when we think of gender, we usually think of a world divided into male and female. And when it comes to sex itself, as was discussed in Chapter 2, we commonly think of a male with a female, end of story. But the reality is that throughout the history of our species, sexuality has always been far more complex.

As noted earlier in the book, humans do not have to create rules prohibiting behaviours that no one wants to do. The fact that every culture has constructed rules pertaining to sexual behaviour tells us immediately that sexuality is a core issue for our species. This should not be surprising. First, for most of human history, birth control methods were insecure. Excessive mating could lead to a dangerously large number of children; for foraging people, unproductive mouths to feed could lead to the destruction of the entire population. At other times in history, when surplus was ample, or when wars or natural disasters destroyed populations, encouraging marital sex would have been in order. In addition, families were the core unit of all societies—minimally a male and female with extended kin. Sex practised outside this framework could create tensions that, again, would be risky for the whole group. Of course, such practices did occur, but while

those with wealth and privilege often got their needs met, for the less advantaged the cost could be high, including death.

Today in Canada we recognize that heterosexuality is not universal in our species, and most of us accept the diversity of sexual practices that exist in our country. The term "LGBT" (for lesbian, gay, bisexual, and trangender) is now commonly used to encompass the various gender and sexual minorities in our society, although we should also include intersex, two-spirited people, and questioning individuals as additional categories.

Although these groups are now acknowledged, they still face many forms of prejudice and discrimination, the degree varying according to geography and circumstance. Paradoxically, around the globe two opposing trends are occurring simultaneously—more openmindedness, acceptance, debate, and interest on the part of some, combined with a rigid fundamentalist, "traditionalist" world-view on the part of others. As one author writes, "Their struggle is one for human rights—the right to be who they are, free from violence and harassment. The right to have consenting sexual relations with others without losing life, liberty or livelihood. And the right to be recognized as equal citizens and to be treated with the respect that is due to all people" (Baird 2005, 8).

---

sexes. For example, men and women have both male and female sex hormones; indeed, some men may have more female hormones than some women and vice versa. In addition, as was noted in Chapter 2, biology itself can be affected by the external environment, making absolute boundaries difficult to determine.

Numerous studies have been undertaken to investigate possible innate differences between the sexes, including activity levels, nurturing behaviour, aggression, and mathematical and visual-spatial ability. Taken as a whole, this research suggests that—both biologically and psychologically—there are few obvious, consistent, and recurring differences between men and women. In other words, there is simply no concrete evidence to support the argument that biology alone is the basis for gender inequality. In the end, such arguments, like all biological determinist arguments, are more *justifications* of inequality than legitimate explanations of them. That is not to say that the biological difference between men and women plays *no* part in gender inequality; however, biology must always be understood within a social context.

Think About It

In what ways is the notion that the difference between men and women is natural or eternal reinforced within our society? Think of what you have learned in school as well as from your religion, parents, peers, and the media.

Feminist Theories of Gender Inequality

If biology alone cannot explain gender inequality, why has such inequality been so widespread? Various theories have attempted to answer this question. We have seen how the growth of capitalist economies brought about a new world-view known as liberalism, an ideology that emphasizes individual freedom, equality, and choice. This ideology developed because it suited the new growing bourgeoisie, but it was taken up by others who also aspired to these laudable goals. One of these groups was women. From the mid-nineteenth century and onward to the present day, groups of women (and some men) have taken on the question of gender inequality. The term **feminism** is used to broadly describe both the belief in the social, political, and economic equality of the sexes, as well as the various social movements organized around this belief.

When we hear the word *feminism* today, many of us have a distorted negative perception of its meaning, linking it to some mythical unhygienic man-hating extremist women. In reality, feminism includes a broad spectrum of beliefs and social activities, and most feminist research today examines the implications of gender inequality for both men and women. A number of writers now speak of three "waves" of feminism. First Wave feminism developed in the mid-nineteenth century, at first in Britain and later in North America. It consisted mostly of privileged White women who wanted to improve their own life situations; the focus was on gaining equal rights for women, especially the right to vote. These women did not refer to themselves as feminists.

This term really developed during the Second Wave of feminism, which began in the late 1960s. Second Wave feminism developed out of other social movements that arose at this time, including the student, anti-war, and civil rights movements in the United States; the revolutionary youth movements in Europe; the Quiet Revolution in Quebec; and various nationalist and socialist movements across Canada. This period of the twentieth century saw the development of a number of theories about gender inequality. As has been noted in previous chapters, the key theoretical frameworks in social analysis in the course of the twentieth century have been linked to either liberalism or Marxism, and two strands of Second Wave feminist theories can be linked to these two traditions. However, the 1960s also saw the development of a new approach to gender inequality that came to be known as *radical feminism*, which is examined later in this chapter.

Second Wave feminism must also be understood in the context of two developments that occurred at that time: first, middle-strata young women in North America started to attend university in increasing numbers, and second, the birth-control pill appeared on the scene. As women were increasingly given occupational choice, they also began to value greater personal choice as well. Many women in this period thus began to challenge the traditional family structure and their expected role of wife and mother; because of the pill, women also began to have expanded choices regarding sexual activities and childbearing.

In this context, women began to oppose the state's right to control their bodies—particularly with regard to reproduction—and, thus, issues relating to contraception and abortion were high on the feminist agenda. Both men and women also began to challenge **heterosexism**, the ideology that heterosexual sex within a state-sanctioned marriage—primarily for the purpose of reproduction—is normal, while all other forms of sexual behaviour are deviant. Lesbians, gay men, bisexuals, and transgendered people (individuals who move from one gender to another or defy gender boundaries) have made great strides in the last thirty years, although many forms of prejudice and discrimination remain.

Culture as the Basis of Gender Inequality: The Liberal View

The most broadly accepted form of feminism that advanced during the Second Wave was that of liberal feminism. For liberal feminists, the main source of gender inequality is the process of socialization. As has been discussed earlier in this book, socialization is the learning process by which we acquire our society's cultural components and social expectations. This process is carried out by various social institutions such as the family, schools, peers, mass media, and so on. While it begins in childhood, it continues throughout our life.

Cross-cultural research done by many anthropologists has demonstrated that the gender behaviours that seem so natural in our own society may be quite different in other times and places. In a broader investigation of more than 200 societies, George Murdock (1937) also found a large degree of cultural variation in the division of labour. While all societies had some division of labour based on gender, what was considered a male or female activity was not consistent. However, hunting and warfare were generally male activities, while cooking and childcare were more often defined as female tasks. Various anthropological studies thus refuted the biological determinist approach and put emphasis on the cultural basis of gender difference. These early studies were part of the broader liberal tradition.

Humans learn accepted gender behaviours from the various agents of socialization. For example, social scientists have noted that parents treat their male and female children differently, even within the first twenty-four hours after birth. In general, baby girls are thought to be more fragile than boys and are held more (MacDonald and Parke 1986). Ample data have also demonstrated the differential treatment of boys and girls in school classrooms, not only by their teachers but also via stereotyping in school materials. Meanwhile, from children's cartoons to adult drama, the mass media continue to portray stereotyped images of men and women. Advertising reinforces the centrality of physical attractiveness for women, who are commonly shown as being young, beautiful, and seductive.

Think About It
Look at a magazine rack as if you were a social scientist studying gender. Which sex is most often on the cover of magazines? What do men and women on the cover of these magazines look like? Do they look like people you know?

Surprisingly, role expectations are in some ways narrower for boys than for girls. Little boys learn very early on not only that they must not simply behave as boys, but also, more importantly, that they must not behave as girls (David and Brannon 1976, 14). This makes sense, since males in our society have a higher status than females: it is more acceptable for those with the lower status to emulate the behaviour of those above them; conversely, it is less permissible for men to act in ways that are seen in our society as "beneath them." Thus in the last forty years, the struggle for gender equality has seen more women entering male-dominated professions than the converse. While the women's movement brought to the fore the negative consequences of narrowly defined social roles for women, more recent works have also begun to notice that traditional expectations of masculinity have negative, although different, consequences for men (see Box 12.2).

The study of gender role socialization has helped social scientists understand that both women and men have a societal "script" imposed on them, and both women and men pay a price for the various restrictions on their behaviour. However, while the study of gender role socialization is fascinating, it helps us understand only one piece of the puzzle. For example, if social behaviour is merely the result of the process of socialization, how do we explain social change? Most of the women who initiated the modern women's movement in the 1960s and 1970s were raised in the very traditional family forms of the 1950s, just as many of you will reject some of the traditional family norms and values you learned as children.

One additional question remains: Where did our ideas about gender come from in the first place? As we noted with regard to race, the question is more than an academic one, for if we fail to eradicate the basis for such ideas then we will never achieve full gender equality. Liberal feminism and its arguments regarding gender role socialization are valuable in helping us understand how gender inequality is reinforced; however, this approach fails to pinpoint both the reasons for its development and the power structures in the distal sphere that help maintain it.

Box 12.2 What Sports Teach Boys

After the Vancouver Riot of 2011 was over, many analysts tried to explain the roots of the rowdy behaviour. While the official report blamed "congestion" and "free-flowing alcohol," the question of whether hockey itself—as a violent sport—played a key role was never addressed. Coincidentally, at around the same time that the report on the riots was released, a third former hockey "enforcer" in one year took his own life.

Although not well reported, troubling behaviour had also occurred during the Olympics in 2010. Gangs of young males took over public space in Vancouver's District 1, where many sports bars are located. According to the police, District 1 saw an increase of 233.3 percent in reported sexual offences during the Olympics; Women Against Violence Against Women saw a spike in the number of women they accompanied to hospital for the rape kit in the twenty-four hours after the gold-medal men's hockey game, while Vancouver's Battered Women's Support Services reported an increase in domestic violence of 31 percent.

The connection between hockey, masculinity, and violence is difficult to address. Hockey is our country's game. Over four million Canadians of all ages play hockey, and millions more watch it. And yet the connection is obvious. Hockey-sanctioned violence reinforces violence as a means of addressing or settling conflicts for men of all ages, but particularly for young males. Hockey, however, is not the only sport that has sparked male violence. In late 2011 the Turkish Football [soccer] Federation responded to previous fan violence by having a match that was open only to women and children under the age of twelve. Over 41,000 fans attended.

In general, competitive sports teach boys how to be males. Boys are expected to learn to control their emotions, especially those considered to be "feminine." Crying on the soccer pitch or the ice is not acceptable. And fear or feelings of physical pain just won't do, with young players being told to "suck it up" or to "stop being a sissy." The link between competitive sports and the military is not accidental, with both reinforcing the warrior image. The language of many sports, particularly North American football, contains military references, and teams have names like the Rough Riders and the Blue Bombers. It was also noted in Chapter 3 that the Winnipeg Jets hockey team launched its logo in 2011 by coming out of the back of a Canadian jet fighter, while the Toronto Raptors basketball team unveiled their new camouflage-style jersey shortly afterward. The names of many sports teams focus on ferocious-sounding animal names (Cougars, Panthers, Lions, Tigers, Sharks, Bruins, etc.). You won't find many boys on teams with names like the Pooh Bears, the Kittens, or the Fuzzy Rabbits.

And although we claim "it's not about whether you win or lose but how you play the game," even young players learn pretty quickly that it's the winners who get the cheers and the rewards, not the losers.

Source: Adapted from Nelson and Robinson 2002; L. Robinson 2011; and Pollett 2009.

Structural Analyses of Power: Radical Feminism and Marxism

As women's issues came into public awareness in the 1970s and onward, a number of writers advanced arguments that tried to move beyond liberal feminism by explaining the root cause of gender inequality. Two core theories were Marxism and **radical feminism**. Both were structural analyses in the sense that they saw gender inequality as rooted in something beyond simply beliefs. For radical feminists, gender inequality is connected to the biological difference between men and women, which led to an unequal power distribution within the family. Radical feminist theories were quite popular in the 1970s as the women's movement expanded.

While there is much diversity among radical feminists, their shared focus has been on the subordination and oppression of women. Thus radical feminists commonly speak of Western societies as a form of **patriarchy**, or rule by men. Men are the main beneficiaries in this power relationship, which may be sustained by the broader legal and cultural institutions; thus they are predisposed to maintain gender inequality. Because radical feminism emphasized the unequal power structures in the proximal sphere of the traditional family and male-female relationships, it touched the real experiences of many women.

Since radical feminists saw inequality as rooted in our biology, the difficult issue was how to attain gender equality. Many radical feminists focused on a separatist solution—that is, the elimination of men and traditional family structures from women's lives—since *compulsory heterosexuality*, a term first coined by Adrienne Rich (1980), was seen as a key way in which women's subordination was maintained. As a result, some lesbian feminists directed their struggle for change mainly in the sphere of personal relationships rather than broader societal issues.

While traditional Marxism also sees the problem of gender inequality as a structural one rather than one simply based on ideology, Marxists see gender inequality as rooted in the variable of class relationships rather than biology. Friedrich Engels, drawing on the work of anthropologist Lewis Henry Morgan, was the first to present a fully developed Marxist position on gender inequality in *The Origin of the Family, Private Property, and the State* ([1884] 1972). According to Engels, the monogamous family with the man at the head was the result of the growth of private property and the transformation of the family form into a means through which property could be inherited.

During the 1970s, there was a heated debate amongst feminists, particularly those in academia, about the cause of women's oppression. By the late 1970s, many feminists became increasingly dissatisfied with what they saw as the narrowness of both radical feminism and classical Marxism. They developed a new framework, which came to be known as **socialist feminism**. Socialist feminists attempted to combine the best insights of both radical feminism and Marxism, with varying degrees of success. In general, socialist feminism stresses the intersection of class and gender as well as the intersection of the public sphere of the economy and the state with the private sphere of the family and household. Many Canadian socialist feminists broadened and deepened the traditional Marxist analysis of gender.

From the mid-1990s and onward feminist theory moved in different directions. These theories are often described as Third Wave feminism. One strong theme of this new wave is diversity. This approach has been given various names, including multicultural feminism and inclusive feminism.

Inclusive feminism argues that radical feminism and Marxism—by focusing on broad categories such as "women" or "workers"—often ignore the lived experiences of individuals who are not only discriminated against as women but are additionally marginalized because of their race, ethnicity, socioeconomic status, age, ability, or sexual preference. Third Wave feminism is also connected to postmodernism, a broad analytical framework that is now found in most universities. Unlike the earlier approaches of Second Wave feminism, postmodernism rejects what are often called grand narratives or totalizing theories. Because postmodernism focuses on cultural elements such as the media, language, and ideas, it is in some ways similar to liberal feminism.

The Roots of Gender Inequality

While not all social scientists agree, most of the evidence seems to indicate that gender inequality was minimal in foraging societies. As was noted in Chapter 3, foraging societies emphasized cooperation, sharing, and mutual support. Family structures in these societies helped to ensure social stability, maximize life chances for offspring, and decrease the likelihood of social conflict. The family linked women to men, children to adults, and individuals to other individuals in often-complex kin networks. Survival depended on the interdependence of men and women.

Certainly there must have been a preference among women for tasks compatible with pregnancy and lactation. While this gave differing tasks to women and men, it in no way implied an unequal distribution of power. The distinction between the public world of men's work and the private world of women's domestic labour had not yet developed, because essentially the collective household was the entire community (Leacock 1972, 33).

Most anthropologists and historians seem to concur with Engels's proposition that dramatic changes in women's status began to occur with the production of food surpluses and the gradual transition to agrarian-based modes of production. As noted in Chapter 3, permanent surpluses led to the growth of structured social inequality, the state, warfare, and ultimately the development of class societies. Gender inequality, beginning about 7,000 to 10,000 years ago, took about 2,500 years to develop. Although we do not know the exact chain of events, we do know that over time productive property passed from collective ownership to family ownership, with the parallel development of the monogamous, or patriarchal, family. The main economic activity of farming came to be dominated by males. In this process, women became a form of property owned by the male.

Central to the changes in women's condition was the rise of slavery, and indeed one author (Lerner 1986, 78) argues that the first slaves were women and children. Thus the concept of women as property is tied to the notion of property in general, and the inequality of the female develops with the rise of social inequality in general. As classes developed, only a few families became the owners of productive property, which included slaves. The central role for women of this ruling class was solely to provide "legitimate" offspring to inherit property; their productive role became irrelevant since there were slaves to perform the work tasks. But even for small land-holding peasants, the question of heirs became important, since land could not be divided infinitely. There was only one way to maximize the likelihood that offspring who could make a claim on property were, indeed, "legitimate": the husband had to have full control over his wife to prevent her from having sexual access to other men.

Public and private spheres became increasingly separated, with women generally restricted to the household. In addition, the perceived role and value of men and women gradually changed. In foraging societies, the supernatural life-giving force was, logically, female. With the growth of gender inequality came gradual changes in religious beliefs. Female goddesses were gradually joined and eventually replaced by male gods, as in Greece and Rome, culminating in the widespread acceptance of the unitary, patriarchal god of the Old Testament, who created all living things and who created the first woman out of the first man (Lerner 1986, 145–46).

Such beliefs were connected to other changing assumptions about men and women: that God had created men and women as different and ultimately unequal; that men were naturally superior, stronger, and more rational, while women were naturally weaker, intellectually inferior, more nurturing, and emotionally unstable; that men's natural characteristics made them suited to explain and order the world, while women's made them suited to household activities and childcare (Lerner 1993, 4). Women were excluded from the world of ideas and, as a result, became invisible. Living in a form of slavery, they were—like all slaves—seen as less than fully human. Masculine behaviour came to be seen as "normal," while feminine was "abnormal." Thus to a greater or lesser degree, all modern societies became infused with notions of **misogyny**, or the hatred of women. These changing notions evolved gradually, as the roles of men and women—and social inequality in general—changed over time. In this way, the various beliefs about the sexes both resulted from societal changes and reinforced them.

The growth of the state also played an important role in legitimating gender inequality. With the development of private property, families became connected to a state system. Marriage, divorce, rights of inheritance, legitimacy of children, and so on came to be legal as well as moral matters. As Box 12.3 notes, women's sexuality also came under increasing control of a public and coercive apparatus—what had previously been a private matter was now regulated by the state. The question of who actually "owns" a woman's body continues to the present day.

Think About It

The issues about the state's right to control a woman's body are very complex. For example, do you think the Canadian government should have the right to prohibit pregnant women from smoking, drinking, or taking drugs?

Box 12.3 The Veiling of Women

In a number of countries of the Western world today, the veiling of some Muslim women has become a point of contention. What is little known, however, are the origins of this tradition, with many assuming it is rooted in the Islamic faith. In fact, the veiling of women actually begins much earlier, in Mesopotamia, the area between the Tigris and Euphrates rivers that was then dominated by two peoples, the Sumerians and the Assyrians. Assyrian law can be traced back to about the twelfth century BCE.

During this period, the sexual control of women of the propertied class became more firmly entrenched, and the virginity of respectable daughters became a financial asset for the family. At the same time poor women were often sold into prostitution, while concubines and harems for rich and powerful men also became common. Thus, prostitution and virginity were essentially two sides of the same coin, both involving the sexual regulation of women. But there was a social need for people to be able to distinguish between "respectable" and "non-respectable" women. There was also a need to keep men from excessively associating with women now defined as "non-respectable." Both purposes were accomplished by the enactment of Middle Assyrian Law number 40, the first that is known to have legislated the veiling of women. Nearly all of the Middle Assyrian laws relate to women and were a limitation on their rights. The law regarding the veiling of women reads as follows:

Neither [wives] of [seigniors] nor [widows] nor [Assyrian women] who go out on the street may have their heads uncovered. The daughters of a seignior... whether it is a shawl or a robe or a mantle, must veil themselves.... When they go out on the street alone, they must veil themselves. A concubine who goes out on the street with her mistress must veil herself.... A harlot [prostitute] must not veil herself; her head must be uncovered.

Thus the veil was as much about class as about gender, and wearing it became a sign of privilege, both for the wife of a propertied male and his concubine. The worst punishment was therefore not inflicted on a woman who *failed* to veil herself, but rather on a woman who tried to "pass" as someone above her station by *wearing* a veil. Punishment was public, including whipping and being forced to strip naked in the street. Moreover, savage punishment was also inflicted on any sympathetic or non-compliant men.

Many cultures and religions with origins in the Mesopotamian region—including the Abrahamic religions of Judaism, Christianity, and Islam—have some form of tradition involving the covering of women's heads. Of course, in Canada today, many women—whether religious or not—still observe the practice of veiling on their wedding day.

Source: Lerner 1986: 123-40.

The state enforced by law what religion enforced by belief, with violators severely punished. As forms of chattel like slaves, women had no, or very few, legal rights until recent times. Both legally and ideologically, women were seen as the property of men. At birth, a woman belonged to her father and remained so until she was "given away" in marriage to her husband. And, until very recently, like any form of property, she was the owner's (man's) to do with as he pleased, including to rape, assault, and, in some jurisdictions, even murder.

Many anthropologists have argued that conditions for women reached their lowest point in agrarian societies. In these societies—which still exist in many parts of the world—women are kept ignorant and often isolated in the family unit, from which there is no escape. In addition, while they may hold a certain degree of power in the domestic sphere, they are legally under the control of their fathers or husbands. Historically, maintaining control over women often involved such acts as foot binding (practised in China for almost a thousand years), suttee (a Hindu custom in which the woman was expected to throw herself on the funeral pyre of her dead husband), and various forms of genital cutting, still practised by many religious groups in North and West Africa.

The industrial era saw women around the world begin their long struggle out of horrific conditions of oppression. Capitalism, from the earliest stages, drew women out of the home. Women were actually sought out by the textile industry in the eighteenth and nineteenth centuries because they had small hands and worked for lower wages. However, it was not until the early 1960s that women, particularly married women with children, began to enter the paid labour force in large numbers. This integration of women into paid labour raised women's status in society and has helped break down the notion of "man's place" and "woman's place," as well as the different value assigned to each.

Gender and Power

We have noted throughout this book that inequalities of power exist at both the distal level and the proximal level. It is often power at the proximal level that we experience most directly and most intensely: on a day-to-day level, one is more likely to feel, and have to respond directly to, the power wielded by one's parents or boss as opposed to that wielded by, say, the prime minister or the CEO of a major corporation. Power at the distal level is rooted in the relationships between classes; in contrast, it is *status* differentials that largely determine power relationships at the proximal, or nearby, level.

When we look at the statuses of male and female, it is obvious that, on all accounts, males have the higher status. It should be noted that this status inequality is so far from being "natural" that it must constantly be reaffirmed in symbolic ways. Even today, men are still expected to date and marry women who are shorter, smaller, younger, and less educated, and who have a lower occupational status.

Think About It
What would you think if you saw an older woman walking in an intimate way with a much younger man?

Radical feminists emphasized the male power over women that results from this unequal status relationship. This power can most clearly be noted in the many forms of physical and psychological violence that men have long inflicted on women. Both in Canada and around the world, women report a much higher incidence of domestic abuse than men. In addition, women who report being abused are more likely to report being physically injured or require medical attention and are much more likely to fear for their lives or the lives of their children. However, while an abused woman may see her abuser as very powerful, in reality men as a group actually have very little structural power. In much of their daily lives—in their world of work, in their control over the world—the majority of men are actually quite powerless.

Thus, while men achieve some real benefits from gender inequality, they have also paid a high price for them, a fact that has now been noted by many men. At the economic level, the lower wages of women exert a downward pressure overall on men's wages as well. Moreover, since most men are members of family units, the lower wages of women reduce their total family income.

Men also pay a high price in physical health and safety. Proportionally more men than women die from suicides and accidents, and many more injured every year in job-related accidents (Statistics Canada 2010c; Human Resources and Development Canada 2011b). We should also not forget the large number of men who die every year in war. The psychological price men pay for their few privileges is much harder to measure, but no less consequential. From a young age many boys are taught not to display those characteristics deemed "feminine," including the ability to express feelings and show vulnerability (Pollack 1998). This can stunt personal relationships, sexual intimacy, and emotional experiences. For many men, a life devoted to occupational mobility has meant higher death rates from diseases of stress and less time to participate in family life.

However, although men as a group do not hold the reins of power, they have traditionally had greater *access* to positions of power than have women. Put differently, we might say that the "access gates" to positions of power within capitalism have been more open to men than to women, even though the reality for most men is that, like most women, they will never hold such structured positions of power. In this way, we can speak of male privilege just as we can speak of White privilege, without assuming that all males, any more than all White people, have all the power.

For Marxists, the main beneficiary of gender inequality is the ruling class in capitalist society. Gender inequality, as noted in this chapter, long predates capitalism; the bourgeoisie inherited a social system with a long history of gender inequality and a deeply held set of beliefs and values that justified and maintained it. Nonetheless, the capitalist owning class has benefited from this already-existing inequality and as a result has had little motivation to eliminate it.

In the previous chapter we saw how capital benefits from the maintenance of racism. To some extent, the benefits to capital of gender inequality are similar. First and most directly, the underpaid labour of women provides huge profits for the employer. More women than men are unemployed, underemployed, or work part-time, ready to take whatever work is available out of economic need. This underpayment of women both in Canada and in the less developed countries—as already noted—exerts a downward pressure on all wages, further enhancing profits. In the domestic sphere, the unpaid labour done by women is also of benefit to the capitalist owning class. Women continue to be the primary caregivers for the next generation of workers, at little cost to this class, which might otherwise have to pay more taxes to provide an extensive state-supported childcare system.

> The increasing packaging of men's bodies in the media— it is now common to see men's bodies displayed in advertising in ways that were conceivable only for women's bodies a generation ago—coupled with increased economic anxiety (which leads us to focus on things we *can* control, like how we look), has led to a dramatic shift in men's ideas about their bodies.
> —Michael Kimmel

Despite the changing gender roles in the workplace, males and females have continued to be socialized into traditional roles. Muscular masculinity is linked to participation in sports, as well as the ability to fight, endure pain, and master machines (Connell 1995). Governments and traditional religions that adhere to historical gender roles have promoted this notion of masculinity to prepare men for their role in the family, their possible role on the battlefield, and for work.

Domestic femininity, meanwhile, prepares women for their role as household workers and family caregivers. Even if women work outside the home, their primary activity is still commonly seen as that within a heterosexual marriage with offspring. Although the latter half of the twentieth century saw women's and men's work activities change substantially, notions of the "traditional" family and gender roles—if modified somewhat to reflect new realities—continue to the present day. Indeed, Wolf (1991) argued that the growing independence of women actually led to an escalation of what she called the "beauty myth," with women more preoccupied with their self-image than with changing structures of power (see Box 12.4).

Think About It
Why do women paint their nails but men don't? What does having one's fingernails done say about the type of work that women are expected to be doing?

Most of us would agree that both men and women have become more absorbed with their appearance. As Box 12.4 notes, while Second Wave feminists sought to discredit the media's hyper-sexualized images of females, many of today's young women have embraced these images. In the late 1960s the "unisex" look was the rage, and it was sometimes hard to tell a male from a female. As women have struggled to advance gender equality—entering the paid labour force and attaining higher levels of education—the idealized body type and fashion style for both men and women have returned to an emphasis on their physiological differences. Such differentials, in their own way, help maintain the notion of gender difference.

Box 12.4 Pretty in Pink

Have you noticed something interesting about the way young children are dressed these days? Little boys are dressed in a variety of colours, while little girls are almost universally dressed in pink. Moreover, it isn't just the colour, it's the style: more and more young girls are looking like little princesses. Is this just a natural phase that all little girls go through or is it something more?

Peggy Orenstein argues that, at least in its current hyper-feminine and highly commercial form, this phase is anything but natural. According to Orenstein, princess products were introduced in 2000 by the Disney Corporation. There are now more than 26,000 Disney Princess items on the market; in 2009, they generated sales of $4 billion for Disney alone, and, of course, these products have been widely imitated.

Orenstein notes that while these products are not sexualized *per se*, they're certainly linked to the growing culture of consumerism and narcissism that was discussed in Chapter 6. Of particular concern for young girls is that they are increasingly playing with toys, wearing clothes, watching videos, and otherwise partaking of a culture that is too mature or sexual for them, and they're encouraged to play-act at being sexy. Orenstein also worries that girls' identity is increasingly focused on performance—how they look, how they act sexually, and how feminine they are. While in some ways none of this is recent, it is worrying that, first, these tendencies are being seen at ever-younger ages and second, that new technologies allow young women to advertise their "sexy" personas in a very public way.

The rise of Second Wave feminism in the 1970s was in some ways a response to the pretty-in-pink (although not sexual) girl culture of the 1950s. By the 1990s, the cry for a social revolution that would liberate women had morphed into struggle for "girl power," for self-actualization and personal fulfillment. For Orenstein, girl power today means "being valued for how you look instead of what you do. And being confident is expressed by being spoiled, pampered, bratty, narcissistic."

Do you agree with Orenstein's assessment?

Sources: Orenstein 2010; Moskowitz 2011.

These images have also proven very profitable to capital. The need of males and females to live up to these images has both women and men spending billions on clothing, gym memberships, make-up, weight-loss products, steroids, Botox treatments, plastic surgery, and so on. And of course, because most of us need money to buy these products as we seek the temporary gratification that comes through their purchase, we are likely to accept our deteriorating workplace conditions. In this way, distinct gender roles and the images that go with them remain very profitable to capital.

How Far Has the Struggle for Gender Equality Come?

From the viewpoint of the early twenty-first century, it may appear that Canadian women of today actually have it pretty good. However, in some ways the main advances for women have come in the personal realm—increasing freedom of lifestyle choices as well as sexual liberation—while certain important structural transformations have been limited.

For example, there continues to be occupational gender segregation, with the labour market divided into male and female segments. One study looked at Statistics Canada data and found that there have been few advances for women in senior management positions (Chenier and Wohlbold 2011). By 2009, 0.32 percent of women had made it to the top echelon compared to 0.64 percent of male workers, virtually unchanged since 1987. As one textbook on work notes, "A potent combination of gender-role socialization, education, and labour market mechanisms continue to channel women into a limited number of occupations in which mainly other females are employed" (Krahn et al. 2007, 182). These female job ghettos often have lower wages, fewer benefits, little job security, and little opportunity for advancement.

Moreover, some of the growing equality between the sexes has come not from women's advances but rather from men's deteriorating position, particularly regarding the increasing numbers of men working in low-wage jobs. Such data are in line with the argument made by Pat Armstrong (1996) that using a male standard to evaluate women's progress often exaggerates women's gains while masking the deteriorating condition for men. While some women—like some men—are doing better than ever, more women and more men are finding themselves in "bad" rather than "good" jobs. Even those who remain in the good jobs find that they are working harder and are under more stress. Overall, workers are putting more time into their paid employment than they did forty years ago (Human Resources and Development Canada 2011a).

And while girls are surpassing boys at all levels of education—females get higher grades in high school, are more likely to graduate from high school, and are more likely to attend postsecondary institutions—their achievements may be coming at the expense of some males. Across North America, the data seem to indicate that White, middle-, or upper-income males are doing as well as, or better than, ever before. However, some racial and ethnic minorities and lower-income males are finding themselves increasingly marginalized at an early age. With some "good" and many "bad" jobs, many disadvantaged students—as noted elsewhere in this book—are being streamed out of programs that would give them access to the postsecondary education required for the high-paying good jobs (Sears 2003).

For both males and females, there is a link between paid employment and work done in the home. However, unlike men, many women continue to make career choices that they feel will be compatible with child-rearing. Men, in contrast, are more likely to see themselves as the breadwinners and choose careers that fit with this assumption. The unequal wages that persist in the workplace simply reinforce differing roles in the heterosexual household, which then reinforce differing roles in the workplace.

Think About It

How did you decide what program to choose when you entered university or college? Do you think your choice was at all gender-related?

Gender inequality persists in male-female households, despite women's increased participation in the paid labour force. For example, when men do participate in housework, they tend to do the more pleasant chores, such as playing with children or shopping. Among heterosexual couples, a central variable affecting the gender division of labour in the home seems to be the wages of the woman relative to those of the man. That is, the narrower the wage gap between male and female partners, the more equal the household division of labour seems to be. A 2005 study of Canadian households concluded that the division of paid labour and housework for male-female couples is more likely to be split equally when wives have an income of $100,000 or more (Statistics Canada 2006a).

The household continues to be seen as privatized and outside of the public sphere, primarily under the control of those within it. For this reason, domestic violence and violence against children have taken so long to be seen as more than a personal problem, while the burdens of child-rearing and household management have received declining support from the state, particularly in Canada. Also troubling is the decision by the federal government in 2011 to eliminate the long-form census, done every 5 years. Data from this census allowed social analysts to assess, among other things, long-term changes to the gender division of labour in Canadian households.

Ironically, governments are touting themselves as "family friendly" while actually reducing the supports that most families need. In 2006, shortly after taking power, the Conservative government under Stephen Harper cancelled plans for the $2.2 billion National Child Care Strategy, which had been over ten years in the making; instead the government returned to a system of funding families, with every child under six receiving a paltry $1,200 per year. (The sole exception to this policy is the province of Quebec, which increased family benefits some years ago and instituted an accessible and affordable childcare system.) Although the government has handed out a total of nearly $3 billion in these monthly benefits to families, no new daycare spaces have been added. Regulated daycare shortages across the country are so severe that families now pay to put their names on multiple waiting lists long before their children are even born. Care for the sick and elderly is also being shifted back into the private sphere of the household.

In all these activities, women constitute the majority of caregivers. Those with higher incomes are increasingly hiring paid workers such as nannies, cleaners, and caregivers for the aged to do such work. Of course, most of these paid household workers are other women—often immigrant women—with low wages, poor working conditions, few benefits, and low status. In many cases these women are forced to leave their own children behind in the care of others while they work abroad.

In recent years both women and men have felt increasing pressures in trying to balance work and home tasks. The "work-family crunch" is currently being aggravated by a number of tendencies. The stagnating wages of men have pressured more women to stay in or rapidly re-enter the paid labour force. Declining government supports for children (particularly in the areas of childcare and education) also mean that two wages (and frequently more than two jobs) are required for parents to acquire some measure of financial security. At the same time, both men and women are finding that they are under increasing pressure from employers to be more productive, which has resulted in longer hours and more intensified work.

Achieving a balance is a particularly serious concern for women, who perform the major share of domestic tasks. Researchers at Laval University found that the combination of high-stress jobs and child-rearing responsibilities was driving women's blood pressure to persistently high levels, putting them at a much higher risk of stroke and heart disease (Picard 1999). Some women opt to become full-time mothers after their children are born. However, women who stay at home to raise children sometimes experience *more* symptoms of depression, such as irritability and sleep disorders, than those who work outside the home. Moreover, staying at home is not a realistic option for most women. In the current economic climate, the majority of women—whether living with a partner or not—have to work and find themselves working harder than ever before. Clearly these stresses are magnified for lower-income earners and in lone-parent families.

Many men are now taking on more child-rearing responsibilities. For example, between 2001 and 2006, the proportion of fathers who took a leave from work for the birth or adoption of their child rose from 38 percent to 55 percent. This rise was likely due to changes in government eligibility for benefits (Statistics Canada 2007b). However, the stresses are different for men, who often find themselves in jobs where no accommodation is made for their family life. Moreover, while men are under pressure to more equitably share household tasks, they are still expected to be "good providers."

The Outlook for the Future

Unlike earlier pre-industrial societies, it is now possible to have full equality between men and women. And yet gender inequality continues to exist. Since this inequality has had negative consequences for *both* men and women, why is change so slow? The process of change is by no means an easy one. Even for many women change does not come easily. This should not be surprising, given that notions of gender inequality have existed for thousands of years and constitute an essential part of many of our strongly held religious or moral belief systems. Moreover, because those with power continue to

Advancing feminist public policy is extremely difficult under neoliberal economic and social conditions. Developing effective strategies will require Amazonian efforts to make women's voices loud enough to be heard by governments; nevertheless, feminist persistence has been a characteristic of significant change in the past, even under poor circumstances.
—Marjorie Griffin Cohen and Jane Pulkingham, Public Policy for Women

Empower women and you will see a decrease in poverty, illiteracy, disease and violence.
—Michaëlle Jean, former Governor General of Canada

As we go marching, marching,
We're standing proud and tall,
The rising of the women means the rising of us all.
—modern lyrics of "Bread and Roses," considered the anthem of the modern women's movement, adapted from a poem written by American James Oppenheim in 1911.

benefit from gender inequality, change has been much slower than one might have imagined even twenty-five years ago.

Governments at all levels have an important role to play in this respect. One key area lies in support for families. Countries that provide the most social and financial supports to families, such as Sweden, where 92 percent of children aged eighteen months to five years get state-funded daytime care, also have the greatest social equality, including gender equality. Such government supports, including adequate subsidies for single parents, improved minimum wages, and so on, have been shown to advance gender equality both in the home and in the workplace, as well as life-expectancy and overall health (Wilkinson and Pickett 2010). Unfortunately, the neoliberal policies of various levels of government in Canada have eroded some of the previous gains made by women, and many policies have had a devastating effect on the family as social supports were reduced or removed. The massive spending cuts over the last thirty years at all levels of government have been particularly hard on women, in part because so many find themselves in poverty.

But there are other concerns for women, not only those who are poor. Women's paid employment occurs in a relatively narrow range of occupations, primarily the service sector. These are the very occupations—such as nurses, early childhood educators, teachers, social workers, and government clerical workers—that have been most under attack by governments since the late 1990s. Some women also find themselves having to take care of aging parents as social supports to the elderly and the sick have declined. Globalization and the elimination of trade barriers have also had a particularly negative effect on women. Many of the jobs held by women in manufacturing (clothing, footwear, textiles, and electrical products) have been lost to cheaper global competition.

The declining rate of unionization is another worrying trend. There is substantial agreement that collective bargaining improves wages and benefits for unionized workers when compared to non-unionized workers, particularly for those with lower skills, while promoting greater equality of wages and working conditions within the unionized sector (Jackson and Schellenberg 1999, 247). Not only do women in unionized workplaces generally earn higher wages than do women in comparable employment who are not unionized, but they also have greater protection via collective-agreement provisions around such issues as maternity leave and sexual harassment.

The same factors that are holding back gender equality in Canada—global capitalism and neoliberalism—have been having a negative effect on women in other parts of the world, and many advances for women have been eroded. The transformation of countries of the former Soviet Union to free market economies meant an end to a range of government supports for women—including free health care and education—which drove many into poverty. In the developing world, global pharmaceutical companies have marketed unsafe or experimental contraceptives to women. Meanwhile, the current backlash against Western society and values in many parts of the world has frequently meant a backlash against women's rights (van der Gaag 2004, 12). Many of the countries that have repressive laws against women continue to severely restrict and punish homosexuality as well.

As emphasized in this chapter, the erosion of women's conditions generally means worsening conditions for men. Such analyses tell us that the struggle for gender equality is not one of women versus men, nor is it simply a struggle to change ideas or gender images. Gender inequality is bound up in the unequal and highly segregated worlds of work, both in the paid labour force and in the household. Gender inequality is inevitable in a society that puts corporate needs ahead of the needs of people.

In the short term, a number of policy changes would lead to greater gender equality in Canada, improving the lives of both women and men. These would be truly "family friendly" policies, including a national child-care program, more affordable housing, minimum wages that are above the Statistics Canada LICO poverty line, the expansion of the living wage (see Box13.3, in the next chapter), the growth of public-sector jobs, improvements to unemployment insurance (EI), union contracts that limit the ability of companies to hire contingent workers, and more protections and benefits for part-time workers.

In the longer term, there is a need for a shorter work week so that both men and women can better combine paid labour with family obligations, the reduction of part-time and contingent workers, and increased rates of unionization. Overall, all family forms require greater financial and social supports from the various levels of government and from employers. Such demands constitute a collective challenge to the present ruling class, which currently sets the limits on such possibilities through its ownership and control of the means of production.

KEY POINTS

1. Assumptions about gender difference have led to gender inequality around the world.

2. Despite gains over the past thirty years, gender inequality continues to be a reality in Canada.

3. Biological determinists and functionalists believe that anatomy is destiny. Overall, the research suggests that there are few obvious, consistent, and recurring differences between men and women.

4. Since the nineteenth century, various feminist theories have developed to explain gender inequality. Many writers now speak of three "waves" of feminism.

5. Liberal feminism sees the main cause of gender inequality within a society's culture, that is, in the ideas we have about men and women and in the way children are socialized. What is missing in this argument, however, is the roots of these cultural elements.

6. Both radical feminism and traditional Marxism see gender inequality as a structural problem, linked to the allocation of power. While radical feminists feel gender inequality is rooted in biology, Marxists argue that it began with the rise of social classes and the patriarchal family.

7. Most anthropologists agree that the development of classes led to the growth of the state, warfare, a changing religious system, and the patriarchal family. All of these played a role in magnifying gender inequality.

8. While men's higher status does lead to some male privilege, most men have little structural power. The real power is held by the capitalist owning class. Traditionally men have had greater access to positions of power, but most men—like most women—seldom achieve such positions.

9. Many of the recent advances made by women in Canada have been under attack as a result of globalization and neoliberal government policies.

10. Both women and men have felt increasing pressures in trying to balance work and home tasks; these stresses are magnified for lower-income earners and in lone-parent families.

11. Gender inequality has had negative consequences for both men and women. The Canadian government could make a number of policy changes that would improve the lives of both men and women.

Fine, Cordelia. 2010. *Delusions of Gender: How Our Minds, Society, and Neurosexism Create Difference*. New York: W.W. Norton.
A critical examination of various biological determinist arguments—both "scientific" and from the popular press—that attempt to convince us that gender inequality is hard-wired in our species.

Griffin Cohen, Marjorie, and Jane Pulkingham, eds. 2009. *Public Policy for Women: The State, Income Security, and Labour Market Issues*. Toronto: University of Toronto Press.
A book of readings that assess the way neoliberal policies have affected women in Canada, with consideration of how public policy needs to be altered.

Knegt, Peter. 2011. *About Canada: Queer Rights*. Black Point, NS: Fernwood.
A brief introduction to the history of the struggle for queer rights as well as an analysis of current issues.

Lerner, Gerda. 1986. *The Creation of Patriarchy*. New York: Oxford University Press.
This is probably the most thorough examination of the evolution of gender inequality in the region of the Middle East. Essential reading for those interested in the way certain religious beliefs about men and women transformed over time.

Nelson, Addie. 2009. *Gender in Canada*. 4th ed. Don Mills, ON: Pearson Education Canada.
A highly readable text that covers a vast array of issues pertaining to gender in Canada.

Tyyskä, Vappu. 2007. *Action and Analysis: Readings in the Sociology of Gender*. Toronto: Nelson.
This book of readings does a nice job of showing how the various feminisms of our time have each added to our understanding of modern gender issues.

Rebick, Judy. 2005. *Ten Thousand Roses: The Making of a Feminist Revolution*. Toronto: Penguin Canada.
The author, herself a long-time feminist activist, weaves together an oral history of four decades of the women's movement in Canada.

Valenti, Jessica. 2007. *Full Frontal Feminism: A Young Woman's Guide to Why Feminism Matters*. Berkeley, CA: Seal Press.
As the title indicates, this book is for young women who may be wondering what feminism has to offer them. Young men might learn a few things as well.

Walter, Natasha. 2011. *Living Dolls: The Return of Sexism*. London, UK: Little, Brown.
An examination of the way women's roles today emphasize youth, sexuality, and beauty.

13 Looking Toward the Future

In This Chapter
- Where is our society headed?
- Can the problems within capitalist societies be corrected without any radical transformation of the entire system?
- Will Canada survive as a country?
- How do societies change from one form to another?

In August 2011, Jack Layton, then head of the New Democratic Party and leader of the Opposition, died unexpectedly. Within hours people were organizing vigils in his honour in a number of cities across Canada. Thousands of people lined up to view the casket in Ottawa and Toronto, and thousands more left notes on message boards. What became clear from these messages was that the outpouring of emotions was not particularly with reference to Layton's politics or his party. Rather, the messages embodied what so many Canadians—from a wide variety of political, ethnic, racial, and economic backgrounds—wanted to see their country become: a more open, tolerant, compassionate, and caring place to live.

There has been a great deal of discussion in this book about change, but up until now we've looked at change from the past—both ancient and recent—up to the present. And although we know that change is constant, it often seems that change is both unpredictable and out of our control. In this context, the notion of being able to make predictions about where our society is headed seems an absurdity. Social scientists, of course, are not mystics or fortune-tellers. Like all scientists, we predict the future based on past patterns.

European social thought of the late nineteenth and early twentieth centuries, including sociology, largely developed out of the turbulent changes brought about by the Industrial Revolution and the transformation to capitalism. From the outset, there was a tension about the ultimate purpose of social analysis. On one side are those analyses—the order theories—that supposedly seek simply to describe the

> The philosophers have only interpreted the world: the point however is to change it.
> —Karl Marx, Theses on Feurbach

> There is no better example of what's wrong with completely unregulated capitalism than the situation we're in right now. It's right there, on the front page of every newspaper…. Step up to the plate and start swinging.
> – Thomas Frank

social universe. While society may need a bit of fixing up here and there, social arrangements are seen as both inevitable and permanent—"The world is just." In contrast are the change theories, which see the world as currently lacking in justice and thus in need of change.

The question of how our social world might change is linked to two elements: the real, material conditions within capitalist societies, and the way humans act on and change such conditions. In other words, change must be understood in terms of both the *objective* and the *subjective* elements in any given society at any particular point in time. This chapter examines some of the growing and increasingly visible contradictions within capitalist systems and the way people are responding to these contradictions.

Where in the World Are We Headed?

It has been noted throughout this book that humans, interacting both with each other and with the physical world, inevitably alter the social world in which we live. Most of the changes humans make are within the existing class relations. Any such change—which can be of a social, legal, economic, or political nature—is generally referred to as a **reform**. Reforms can be of benefit to ordinary people (for example, human rights legislation) or work against their interests (for example, government cuts to social spending).

Reforms can sometimes be major transformations within a society and therefore can be quite controversial. Over the past fifty years Canada has seen the social institutions of both marriage and the family change in dramatic ways. The expansion of divorce, the right to disseminate birth control information, the right of women to obtain legal abortions, and the right of gays and lesbians to marry were all very controversial developments in their time.

Even when reforms involve major alterations to a social institution, they must be distinguished from the rare instances of **revolution**. Sometimes this term is used to refer to any kind of major social, political, or technological change. However, social science requires greater precision of terminology. For this reason, revolution should more correctly be defined as a radical transformation of the social order. In the traditional Marxist definition, it is legitimate to use the term *revolution* only when there has been a basic altera-tion in the relationships between social classes, such as the transformation from a feudal to capitalist order. Even dramatic political events that result in some form of "regime change" without altering the existing class structure are not revolutions.

However, it is important to understand that no social transformation, however radical, totally eliminates what came before. Humans are an essen-tially conservative species, always building the new on the foundation of the old. Many of our current religious and philosophical beliefs are thousands of years old. Capitalism itself is rooted in the European feudal order, and an advanced capitalist country such as ours still has a number of feudal remnants, including a queen of Canada.

There is a dialectical relationship between reform and revolution, with reforms constituting the *quantitative* component of change, and revolution constituting the *qualitative*. In other words, people do not just wake up one day, say to themselves simultaneously, "Hey, I've got a great idea—how about a new socioeconomic formation?" and then go out and overturn the old order. On the other hand, reforms within a given socioeconomic formation cannot simply go on forever. When the "boiling point" of a society is reached, when the contradictions within it have become so great that it can no longer continue in its present form, then a qualitatively distinct moment for change has arrived.

There is nothing in the concept of revolution that requires physical violence as a necessary component. If a ruling class is defeated by a previously subservient class (or classes), then this is a revolutionary change no matter whether it occurred peaceably or through armed force. While historically all revolutions have included some violence, the actual degree of it—for example, the presence or absence of civil war—has varied. Frequently, the revolution itself has been relatively peaceful, but the counter-revolution instigated by the defeated ruling classes has been quite ruthless and of considerable duration. This is exactly what happened following the Russian Revolution of 1917.

Of course, to speak of revolution in the present Canadian context seems an absurdity for most of us, clearly an indication that the boiling point for radical change in this country is not yet at hand. Most of us in Canada continue to believe either that certain social problems are inevitable or that reforms within the capitalist system will be enough to improve our social world. However, in many other parts of the world today, the "boiling point" has been reached, with more and more calling for radical transformations within their countries.

The view that we can change the world through reforms alone is referred to as **reformism**. This approach acknowledges the imperfections of our society but denies the class nature—and therefore the power inequities—of capitalism. Reformism is reflected in the political tendency known as *social democracy*. Social democrats acknowledge the inequities and unfairness created by capitalist systems. While they are likely to identify with workers and disadvantaged groups, they believe that the worst tendencies of capitalism can be brought under control. For social democrats, the primary solution to the excesses and inequities of capitalism is to put their political party into power. In Canada, social democracy is most clearly embodied in the New Democratic Party.

At certain moments in history, social democratic parties have been one of the leading political forces for change that helped ordinary people. In 1933, the Cooperative Commonwealth Federation (CCF)—the predecessor of the New Democratic Party—approved a fourteen-point program for change at its founding convention. The Regina Manifesto, as it was called, opened with these words:

We aim to replace the present capitalist system, with its inherent injustice and inhumanity, by a social order from which the domination and exploitation of one class by another will be eliminated, in which economic planning will supersede unregulated private enterprise and competition, and in which genuine democratic self-government, based on economic equality, will be possible.

However, following World War II and particularly since the rise of neoliberalism, many of these parties have become indistinguishable from their more conservative opponents. Social democratic parties are commonly spoken of as "socialist" parties (particularly by their opponents on the right). However, although social democrats have achieved parliamentary majorities in a number of provinces and in many countries, often for considerable periods of time—for example, Nova Scotia, Saskatchewan, Manitoba, Sweden, Great Britain, Australia, and New Zealand—the capitalist ruling class has retained both its wealth and its power, and the private appropriation of surplus has continued or even escalated. In fact, some analysts argue that the ruling class does better under social democracy because it silences or reduces broad opposition from the population. Indeed, the United States is one of the few advanced capitalist countries of the world that never developed a national social democratic party.

In contrast to the social democrats are those on the left who feel that, in the end, capitalism cannot be reformed to any great extent. If we examine history, it is clear that all socioeconomic formations up to the present have come into being, developed for a time, decayed, and finally disappeared. Nonetheless, capitalism has shown itself to be an extremely flexible societal form. Marxists have frequently predicted the imminent demise of capitalism, and yet it still dominates the globe. However, the increasingly visible contradictions within capitalist systems give us a clue that capitalism as we know it may now be on the decline.

The Contradictions of Capitalism

More and more analysts—not simply those with a Marxist orientation—have been noticing a number of disturbing developments within modern capitalist societies. None of them are new, but there seems to be an increased visibility of such tendencies, as well as escalating discomfort with them. Particularly since the economic downturn that began in 2008, many have been questioning whether the interests of corporate leaders mesh with the interests of the rest of us. A look beneath the surface reveals a troubling and uncertain future for capitalism.

Doomsday scenarios that see a society declining economically or morally and headed into a "dark age" are not new, and the prevalence of this theme—among

> It must be recognized that organized capital has become—together with, but to an even greater extent than organized crime—a parasite so voracious that it is killing the body it feeds off.
> —*Harry Shutt*, The Trouble With Capitalism

religious leaders, philosophers, and cultural critics—may make some of us wonder about their legitimacy. Nonetheless, there do seem to be a number of major fault lines in our current social arrangements that appeared even before the crisis of 2008. Morris Berman (2006), an American sociologist, argued that the United States was heading into a "dark age," which he links to such elements as cultural deterioration, erosion of both civil liberties and the rule of law, the development of a permanent state of war, and the decline of the United States as a global economic and moral power. Jane Jacobs (2004, 163), focusing on broader North American culture, argued that a decay in the five central pillars of our society—community and family; higher education; science and technology; governmental representation; and self-regulation of the learned professions—has been leading to what she calls an "unprecedented crisis."

As was noted in Chapter 1, dialectics asserts that change is the result of the unity and struggle of opposites—that, in effect, all societies contain the seeds of their own destruction. Capitalism certainly displays such tendencies. Strangely, the inner contradictions of capitalism are escalating at the very time when its supposed enemies—that is, Marxist political movements, the Soviet empire, the trade union movement, and so on—are either weak or have disappeared entirely. Thus, ironically, the current global economic crisis can be blamed on nothing other than capitalism itself. This may explain why a number of mainstream economists have recently expressed the opinion that Marx was the only one to correctly predict the current economic crisis (see, for example, the Roubini quote later in this chapter). It also helps us understand the sudden appearance and rapid spread of the Occupy movements in 2011.

Growing Social, Political, and Economic Instability

The capitalist owning class seeks stability, but, in carrying out its competitive activities in the marketplace, it always ends up with its opposite, growing instability. New policies and directions are sought in an attempt to restore stability until the inevitable instability appears again. This is the irresolvable crisis of capitalism. Capitalism inevitably suffers from excess production—of goods, of workers, and of capital itself, and overproduction leads to growing economic instability, which in turn creates increasing social and political instability. The highly competitive global economy of today has increased economic instability and the risk of global economic collapse.

Some government policies were developed in the late nineteenth and early twentieth centuries in an attempt to control the worst tendencies of the ruling class, in particular, its propensity to do anything required to maximize profits, regardless of the consequences. Nonetheless, the first half of the twentieth century was marked by two world wars and one severe global depression. In an attempt to prevent such major upheavals from happening again, the governments of the developed world became more involved in economic issues in the second half of the twentieth century. This role played by governments was not primarily to help the average citizen—although it often did that—but, rather, to keep capitalist economies from destroying themselves.

In Chapter 9 we saw that, following World War II, two other important changes occurred within the world capitalist economies. First, the United States became the pre-eminent global superpower economically, politically, and militarily. Second, a wide range of organizations such as the United Nations and World Bank were developed in order to integrate and oversee the various capitalist nations of the world. The goal was to prevent a repeat of the economic collapse in the earlier part of the century and, at the same time, to remove all constraints on the ability of capital to move anywhere in the world to secure profits.

The push by the owning class to maximize profits has created what has been termed *hypergrowth*, the ever more rapid and expanding corporate economic growth that is caused by the search for new markets, cheaper labour, and new resources (Cavanagh et al. 2002). To achieve this end, corporations called for increasing "free trade." However, trade was never the issue. In reality, what corporations sought was the freedom to secure profits anywhere in the world and by any means without the constraints of governments. As neoliberal agendas around the world deregulated and freed corporations from "impediments"—such as laws that protected the environment, workers' rights, public health, and national sovereignty—nation-states and local governments have been less able to protect their resources and their citizens. In this way, the tension between the needs of the few in the ruling class—to secure and constantly expand their profits at any cost—and the rest of us are becoming more visible and more direct.

Social and political instability are the inevitable result of a growing disparity between rich and poor, environmental degradation, and the loss of a shared sense of social values. Moreover, in a world that appears to be out of our control with increasing competition for scarce resources, people tend to turn inward—to their clan, ethnic group, language group, religion, or region. As noted in Chapter 9, this growing "us" versus "them" world leads to growing tensions, an increase in social instability, and increased violence (see Box 13.1).

As part of this process, we are seeing a growing threat of terrorism around the world. Although terrorism usually refers to small groups using violent means to achieve their goals, we should also include the expansion of state terrorism. As noted in Chapter 8, the repressive arm of the state has been growing in most countries, including Canada, and there has been an increased criminalization of dissent. Moreover, the use of military force abroad by the major Western powers has continued despite the great financial and human costs.

The contradictions and irrationality of capitalism are so embedded in our society—and in our psyches—that we rarely even notice them. For example, we rarely think about the fact that people around the globe are suffering untold misery as a result of unemployment and underemploy-

Box 13.1 The Dialectics of Change

Dialectics helps us understand that those with power—seeking to advance their own agendas—often go down paths that end up doing the very opposite of what was intended. Historians such as Paul Kennedy and Barbara Tuchman have noted this repeated pattern, in which great powers follow policies that lead to their own destruction.

One clear example of this tendency can be observed in the foreign policy of the United States since 9/11. After the attacks in New York and Washington, many around the world expressed sympathy and solidarity with the American people. However, the U.S. government (via a compliant media) framed its story in very simple "us" versus "them" terms. What the world was facing—or so everyone was told—was a "clash of civilizations," a term first coined by political scientist Samuel P. Huntington. The enemies of the "West" were supposedly crazed Muslim fanatics who hated, as President George W.

Bush said at the time, American freedoms, values, religion, and way of life.

A decade later, what has been the outcome for the United States and its allies such as Canada? First, two wars cost the U.S. about $4 trillion and thousands of military casualties. Excessive spending on the military and intelligence by successive U.S. governments, while they were simultaneously cutting taxes, has been a key factor in the economic downturn in the U.S. and has aggravated the global capitalist economic crisis.

In addition, polls indicate that a majority in Muslim nations—even so-called "moderate" ones like Egypt, Indonesia, and Morocco—now believes the U.S. is out to destroy Islam, while conditions in Afghanistan and Iraq remain highly volatile. Both economically and militarily, the world is now a far *less* stable place than it was a decade ago.

---

ment, while there are an enormous number of jobs that need to be done. For example, there are housing shortages, deteriorating roads, overcrowded classrooms, illiterate children, rampant diseases, short-staffed hospitals, and so on. Thus there is no shortage of tasks to be done, nor is there a shortage of money to train and employ people to do these tasks, as the wealthiest individuals are financially better off than ever before. However, aside from the occasional act of charity, those who have the means to fund various work-creating and socially useful projects do not do so because they will not make sufficient return on such investments. Not only is this perfectly legal in all capitalist countries, but—as was seen after the economic crisis of 2008—we don't financially reward those who improve the world, but rather the corporate leaders who cause massive human and social destruction by constantly seeking to maximize their profits.

The Limits of Growth

We have seen throughout the book that a basic underlying element of all capitalist economies is perpetual growth. This growth is the inevitable result of individual units of capital competing with each other in the marketplace and constantly self-expanding. In the capitalist marketplace, "you grow or you die." Without thinking about it, most of us see this never-ending growth as a positive thing. The media are always reporting that it is good when the gross domestic product (GDP) increases, bad if the economy shrinks. This notion is not totally incorrect, for in a capitalist system, an expanding economy is more likely to see the number of jobs increase than a shrinking one. Moreover, many Canadians have investments or pensions that depend on the success of specific corporations and the stock market in general. If corporations are losing money or go out of business, this may, indeed, be bad for some Canadians. And a serious economic downturn, as evidenced in Europe and the United States since 2008, can prove disastrous for many as unemployment grows.

However, events of the last thirty years have called into question whether perpetual growth in and of itself is good for Canadians or the world as a whole. The advance of the neoliberal agenda has seen an improvement of life conditions for a select few while many others have seen their standard of living stagnate or decline. This began when the economy was in a boom period, as companies cut costs by downsizing and outsourcing. While "good" jobs continued to be available for some, more and more "bad" jobs—insecure and poorly paying—have appeared on the scene. While some individuals have been able to secure huge amounts of wealth, many others cannot get their most basic needs met.

> For more than 20 years we have exceeded the earth's ability to support a consumptive lifestyle that is unsustainable and we cannot afford to continue down this path.
> —James Leape, World Wildlife Fund Director-General, 2006

> We are a profligate, consumption-mad society, in a world in which unsustainable living arrangements are the norm in the developed world and spreading quickly in the developing world. We can't predict the time frame for collapse if we continue on this trajectory, but we can be reasonably certain that without major changes in our relationship to the larger living world the ecosphere will at some point (likely within decades) be unable to support large-scale human life as we know it.
> —Robert Jensen, 2011

There has been a growing critique of the effects this agenda has had on ordinary people. Some critics are advocating a return to the "golden age" when governments intervened more directly in economies to moderate the worst effects of capitalism for the average Canadian. Others are criticizing corporations for their excessive greed and lack of social conscience, urging them to be more socially responsible. Such individuals believe that mere reforms can improve the lives of most people in this country. They accept that capitalism is an essentially workable system that has simply lost its bearings and has become more and more unfair and unjust. From this point of view, a few adjustments—both political and economic—can create a better world for all.

In contrast are those who feel that the perpetual growth required by capitalist economies has reached its limits; indeed, many now feel perpetual growth is itself one of the major problems of the twenty-first century. Many scientists have noted that, beginning in the 1970s, global economic growth began to surpass the capacity of the planet's ecosystems to sustain it. If economic growth and population increases continue at their current rate, it is unlikely that the earth—and the humans that occupy it—will survive the next hundred years. For those who see capitalism and its need for perpetual growth as the core problem, the whole socioeconomic system has to be transformed.

The Consequences of Perpetual Growth

Humans have always had to exploit nature in order to survive. Foraging peoples understood that they were in a delicate balance with the natural world and, indeed, considered nature holy. If nature didn't provide, these people would not survive. The rise of social classes and the growth of technology changed the relationship between humans and nature. For the first time, the environment was seen as something to be dominated and conquered. However, it was not until the industrial age that advancing technologies made massive environmental destruction a reality. Capitalist growth is infinite, but the planet's resources are finite.

Evidence is mounting that our natural world—without which there can be no life—is seriously under threat. In the twentieth century, the world population increased by more than four billion, over three times what it was at the beginning of the century. However, the use of energy and raw materials grew more than ten times (Brown and Flavin 1999). Our planet simply cannot sustain its current level of environmental degradation. In this context, we are coming to realize that environmental protection is both a local and a global issue. Whether it is the disappearance of the Amazon rainforest, the rapid melting of Arctic sea ice and permafrost, the extreme degradation of the Great Lakes ecosystem, the destruction of the oceans from oil spills and other chemical contamination, the air pollution resulting from automobile exhausts and industrial activities, the irreversible contamination resulting from nuclear accidents (see Box 13.2), or the decline of safe drinking water—all of us, regardless of nationality, are affected by environmental degradation.

According to the Conference Board of Canada (2011), while Canada's environmental performance has improved in some areas over the past few decades, it has deteriorated in others. For example, the amount of municipal waste generated per capita in Canada increased steadily from 510 kg. in 1980 to 894 kg. in 2007, far above the OECD average. Water consumption is also a key environmental issue. Sustainable water management helps maintain adequate water supplies for people and ecosystems. Canada's water use per capita is over eight times higher than that of Denmark. Industry is Canada's largest water user, accounting for nearly 70 percent of total water used in 2000. Two major reasons for Canada's excessive use of water are inadequate water conservation practices and prices that are too low to encourage efficiency.

The need for corporations to seek new sources for profit expansion has led to the increasing privatization of the commons, as was discussed in Chapter 9. Some of the commons can be thought of as global—the atmosphere, the oceans, outer space, and plant and animal biodiversity; other elements of the commons can be thought of as community commons,

Box 13.2 What Have Nuclear Disasters Taught Us?

Here are ten lessons that can be learned from the nuclear disasters in Chernobyl, Ukraine (1986) and Fukushima, Japan (2011):

1. Nuclear power is a highly complex, expensive, and dangerous way to boil water to create steam to turn turbines.

2. Accidents happen, and the worst-case scenario often turns out to be worse than imagined or planned for.

3. The nuclear industry and its experts cannot plan for every contingency or prevent every disaster.

4. Governments do not effectively regulate the nuclear industry to assure the safety of the public. Regulators of the nuclear industry often come from the nuclear industry itself and tend to be too close to it to regulate it effectively.

5. Hubris, complacency, and high-level radiation are a deadly mix. Hubris on the part of the nuclear industry and its government regulators—along with complacency on the part of the public—has led to the creation of vast amounts of high-level radiation that must be guarded from release to the environment for tens of thousands of years.

6. The corporations that run the nuclear power plants are protected from catastrophic economic failure by government limits on liability. If the corporations that own nuclear power plants had to bear the burden of potential financial losses in the event of a catastrophic accident, they would not build the plants because they know the risks are unacceptable. No other private industry is given such liability protection, which leaves the taxpayers on the hook.

7. Radiation releases from nuclear accidents cannot be contained in space and will not stop at national borders.

8. Radiation releases from nuclear accidents cannot be contained in time and will adversely affect countless future generations.

9. Nuclear energy—as well as nuclear weapons—and human beings cannot coexist without the risk of future catastrophes. The survivors of the atomic bombings of Hiroshima and Nagasaki have long known that nuclear weapons and human beings cannot coexist. Fukushima, like Chernobyl before it, makes clear that human beings and nuclear power plants also cannot coexist.

10. The accidents at Fukushima and Chernobyl are a bracing reminder to phase out nuclear energy. We need to move as rapidly as possible to a global energy plan based upon conservation and various forms of renewable energy: solar cells, wind, geothermal, and energy that is extracted from the oceans and the tides and the currents.

Source: Adapted from Krieger 2011.

---

such as public spaces, common lands, local knowledge and wisdom, and the gene pool of populations. All of these elements are now under threat as transnational corporations seek to privately own and control that which has historically been shared by all.

One worrying trend, particularly for Canadians, is the privatization of fresh water. The supply of available fresh water represents less than half of 1 percent of the world's total water stock. Thirty-one countries face water scarcity, and more than a billion people lack adequate access to clean drinking water. A child dies from a water-related disease every twenty seconds. For those who bottle and sell water, increased consumption that generates higher prices is a central goal, rather than the promotion of water conservation.

Companies that control water resources are not local enterprises but rather giant transnational corporations, and governments are often required to financially support these corporations with public money. In Cochabamba, Bolivia, in 2000, the government raised water rates and planned to privatize the water supply. A massive general strike by locals forced the government to cancel these plans.

Another serious concern is the threat to the genetic commons as a result of recent advances in genetic engineering and the patenting of life forms and biodiversity. Corporations such as Monsanto, Novartis, DuPont, Pioneer, and others are now scouring the globe for life forms they can own or engineer. Monsanto has intellectual property rights to more than 80 percent of all genetically engineered seeds. It also owns broad species patents on cotton, mustard, and soybeans, species that were developed over thousands of years in small farming communities. Even the genes of humans are in the process of being patented. This process is sometimes referred to as "biopiracy" (Shiva, in Cavanagh et al. 2002, 87).

The commons is also being appropriated as a free dumping ground for the waste materials produced by corporations. The need to secure profits pushes corporations toward planned obsolescence, for there is more money to be made if your car, computer, or cell phone is replaced every few years. Not only does this use up our limited natural resources at a rapid pace, it also leads to the increasing problem of where to store the ever-mounting waste. And increasingly, that waste is full of toxic ingredients. One solution has been the shipping of waste to the poorest countries in the world, which are becoming toxic dump sites for the excesses of corporate capitalism. However, even in Canada, the growing accumulation of toxic waste has become a serious problem.

Think About It

Most of us think a lot about what new piece of technology we would like to buy next. Have you ever thought about where your old devices go? Why do so few of us think of the downside of all the new technologies we are currently purchasing?

Lastly, we are all increasingly aware that human activities have led to dramatic climate change. Such change has already, at least in part, affected food supplies and caused severe storms, droughts, and forest fires in many parts of Canada and elsewhere around the globe, while many plants and animals are going extinct as their habitats are destroyed. A 2011 scientific report presented to the United Nations noted with concern that the health of the world's oceans was declining much faster than originally thought as a result of global warming, pollution, overfishing, and other human-caused problems interacting all at once, which could lead to a mass extinction in the world's oceans (CBC News online, June 21, 2011).

A major cause of global warming is greenhouse gas (GHG) emissions. Canada's per capita GHG emissions increased 3.2 percent between 1990 and

2008, while total GHG emissions in Canada grew 24 percent (Conference Board of Canada 2011). The tar sands are the fastest growing source of pollution in Canada that is affecting global warming. These enormous operations in northern Alberta are also creating toxic waste ponds, air and water pollution, as well as habitat and species destruction. Canada's carbon footprint more than doubles if exports are included. Approximately one-fifth of Canada's exports in 2009, valued at about $80 billion, were fossil fuels. About half of the export-related emissions are from the tar sands, with the rest coming from coal, natural gas, and other petroleum products (Lee 2011).

For some years, scientists have argued that global warming had to be kept to less than two degrees Celsius if there was any hope of preventing major environmental disasters in the future. A 2011 scientific study concluded that without putting the brakes on CO_2 emissions very soon, large parts of Africa, most of Russia and northern China will be two degrees Celsius warmer in less than ten years, while Canada and Alaska will soon follow (Leahy 2011). If the planet continues to warm, as most scientists are now predicting, we can look forward to rising sea levels, the disappearance of the rainforests, major social dislocation and global malnutrition leading to large-scale movement of populations.

Many of us are concerned about these frightening scenarios and want our three levels of government to take action. Unfortunately, in late 2011 the federal government decided to withdraw from the landmark Kyoto Protocol, reached in 1997, which is the only global treaty—signed by thirty-seven industrialized countries and the European community—that set down binding targets for curbing global carbon emissions. By signing the pact, the Canadian government committed to reduce CO_2 emissions to 6 percent below 1990 levels by 2012. However, these emissions have actually risen by around a third (Vaughan 2011).

Meanwhile, the federal government is pushing ahead in its support of expanded tar sands production and pipelines that would move corrosive and highly diluted bitumen to coastlines of either Canada or the United States. There it would be loaded onto ships, to be processed and used abroad, primarily in China. Until now, the movement of such giant vessels along the hazardous northern British Columbia inland waterways has been off-limits due to concerns that an oil spill would ruin precious coastal natural resources.

To some extent, the ability of all levels of government in Canada to act decisively regarding climate change and other pressing issues has been limited by the policies of our neighbour to the south.

> Socialism failed because it could not tell the economic truth, and capitalism may fail because it cannot tell the ecological truth.
> —Oysten Dahle, Exxon's former VP North Sea operations

> Ultimately, in a globalizing world corporate power grows at the expense of workers, communities, and the ecosystem itself…. The stakes [in contesting this power] are higher than ever before, and the struggle epochal. The ticking bomb can be defused only by transfiguring corporate power into economic democracy.
> —William K. Carroll, Corporate Power in a Globalizing World

Will Canada Become Part of the United States?

For Canadians, a key issue that will face us in this century is whether we will survive as a nation. The first half of the twentieth century saw Canada slowly separate from Britain. By the 1960s Canada had its own flag and got its own constitution in 1982. Ironically, the 1980s was also the time when neoliberal policies began to dominate in Canada. One key aspect of neoliberalism in Canada has involved an increasing integration with the United States, politically, economically, militarily, and culturally. In poll after poll, the majority of Canadians have indicated that they like the Canadian way of life and want to protect Canadian sovereignty. And yet almost imperceptibly over the last thirty years, Canada has become increasingly Americanized.

If Canadians want to retain their independence from the United States, why does there seem to be growing integration with that country? The answer involves understanding the interests of those with power, the corporate owning class, and the politicians who support them. In the nineteenth century, the majority of Canadian corporate leaders saw U.S. businesses as worrying competitors. They sought to build a sovereign country where their smaller units of capital would not be threatened by the much bigger competitors to the south. However, maintaining Canadian independence from the United States has never been easy, given our shared border, language, and cultural elements. Numerous governments created policies to try to promote and protect Canadian economic and cultural entities. Things began to change drastically when Prime Minister Brian Mulroney pushed greater economic integration with the United States via the North American Free Trade Agreement (NAFTA), as part of the overall neoliberal agenda.

Economic protection for Canadian-owned companies began to decline with the advance of free trade (which a number of analysts have noted was neither free nor actually about trade), and some key sectors of our economy became increasingly owned by U.S. and other international corporations, or dependent on them. At the same time, successive Canadian and provincial governments, such as that in Alberta, have become more closely tied to the U.S in terms of sales of natural resources to that country.

Many Canadians have begun to wonder whether, in a time of crisis, Canadian oil, gas, and water will be shipped south of the border, while Canadians could face shortages of their own natural resources. It is now known that the governments of Canada and the United States have been meeting regularly—sometimes in secret—to proceed with what is referred to as *deep integration*. **Deep integration** is the harmonization of policies and regulations between Canada and the United States (although Mexico was originally included, problems in that country led to its subsequent exclusion). In recent years Canadian and American regulations and standards governing health, food safety, and the environment began to move toward harmonization (Barlow 2007). In 2011, Prime Minister Stephen Harper and U.S. President Barack Obama signed the Declaration on a Shared

Vision for Perimeter Security and Economic Competitiveness. The core of this "vision" is to create a single security perimeter between the two countries, boosting integration of Canadian and American police, border, and intelligence services. Many are concerned that this is further integration of the two countries by stealth.

Many are also afraid that the collapsing U.S. economy will spread to Canada and that their increasingly gridlocked political system—with its culture of paranoia, unending war, and declining freedoms—will also spread to our country.

It is interesting to note that while developing closer ties with the U.S., the Harper government simultaneously moved to re-establish ties to our past by making the monarchy more visible in Canada. In late 2011, it restored the word "Royal" to the front of the names of Canada's navy and air force, and all Canadian embassies were instructed to have pictures of the Queen prominently displayed. The government also committed $7.5 million in 2012 to celebrate the sixtieth anniversary of Queen Elizabeth's accession to the throne.

> The end results of a fully integrated continental security perimeter could sacrifice what is left of Canadian sovereignty and independence. This could bring its military, security and foreign policy under the umbrella of a single, U.S.-dominated North American Command.
> —Dana Gabriel

Think About It
Do you care whether Canada continues as a country? Why or why not? Why do you think the Harper government is promoting the monarchy at this time?

The Changing Nature of Classes

It comes as no surprise that Marx and other social critics of the nineteenth century disliked the capitalist owning class. It was felt that this class, in the name of profits, committed horrible crimes against the vast majority in the capitalist world. However, while many people in the nineteenth and early twentieth centuries may have hated the capitalist class, it was the only class at that time that had the capacity to advance the productive forces. Thus moral opposition to the capitalist system could not be transferred into viable economic alternatives.

A century later, this is no longer the case. The concentration and centralization of capital has led to a decline in the size of the owning class, as well as an almost complete separation of the function of ownership from the function of management. Moreover, it seems that we have now reached a stage in social development where the owning class no longer performs the essential economic role it once did. Less and less is capital interested in questions of production of actual goods and services. With the growing financialization of capitalist economies, groupings of capital now commonly purchase large corporations without any real interest at all in the productive process. Often their only goal is to restructure or simply hold on to a company until, it is hoped, share prices rise, and then re-sell it in the marketplace at a hefty profit.

Nor is the owning class, on the whole, any longer seen by the rest of us as the arbiter of societal values. Indeed, there are many who see a moral vacuum in both the economic and political spheres. Capitalism as a whole is increasingly facing a crisis of legitimacy that is the result of the widespread incidence of fraud, corruption, scandals, organized crime, and abuses of power within both the corporate and political spheres. This is being noticed in the developed capitalist world and in developing countries as well (see Box 13.4).

Concurrent with changes to the ruling class were changes to the working class that occurred over the course of the twentieth century. No longer the unskilled, uneducated workers of a hundred years ago, most working people are now highly trained and educated. People are educated not simply in specific skills but in the general capacity to work with others collectively, in an organized and disciplined fashion, to achieve a particular set of goals. Working people also constitute a proportionally larger sector of the population, as more people on a global scale have to sell their labour power for a wage. It is these characteristics—size, organizational capacity, education, and discipline—that led Marx and Engels to argue that the working class, created by the bourgeoisie, would be "the gravediggers of capitalism."

In addition, the notion that the state can be directly involved in the economy is no longer an alien or frightening notion. In the nineteenth and early twentieth centuries, large-scale economic intervention by the state seemed like a foreign and dangerous concept, impossible to bring into reality. It is hard for us today to believe that the early proponents of a state-run health-care system in Canada were attacked for being "communists." The growth of the welfare state in the latter half of the twentieth century made a large number of people less fearful of state intervention in the economy. Canadians have seen that their governments can lessen the worst effects of unfettered capitalism, and in general Canadians have supported government-provided pensions, health care, and social services.

On the other hand, there are many Canadians who continue to disapprove of policies promoting direct government involvement in the Canadian economy. There is a strong libertarian sentiment (that is, one that gives priority to individual freedoms over government intervention) in Canada, particularly in the West. Such opposing views regarding the state and its role, which is part of the larger political and social instability within many capitalist societies, are discussed later in this chapter.

For thousands of years, religious leaders and philosophers have envisaged a better world, often a paradise to be reached after death. Given the limited life chances of most humans, it is not surprising that so many needed to believe in a better tomorrow. Thomas More created the word *utopia* in the sixteenth century, and since that time many writers have described their visions of a heaven on earth. If the real world were one of exploitation, oppression, poverty, injustice, inequality, cruelty, and hatred, a future utopia would be one with equality and social justice, where humans were kind, cooperative, and loving.

By the end of the eighteenth century, a number of utopian socialists, such as Claude Henri Saint-Simon, Charles Fourier, and Robert Owen, were describing their vision of an alternative to capitalism. Owen, a British factory owner, actually put his ideas into practice by creating more humane conditions for his workers, reducing the working day, setting up nurseries for workers' children, and raising wages. In the end, the utopian socialists failed because they did not understand the class relations of power within capitalist societies. They thought socialism could be attained simply by winning people over to their vision of a more humane society.

Today few of us have even heard of such individuals, let alone read their work. Yet the names of Karl Marx and Friedrich Engels are known around the globe. While they acknowledged their debt to the utopian socialists, Marx and Engels stood apart from them. It sometimes comes as a surprise to learn that Marx and Engels wrote relatively little about exactly what the alternative to capitalism would look like. In this sense, they were being true both to their philosophical materialism and to the methods of science. Unlike the mystics who conjured up the future from crystal balls or tea leaves, or the intellectuals who imagined a better world inside their heads, the first "scientific socialists" (as they called themselves) felt that the only way to predict the future was to look for past patterns. Thus Marx and Engels concentrated on studying the history of human societies, the political economy of human social life, and the patterns of social change.

Marx and Engels felt that the conditions within capitalism—the development of the working class, the large-scale socialization of production, and the growing tension between the needs of an ever-shrinking ruling class and an expanding working class—set the stage for social transformation. What is most clear in the writing of Marx and Engels is that they envisaged a future society where the interests and goals of ordinary working people would dominate in all spheres—the economic, the social, and the political. They believed that current class relations would be replaced by a new set of class relations in which power—via the state—would be transferred to the working class, that is, the vast majority. Production would no longer be for corporate profits and personal gain but rather to meet human needs. Marx and Engels thought this new socioeconomic formation would appear when capitalism had reached its limits of development; that is, when the forces of production could no longer advance under the current capitalist class relations.

> Karl Marx got it right, at some point capitalism can destroy itself. We thought markets worked. They're not working.
> —economist Nouriel Roubini, Wall Street Journal, 2011

> To avoid the instability of capitalism and its huge social costs requires changing the system.
> —economist Richard Wolff, Guardian (U.K.), 2011

It is worth noting that this was not the case for the socialist societies that appeared in the twentieth century. While a complete explanation for the failure of such societies would constitute a book in itself, the low level of development of the forces of production must certainly be one key factor. At the time of its revolution, Russia was largely a backward, peasant-based society. All twentieth-century socialist societies had to focus on advancing their forces of production, including the development of a workforce with appropriate skills and knowledge. Many were devastated during World War II. While this by no means fully explains the failure of such societies, it certainly points out the vast difference between these and any future society that would develop out of advanced capitalism.

While the objective preconditions for social transformation may currently exist within the developed capitalist world, the actual process of transformation will depend on the willingness and capacity of the people within these societies to act for change.

Modern Social Movements for Change

To this point we have been discussing the *objective* factors that may lead to future social transformations. We should now briefly address the *subjective* element of how real people come to change the conditions of their lives. Dialectics helps us understand that societies contain opposing tendencies and that elements within a society give rise to their opposites. Humans persistently join together to oppose the negative conditions that arise in societies.

We can begin to examine this process by thinking of a simple situation that any one of us might experience. Suppose you are taking a course in sociology and you fail a major term paper. What do you do? You might see the teacher, appeal the grade, complain to your friends, or, perhaps, you might do nothing at all. Now, suppose you find out the following week that the teacher has failed two-thirds of the class. You also discover that this professor has been failing most of her students for years. At this point, you have discovered that what started out (in C. Wright Mills's terms) as a "personal trouble" is actually a "public issue." What do you do now? You may still decide to do nothing, but it becomes more likely that you will get together with some of the other students who failed and plan a strategy—perhaps you will start a petition, get a group to speak to the chair or dean, or go to the student newspaper. The more radical among you might suggest staging a sit-in at the president's office or hiring a lawyer. Perhaps you will do all of these things or just some of them. What you have probably realized is that, in order to oppose someone with more power than yourself, you have to act in a collective and organized fashion.

This is exactly how opposition to structures of power occurs in the broader society. People lose their jobs, get sexually abused, get hurt in industrial accidents, are denied housing because of their skin colour, are harassed for being gay, and so on. Given the nature of power and the lack of understanding most of us have about our social world, a good many of us will direct our anger or frustration at ourselves or others. Not being able to grasp the power that exists at the distal realm, we are likely to see ourselves as the victims of personal problems rather than as being a part of broader public issues.

Obviously, as long as most people can get their needs met within a given socioeconomic formation, they will not be particularly interested in risking what they have for some unknown future. At the moment—both in Canada and across the developed capitalist world—it is likely most people want to keep their privileges and do not want the world to change in any major way. However, it is also likely that this world of privilege will change in the next fifty years. In times of increasing social and economic deterioration or uncertainty, as we are seeing now even in the developed world, more and more people may feel frustrated by failed attempts to better, or simply maintain, the conditions of their lives. At this point, many formerly passive individuals will join the struggle for change, and organized attacks on the social order will grow. What no one can predict at the moment is whether sufficient changes will occur in time to save our planet from ecological destruction.

Organizing for Change

There are many ways that people struggle to change elements within a society. Some people feel that the only way to effect change is by altering their own personal behaviour. For example, if they believe that the environment is at risk they may decide not to fly or may decide to grow their own vegetables. Others will decide that the best way to change existing social institutions is to become involved in the political structures of society in the hopes of creating new social policies, and thus they become active in—or create their own—political parties. Yet others decide to take some sort of collective action in what are sometimes referred to as *civil society groups*, that is, voluntary organizations that are outside of both the corporate world and the state (for an example, see Box 13.3). There are a wide variety of such groups currently advocating for change in Canada and around the world. Some may develop because of a local issue and exist only for a short period of time, such as those opposing a new highway or struggling for more social housing. Others may be larger, may be more permanent, and may have broader aims.

Social movements are broader networks of groups and individuals that work for change, and there are many such movements in Canada, including those struggling for social justice, peace, environmental protection, and the advancement of women, minorities, and Indigenous people. However, in recent years such groups have found themselves under attack and weakened by lack of government funding and popular support. Because of Canada's large size and regionalism, many groups have had greater success at the local level than at the national level. Moreover, while many in Canada may feel despair at the decline in social activism, in many other parts of the world social movements have been expanding.

Box 13.3 Fighting for a Living Wage

When a "ragtag band of church groups and trade unionists" in the U.K. called London Citizens began campaigning for workers to be paid a living wage back in 2001, they were branded as "unrealistic" by employers and politicians. But by the time the campaign celebrated its tenth anniversary, it had persuaded scores of major employers to pay their staff well above the legal minimum. At a rally in the run-up to the 2010 election, Prime Minister David Cameron described the living wage as "an idea whose time has come." The 2012 Olympics in London was officially declared a Living Wage Olympics. In addition to the issue of wages, concerns about housing, education, and local employment were also addressed.

The *living wage* is the amount that earners in a family need in order to meet their basic needs, based on the actual costs of living in a specific community. As real wages have fallen over the past thirty years, workers have increasingly struggled to earn enough to cover even a "bare-bones" budget. The result can be seen in growing number of poor children living in working families with parents doing two and three jobs just to pay the bills. In turn, this means more illness, more social problems, and more social unrest.

Since whole communities are damaged by low pay, it stands to reason that the whole communities have a stake in securing a living wage for the lowest paid workers. Using this analysis, living wage campaigns have built wide coalitions of union, faith, and community groups, as well as finding allies among politicians, professionals, and business leaders. Where employers have proved reluctant, living wage campaigners have used creative actions—rallies, concerts, flash mobs, and community hearings—to bring pressure to bear, often with great success.

The first living wage policy in Canada was adopted by the city council of New Westminster, B.C., in May 2010. As with any new idea, there are concerns and questions: Will it cost jobs? How will it be paid for? Will it make any difference? However, the empirical evidence from London is that living wages are a resounding success, so much so that the Conservative mayor of London, Boris Johnson, remarked, "Paying the London living wage is not only morally right, but makes good business sense too. What may appear to a company to be an unaffordable cost in a highly competitive market should more often be viewed as a sound investment decision."

Source: Deborah Littman, Lead Organizer, Metro Vancouver Alliance, and former vice-chair of London Citizens, one of Britain's largest citizen organizations.

Think About It

Have you ever been involved in a movement for social change? Why or why not? Why do you think most young people are not involved in such movements?

Populist Movements

In Chapter 7 you were introduced to the concepts of "left-wing" and "right-wing." It was explained that in times of social upheaval, some people (particularly the "small fish" and "middle fish") may be drawn to the left, where the "we" of our social world is emphasized—movements for democracy and social justice for example—while others are drawn to the right, which emphasizes the "me."

In North America, "middle fish" have often been drawn to social movements that espouse an ideology known as **populism**. Populism comes from the Latin word *populi*, meaning "of the people." It presents itself as a movement of "the little guy," opposing big government, big business, and (for the right-wing variant of populism) big unions. Western Canada has long been fertile ground for populist movements of both the left (the Co-operative Commonwealth Federation, forerunner of the NDP) and the right (Social Credit, forerunner of the Reform Party, which became the Canadian Alliance and later merged with the federal Progressive Conservative Party, predecessor to the current Conservative Party). While "middle fish" accept the general organization of our society, they feel they're been given unfair treatment in it. We saw in earlier chapters how small business and others of the middle strata are currently feeling stress: increasing competition with big business, declining profits, layoffs, and, overall, less control over their lives. Such individuals continue to support the system as a whole, but feel their share in it is declining. As noted earlier in the book, White males, in particular, may feel their share has been declining because others have been getting a bigger share.

Right-wing populist groups—while in theory defending the rights of the "little guy"—are often funded by wealthy corporate donors. For example, the Tea Party in the United States—a classic example of right-wing populism—has received major funding from the enormously wealthy Koch family, which has also funded a variety of extreme right-wing organizations over the past few decades (Mayer 2010). While funding various populist movements, they have simultaneously spent many millions of dollars lobbying the U.S. government on behalf of their corporations. Since their main interest is in oil, they have also become big supporters of the Alberta tar sands and the Keystone XL pipeline project, which would transport oil from Alberta down to the United States for refining or export. Flint Hills Resources Canada LP, an Alberta-based subsidiary of Koch Industries, applied for—and won—"intervenor status" in the National Energy Board hearings that led

History never actually repeats itself, of course, though it does occasionally seem strikingly familiar. There are only a handful of times in history when rising tides of democracy have simultaneously washed over multiple countries: 1848, 1968, 1989, and 2011. We are reminded, yet again, that what seems impossible—even unthinkable—can quickly become inevitable.
—*sociologist Dan Brook*

Their message is very clear and simple: get money out of the political process; strive for equality in taxation and equal rights for all regardless of race, gender, social status, sexual preference or age. We must stop poisoning our food, air and water for corporate greed. The people on Wall Street and in the banking industrial complex that destroyed our economy must be investigated and brought to justice.... America has been debased and degraded by greed. This has touched 99 percent of America's population. The other 1 percent is doing just fine—with more than a third of the wealth of this nation.
—*actor Mark Ruffalo, after spending two days with the Occupy Wall Street activists in New York City*

My favourite sign [at the Occupy Wall Street protests] says "I care about you." In a culture that trains people to avoid each other's gaze—to say "Let them die"—that is a deeply radical statement.
—*Naomi Klein*

to Canada's 2010 approval of its 327-mile portion of the pipeline (*Guardian* online, October 5, 2011).

Right-wing populist movements and ideologies have expanded in recent years by appealing to the real fears of the middle strata. For example, some political parties in Canada, such as the Reform Party, gained popularity primarily by promoting the notion that individuals were being held hostage by "special interest groups," such as the poor, women, racial minorities, and people with disabilities (Harrison et al. 1996, 174). In the United States, the Tea Party gained influence as economic conditions in that country deteriorated. Right-wing populist movements also tend to be connected to a broader social and religious conservatism, such as hostility to feminism and gay rights, sex education in the schools, abortion rights, and so on. In times of social instability, when many people feel that moral standards and traditions are rapidly eroding, such views can have wider appeal. Christian conservatism in the United States has drawn in many supporters because it speaks directly to the losses felt by "middle Americans"—the loss of community and connection, the fear of crime, the fear for their children's futures, and the absence of spirituality in their lives. In Canada, the current federal Conservative government and some provincial governments have advanced many neoliberal policies by utilizing populist narratives.

Because the political left in North America has been relatively weak in recent years, there has not been much evidence of left-wing populist movements. However, in late 2011, a loose grouping of individuals—a classic left-wing populist movement—began a sit-in near Wall Street in New York City. It had no party affiliations or connections to either labour or wider social movements. Clearly, its demands touched a raw nerve with the general population of the United States and Canada, not known in this period for political activism. Put simply, in an "us" versus "them" narrative, the "them" became the wealthiest and most powerful financiers, who were not acting in the interests of the majority of Americans. Soon many mainstream groups and some politicians expressed support for the Occupy movement.

Think About It

How are protest movements generally portrayed in the mass media? Do such portrayals make you want to be a participant in future protests?

Older movements of the left have long struggled to change class relations and the consequences of capitalist economies. One of the interesting aspects of the newer movements is that they are not simply opposed to various negative aspects of capitalism; they are beginning to draw a blueprint of what a future society not dominated by the interests of global corporations might look like. Another interesting feature of the new social movements is the coming together of old and new types of activists. Labour unions— the organized sector of the working class—continue to be at the heart of most such movements because of their centrality to the productive process.

However, a wide spectrum of new groups—such as the environmental and anti-poverty movements—have become involved in opposition to corporate globalization as well. Despite somewhat differing agendas and different strategies, there is a commonality of goals. Most groups are fighting for an advance of democratic rights along one or more of the following lines: subsistence rights, economic rights, environmental rights, social rights, cultural rights, and human rights. Within these demands is the call for a fundamental redistribution of wealth and power (Barlow and Clarke 2001, 207).

Conclusion

People in general, and Canadians in particular, are not especially prone to rebelliousness; given alternatives, most of us will accept the social order and our place in it. Moreover, many of you reading this book may feel that you simply want to graduate, get a good job, buy a house, and live the good life promised in the ads; changing the world may be the last thing on your mind. However, we have now reached a point where the need for dramatic social change is no longer a debatable question. If our planet is to survive, we must come up with creative and immediate solutions to major economic, environmental, social, and political problems.

As noted in this chapter, we are reaching the limits of capitalist growth. The two central issues that now face humankind, climate change and global militarization, are both being fuelled by the greed of transnational corporations and their government supporters. The issue of whether humans can continue in the destructive manner of the last two centuries is literally one of life or death.

It is easy to feel powerless in the face of the growing concentration of global capital, and at the moment there can be no question that the power of capital remains ascendant. However, history has shown that even the most powerful can be defeated by determined and persistent opposition. All the territorial empires of the last few hundred years—regardless of their military might—such as the Austro-Hungarian empire, the Ottoman empire, and the colonial empires of Europe either declined or disappeared entirely. These empires declined primarily because of political and civil resistance from within, rather than via defeats on the battlefield. Indeed, the nature of the technology of modern warfare makes it increasingly necessary to seek non-military solutions to global crises. With regard to opposition to capitalism itself, there has certainly been some very successful opposition to corporate rule around the world, although such opposition up to this point has been erratic and mostly localized. As this book demonstrates, it is distal relations of power that are both hardest to understand and most difficult to oppose.

The problem, of course, is that most of us do not want to be—or are unable to be—activists. Most people around the world spend their days caught up in the problems of their lives in the proximal realm—working, spending time with family and friends, getting their basic daily needs met, and so on. It is therefore unreasonable to expect a majority of people in

Box 13.4 Youth Lead the Struggle for Social Change

What has been termed the "Arab Spring" began at the end of 2010 when a young man in Tunisia set himself on fire. However, while this act was the first to capture international attention, struggles had been going on for a number of years prior to this action, including labour protests in Tunisia and Egypt. Beginning in early 2011, a wave of demonstrations and protests occurred in the Arab world, including the overthrow of the autocratic leaders of Tunisia and Egypt; a civil war in Libya; civil uprisings in Bahrain, Syria, and Yemen; major protests in Algeria, Iraq, Jordan, Morocco, and Oman; and minor protests in a number of other countries. However, protests were not limited to the Arab world; inspired by the "Arab Spring," many large protests also took place in Greece, Spain, Italy, and France. Later in the year protests spread to North America.

In the Western media, some analysts speculated that the protests—particularly in the Middle East and North Africa—were the result of the new social media that allowed young people to organize. At times opposition to the repressive governments of those countries was also noted. Certainly new technologies, as well as the extreme wealth of autocrats, political repression, and a long history of corruption played a role.

But these conditions are not new. Why did 2011 see such widespread and radical actions? One analysis argued that the rise in food prices in the Arab world, a result of growing droughts, was a key factor, and that these conditions were similar to protests first seen in 2008, when food prices rose substantially (Lagi, Bertrand, and Bar-Yam 2011). Also central to the protests in many parts of the world were the deteriorating economic conditions and dismal futures facing many young people as a result of education cuts, low pay, and cuts to much-needed public services. In Spain in 2011, nearly half of all young people were unemployed.

any country to be swept into a struggle for social change until conditions of their lives have eroded to the point where they cannot continue as they are (see Box 13.4). One thing Marx and Engels could not have predicted is the rapid destruction of our physical environment. Unfortunately, current scientific evidence seems to indicate that—with regard to climate change—if we wait until our lives are negatively affected to the point where we are prepared to struggle for change, it may be too late.

We are living in a time of great cynicism and despair. Many of us feel that the world is changing rapidly, but that such changes are beyond our understanding and out of our control. Although some young people are front and centre in the struggle for change, many more continue to be quite detached from both the struggles for change and mainstream social institutions. This detachment, of course, is exactly what the ruling class prefers, as it ensures the maintenance of relationships of power and inequality. Nonetheless, this book shows that there is every reason to be optimistic rather than pessimistic about the future. Humans are social animals; as history has confirmed again and again, people—organized and united—can determine the future course of their lives.

KEY POINTS

1. There has always been a tension in sociology between those theorists who focus on simply describing society and those who feel the social world needs to be changed.

2. Change must be understood in terms of both the *objective* and the *subjective* elements in any given society at any particular point in time.

3. While the real material conditions of capitalism set the stage for social transformation, the future will depend on how human beings act on and change such conditions.

4. Changes that occur within a given socioeconomic formation are referred to as reforms, while a revolution is a radical transformation of the social order in which there is a basic alteration of the relationship between social classes. There is a dialectical relationship between reform and revolution.

5. The view that reforms alone will eventually eliminate the problems of working people in capitalism is referred to as reformism. Social democracy is reformism in the political sphere.

6. Around the world, there is growing instability and an escalation of the inner contradictions of capitalist systems.

7. Many analysts feel that the perpetual growth required by capitalist economies has reached its limits and the resulting climate change may be one of the major problems of the twenty-first century.

8. For Canadians, a key issue that will face us in this century is whether we will survive as a nation.

9. The nature of both the owning class and the working class in capitalist societies has changed dramatically over the past century.

10. Many individuals get involved in the struggle for change outside the formal institutions of the state, in civil society groups and in social movements.

11. In times of social instability, many of the middle strata are often drawn to the ideology known as populism.

12. Humans are social animals; history has repeatedly shown that people—organized and united—can determine the future course of their lives.

Barlow, Maude. 2009. *Blue Covenant: The Global Water Crisis and the Coming Battle for the Right to Water.* Reprint edition. New York: New Press.
Activist Barlow looks at the water crisis facing the globe, and offers suggestions for solving it.

Cullis-Suzuki, Severn, et al. eds. 2007. *Notes from Canada's Young Activists: A Generation Stands Up for Change.* Vancouver: Greystone.
Twenty-five young activists explain how they were inspired to become active in an attempt to make the world a better place.

Frank, Thomas. 2012. *Pity the Billionaire: The Hard-Times Swindle and Unlikely Comeback of the Right.* New York: Metropolitan Books.
A critical look at the resurgence and growth of right-wing populism in the United States.

Magdoff, Fred, and John Bellamy Foster. 2011. *What Every Environmentalist Needs to Know About Capitalism.* New York: Monthly Review.
The authors argue here that trying to solve the impending ecological crisis is impossible within a capitalist economy.

Marsden, William. 2008. *Stupid to the Last Drop: How Alberta is Bringing Environmental Armageddon to Canada and Doesn't Seem to Care.* Toronto: Vintage Canada.
The author shows how corporations and governments are pushing ahead with the tar sands, despite the effect on the land, water, wildlife, atmosphere, and of course, on the people of Alberta.

McNally, David. 2006. *Another World Is Possible: Globalization and Anti-Capitalism.* Revised Expanded Edition. Winnipeg: Arbeiter Ring.
This clearly written book offers both a critique of globalizing capitalism and a set of proposals for change.

Roberts, Wayne. 2008. *No-Nonsense Guide to World Food.* Toronto: Between the Lines.
Another in the No-Nonsense Guide series, this one looks at the issues pertaining to global food production and distribution. Suggestions for change are offered.

Veltmeyer, Henry, ed. 2011. *21st Century Socialism: Reinventing the Project.* Black Point, NS: Fernwood.
A number of authors explore the ways that the notion of socialism needs to be re-imagined for our times.

Wittman, Hannah, Annette Aurélie Desmarais, and Nettie Wiebe. 2011. *Food Sovereignty in Canada: Creating Just and Sustainable Food Systems.* Black Point, NS: Fernwood.
This book provides an alternative to the industrialized food production sector, with concrete examples of how groups across the country are moving to a new model of sustainable food production and consumption.

Glossary

Numbers in parentheses refer to the chapter(s) containing the main discussion of the term.

Absolute poverty
A way of measuring poverty in which only those who are not getting their most basic daily needs met—that is, those who are not able to acquire a minimum of nutrition, basic shelter, and adequate clothing—are defined as poor. (10)

Alienation
In Marxist terminology, the separation of workers from their labour, and all that this entails. In capitalist societies, workers lose control over the workplace, the product, and the surplus value that they produce. In non-Marxist terminology, the term is used to describe more general feelings of powerlessness, meaninglessness, or isolation. (6)

Anarchy of production
In Marxist terminology, an inevitable consequence of capitalist production, with each individual productive unit making production decisions on the basis of maximizing profit. For this reason, production cannot be planned, which leads inevitably to the crisis of overproduction. (5)

Anti-Semitism
Hostility directed toward those of Jewish origin. (11)

Assimilationism
A theory proposing that particular racial or ethnic groups will cease to be disadvantaged once they integrate into the dominant group. (11)

Biological determinism
Any theoretical explanation of human behaviour that focuses on the biological or genetic basis for that behaviour. (1, 2)

Bipedalism
The ability to stand upright on two feet. (2)

Bourgeoisie
The class in capitalist society that owns and controls the means of production and hires workers to produce the surplus value that is converted into profits. This class is also referred to as the owning class, the ruling class, or capitalists. (4)

Capital
Money invested with the purpose of increasing its value. (4)

Capitalism

An economic system in which all production is subordinated to the imperatives of the market, i.e., accumulation, labour productivity, competition, and profit maximization. (4)

Change theories

Theories that critique the current distribution of power and focus on how societies change. They are generally linked to a Marxist analysis. (1)

Class

See Social class. (3)

Class conflict

Also referred to as class struggle, it is a structural conflict between the owning and producing classes in all class-based societies. (3))

Class consciousness

A person's understanding of her or his place in the class structure and of shared interests with others in the same class. (5)

Commodity

Any object that is exchanged in the marketplace. (4)

Commons

Areas of a society that have traditionally been considered out of bounds for private ownership or trade because they have been accepted as collective property, existing for everyone to share. (9)

Concentration and centralization of capital

An inevitable process in capitalism, it is the coming together of small aggregates of capital to form huge enterprises located in a few centres around the globe. (4)

Convergence

The merging of the technology and content of the telecommunications, computer, entertainment, publishing, and broadcasting industries, among others. (7)

Credentialism

The use of paper credentials as a means of limiting access to certain job categories, even if the credentials are of questionable utility in actual job performance. (7)

Crisis of overproduction

In Marxist terminology, an inevitable consequence of the anarchy of production in all capitalist societies. As individual productive units compete in the marketplace in an attempt to maximize profits, there will ultimately be overproduction of goods. Capital tries to solve this problem in a variety of ways, but the crisis keeps recurring. (5)

Culture

The complete way of life shared by a people, including both the material and non-material elements. (3)

Deep integration

The harmonization of policies and regulations between Canada and the United States in the interest of the corporate sectors of these countries. (9)

Dialectics

A philosophical approach to the world that emphasizes the constancy of change and the interrelationship of elements. A concept first developed in ancient Greece, it was advanced as a tool for modern social analysis by Karl Marx and Friedrich Engels. (1)

Discrimination

The denial of equal treatment or opportunities to individuals on the basis of their membership in a particular social group. (11)

Distal relations of power

Relations of power that exist in society as a whole rather than within personal social relationships. This is a term used to describe the power wielded by governments or corporations that affect both individuals or groups. The opposite of *proximal relations of power*. (1)

Division of labour

The assigning of tasks to particular individuals or groups of people. All societies have minimally had a division of labour by sex and by age. (2)

Ethnic chauvinism

Hostility directed toward people on the basis of their membership in a particular ethnic group. (11)

Ethnicity

A collectivity of people with shared cultural traits, including language, religion, or ancestry. (11)

Ethnocentrism

The tendency of people to see the world in terms of their own culture, and to evaluate their group or culture favourably in relation to others. (3)

Eugenics

First developed by Francis Galton, a theory and later a social movement that believed in the improvement of the human species through selective mating. Eugenics theories were used to sterilize thousands of individuals considered "feebleminded" and became the basis for the mass exterminations undertaken by the Nazi regime. (2)

Exogamy

Rules or social preference for marriage outside the immediate group. (2)

Fascism

Capitalism in its most repressive, undemocratic, and militaristic form, with a police state to control populations while corporations increasingly control the economy. As an ideology, fascism emphasizes a strong leader and a strong state, while opposing egalitarianism, democracy, pacifism, or collectivism. (8)

Feminism

A term that broadly describes the belief in the social, political, and economic equality of the sexes, as well as the various social movements organized around this belief. (12)

Feudalism

A socioeconomic formation that grew out of the ruins of the old slave societies in the Middle Ages, which centred on duties and obligations between individuals. The major classes were the appropriating class, the aristocracy, and the producing class of peasants, or serfs. (4)

Financialization

The tendency of advanced capitalist economies to become dominated by the financial sector. (4)

Fordism

A term used to describe that period of capitalist development marked by intensive production, maximum use of machinery, and minute divisions of labour. Such developments were combined with higher wages, which would allow workers to buy the mass-produced goods created through these new production techniques. (6)

Free enterprise

An economic system in which no single buyer or seller can affect the price of a commodity by withdrawing purchasing power or a product. (4)

Functionalism

Also referred to as structural functionalism. A sociological framework that sees society as similar to an organism, with a number of interrelated and necessary elements. Each element, or structure, is seen as having an equally important function for the maintenance of a particular society. (1)

Gemeinschaft

A term created by Ferdinand Tönnies to describe traditional societies where social relationships were based on personal bonds of family or friendship that were held together by shared moral values usually tied to religion. The opposite of *gesellschaft*. (6)

Gender division of labour

Assigning different tasks in a society to men and women. (2)

Gesellschaft

A term created by Ferdinand Tönnies to describe large urban societies where social bonds were eroded by the complex division of labour, individualism and competitiveness. The opposite of *gemeinschaft*. (6)

Heterosexism

The ideology that heterosexual sex within a state-sanctioned marriage—primarily for the purpose of reproduction—is normal, while all other forms of sexual behaviour are deviant. (12)

Ideological hegemony

The control of the ruling class over a society's belief system. The term, developed by Antonio Gramsci, has embedded in it the notion that the dominant class maintains its power through a combination of coercion and persuasion. (7)

Ideology

A body of assumptions, ideas, and values that coalesces into a coherent world-view. In Marxist terminology, ideologies are connected to specific social classes and their particular class interests. (7)

Imperialism

The global stage of capitalism in which large monopolies come to control the economy, and capital—rather than commodities—becomes the primary export. (4)

Incest taboo

A societal rule that forbids sexual relations between those defined as kin, or family. (2)

Income

The economic gain derived from wages, salaries, or various forms of government assistance. (10)

Instinct

An inborn complex pattern of behaviour that must exist in every member of a species and, because it is embedded in the genetic code, cannot be overcome by force of will. (2)

Institutional racism

Racism that is embedded within a society's various social institutions, such as the education system, the judiciary, and the mass media. (11)

Islamophobia

The fear of or prejudiced viewpoint toward Islam, Muslims, and matters pertaining to them. (11)

Keynesianism

An approach to capitalism that advocates increased levels of state intervention and regulation of the economy. Named after economist John Maynard Keynes, it was adapted by many capitalist countries after World War II to help maintain economic and social stability. (8)

Labour power

The sum total of a worker's physical and mental capacities that go into a particular work task. In capitalist societies it is a commodity that is purchased by the employer because workers add value to the business. (4)

Labour union

A group of workers who join together to bargain with an employer or group of employers with regard to wages, benefits, and working conditions. (5)

Laissez-faire capitalism

An early stage of capitalism, when free enterprise still dominated, there were many small or medium-sized productive units, and there was a minimum of state intervention to control the worst excesses of capital. (4)

Liberalism

The dominant ideology of capitalism, it emphasizes individual freedom, equality, and choice, all perceived within the framework of a capitalist market economy. (7)

Lumpenproletariat

In Marxist terminology, the underclass within capitalist societies, made up of those marginal to production, such as the long-term unemployed, who historically have been used by the bourgeoisie against the organized working class (as strikebreakers, for example). (5)

Macrosociology

The branch of sociology that primarily examines societies as a whole, with analysis focusing on large-scale and long-term social processes. (1)

Market

People offering goods and services for sale to others in a more or less systematic and organized way. The concept of the market embodies not simply a physical place but rather a set of social relationships organized around the buying and selling of objects. (4)

Means of production

The various items that humans use in order to produce what they need. These include tools, natural resources, the land on which production occurs, and the buildings (if any) where production takes place. (3)

Mechanical solidarity

A term developed by Émile Durkheim to describe a society with a minimal *division of labour* and people united by shared values and common social bonds. The opposite of *organic solidarity*. (6)

Meritocracy

A society where advancement is based on individual ability or achievement. (10)

Microsociology

The branch of sociology that examines primarily individual and small-group behaviour, with analysis focusing on individual perceptions and communications. (1)

Misogyny

The hatred of women. (12)

Mode of production

The economic underpinning of a society, it is composed of the forces of production and the relations of production. (3)

Monopolization

An economic situation where there are so few companies in a given industry that free-enterprise competition no longer effectively exists. There is a high degree of monopolization in the current world economy. (4)

Nation

An aggregate of people within a particular territory who share a common history, language, and culture, and who possess—or seek to possess—a politically independent unit. (4)

Neoliberalism

The theoretical underpinning of the modern corporate agenda, it argues for the centrality of the individual, the importance of the marketplace, and a minimal role for government intervention. (9)

Neolithic Revolution

The historical technological transformation beginning about 10,000 years ago that led to the growth of agrarian societies. (3)

Norms

The expected patterns of behaviour. (1)

Order theories

Theories that ultimately support the current arrangements of power within a society. (1)

Organic solidarity

A term developed by Émile Durkheim to describe a society with a complex division of labour, with people performing highly specialized tasks, and people united by their interdependence. Such patterns were to be found in industrial societies. The opposite of *mechanical solidarity.* (6)

Patriarchy

In radical feminist analysis, a social system characterized by male dominance and female subordination, with men in control of the political, economic, and ideological spheres. The term is also used more generally to mean any society where males as a category have social advantages over women (for example, access to better jobs or higher wages). (12)

Petite bourgeoisie

The class that owns some means of production, but not a sufficient amount to survive by ownership alone. This class includes small-business people, farmers, fishers, and self-employed professionals. (4)

Pluralism

A theoretical position that argues that power in capitalist societies is spread among a wide number of equally influential interest groups and associations, which guarantees that no one group can dominate the others. (8)

Populism

A political orientation that presents itself as a movement of "the little guy," opposing big government and big business. There are left- and right-wing variants of populist movements. (13)

Post-Fordism

The stage of capitalist development characterized by more flexible forms of work that differ from the rigid Fordist assembly-line model. Post-Fordist production is centred on new information-based technologies. (6)

Power

The ability of an individual or a group to carry out its will even when opposed by others. Power is largely a result of the control one has over the resources of a society, including its "human resources." (1)

Precarious employment

Those forms of work characterized by limited social benefits and statutory entitlements, job insecurity, low wages, and high risks of ill health. (6)

Prejudice

The holding of biased attitudes and beliefs toward individuals on the basis of their membership in particular social groups. (11)

Progressive taxation

A form of taxation in which citizens are taxed on the basis of their ability to pay. The opposite of *regressive taxation*. (8)

Proletariat

The class in capitalist societies that does not own any means of production. As a result, members of this class must sell their labour power for a wage in order to survive. (4)

Proletarianization

The process in which higher status jobs, such as those of professionals, increasingly take on the characteristics of factory workers. (5)

Proximal relations of power

Relations of power that exist between individuals within social groups—for example, the power a parent has over a child in the family. The opposite of *distal relations of power*. (1)

Race

A category of people who share common physical traits deemed to be socially significant. Racial categories are most commonly linked to differences in skin colour. (11)

Racialized groups

Groups of people that are singled out for unequal treatment on the basis of real or imagined physical characteristics. (11)

Racism

Hostility directed toward those with real or perceived physiological traits, most centrally skin colour. (11)

Radical feminism

A theory that sees gender inequality as rooted in *patriarchy*, or the power men hold over women in society. (12)

Reformism

The belief that a series of reforms to the current structure can eliminate the major contradictions of capitalism, create societies where social justice reigns, and, in the long run, eventually lead to socialism. (13)

Reforms

Any change to society—whether legal, political, social, or economic—that occurs within a particular socioeconomic formation. There is no change in class relations. (13)

Regressive taxation

A form of taxation in which there is no connection between the amount of wealth or income one has and the tax paid. The opposite of *progressive taxation*. (8)

Relations of production

The type of relations that occur between humans in the process of production and are the result of their relationship (ownership or non-ownership) to the means of production. (3)

Relative poverty

A definition of poverty in which those whose incomes are far less than the average in their locale are deemed to be poor, even if they are above the barest subsistence level. (10)

Reserve army of the unemployed

In Marxist terminology, a group of people who exist in all capitalist societies as a result of the anarchy of production. They move in and out of the labour force as they are required by capital and are frequently unemployed for long periods of time. (6)

Revolution

Any major social transformation. In Marxist terminology, revolutions can be said to have occurred only when there is a transformation of class relations in a society. (13)

Rule of law

A formally determined set of rules or principles that applies, in theory at least, to all within its jurisdiction. (8)

Scientific management

A concept of managerial control of workers that developed in the early twentieth century. The goal was increased worker efficiency in order to maximize worker output and, therefore, profits. (6)

Social capital

The social networks connecting individuals to each other that are based on reciprocity, shared norms, and trust. (6)

Social class

A group of people with a common relation to the means of production. Where private appropriation of surplus occurs, there must always be a minimum of two classes: a superor class that, through ownership or control of the means of production, appropriates the surplus; and a subordinate class that produces the surplus. (3)

Social Darwinism

Any theoretical approach arguing that social inequality is based on biological differences and is simply the working out of the laws of nature. Often this refers specifically to a group of theories justifying social inequality that came out of the United States in the late nineteenth and early twentieth centuries. (2)

Socialist feminism

A theory that attempts to explain gender inequality by combining insights from both *radical feminism* and Marxism. In this framework, power is linked to both gender and class. (12)

Social mobility

The upward or downward movement of individuals in terms of their class position or their socioeconomic status. (10)

Social wage

The part of surplus value that is used, via transfers to the state, to provide such social necessities as health care, education, unemployment insurance, old age pension, and so on. (9)

Socialization

An ongoing process by which individuals learn a society's cultural components and social expectations. (3)

Society

A group of people within a limited territory who share a common set of behaviours, beliefs, values, material objects (together referred to as culture), and social institutions, all existing together as a coherent system. (1)

Sociocultural system

A term commonly used by anthropologists, it embodies the same meaning as society. (1)

Socioeconomic formation

In Marxist terminology, a society with a specific mode of production. Marxists sometimes refer to the mode of production as a society's base, and the other components—ideological, political, and social—as its superstructure. (3)

Socioeconomic status (SES)

The position one has in society, usually based on some combination of occupation, income, and education. Often used interchangeably—but incorrectly—with social class. (5)

Sociological imagination

The ability to go beyond the personal issues that all humans experience and connect them to broader social structures. Put differently, the sociological imagination is the ability to link distal relations of power to our immediate life situations. (1)

State

An organized political structure that carries out tasks required by more complex societies as their population and geographic size increase, as warfare and trade expand, and as social inequalities become more extreme. The state also acts as a major institution of social control. (8)

Status

A position within the social structure; statuses are usually ranked in relation to each other. Status can also be used to mean honour or prestige. (1, 5)

Status symbols

Those cultural objects, primarily although not totally material, that reflect an individual's socioeconomic status. (10)

Structural adjustment policies

A set of policies implemented by the World Bank and the International Monetary Fund that are linked to the expansion of neoliberalism. Its guiding principles include export-led growth; privatization and trade liberalization; and the efficiency of the free market. (9)

Structural functionalism

See Functionalism. (1)

Surplus value

That which is created by the unpaid labour of workers. In Marxist analysis, the production of surplus value and its appropriation by capitalists is the motive force of the capitalist mode of production. (4)

Symbol

Any object or act that has a socially shared meaning. It is anything that stands for or represents something else. (2)

Systemic racism

See Institutional racism. (11)

Transfer payments

Payments from one level to another level of government. It can also be used to describe payments made from one level of government to a family or an individual. (8)

Transnational corporations (TNCs)

Large capitalist monopolies, national in their capital, but international in the sphere of economic activity due to the export of capital. Such companies generally conduct at least 25 percent of their business outside of their own country. (4)

Wealth

All one's assets—including real estate holdings and money in bank accounts, stocks, bonds, and so on—minus debts. (10)

Welfare state

A form of capitalism in which governments played an increasing role in economic affairs, the public sector and social safety net expanded, and there was general economic prosperity for large numbers of working people. Most developed capitalist economies developed this form following World War II until the 1970s. (4, 8)

References

Abella, Irving, and Harold Troper. 1982. *None Is Too Many: Canada and the Jews of Europe, 1933–1948*. Toronto: Lester and Orpen Dennys.

Afanasiff, Kevin. 2011. "Canada's Participation in the Global Arms Race." *In Tel Daily*, April 29.

Agrell, Siri. 2007. "The Science of Soul." *Globe and Mail*, 3 May: L1.

Anderson, Mitchell. 2003. "The Cod's Gone, yet the Deadly Draggers Remain." *Globe and Mail*, 30 April: A17.

Anderssen, Erin. 2007. "Cut Your Spending, Save the World." *Globe and Mail*, 21 April.

Armstrong, Pat. 1996. "Feminization of the Labour Force." In Isabella Bakker (ed.), *Rethinking Restructuring: Gender and Change in Canada*. Toronto: University of Toronto Press.

Arundel Caral and Associates. 2009. *How Are Canadians Really Doing? A Closer Look at Select Groups. Canadian Index of Wellbeing*. At <http://www.ciw.ca/Libraries/Documents/ACloserLookAtSelectGroups_FullReport.sflb.ashx>.

Axelrod, Paul. 2010. "The Trouble with University Rankings: It's Maclean's Magazine Time Again." *University Affairs/Affairs Universitaire*, December 6. At <universityaffairs.ca/the-trouble-with-university-rankings.aspx>.

Bakan, Joel. 2011. *Childhood Under Siege: How Big Business Targets Children*. N.Y: Free Press.

Baran, Paul A., and Paul M. Sweezy. 1966. *Monopoly Capital: An Essay on the American Economic and Political Order*. New York: Monthly Review Press.

Barlow, Maude. 2007. "Integrate This! A Citizen's Guide to Fighting Deep Integration." At <canadians.org/DI/issues/guide/index.html>.

Barlow, Maude, and Tony Clarke. 2001. *Global Showdown: How the New Activists Are Fighting Global Corporate Rule*. Toronto: Stoddart.

Barlow, Maude, and Heather-Jane Robertson. 1994. *Class Warfare: The Assault on Canada's Schools*. Toronto: Key Porter.

Baron-Cohen, Simon. 2011. *The Science of Evil: On Empathy and the Origins of Human Cruelty*. Basic Books.

Basen, Ira. 2011. "Temporary Foreign Workers: Why so Many All of a Sudden?" CBC News online, April 14. At <cbc.ca/news/politics/canadavotes2011/reality-check/2011/04/temporary-foreign-workers-why-so-many-all-of-a-sudden.html>.

Battle, Ken, Sherry Torjman, and Michael Mendelson. 2011. *Prisons or Poverty? The Choice Is Clear*. Caledon Institute for Public Policy, March. At <caledoninst.org/Publications/PDF/934ENG%2Epdf>.

Berman, Morris. 2006. *Dark Ages America: The Final Phase of Empire*. New York: W.W. Norton.

Black, Errol, and Jim Silver. 2011. "Fast Facts: How Unions Protect Our Human Rights." Canadian Centre for Policy Alternatives, Manitoba Office, June 10. At <policyalternatives.ca/publications/commentary/fast-facts-how-unions-protect-our-human-rights>.

Block, Sheila. 2010. *Ontario's Growing Gap: The Role of Race and Gender*. Canadian Centre for Policy Alternatives, Ontario Office, June. At <policyalternatives.ca/sites/default/files/uploads/publications/reports/docs/The%20Role%20of%20

Race%20Ontario%20Growing%20Gap.pdf>.

Blum, William. 1998. *Killing Hope: U.S. Military and CIA Interventions Since World War II*. Montreal: Black Rose.

____. 2000. *Rogue State: A Guide to the World's Only Superpower*. Monroe, ME: Common Courage.

Boesveld, Sarah. 2011. "Ask for Higher Pay, Young Women Told." *National Post* online, 20 May. At <nationalpost.com/news/higher+young+women+told/4813703/story.html>.

Bolaria, B. Singh, and Peter S. Li. 1988. *Racial Oppression in Canada*. Second ed. Toronto: Garamond.

Bowles, Samuel, and Herbert Gintis. 1976. *Schooling in Capitalist America*. New York: Basic Books.

Bramham, Daphne. 2011. "Tough on Crime and Good for Profits," *Vancouver Sun*, July 22: A5.

Brannigan, Augustin. 1984. *Crimes, Courts and Corrections*. Toronto: Holt, Rinehart and Winston.

Brown, Lester, and Christopher Flavin. 1999. "It's Getting Late to Switch to a Viable World Economy." *International Herald Tribune*, 19 January.

Brownlee, Jamie. 2005. *Ruling Canada: Corporate Cohesion and Democracy*. Halifax: Fernwood.

Burke, Mike, and John Shields. 2002. "The Hour-Glass Workforce: Measuring the Deterioration of Job Quality in Canada." Paper presented at the Annual Meeting of the Society for Socialist Studies, 30 May.

Campaign 2000. 2010. *Report Card on Child and Family Poverty in Canada: 1989–2010*. At <campaign2000.ca/reportCards/national/2010EnglishC2000NationalReportCard.pdf>.

Canadian Taxpayers Federation. 2007. *On the Dole: Businesses, Lobbyists and Industry Canada's Subsidy Programs*, January 10. At <taxpayer.com/pdf/2007_corporate_welfare_report.pdf>.

Carey, Elaine. 2003. "Gambling a Real Growth Industry." *Toronto Star*, 23 April: A4.

Cardinale, Matthew. 2011. "First Federal Reserve Audit Reveals Millions in Secret Bailouts." Centre for Research on Globalization, August 29. At <globalresearch.ca/index.php?context=va&aid=26276>.

Carroll, William K. 2010. *Corporate Power in a Globalizing World*. Don Mills, ON: Oxford University Press.

Catalyst. 2010. *Women MBAs: Women's Enrollment and Degrees Around the World*. At <catalyst.org/file/194/qt_women_mbas.pdf>.

Cavanagh, John, Jerry Mander, et al. 2002. *Alternatives to Economic Globalization: A Better World Is Possible. A Report of the International Forum on Globalization*. San Francisco, CA: Berrett-Koehler.

Certified General Accountants Association of Canada. 2011. *A Driving Force No More: Have Canadian Consumers Reached Their Limits?* June. At <cga-canada.org/en-ca/ResearchReports/ca_rep_2011-06_debt-consumption.pdf>.

____. 2010. *Where Is the Money Now? The State of Canadian Household Debt as Conditions for Economic Recovery Emerge*. May. At <cga-canada.org/en-ca/ResearchReports/ca_rep_2010-05_debt-consumption.pdf>.

Chase, Allan. 1977. *The Legacy of Malthus: The Social Costs of the New Scientific Racism*. New York: Alfred A. Knopf.

Chenier, Louise, and Elise Wohlbold. 2011. *Women in Senior Management: Where Are They?* The Conference Board of Canada, August. At <conferenceboard.ca/

documents.aspx?did=4416>.

Church, Elizabeth. 2007. "Tax Credits Provide Little Help to Low-Income Students, Study Finds." *Globe and Mail*, 29 May: A7.

Clement, Wallace. 1975. *The Canadian Corporate Elite: Economic Power in Canada.* Toronto: McClelland and Stewart.

___. 1983. *Class, Power, and Property: Essays on Canadian Society.* Toronto: Methuen.

Clement, Wallace, and John Myles. 1994. *Relations of Ruling: Class and Gender in Postindustrial Societies.* Montreal: McGill-Queen's University Press.

Cohen, Lizabeth. 2003. *A Consumers' Republic: The Politics of Mass Consumption in Postwar America.* New York: Vintage.

Collins, Randall. 1994. *Four Sociological Traditions.* New York: Oxford University Press.

Conference Board of Canada. 2011. "Is Canada Becoming More Unequal?" At <conferenceboard.ca/hcp/hot-topics/canInequality.aspx>.

Connell, R.W. 1995. *Masculinities.* Berkeley, CA: University of California Press.

Corak, Miles, and Andrew Heisz. 1996. *The Intergenerational Income Mobility of Canadian Men.* Analytical Studies Branch no. 89. Ottawa: Statistics Canada.

Cox, Oliver C. 1970 [1942]. *Caste, Class, and Race.* Reprint, New York: Monthly Review Press.

Daniels, Ronald J., Patrick Macklem, and Kent Roach. 2001. *The Security of Freedom: Essays on Canada's Anti-Terrorism Bill.* Toronto: University of Toronto.

David, Deborah, and Robert Brannon (eds.). 1976. *The Forty-Nine Percent Majority: Readings on the Male Role.* Reading, MA: Addison-Wesley.

Davis, Jeff. 2011. "Prison Costs Soar 86% in Past Five Years: Report," *National Post* online, July 18. At <news.nationalpost.com/2011/07/18/prison-costs-soar-86-in-past-five-years/>.

Davis, Kingsley, and Wilber E. Moore. 1945. "Some Principles of Stratification." *American Sociological Review* 10.

de Botton, Alain. 2004. *Status Anxiety.* London: Viking.

de Wolff, Alice. 2000. *Breaking the Myth of Flexible Work: Contingent Work in Toronto.* Toronto: Contingent Workers Project.

DeManno, Rosie. 2010. "Make It Right, Chief Blair." *Toronto Star* online, Dec 8. At <thestar.com/news/crime/article/903363--dimanno-make-it-right-chief-blair?bn=1>.

Diamond, Jared. 1999. *Guns, Germs and Steel: The Fates of Human Societies.* New York: W.W. Norton.

Durkheim, Émile. 1933. *The Division of Labor in Society.* New York: Free Press.

___. 1951 [1897]. *Suicide.* New York: Free Press.

Ehrenberg, Margaret. 2001. "The Role of Women in Human Evolution." In Caroline Brettell and Carolyn Sargent, eds., *Gender in Cross-Cultural Perspective.* NJ: Prentice Hall.

Engels, Friedrich. 1972 [1884]. *The Origin of the Family, Private Property, and the State.* Eleanor Burke Leacock, ed. New York: International Publishers.

Engler, Yves. 2009. *The Black Book of Canadian Foreign Policy.* Vancouver, B.C. & Black Point, NS: Red/Fernwood.

Estulin, Daniel. 2007. *The True Story of the Bilderberg Group.* TrineDay LLC.

Fleming, James. 1991. *Circles of Power: The Most Influential People in Canada.* Toronto: Doubleday.

Francis, Diane. 1986. *Controlling Interest: Who Owns Canada?* Toronto: Macmillan.

Frenette, Marc. 2007. *Why Are Youth from Lower-Income Families Less Likely to Attend University? Evidence from Academic Abilities, Parental Influences, and Financial Constraints,*

February. Statistics Canada Analytical Studies Branch Research Paper Series, 11F0019MIE–No. 295. At <statcan.ca>.

Frideres, James S. 1988. "Institutional Structures and Economic Deprivation: Native People in Canada." In B. Singh Bolaria and Peter S. Li (eds.), *Racial Oppression in Canada*. Second ed. Toronto: Garamond.

Fudge, Judy. 2005. "Beyond Vulnerable Workers: Towards a New Standard Employment Relationship." *Canadian Labour and Employment Law Journal* 12 (2).

Galabuzi, Grace-Edward. 2006. *Canada's Economic Apartheid: The Social Exclusion of Racialized Groups in the New Century*. Toronto: Canadian Scholars' Press.

Garfinkel, Simson L. 2011. "Mind Your Own Browser." *Utne Reader* 166, July–August.

Gonick, Cy. 2011. "Precarious Labour." *Canadian Dimension* 45, 3 (May–June): 24–25.

Goodyear, Sheena. 2011. "U.S. Health-Care System Less Efficient: Study." *Toronto Sun* online, August 5. At <torontosun.com/2011/08/05/us-health-care-system-less-efficient-study>.

Gould, Stephen Jay. 1977. *Ever Since Darwin*. New York: W.W. Norton.

___. 1981. *The Mismeasure of Man*. New York: W.W. Norton.

Government of Canada Standing Committee on Human Resources, Skills and Social Development and the Status of Persons with Disabilities. 2010. *Federal Poverty Reduction Plan: Working in Partnership Towards Reducing Poverty in Canada*, November. At <parl.gc.ca/content/hoc/Committee/403/HUMA/Reports/RP4770921/humarp07/humarp07-e.pdf>.

Gray, John. 1993. *Men Are from Mars, Women Are from Venus*. New York: HarperCollins.

Gwyn, Richard. 2007. "The Rich Get Their Own Nationality." *Toronto Star* online, 26 June. At <thestar.com/comment/article/229382>.

Gue, Lisa. 2011. "Federal Budget Will Outline the Value the Government of Canada Places on The Environment," March 21. At <davidsuzuki.org/blogs/panther-lounge/2011/03/money-talks-tomorrows-federal-budget-will-outline-the-value-the-government-of-ca/>.

Gutstein, Donald. 2010. "New Citizen Handbook Twists the Canadian Story." The Tyee, March 3. At <thetyee.ca/Mediacheck/2010/03/03/DiscoverCanada/>.

Harris, Marvin. 1989 [1974]. *Cows, Pigs, Wars and Witches*. New York: Random House.

Harris, Misty. 2011. "Female Artists' Airplay, Sales Lag Behind Male Counterparts." December 21, Postmedia news online. At <2.canada.com/topics/news/national/story.html?id=5895137>.

Harrison, Trevor, Bill Johnston, and Harvey Krahn. 1996. "Special Interests and/or New Right Economics? The Ideological Bases of Reform Party Support in Alberta in the 1993 Federal Election." *Canadian Review of Sociology and Anthropology* 33, 2 (May).

Hedges, Chris. 2009. *Empire of Illusion: The End of Literacy and the Triumph of Spectacle*. Toronto: Alfred A. Knopf Canada.

Henry, Frances, Carol Tator, Winston Mattis, and Tim Rees. 2000. *The Colour of Democracy*. Second ed. Toronto: Harcourt Brace.

Henton, Darcy. 1996. "Faith in Eugenics Ran Deep in Alberta." *Toronto Star*, 11 February: F1.

Herman, Edward, and Noam Chomsky. 1988. *Manufacturing Consent: The Political Economy of the Mass Media*. New York: Pantheon.

Higham, Charles. 1983. *Trading with the Enemy: An Exposé of the Nazi-American Money Plot, 1933–1949*. New York: Dell.

Himelfarb, Alex. 2011. "Is It Getting Tough on Crime or Getting Tough on the Poor?" *CCPA Monitor* 18, 3 (July–August): 14–15.

Hubbard, Ruth, and Elijah Wald. 1993. *Exploding the Gene Myth*. Boston: Beacon Press.

Human Resources and Skills Development Canada. 2011a. "Indicators of Well-Being in Canada: Weekly Hours Worked." At <4.hrsdc.gc.ca/.3ndic.1t.4r@-eng.jsp?iid=19>.

___. 2011b. "Indicators of Well-Being in Canada: Work Related Injuries." At <hrsdc.gc.ca/.3ndic.1t.4r@-eng.jsp?iid=20>.

Industry Canada. 2008. "Key Small Business Statistics." July 2008. At <ic.gc.ca/eic/site/sbrp-rppe.nsf/eng/rd02300.html>.

Innis, Harold Adams. 1964 [1951]. *The Bias of Communication*. Toronto: University of Toronto Press.

Jackson, Andrew, and Grant Schellenberg. 1999. "Unions, Collective Bargaining and Labour Market Outcomes for Canadian Working Women: Past Gains and Future Challenges." In Richard P. Chaykowski and Lisa M. Powell (eds.), *Women and Work*. Montreal and Kingston: McGill–Queen's University Press.

Jackson, Andrew and Sylvain Schetagne. 2010. *Is EI Working for Canada's Unemployed? Analyzing the Great Recession*. Canadian Centre for Policy Alternatives, January. At <policyalternatives.ca/sites/default/files/uploads/publications/reports/docs/Is_EI_Working_For_Canadas_Unemployed.pdf>.

Jackson, Michael and Stewart, Graham. 2009. *A Flawed Compass: A Human Rights Analysis of the Roadmap to Strengthening Public Safety*, September 24. At <justicebehindthewalls.net/resources/news/flawed_Compass.pdf>.

Jacobs, Jane. 2004. *Dark Age Ahead*. Toronto: Random House Canada.

Jedwab, Jack. 2010. "Getting Ahead: Rightly or Wrongly Canadians Believe Their Society Is Egalitarian." Association for Canadian Studies.

Jin, R.L., C.P. Shah, and T.J. Svoboda. 1995. "The Impact of Unemployment on Health: A Review of the Evidence." *Canadian Medical Association Journal* 153, 5.

Johnson, Gail. 2011. "Soaking up Nature May Help Cure What Ails You." *Georgia Strait*, September 15–22: 31.

Johnson, Leo. 1972. "The Development of Class in Canada in the Twentieth Century." In Gary Teeple (ed.), *Capitalism and the National Question*. Toronto: University of Toronto Press.

Kinsman, Gary. 2001. "Gays and Lesbians: Pushing the Boundaries." In Dan Glenday and Ann Duffy (eds.), *Canadian Society: Meeting the Challenges of the Twenty-First Century*. Don Mills, ON: Oxford University Press.

Kinsman, Gary, Dieter K. Buse, and Mercedes Steedman (eds.). 2000. *Whose National Security? Canadian State Surveillance and the Creation of Enemies*. Toronto: Between the Lines.

Klaffke, Pamela. 2003. *Spree: A Cultural History of Shopping*. Vancouver: Arsenal Pulp Press.

Korten, David C. 1996. *When Corporations Rule the World*. West Hartford, CT: Kumarian Press.

Krahn, Harvey J., Graham S. Lowe, and Karen D. Hughes. 2007. *Work, Industry and Canadian Society*. Fifth ed. Toronto: Thomson Nelson.

Kraus, Michael W., Paul K. Piff, and Dacher Keltner. 2011. "Social Class as Culture: The Convergence of Resources and Rank in the Social Realm." *Current Directions in Psychological Science* 20, 4 (August).

Krieger, David. 2011. "Ten Lessons From Chernobyl And Fukushima." *The Progressive* online. At <progressive.org/mpkrieger051311.html>.

Kuypers, Jim A. 2009. *Rhetorical Criticism: Perspectives in Action*. Lexington Press.

Lagi, M., K.Z. Bertrand, and Y. Bar-Yam. 2011. *The Food Crises and Political Instability in North Africa and the Middle East.* arXiv:1108.2455. At <necsi.edu/research/social/foodcrises.html>.

Laird, Gordon. 2007. *SHELTER—Homelessness in a Growth Economy: Canada's 21st Century Paradox.* Calgary: Sheldon Chumir Foundation. At <chumirethicsfoundation.ca/files/pdf/SHELTER.pdf>.

Lasch, Christopher. 1979. *The Culture of Narcissism.* New York: W.W. Norton.

Leacock, Eleanor Burke. 1972. "Introduction." In Friedrich Engels, *The Origins of the Family, Private Property, and the State.* New York: International Publishers.

Leakey, Richard E., and Roger Lewin. 1977. *Origins.* London: E.P. Dutton.

Lee, Marc. 2011. "On Climate, Canada Is a Rogue State." Behind the Numbers: A Blog from the Canadian Centre for Policy Alternatives, November 29. At <behindthenumbers.ca/2011/11/29/on-climate-canada-is-a-rogue-state/>.

Lee, Richard. 1978. "Politics, Sexual and Nonsexual, in an Egalitarian Society." *Social Science Information* 17.

Lemonick, Michael D., and Andrea Dorfman. 2006. "What Makes Us Different." *Time*, Canadian ed., 9 October.

Lerner, Gerda. 1986. *The Creation of Patriarchy.* New York: Oxford University Press.

___. 1993. *The Creation of Feminist Consciousness: From the Middle Ages to 1870.* New York: Oxford University Press.

Lewis, Charles. 2011. "Number of Muslims in Canada Predicted to Triple over Next 20 Years: Study." *National Post* online, January 31. At <life.nationalpost.com/2011/01/31/number-of-muslims-in-canada-predicted-to-triple-over-next-20-years-study/>.

Lewis, David. 1972. *Louder Voices: The Corporate Welfare Bums.* Toronto: James Lewis and Samuel.

Lewontin, Richard. 2001. *It Ain't Necessarily So: The Dream of the Human Genome and Other Illusions.* New York: New York Review of Books.

Li, Peter (ed.). 1990. *Race and Ethnic Relations in Canada.* Toronto: Oxford University Press.

Lichtenstein, Nelson. 2006. *Wal-Mart: The Face of Twenty-First-Century Capitalism.* New York: New Press.

Livingstone, D.W. 1999. *The Education–Jobs Gap: Underemployment or Economic Democracy.* Toronto: Garamond.

Livingstone, Sonia. 2008. "Taking Risky Opportunities in Youthful Content Creation: Teenagers' Use of Social Networking Sites for Intimacy, Privacy and Self-Expression." *New Media & Society* 10 (3): 393–411.

Lorimer, Rowland, and Jean McNulty. 1996. *Mass Communications in Canada.* Third ed. Toronto: Oxford University Press.

Louv, Richard. 2005. *Last Child in the Woods: Saving our Children from Nature-Deficit Disorder.* Chapel Hill: Algonquin Books.

Macdonald, David. 2011a. *Corporate Income Taxes, Profit, and Employment Performance of Canada's Largest Companies.* Ottawa: Canadian Centre for Policy Alternatives, April. At <policyalternatives.ca/sites/default/files/uploads/publications/National%20Office/2011/04/Corporate%20Income%20Taxes%2C%20Profit%2C%20and%20Employment.pdf>.

___. 2011b. *The Cost of 9/11: Tracking the Creation of a National Security Establishment.* Ottawa: Rideau Institute, September. At <rideauinstitute.ca/file-library/cost-of-9-11.pdf>.

MacDonald, Kevin, and Ross D. Parke. 1986. "Parental-Child Physical Play: The Effects of Sex and Age of Children and Parents." *Sex Roles* 15.

MacKenzie, Hugh. 2011. *Recession-Proof: Canada's 100 Best Paid CEOs*. Ottawa: Canadian Centre for Policy Alternatives, January. At <policyalternatives.ca/sites/default/files/uploads/publications/National%20Office/2011/01/Recession%20Proof.pdf>.

Marshall, Katherine. 2010. *Gambling 2010*. Statistics Canada Catalogue no. 75-001-X. At <statcan.gc.ca/pub/75-001-x/2010108/pdf/11297-eng.pdf>.

Martin, M. Kay, and Barbara Voorhies. 1975. *Female of the Species*. Toronto: Methuen.

Mayer, Jane. 2010. "The Billionaire Brothers Who Are Waging a War Against Obama." *The New Yorker* online, August 30. At <newyorker.com/reporting/2010/08/30/100830fa_fact_mayer>.

McBride, Stephen, and John Shields. 1997. *Dismantling a Nation: The Transition to Corporate Rule in Canada*. Second ed. Halifax: Fernwood.

McCracken Jeffrey, and Brett Foley. 2011. "Dealmaking Hits Bump as Market Slump Overshadows Cash Pile." Bloomberg online. June 29. At <bloomberg.com/news/2011-06-29/global-dealmaking-hits-june-bump-as-economic-slump-overshadows-cash-piles.html>.

McLaren, Angus. 1990. *Our Own Master Race: Eugenics in Canada, 1885–1945*. Toronto: McClelland and Stewart.

McMullen, Kathryn, Jason Gilmore and Christel Le Petit. 2010. *Women in Non-Traditional Occupations and Fields of Study*. Statistics Canada Catalogue number 81-004-X. At <statcan.gc.ca/pub/81-004-x/2010001/article/11151-eng.htm>.

McNally, David. 2002. *A Better World Is Possible: Globalization and Anti-Capitalism*. Winnipeg: Arbeiter Ring.

___. 2011. *Global Slump: The Economics and Politics of Crisis and Resistance*. Black Point, N.S.: Spectre/Fernwood.

McQuaig, Linda. 1992. *The Quick and the Dead: Brian Mulroney, Big Business, and the Seduction of Canada*. Toronto: Penguin Books.

___. 1999. *The Cult of Impotence*. Toronto: Penguin Books.

McQuaig, Linda, and Neil Brooks. 2010. *The Trouble With Billionaires*. Toronto: Viking Canada.

Mensah, Joseph. 2002. *Black Canadians: History, Experiences, Social Conditions*. Halifax: Fernwood.

Menzies, Heather. 2005. *No Time: Stress and the Crisis of Modern Life*. Vancouver: Douglas & McIntyre.

Milan, Anne, and Kelly Tran. 2004. "Blacks in Canada: A Long History." *Canadian Social Trends* Spring. Statistics Canada Catalogue No. 11-008. At <statcan.ca/english/studies/11-008/feature/11-008-XIE20030046802.pdf>.

Miles, Robert. 1989. *Racism*. London: Routledge.

Mills, C. Wright. 1961. *The Sociological Imagination*. New York: Grove Press.

Minsky, Amy. 2011. "Not All Native Land Claims Face Final Offer, Aboriginal Affairs Minister Says." *National Post* online, July 26. At <2news.nationalpost.com/2011/07/26/minister-denies-reports-of-limit-on-native-land-claims-negotiations/>.

Miranda, Veerle. 2011. "Cooking, Caring and Volunteering: Unpaid Work Around the World." *OECD Social, Employment and Migration Working Papers* 116, OECD Publishing. At <10.1787/5kghrjm8s142-en>.

Mithen, Steven. 2006. *The Singing Neanderthals: The Origins of Music, Language, Mind and Body*. Cambridge, MA: Harvard University Press.

Mohammad, Susan, and Duncan Hood. 2009. "Cashing In: Canada's CEO Salary Surge." May 1. Macleans.ca. At <2.macleans.ca/2009/05/01/the-rising-salaries-of-canadas-top-50-ceos/>.

Monk, Katherine. 2010. "Hollywood Is a Near-Wasteland for Good Female Roles." *Vancouver Sun* online, March 5. At <vancouversun.com/health/praise+ofstronger+women/4389216/story.html>.

Mooers, Colin (ed.). 2006. *The New Imperialists: Ideologies of Empire.* Oxford: Oneworld Publications.

Moskowitz, Clara. 2011. "The Destructive Culture of Pretty Pink Princesses." Live Science, 24 January. At <livescience.com/11625-destructive-culture-pretty-pink-princesses.html>

Mugyenyi, Bianca, and Yves Engler. 2011. *Stop Signs: Cars and Capitalism on the Road to Economic, Social and Ecological Decay.* Vancouver and Black Point, NS: Red/Fernwood.

Murdock, George. 1937. "Comparative Data on the Division of Labour by Sex." *Social Forces* 15, 4 (May).

Murphy, Jessica. 2011. "Offshore Financial Centres Keep Canada Competitive, MPs Hear." *Toronto Sun* online, March 3. At <torontosun.com/news/canada/2011/03/03/17484606.html>.

Nagler, Mark. 1972. "Minority Values and Economic Achievement: The Case of the North American Indian." In Mark Nagler (ed.), *Perspectives on the North American Indian.* Toronto: McClelland and Stewart.

Nelson, Adie, and Barrie W. Robinson. 2002. *Gender in Canada.* Second ed. Toronto: Pearson Education Canada

Newman, Peter C. 1975. *The Canadian Establishment.* Toronto: McClelland and Stewart.

___. 1998. *Titans: How the New Canadian Establishment Seized Power.* Toronto: Viking.

Niosi, Jorge. 1981. *Canadian Capitalism: A Study of Power in the Canadian Business Establishment.* Toronto: Lorimer.

O'Connor, James. 1973. *The Fiscal Crisis of the State.* New York: St. Martin's Press.

Orenstein, Peggy. 2011. *Cinderella Ate My Daughter: Dispatches from the Front Lines of the New Girlie-Girl Culture.* HarperCollins.

Panitch, Leo. 1977. "The Role and Nature of the Canadian State." In Leo Panitch (ed.), *The Canadian State: Political Economy and Political Power.* Toronto: University of Toronto Press.

Parenti, Michael. 1993. *Inventing Reality: The Politics of the News Media.* Second ed. New York: St. Martin's Press.

Parsons, Talcott. 1961. "The School as a Social System: Some of Its Functions in American Society." In A.H. Halsey, Jean Floud, and C. Arnold Anderson (eds.), *Education, Economy and Society.* New York: Free Press.

Paxton, Robert. 2004. *The Anatomy of Facism.* New York: Knopf.

Perriera, Richard. 2009. "The Costs of Unpaid Overtime Work in Canada: Dimensions and Comparative Analysis." Masters thesis, Athabasca University, August 2009.

Picard, Andre. 1999. "Balancing Work and Home Tasks Raising Women's Blood Pressure." *Globe and Mail*, 29 March: A6.

Piff, Paul K., Michael W. Kraus, Stéphane Côté, Bonnie Hayden Cheng, and Dacher Keltner. 2010. "Having Less, Giving More: The Influence of Social Class on Prosocial Behavior." *Journal of Personality and Social Psychology* 99, 5 (November).

Polanyi, Karl. 1957 [1944]. *The Great Transformation: The Political and Economic Origins of Our Time.* Boston: Beacon Press.

Pollack, William. 1998. *Real Boys: Rescuing Our Sons from the Myths of Boyhood.* New

York: Owl Books.

Pollett, Graham. 2009. *Violence in Amateur Hockey.* Middlesex-London Health Unit.

Porter, John. 1965. *The Vertical Mosaic.* Toronto: University of Toronto Press.

Potter, Andrew. 2011. "Inequality." *Canadian Business* 83, 21/22 (January 18): 78–81.

Putnam, Robert D. 2000. *Bowling Alone: The Collapse and Revival of American Community.* New York: Simon & Schuster.

Reiman Jeffrey, and Paul Leighton. 2010. *The Rich Get Richer and the Poor Get Prison: Ideology, Class, and Criminal Justice.* Ninth ed. Allyn & Bacon.

Robinson, Bill. 2011a. *Canadian Military spending 2010–11.* Canadian Centre for Policy Alternatives Foreign Policy Series, March. At <policyalternatives.ca/sites/default/files/uploads/publications/National%20Office/2011/03/Canadian%20Military%20Spending%202010.pdf>.

___. 2011b. "More Is Being Spent on Military Than at Any Time Since WW-II." *CCPA Monitor* 18, 1 (May):12–13.

Rodney, Walter. 1972. *How Europe Underdeveloped Africa.* London: Bogle-L'Ouverture.

Rosenzweig & Company. 2011. *The 6th Annual Rosenzweig Report on Women at the Top Levels of Corporate Canada.* At <rosenzweigco.com/media/2011/2011-pdf/6thAnnualReport-WomenAtTopLevel.pdf>.

Russell, Frances. 2010. "Socialism for the Rich Is Tory Way." *Winnipeg Free Press* online, March 3. At <winnipegfreepress.com/opinion/westview/socialism-for-the-rich-is-tory-way-87204607.html>.

Ryan, William. 1971. *Blaming the Victim.* New York: Vintage Books.

Samuelson, Leslie. 1995. "The Canadian Criminal Justice System: Inequalities of Class, Race, and Gender." In B. Singh Bolaria (eds.), *Social Issues and Contradictions in Canadian Society.* Second ed. Toronto: Harcourt Brace.

Sanders, Richard. 2004. "Canada and the Big Business of War." *Canadian Dimension* March/April. At <canadiandimension.com/articles/2004/03/01/150/>.

___. 2011. "Canada's Military Exports Arm World's Most Belligerent Nations." *CCPA Monitor* 18, 1 (May).

Sanderson, Steven K. 1999. *Macrosociology: An Introduction to Human Societies.* Fourth ed. Boston: Allyn and Bacon.

Sanger, Toby. 2011. *Fair Shares: How Banks, Brokers and the Financial Industry Can Pay Fairer Taxes,* Canadian Centre for Policy Alternatives, April. At <policyalternatives.ca/sites/default/files/uploads/publications/National%20Office/2011/04/Fair%20Shares.pdf>.

Satzewich, Vic. 1999. "The Political Economy of Race and Ethnicity." In Peter S. Li (ed.), *Race and Ethnic Relations in Canada.* Second ed. Toronto: Oxford University Press.

Schechter, Danny. 2007. "Manufacturing Indifference: Searching for a New 'Propaganda Model.'" CommonDreams.org. At <commondreams.org/archive/2007/05/19/1317/>.

Schwartz, Nelson D. 2010. "Industries Find Surging Profits in Deeper Cuts." *New York Times* online, July 25. At <nytimes.com/2010/07/26/business/economy/26earnings.html>.

Sears, Alan. 2000. "Education for a Lean World." In Mike Burke, Colin Mooers, and John Shields (eds.), *Restructuring and Resistance: Canadian Public Policy in an Age of Global Capitalism.* Halifax: Fernwood.

___. 2003. *Retooling the Mind Factory: Education in a Lean State.* Aurora, ON: Garamond.

___. 2005. *A Good Book, in Theory: A Guide to Theoretical Thinking.* Peterborough, ON: Broadview Press.

Shaker, Erika. 2011. "The Riddle of the Middle." Canadian Centre for Policy Alternatives, July 8. At <behindthenumbers.ca/2011/07/08/the-riddle-of-the-middle/>

Shields, John, Susan Silver, and Sue Wilson. 2006. "Assessing Employment Risk: Dimensions in the Measurement of Unemployment, Research Note." *Socialist Studies: The Journal of the Society for Socialist Studies* 2, 2 (Fall).

Sklar, Holly (ed.). 1980. *Trilateralism: The Trilateral Commission and Elite Planning for World Management*. Boston: South End Press.

Slater, Philip. 1970. *The Pursuit of Loneliness: American Culture at the Breaking Point*. Boston: Beacon Press.

Smail, David. 1999. *The Origins of Unhappiness: A New Understanding of Personal Distress*. London: Constable.

Smith, Mark. 2006. "How Do Teens Use the 'Net?" *Technology & Learning* 26, 6, January.

Sorenson, John. 2003. "I'm Not a Racist, and Nobody I Know Is Either." In Judith Blackwell, Murray Smith, and John Sorenson (eds.), *Culture of Prejudice: Arguments in Critical Social Science*. Peterborough, ON: Broadview Press.

Stanford, Jim. 1999. *Paper Boom*. Toronto: CCPA and Lorimer.

____. 2008. *Economics for Everyone: A Short Guide to the Economics of Capitalism*. Black Point, NS and Ottawa, ON: Fernwood Publishing and the Canadian Centre for Policy Alternatives.

____. 2011. "Another Indicator of Canada's Deindustrialization." Progressive Economics Forum, February 22. At <progressive-economics.ca/2011/02/22/another-indicator-of-canadas-deindustrialization/>.

Staples, Steven. 2006. "Marching Orders: How Canada Abandoned Peacekeeping— and Why the U.N. Needs Us Now More Than Ever." A report commissioned by the Council of Canadians. At <canadians.org/peace/issues/Marching_Orders/index.html>.

Statistics Canada. 2003. *Earnings of Canadians: Making a Living in the New Economy*. Catalogue No. 96F0030XIE2001013. At <12.statcan.ca/english/census01/Products/Analytic/companion/earn/pdf/96F0030XIE2001013.pdf>.

____. 2006. "Women in Canada." *The Daily*, 7 March. At <statcan.ca/Daily/English/060307/d060307a.htm>.

____. 2006a. *Women in Canada: A Gender-Based Statistical Report*. Fifth ed. No. 89-503-XPE. Ottawa: Ministry of Industry. At <statcan.ca/bsolc/english/bsolc?catno=89-503-X>.

____. 2007a. "Average Earnings by Sex and Work Pattern." At <www40.statcan.ca/l01/cst01/labor01a.htm>.

____. 2007b. *The Daily*. "General Social Survey: Navigating Family Transitions," 14 June. At <statcan.ca/Daily/English/070613/d070613b.htm>.

____. 2007c. *Self-employment, Historical Summary*. Cat. no. 89F0133XIE. At <www.statcan.ca>.

____. 2008a. *Educational Portrait of Canada, Census 2006*. Cat. no. 97-560-X2006001. At <statcan.ca/census-recensement/2006/as-sa/97-560/pdf/97-560-XIE2006001.pdf >.

____. 2008b. "University Tuition Fees 2008/2009." *The Daily*, Oct 9. Cat. no. 11-001-XIE.

____. 2009. "The 2008 Canadian Immigrant Labour Market: Analysis of Quality of Employment." The Immigrant Labour Force Analysis Series, no. 5 (71-606-X2009001), November. At <statcan.gc.ca/bsolc/olc-cel/olc-cel?catno=71-606-

X2009001&lang=eng>.

___. 2010a. *Education Indicators in Canada: An International Perspective*. Cat. no. 81-604-X. At <statcan.gc.ca/pub/81-604-x/81-604-x2010001-eng.pdf>.

___. 2010b. "Homicide in Canada," *The Daily*, October 26. At <statcan.gc.ca/daily-quotidien/101026/dq101026a-eng.htm>.

___. 2010c. *Leading Causes of Death in Canada 2007*. Catalogue 84-215-X. At <statcan.gc.ca/pub/84-215-x/2010001/hl-fs-eng.htm>.

___. 2010d. "Self-Employment in the Downturn, October 2008 to October 2009." *The Daily*, March 29. At <statcan.gc.ca/daily-quotidien/100329/dq100329a-eng.htm>.

___. 2010e. "Study: Aboriginal Labour Market Update, 2008–2009." *The Daily*, May 13. At <statcan.gc.ca/daily-quotidien/100513/dq100513b-eng.htm>.

___. 2010f. *Pension Plans in Canada Survey*. Record No. 2609. At <statcan.gc.ca/cgi-bin/imdb/p2SV.pl?Function=getSurvey&SDDS=2609&lang=en&db=imdb&adm=8&dis=2>.

___. 2010g. *Women in Canada, A Gender-Based Statistical Report: Economic Well-being*. Catalogue no. 89-503-X. At <statcan.gc.ca/pub/89-503-x/2010001/article/11388-eng.pdf>.

___. 2011a. "Average Earnings by Sex and Work Pattern." At <statcan.ca/l01/cst01/labor01a-eng.htm>.

___. 2011b. "Latest Release from the Labour Force Survey." *The Daily*, October 11. At <statcan.gc.ca/subjects-sujets/labour-travail/lfs-epa/lfs-epa-eng.htm?WT.mc_id=twtB0063>.

___. 2011c. "Police Reported Crime Statistics 2010." *The Daily*, July 21. At <www.statcan.gc.ca/daily-quotidien/110721/dq110721b-eng.htm>.

___. 2011d. "Violent Victimization of Aboriginal People in the Provinces." *The Daily*, March 11. At <statcan.gc.ca/daily-quotidien/110311/dq110311c-eng.htm>.

Stretton, Hugh, and Lionel Orchard. 1994. *Public Goods, Public Enterprise, Public Choice: Theoretical Foundations of the Contemporary Attack on Government*. New York: St. Martin's.

Stringer, Chris. 2011. "Human Evolution: The Long, Winding Road to Modern Man." *The Observer*, 19 June. At <guardian.co.uk/science/2011/jun/19/human-evolution-africa-ancestors-stringer>.

Sverke, Magnus, Johnny Hellgren, and Katharina Näswall. 2002. "No Security: A Meta-Analysis and Review of Job Insecurity and Its Consequences." *Journal of Occupational Health Psychology* 7, 3 (July): 242–64.

Sweeney, John. 2006. "Wal-Mart's Dirty Secret Is Out." *Seattle Post-Intelligencer*, 6 April.

Tanovich, David. 2006. *The Colour of Justice: Policing Race in Canada*. Toronto: Irwin Law.

Taylor, Paul. 1993. "Why the Rich Live Longer, Healthier." *Globe and Mail*, 16 October.

Teeple, Gary. 2000. *Globalization and the Decline of Social Reform: Into the Twenty-First Century*. Toronto: Garamond.

Telford, Adrienne, and Jeff Carolin. 2011. "A Tale of Two Police Forces." *Toronto Star* online, June 25. At <thestar.com/opinion/editorialopinion/article/1014920--a-tale-of-two-police-forces>.

Therien, Emile. 2011. "The National Shame of Aboriginal Incarceration." *Globe and Mail* online, July 20. At <theglobeandmail.com/news/opinions/opinion/the-national-shame-of-aboriginal-incarceration/article2102814/>.

Thomas, Derrick. 2010. "Foreign Nationals Working Temporarily in Canada."

Canadian Social Trends 9. Cat. No. 11-008-XWE. At <statcan.gc.ca/pub/11-008-x/2010002/article/11166-eng.htm>.

Thio, Alex. 1994. *Sociology: A Brief Introduction*. Second ed. New York: HarperCollins.

Toynbee, Polly. 2003. *The Guardian*, 7 March.

Turcotte, Martin. 2007. "Time Spent with Family During a Typical Workday, 1986 to 2005." *Canadian Social Trends* February. Cat. No. 11-008-XWE At <statcan.ca/bsolc/english/bsolc?catno=11-008-X>.

Twenge, Jean M. 2006. *Generation Me: Why Today's Young Americans Are More Confident, Assertive, Entitled—and More Miserable Than Ever Before*. New York: Free Press.

Twenge, Jean, and W. Keith Campbell. 2009. *The Narcissism Epidemic: Living in the Age of Entitlement*. New York: Free Press.

U.N. General Assembly Economic and Social Council. 2011. *Ten-Year Appraisal and Review of the Implementation of the Brussels Programme of Action for the Least Developed Countries for the Decade 2001–2010*. February. At <unohrlls.org/UserFiles/File/Ten-Year%20appraisal%281%29.pdf>.

van der Gaag, Nikki. 2004. *The No-Nonsense Guide to Women's Rights*. Toronto: New Internationalist Publications.

Vallance-Jones, Fred. 2011. *National Freedom of Information Audit 2011, Part 1*. Newspapers Canada. <newspaperscanada.ca/sites/default/files/FOIAudit%202011%20ReportFINAL%20.pdf>.

Valpy, Michael. 2009. "Canada's Military: Invisible No More." *Globe and Mail* online, November 20. At <theglobeandmail.com/news/politics/canadas-military-invisible-no-more/article1372117/page1/>.

Vaughan, Adam. 2011. "What Does Canada's Withdrawal from Kyoto Protocol Mean?" *The Guardian* online, December 13. At <guardian.co.uk/environment/2011/dec/13/canada-withdrawal-kyoto-protocol>.

Veblen, Thorstein. 1994 [1899]. *The Theory of the Leisure Class*. New York: Dover.

Veltmeyer, Henry. 1986. *Canadian Class Structure*. Toronto: Garamond.

Vosko, Leah F. 2006. "Precarious Employment: Towards an Improved Understanding of Labour Market Insecurity." In Leah F. Vosko (ed.), *Precarious Employment: Understanding Labour Market Insecurity in Canada*. Montreal & Kingston: McGill-Queen's University Press.

Walker, James W. St-G. 1980. *The History of Blacks in Canada: A Study Guide for Teachers and Students*. Ottawa: Minister of State for Multiculturalism.

Watson, Jane Werner. 1980. *Dinosaurs*. Racine, WI: Golden Press.

Weir, Erin. 2010. "Wages Lag Inflation." Progressive Economics Forum, Feb. 18. At <progressive-economics.ca/2010/02/18/wages-lag-inflation/>.

Western, Bruce, and Jake Rosenfeld. 2011. "Unions, Norms, and the Rise in U.S. Wage Inequality." *American Sociological Review* 76, August: 513–37.

White, Leslie. 1965. "Summary Review." In J.N. Spuhler (ed.), *The Evolution of Man's Capacity for Culture*. Detroit: Wayne State University Press.

Whittington, Les. 2009. "Foreign Workers Vulnerable, Fraser Warns." At *Toronto Star* online, November 3. At <thestar.com/news/canada/auditorgeneral/article/720490>.

Wilkinson, Richard, and Kate Pickett. 2010. *The Spirit Level: Why Equality is Better for Everyone*. London: Penguin Books.

Wilson, Daniel, and David Macdonald. 2010. *The Income Gap Between Aboriginal Peoples and the Rest of Canada*. Canadian Centre for Policy Alternatives, April. At <policyalternatives.ca/sites/default/files/uploads/publications/reports/docs/Aboriginal%20Income%20Gap.pdf>.

Winseck, Dwayne. 2011. "Media and Internet Concentration in Canada, 1984–2010." *Mediamorphis*, September 3. At <dwmw.wordpress.com/2011/09/03/media-and-internet-concentration-in-canada-1984---2010/>.

Wolf, Naomi. 1991. *The Beauty Myth*. Toronto: Vintage.

Wood, Ellen Meiksins. 1999. *The Origin of Capitalism*. New York: Monthly Review Press.

Wright, Erik Olin. 1980. "Varieties of Marxist Conceptions of Class Structure." *Politics and Society* 9.

Wu, Tim. 2010. *The Master Switch: The Rise and Fall of Information Empires*. Toronto: Knopf.

Yalnizyan, Armine. 2010. *The Rise of Canada's Richest 1%*. Canadian Centre for Policy Alternatives, December. At <policyalternatives.ca/sites/default/files/uploads/publications/National%20Office/2010/12/Richest%201%20Percent.pdf>.

Zeman, Klarka, Kathryn McMullen and Patrice de Broucker. 2010. "The High Education/Low Income Paradox: College and University Graduates with Low Earnings, Ontario, 2006." Statistics Canada. Cat. no. 81-595-M. At <statcan.gc.ca/pub/81-595-m/81-595-m2010081-eng.htm>.

Name Index

Subject Index

Aboriginal people
  incarceration rate of,
    182, 231
  median income of, 249
  poverty and, 227, 250,
    256
  struggle of, 259–260
  and suicide, 4, 7
  See also First Nations;
    Indigenous people
Absolute poverty, 225
Acadian culture, 49
Accord between capital and
  labour, 194–196, 201
Accountability, 185
Activism, social, 113, 136,
  138, 139, 305, 308
Addiction, 42, 124, 182
Advertisers, power of, 150–
  151
Advertising
  corporate, 39, 132, 147–
    148, 156, 198
  elections and, 147, 155
  improvement and, 77,
    151, 271
  and symbols, 39, 216
  tobacco, 182
Afghanistan, 88, 180
Africa, 37, 41, 55, 57, 72, 90,
  188
African-Canadians, 250
  See also Blacks
Agency, human, 9, 21
Agents provocateurs, 147
Agrarian societies, 60, 62–64,
  70–71, 133, 144, 166,
  274
Agriculture, 54, 57, 58, 76
  See also Agrarian
    societies; Horticultural
    societies; Neolithic
    Revolution

Air Canada, 192
Alaska, 299
Alberta, 31, 32, 109, 113,
  147, 251, 299, 300, 307
Alberta Eugenics Board, 32
Alienation, 125–127, 135–
  136
Alliance of Manufacturers
  and Exporters of
  Canada, 105
Al-Quaeda, 187
American Revolution, 30
American Union of
  Concerned Scientists, 14
Anarchy of production, 84,
  85, 313, 314, 321
Anatomy, human, 20, 42
Anti-Ballistic Missile Treaty,
  202–203
Anti-Scmitism, 242 243,
  245, 252
Anxiety, youth and, 137
Apartheid, 255
Apes, 29, 35, 36, 37
Apple, 118, 150
Apprenticeship, 156
Appropriating class. *See*
  Owning class
Arabs, 153, 242, 243
Arab Spring, 9, 310
Arms industry, 179, 180
Asia, 90, 188
Assimilationism, 254
Associated Press, 205
Assyrian, 276
Astral Media, 149
Atlantic provinces, 129
Australia, 90, 291
Automobile, 84, 132

Baby boomers, 136, 137
Bailouts, bank, 87, 173, 178
Bank of America, 178

Bargaining, collective, 110,
  194, 220, 284
Barter system, 69
Battered Women's Support
  Services, 272
Beauty myth, 279
Behaviour. *See* Human
  behaviour
Belgium, 90
Beliefs
  conflicting, 8, 49
  culture and, 45–47, 62
  and ideology, 29,
    141–142, 143, 146,
    161, 213, 218, 278,
    283–284
  religious, 12, 95, 134,
    143, 208, 253, 275–
    277, 289
Bcll, 149
Belonging, human, 8–9, 47,
  48
Benefits, worker, 194
Berlin Wall, 200, 205
Bias
  and ideology, 142
  in media, 147, 152
  in social science, 13–14,
    18, 22
"Big-fish" theories, 17
Bilderberg Group, 106, 107,
  160, 201
Biodiversity, 298
Biological determinism
  criminal behaviour and,
    29
  eugenics and, 31–32
  gender inequality and,
    267–268, 270
  genetics and, 28, 33–34,
    42
  social inequality and,
    29–31, 158, 212, 229,

235, 246–247
theories of, 20, 25–26, 28, 34
Biology. *See* Biological determinism; Human behaviour
Biopiracy, 298
Bipedalism, 36, 37, 42
Blackwater, 89
"Blaming the victim," 208, 228, 229–230, 234, 235
Blue-collar jobs, 101, 124–125, 220
Bolivia, 97, 298
Bonding, human, 42
Bourgeoisie
in Canada, 103, 171
as capitalist class, 70–71, 76, 89, 100–101, 102, 104, 302
ideology of, 74, 144, 213, 269, 278
petite, 79, 96, 98, 101, 102, 108–109
Bowling Alone: The Collapse and Revival of American Community (Putnam), 136, 137–138
Brain, human, 39–40
Branding, corporate, 130, 147–148
"Bread and Roses," 284
Bretton Woods conference, 201
Britain, 48, 127, 245, 269, 300, 306
See also Great Britain
British Columbia, 1, 31, 129, 172, 251, 260, 299
British South Sea Bubble, 84
Business Council on National Issues (BCNI), 106
Business Roundtable, 106

Calgary Herald, 50
Canada
capitalism, development of, 67, 76–77, 83, 87,

98–100, 131
consumerism and, 131, 133, 135
culture, 26, 45, 47–50, 51, 152–156, 160–161, 207, 272, 279–281, 289
education, 157–160, 214
and the environment, 147, 296–299
federal-provincial relations, 197–198
gender inequality in, 265–267, 282–285
immigration, 109, 157, 218
integration with U.S., 159, 196–197, 198, 300–301
justice in, 182, 184–185, 232
military spending in, 50, 179–181, 197, 205, 206
neoliberalism in, 196–198
owning class, 83–88, 102–107, 149–150, 171–172, 220
poverty in, 225–235
racism in, 241–242, 244, 247–254, 255–256, 258, 261
social inequality and, 216–218, 220–224
social spending in, 177–179, 191, 192, 196, 198–199
spy agencies, 183–184
taxation in, 174–177
unemployment in, 122, 295
working class in, 110, 111–112, 113, 123–124, 126, 127–129
Canada Pension Plan (CPP), 180
Canadian Alliance, 307

Canadian Arab Federation, 253
Canadian Border Service Agency, 185
Canadian Broadcasting Corporation (CBC), 155–156, 168
Canadian Centre for Occupational Health and Safety, 126
Canadian Centre for Policy Alternatives, 99, 175
Canadian Chamber of Commerce, 105
Canadian Charter of Rights and Freedoms, 10, 11, 229, 258, 265
Canadian Council of Chief Executives (CCCE), 106, 107, 171
Canadian Federation of Independent Business, 106
Canadian Imperial Bank of Commerce, 123
Canadian Pacific Railway, 251
Canadian Radio-television and Telecommunications Commission (CRTC), 155–156
Canadian Security and Intelligence Service (CSIS), 183, 185
Canadian Taxpayers Federation, 177
Canadian Wheat Board, 77
Cancer, 33
Capital
accumulation of, 71–74, 168, 173–174, 196
circulation of, 80
concentration and centralization of, 83, 92, 150
Capitalism
in agrarian societies, 70–71, 87, 95, 274

in Canada, 67, 76–77, 83, 87, 98–100, 131
classes in, 96
contradictions of, 88, 202, 215, 261, 289, 291–299
culture of, 129–138
defined, 69, 78
democracy and, 144, 169–173
economic cycles and, 85, 122, 195
Enlightenment thought and, 11, 74–75, 143
instability of, 292–294
liberalism and, 143–146, 161
limits to growth, 294–299, 309
profit as driving force in, 80–87
technological change and, 124–125, 133, 289
welfare state and, 89–90, 193–199
Capitalist class. *See* Owning class
Carbon footprint, Canada, 299
Carnivores, 37–38
Catholic Church, 12, 71, 75
CBS, 150
CCCE. *See* Canadian Council of Chief Executives
C.D. Howe Institute, 107, 199
Celebrity culture, 151, 153
Censorship, 153
Census, data, 158, 217, 223, 242, 250–251, 255, 256
Census, long form, 282
Central Intelligence Agency (CIA), 183, 203
Centralization of capital, 83, 301
Certified General

Accountants Association of Canada, 133
Change, social, 7–8, 9, 70
Change theory
class analysis and, 167–168
defined, 18–19, 21, 22, 23
education and, 158
imperialism and, 90
inequality and, 213–215, 220, 223–224, 235–236
social change and, 289
Charter of Rights and Freedoms, 10, 11, 229, 258, 265
Chernobyl, Ukraine, 297
Chief executive officer (CEO), pay, 81, 103, 217, 220
Children, 6, 55, 130, 132, 148, 280, 282–284, 306
Chimpanzees, 41
China, 47, 57, 72, 91, 122, 132, 203, 204, 237, 251–252, 299
Chinese-Canadians, discrimination against, 251
Christianity, 74, 275, 276
Circulation of capital, 80
Cities, 132, 133–134
Citigroup, 178, 217
Civil society groups, 186, 305
Class. *See* Social class
Class analysis, 97–98, 100–101, 114, 167–168, 172, 219, 255
Class conflict, structural basis for, 63–64, 81, 92, 101
Class consciousness, 102, 105–107, 110, 111–113, 114, 220
Classical liberalism, 196
Climate change, 14, 50, 57, 202, 208, 209, 237, 298–300, 309–310

See also Global warming
CN Rail, 192
Cochabamba, Bolivia, 298
CO_2 emissions, 299
Coercion
and appropriation of surplus, 60, 75
forms of, 68, 70, 79
ideological hegemony, 143
and the state, 168, 173, 181–189, 200
Cogeco, 149
Cold War, 113, 206
Collective action, 305
Collective bargaining, 90, 194, 220, 284
Colonialism
expansion of capitalism and, 71, 72, 74, 245
underdevelopment and, 90–91, 200, 236, 246
Commodification
of the commons, 192
of debt, 86
of labour, 72, 78, 126, 134
Commodity, 69, 82, 84
Commodity market, 86
Commons, 72–73, 191–192, 193, 197, 296–299
Communication, human, 38–39
Communication, mass. *See* Mass media
Communism, 172, 206
Competition
biological basis for, 30, 56
capitalism and, 51, 70, 71, 72, 74, 86, 119, 127, 134, 214, 307
global, 196, 202, 284
for scarce resources, 41, 54, 154, 257, 293
Comprehensive Nuclear Test Ban Treaty, 202
Concentration of capital, 83,

92, 150
Confederation, 76–77
Conference Board of
    Canada, 207, 226, 227,
    296, 299
Conflict theory. *See* Change
    theory
Conformist behaviour, 8–9,
    159
Conglomerates, 91, 150, 152
    See also Transnational
    companies (TNCs)
Conseil du patronat du
    Québec, 106
Consensus, 55
Conservative Party, 156, 170,
    182, 188–189, 206, 232,
    259, 307
Conspicuous consumption,
    131, 135
Constitution Act of 1982,
    300
Constitutional monarchy, 74
Consumerism, 85, 131–133,
    139, 280
Consumer Price Index, 160
Contigent workers, 122
Continuous Passage Act, 252
Convergence, 149, 156
Cooperative Commonwealth
    Federation (CCF),
    290–291
Co-operative
    Commonwealth
    Federation (CCF), 307
Corporate branding, 130,
    147–148
Corporate network, 104
Corporate rule, 102
Corporations
    and corporate
    concentration, 83, 92,
    98, 102–105, 149–
    150, 154, 301–302
    as "fictitious persons,"
    83, 102, 181–182
    foreign control of, 129,
    300

mergers, 83
and Nazi Germany, 188
power of, 91–92, 102–
    107, 117–118, 193,
    209, 300
and public interest, 107,
    170
and taxation, 174–177,
    193, 235
and transnational
    corporations (TNCs),
    91–92, 117–118, 119,
    139, 159, 193, 202–
    205, 309
Correctional Services
    Canada, 182
Cost/Benefits, 166
Cost of labour, 119
Council on Foreign Relations,
    107, 201
Crash, economic, 83, 84
Credentialism, 157
Crime, 29, 34
Crime Severity Index, 182
Criminalization of dissent,
    184–186, 293
Criminal justice system, 182–
    183, 231–232, 252, 258
Crisis of overproduction,
    83–85, 195, 292
Critical theory. *See also*
    Change theory
CTVglobemedia, 149
Cultural universals, 46, 47
Culture, Canadian
    and American culture,
    49, 155, 156, 162,
    193, 300
    Canadian, 45, 47–50,
    156
    of capitalism, 129–131,
    146
    characteristics of, 45
    of consumerism, 131–
    133
    corporate, 129–131, 139
    cultural integration,
    159, 196–197, 198,

300–301
    cultural universals, 46,
    47
    cultural values, 45, 64,
    235
    dialectic of, 51–52
    of narcissism, 136
    and socialization, 146–
    148
Currency exchange, 86
Customs, 10

Dark age, 291–292
Daycare, 282, 283, 284
DDT, 35
De Beers Corporation, 39
Debt
    corporate, 195
    government, 195
    household, 133, 137, 226
    national, 236–237
    student, 7, 160, 226
Debt, as commodity, 86–87
Declaration of
    Independence, United
    States, 11
Declaration of the Rights of
    Man and the Citizen, 11
Declaration on a Shared
    Vision for Perimeter
    Security and Economic
    Competitiveness, 300
Deep integration, 300–301
Deficit, government, 175,
    176, 199
Democracy
    capitalism and, 89, 144,
    169–173
    education system and,
    162
    government and, 185,
    186, 197
    media ownership and,
    155, 162
    racial inequality and,
    261
    social, 290–291
    See also Elections;

34, 35
sexuality and, 36, 40–41
tool making and, 36, 37
Exceptionalism, American, 202–203
Exogamy, 54
Expectations, social, 8–9, 9–10
Exxon, 299

Facebook, 151, 184
Factory worker, 110
Failed states, 207, 208
Family
gender roles and, 279
"Generation Me," 137
oriented policy, 282–283, 284, 285
as property, 273, 274–275
"work-family crunch," 283
Farming, decline of, 127–129
Fascism, 113, 186–188
Fashion industry, 84, 85
Feminism, 269–274, 280, 308
Feudalism
decline of, 69–76, 143, 144
defined, 68
and roots of capitalism, 67–70, 78–79, 87, 105, 169, 192, 236, 289
social inequality and, 213
Financialization, 82, 86–87, 195, 301
First Nations, oppression of, 247–250, 259–260
See also Aboriginal peoples; Indigenous peoples
First Wave feminism, 269
Fishing, decline of, 128, 129
Fishpond analogy
"big-fish" theories, 17, 18, 19, 21, 22, 31,

154, 167
"middle-fish" theories, 17, 18, 20, 154, 188, 306–307
"small-fish" theories, 17, 18, 19, 22, 142, 154, 167, 214, 306
Flag, Canadian, 49
Flint Hills Resources Canada LP, 313
Food security, 129
Foraging societies
characteristics of, 52–57
decline of, 57–58, 59
division of labour in, 38, 54
gender roles in, 274, 275
kinship and sharing in, 54, 55–56, 133, 244, 274
leadership in, 165–166
Fordism, 119
Foreign Affairs and International Trade, 185
Foreign direct investment (FDI), 91
Foreign exchange rate, 86
Fortune 500 Global Companies, 132
Fractions, 104, 109
Framing, 147, 199, ix
France, 12, 47, 48, 68, 76, 179, 310
Fraser Institute, 107, 171, 199, 225
Freedom of information (FOI), 185
Free enterprise system, 82, 89, 118
Free trade, 197, 202, 293
See also NAFTA
Free will, 8
French Revolution, 30, 154
French-speaking Canadians, 48, 49
Front de libération du Québec (FLQ), 184
Fukushima, Japan, 297

Functionalism, 20, 158, 218–219
Fundamentalism, 144–145

Gambling, revenues from, 176–177
Gathering societies, 37, 38, 53, 54, 57
Gay marriage, 10
GDP. *See* Gross domestic product, 294–295
Gender
defined, 264–265
difference, 264, 267–269, 270–271, 279, 280
division of labour, 54
and functionalism, 218–219
and occupational mobility, 265–266, 280–281, 284
and physiological differences, 267–269
segregation, occupational, 280–283
and socialization, 49
stereotypes in the media, 152
Gender inequality
beneficiaries of, 273, 278, 283–284
biological determinism and, 267–269
and biology, 272–274
in Canada, 265
defined, 264–265
liberal feminism and, 270–272, 274
Marxism and, 272, 273–274, 278
neoliberalism and, 285
roots of, 274–277
and social change, 283–284
and the state, 275–277
Gender roles
in the home, 281–282,

Merchants, 70–71, 72, 80
Mergers and acquisitions, 83
Meritocracy, 218, 219, 223–224
Mesopotamia, 276
Metro Vancouver Alliance, 306
Mexico, 117
Microsociology, 21
Microsoft, 80
Middle Ages, 67–68
Middle Assyrian Law number 40, 276
Middle class society, 98–100, 108, 109, 111, 223, 226
Middle East, 52
"Middle fish," 17, 18, 20, 154, 188, 306–307
Migration, population, 208
Military-industrial complex, 179, 180
Military spending in Canada, 179–181
Minimum wage, 123
Minorities, racial, 144, 153
    See also Immigrants; Race; Racism
Misogyny, 275
Model Eugenical Sterilization Law (U.S.), 31
Mode of production, 51–52, 53, 69, 73, 78–79
Monarchy, 72, 73, 74, 301
Money economy, emergence of, 68–69
Monkeys, 36
Monopolization
    of media ownership in Canada, 150–151, 155, 156
    of the military, 179–180
    and small-business decline in Canada, 127–129
Monopoly, 82–85, 83, 90
Monsanto, 298
Montreal, 77
Morgan Stanley, 178

Mortality rates, 127
Multicultural feminism, 273
Multiculturalism, 259, 261
Multinational enterprises (MNE), 91–92
    See also Transnational corporations (TNCs)
Music, 39
Muslims. See Islamophobia
Mutual Funds, 105

Nagasaki, 297
Narcissism, 136, 139
Nation, 74, 207, 300
National Child Care Strategy, 282
National Defence, 185
National Energy Board, 307–308
National Freedom of Information Audit, 185
National Post, 253
National security establishment, 185
Nation-state, 73–74, 83, 91, 102, 199–200, 201, 202, 207, 243, 293
Natural behaviour. See Instinct
Natural selection, 34–35, 240
Nature deficit disorder, 55
Nazi Germany, 10, 32, 187–188
Neoliberalism
    agenda, 196–198, 199, 209
    families, impact on, 284
    gender inequality, impact on, 285
    labour, attack on, 219–220
    promotion of corporate agenda and, 198–199, 209, 300
    and the state, 199, 229, 233
    and structural adjustment policies,

196
Neolithic Revolution, 57
Neutral state, myth of, 168
New Democratic Party, 177, 288, 290–291
Newfoundland, 49, 129
New Guinea, 52
New middle class, 108, 109
News
    and advertising, 151
    and entertainment, 153
    and ideas, 146, 147, 149–150, 152, 153, 154
News Corporation, 150
Newspapers Canada, 185
New technologies, 125
New Westminster, 306
New World Order, 201–206
New York City, 9, 83
New Zealand, 291
Niche, market, 128
9/11, 185, 188, 294
Nobility, 68, 69, 74, 75
Nonconformist behaviour, 8–9
Non-material culture, 45
Non-status Indians, 248
North America Command, 301
North American Free Trade Agreement (NAFTA), 300
North American Treaty Organization (NATO), 179, 201
Novartis, 298
Nova Scotia, 129, 291
Nuclear disasters, 296, 297
Nurture, 33

Obesity, 33
Objectivity, myth of, 152–155
Objects, as symbols, 38–39
Occupation and social class, 96, 98, 99
Occupy movement, 9, 83, 95, 96, 102, 113, 142, 292

OECD. *See* Organisation for
    Economic Co-operation
    and Development
Oligopoly, 82
Olympics 2010, 272, 306
Omnivores, 37
One Big Union (OBU), 112
Ontario, 32, 186, 223, 227,
    250
Opportunity, equality of, 145
Opposable thumb, 37
Orangutans, 41
Order theory
    defined, 18, 20–21, 22,
        288–289
    education and, 223
    functionalism and, 158,
        218
    pluralism, 167
    and social inequality,
        212, 218, 254
    stratification theories,
        97–98
Organic solidarity, 134
Organisation for Economic
    Co-operation and
    Development (OECD),
    109, 133, 175, 196, 198,
    296
Organizational structure, 5
Origin of Species (Darwin), 30
*The Origin of the Family, Private
    Property, and the State*
    (Morgan), 273
Outsourcing, 113, 121–122,
    295
Overproduction, crisis of,
    83–85, 195, 292
Over-qualification, job, 157
Overtime, unpaid, 123
"Own account" workers, 128
Owning class
    in Canada, 102–107,
        194–195, 300–301,
        302
    class consciousness,
        105–107
    composition of, 83, 92,

102–105
    and hypergrowth, 293
    ideological power of, 113
    involvement in
        education, 158–160
    and liberal democratic
        rule, 169–172, 187
    and maintenance of
        power, 92, 194
    nature of, 59, 71, 79–80,
        126, 130, 166, 200,
        292, 301
    wealth, 82, 237

Pakistan, 97, 122, 266
Palaeontology, 42
Paper economy, 86
Paradigm, 15
Pastoralism, 58
Patriarchy, 273
Pentagon, 184
Periphery, 83
Pesticide, 35
Petite bourgeoisie, 79, 96, 98,
    101, 102, 108–109
    See also Bourgeoisie
PetroCanada, 192
Philippines, 122
Physiology, human, 20
Planned obsolescence, 131,
    298
Pluralism, 167–168, 188–189
Polar bear, 36
Police, role of, 147, 168,
    181–183, 184, 186
Political economy, 20, 303
Political movements, left-
    wing, 208, 308–309
Political power, 101
Populism, 307–309
Portugal, 90
Possessions, personal, 58
Post-Fordism, 120
Postmedia, 149
Postmodernism, 13, 114, 274
Postsecondary education,
    157, 158, 160, 198
Potlatch, 61

Poverty
    "blaming the victim"
        and, 208, 228, 229–
        230, 234, 235
    capitalism and, 230–231,
        233, 285
    contributing factors of,
        227–229
    culture of, 254–255
    global inequality of, 170,
        230, 235–237
    measures of, 225–226
    policy options, 233–235,
        285
    social impact of, 231
    victims of, 226–227,
        229–230, 266–267
Power
    of advertisers, 150–151
    in agrarian societies,
        62–63, 274
    in capitalist societies, 72,
        73–74, 75, 79, 92–93,
        110, 130, 173
    of corporations, 91–92,
        102–107, 117–118,
        193, 209, 300
    in foraging societies, 56
    and gender, 64, 271,
        277–283, 283–284
    in horticultural societies,
        59
    ideology and, 113, 141,
        142, 143, 144, 161–
        162, 205
    in Marxist theory, 97,
        114, 142, 273–274,
        303
    and order theories, 158
    relations in society, 6–7,
        21–23
    and the state, 165–168,
        171–172, 181
    and stratification
        theories, 97–98
    and structured
        inequality, 58–62, 64,
        92–93, 101, 213–215,

Religious belief systems, 275, 276, 278, 283
Rent system, 68, 70
Representative government, 171
Reserve army of the unemployed, 122
Residential schools, 248–249, 259
Retirement, 222, 234
Revolution, 289–290
    See also French Revolution; Industrial Revolution; Neolithic Revolution; Russian Revolution
The Rich Get Richer and the Poor Get Prison (Reiman and Leighton), 182
"Riddle of the middle," 99
Right, political, 154, 155, 306
Right-wing, 154, 187, 307–308
Rioting, 148
Riots, Vancouver, 1–2, 3
Rogers, 149
Rotman School of Business, 31
Royal Canadian Mounted Police (RCMP), 183, 184, 185
Royal Commission on Equality in Employment, 258
Royal Commission on the Status of Women in Canada, 152, 265
Rule of law, 112, 181, 188, 292
Ruling class. *See* Owning class
Russia, 299, 304
Russian Revolution, 113, 290, 304

Safety standards, 126–127
Salary expectations, gender gap in, 265, 266

Sales tax, 166, 176, 197
Same-sex marriage, 10
Saskatchewan, 129, 291
Save the Fraser Declaration, 260
"The School Class as a Social System: Some of Its Functions in American Society" (Parsons), 158
Schools, socialization function of, 142, 158
Science, 11–15, 16, 18, 22
Scientific management, 119
Scientific principles, 12
Second Wave feminism, 269–270, 274, 279
Securitization, 86–87
Segmented markets, 150–151
Self-employment, 127, 128, 129, 234
Serfs, 68, 79, 169
Service sector, 101, 108, 284
SES. *See* Socioeconomic status
Sex. *See* Gender
Sexism. *See* Gender inequality
Sexuality
    and diversity, 267, 268, 270
    human, 36, 40–41
    and instinct, 25, 26, 27, 28
    women's, 274–275, 276, 280
    See also Heterosexism
Sexual Sterilization Act (Can), 32
Shareholders, 81–82
Shaw Communications, 149
The Shock Doctrine: The Rise of Disaster Capitalism (Klein), 172
Similarity, 34
Slavery
    and African-Canadians, 250
    in agrarian societies, 63–64

    and colonialism, 72, 90, 208, 244–246
    in feudal societies, 70
    women as slaves, 274, 275–277
    workers as slaves, 79
Small-business
    decline of, 101, 127–129
    immigrants and, 251, 252
    owner, 79, 92, 100
    struggle of, 78, 101, 127–129, 307
    See also Self-employment
"Small-fish" theories, 17
Smartphones, 151
"Snapshot" of society, 7
Soccer, 2
Sociability, human, 36–37, 39, 41–42, 53
Social assistance, 177, 226, 229
Social capital, 136
Social change
    and dialectics, 15, 294
    and gender inequality, 283–284
    need for, 309–310
    pace of, 75, 138, 188, 208, 213
    patterns of, 9, 288–289, 303
Social class
    and class conflict, 63–64, 81, 92, 101
    and class consciousness, 102, 105–107, 110, 111–113, 114, 220
    and gender relations, 98, 264, 273–274, 278
    Marx on, 59, 97–98
    and the middle class, 98–100
    stratification theories and, 97–98
    structured inequality and, 96, 97

structure of, 100–102
Weber on, 96–97
Social conservatism, 144–145
Social Darwinism, 30
Social democracy, 290–291
Social expectations, 8–9, 9–10
Social inequality
 biological determinism and, 29–31, 158, 212, 229, 235, 246–247
 education and, 157–158, 224, 227, 233–234, 250, 256, 257, 261
 income and wealth inequality, 212–213, 216–218
 structured inequality and, 58–64
 See also Class; Gender inequality; Poverty
Socialism, 173, 178, 299, 303
Socialist feminism, 273
Socialization
 agents of, 49, 146–148, 161
 in corporate culture, 146–148
 defined, 45, 46
 education system and, 142, 156–160
 gender inequality and, 270–272
 ideology and, 141
 mass media and, 142, 148, 150–155
Social media, 1, 151, 310
Social movements
 for change, 304–309
 defined, 305
 eugenics, 31
 feminist, 269
 infiltration of, 147
 populist, 306–309
 young people in, 310
Social networks
 iGeneration, 137–138
 as social capital, 42, 136

Social order, 7–8, 22, 134–135
Social participation, 124
Social safety net, 89, 114, 195
Social sciences, bias in, 18, 22
Social solidarity, 38
Social spending, 90, 178, 179, 196, 199
Social stratification, 97–98, 218
Social structure, 5–7, 16, 18, 142
Social theory. *See* Biological determinism; Eugenics; Functionalism; Marxism
Society
 and change, 7–8, 9
 defined, 5–6
 and freedom, 9–10
 human behaviour and, 2–4
 as process, 7–8
 as social structure, 5, 7, 16, 18, 142
Sociocultural system, 5, 6, 10, 51–52, 56
Socioeconomic formation
 and capitalist societies, 75, 78, 96, 124, 129, 172, 246–247
 defined, 51
 feudal societies and, 68–69, 89
 foraging societies and, 52–58
 rights and freedoms in, 145
 and the state, 168
 and transformation, 290, 291, 303, 305
Socioeconomic status (SES), 96–98, 114, 150, 158, 182
Sociological imagination, 7
Sociology
 bias in, 13–14

boundaries of, 21–22
class, concepts of, 59
and distal relations of power, 7, 21, 22
major theoretical frameworks, 12–13, 18–21
roots of, 11, 22
and science, 11–15
and the study of ideas, 28–29
Solidarity, 134
South Asians, 153, 242, 252
Southeast Asia, 57
South Sea Bubble, 84
Soviet Union, 113, 187, 200, 205, 285
Spain, 90, 186
Specialization, 57
Speculation, 83, 84, 86, 87, 171
Sports, 2, 3, 82, 272, 279
Spy agencies in Canada, 183–184
Stalinism, 114
Standard Oil, 188, 203
Stanley Cup, 1
State
 accumulation function of the, 173–181, 200
 class approach, 167–168
 coercive power of the, 181–186, 200–201
 and the commons, 191–193
 defined, 165–168
 and democracy, 169–173
 failed, 207, 208
 and gender inequality, 275–277
 and globalization, 199–209
 as mediator between capital and labour, 194–195
 neoliberalism and the, 195–199, 209
 pluralist approach, 167–

114, 304–309
transition to capitalism,
  62–63, 73–76
Transnational corporations
  (TNCs)
  agribusiness, 128
  development of, 91–92
  power of, 117–118,
    202–205, 209
  public funding for, 298,
    309
Treaty of Berlin (1885), 90
Triad, 91
Tribute, 60–61, 166
Trilateral Commission, 107,
  201
Tuition fees, 160, 198
Turkish Football Federation,
  272
Twins, 33
Twitter, 184

Ultimate Fighting
  Championships (UFC), 3
Underdevelopment, 91,
  235–236
Underemployment, 122, 124,
  233, 255, 279, 293
Unemployment
  and business cycle, 109
  in Canada, 122, 124,
    223, 234, 250, 254
  lumpenproletariat, 96,
    122, 255
  and poverty, 228, 231,
    232, 233, 235
  stress of, 127
  and suicide, 3, 7, 127
  threat of, 122, 233
Unions. See Labour unions,
  234
United Arab Emirates, 266
United Farm Women, 32
United Nations, 179, 201,
  203, 235, 236, 293, 298
United Nations International
  Convention on the
  Elimination of All

Forms of Racial
  Discrimination, 258
United States
  and Canadian
    integration, 159, 196–
    197, 198, 300–301
  as classless society, 97
  and cultural domination,
    48, 193
  exceptionalism, 202–203
  and foreign policy
    decisions, 204, 294
  as global police officer,
    200, 203–206
  as global superpower,
    200–201, 293
  health care in, 193, 199
  incarceration rates in,
    232
  media in, 150, 155
  military activities, 188,
    203, 294
  military spending, 179,
    180, 204, 206, 294
  and the New World
    Order, 201–206
  and social inequality,
    218, 230, 231
  unions in, 112, 220, 256
United States Federal
  Reserve, 106, 173, 178
United Technologies, 180
Universal Declaration of
  Human Rights, 121
Universities, 157, 158, 160
University of Toronto, 31
University professors, 109–
  110
Unpaid work, 266
Urban environment, 118
Urbanization, 55, 70, 72,
  133–135, 252, 254
User-pay services, 176, 197
Usury, 71
'Us' versus 'them,' 48, 154,
  188, 207, 230, 244, 253,
  293, 294, 308
Utopian socialism, 302–303

Values
  media promotion of,
    161–162
  socialization of, 157, 158
Vancouver, 1, 2, 3, 148, 184,
  186, 272
Variation, 34, 35
Vertical integration, 149
The Vertical Mosaic (Porter),
  98, 149
Viacom, 150
Video games, 151
Vietnam, 97
Violence
  domestic, 266, 272,
    277–278, 282
  in the media, 161–162
  and revolution, 290
  sport and, 3, 272
  and the state, 165
Volunteer work, 138

Wages
  decline of real, 122–123,
    193, 306
  gender gap in, 266
  and labour productivity,
    119
  price of labour, 71, 81,
    82
Wage workers. *See* Working
  class
Wall Street, 83, 87, 203, 307,
  308
  See also Occupy
    movement
Wal-Mart, 117–118, 120,
  122
War
  in agrarian societies,
    61–62
  in foraging societies,
    54–55
  in horticultural societies,
    61–62
  profits from, 88–89
  as social function, 20